Devon's Last Slave-Owners

Ira Aldridge as 'The Captive Slave', by John Philip Simpson, 1827. This celebrated American actor, known as the African Roscius, performed across Devon in the 1840s and 1850s in plays including Thomas Morton's *The Slave* (1818).

DEVON'S LAST SLAVE-OWNERS

Plantations, Compensation and the Enslaved, 1834

Todd Gray

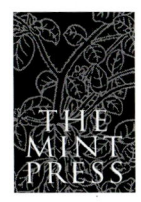 

© Todd Gray 2021

All Rights Reserved. Except as permitted under current legislation no part of this work may be photocopied, stored in a retrieval system, published, performed in public, adapted, broadcast, transmitted, recorded or reproduced in any form or by any means, without the prior permission of the copyright owner

First published 2021

A publication of The Mint Press
Taddyforde House South
Taddyforde Estate
New North Road, Exeter EX4 4AT

website: www.stevensbooks.co.uk

ISBN 978 1903 356 760

A CIP catalogue record for this book is available from the British Library

The publisher has no responsibility for the continued existence or accuracy of URLs for external or third-party internet websites referred to in this book, and does not guarantee that any content on such websites is, or will remain, accurate or appropriate.

Typeset, printed and bound in Great Britain by
Short Run Press Ltd, Exeter, Devon

This publication is printed on acid-free paper

*To the memory of Maya Angelou,
who nearly thirty years ago first encouraged me to
pursue Devon's history of slavery*

Contents

Preface ix
Foreword xix

Introduction 1

Part One: Slavery & Devon, 1562–1834   17

1. Slavery and the language of race   19
    Terminology   21
    Interracial children of slaveholders   30
    Interracial slaveholders   32
    Character   36

2. From slavery to emancipation   43
    Europeans and African slavery   44
    Earlier slaveholders   45
    Abolition and emancipation   60

3. The slave colonies in 1834   64
    The West Indies   68
    The Indian Ocean   04

4. Devon in 1834   97
    Coastal resorts   99
    Urban areas   115
    Devon's Black population   129

Part Two: Devon and slave ownership, 1834 — **139**

5. Devon's veiled slave-owners — **157**
    Agents — 157
    Beneficiaries — 161
    Unsuccessful claimants — 165

6. Devon's slave-owners — **170**
    Devon-born — 173
    Armed services — 184
    The British at leisure — 186
    Country house builders and emancipation — 196
    Colonials — 205

Conclusion — 240

Appendix
Letter of A. J. Lees to Lord Rolle, 22 January 1835 — 247

Illustration sources — 249
Abbreviations — 250
Notes — 251
Index — 283

Preface

*Devon's Last Slave-Owne*rs was written during the COVID-19 Pandemic which has been, so far, eighteen months of general uncertainty in understanding waves of infection, periodic lockdowns, vaccination levels and new variants. But what might have been a happy escape into the past has been far from that; the last two years have been a relentless immersion into the horrors of slavery. I have become reacquainted with its early beginnings, the cruelty of slave colonies and the mechanics of emancipation. The terrors of the past have jostled with the insecurities of the present day.

Why pick this dispiriting topic at this time? One reason is that the long closure of public archives forced me to revisit slumbering projects and this is one which I had promised myself to finish *once I had spare time*. I have been able to utilise a store of pre-COVID electronic copies of documents and thus continue working at home. The second reason is that I have long seen this as an important topic which needs addressing. For nearly forty years I have studied Devon and have concentrated on untold aspects of history. In my youth the most prominent figures in the field were W. G. Hoskins, Joyce Youings and Harold Fox who were proud to devote most of their careers to pursuing Devon's history but they passed away during my middle years. Most other academic historians working on Devon retired or faded away as institutional appraisals disregarded local history in the mid 1990s. For some twenty years nearly all abandoned local studies while I did the opposite: as friends and colleagues reinvented themselves as national historians, I embraced Devon. I have spent these years burrowing through every substantial manuscript collection in the county and threw myself into researching Devon in every public archive across England and Wales. I began my career working on the Elizabethan and Early Stuart period but became fascinated by all things Devonian and pursued the nature and character of the county in all its forms. My field of study became Devon. Academia has recently returned to local studies mostly through research grants but today only a handful of academics have an understanding of Devon's archives: the core knowledge lies with independent scholars and with those who enjoy history as a leisure interest. My electronic archive of thousands of documents had suddenly proved unexpectedly useful.

The reasons for choosing the topic of this book are more complex. I pick some subjects in order to correct outdated or distorted impressions of Devon's past but each project has centred on unearthing previously-unknown documents with which I have fashioned an understanding of an untold facet of Devon's past. They have also recast to some degree the county's general history. So it is with the unexplored topic of slave-ownership. There is much that is new and previously unimagined in this volume, some details and analysis run counter to common assumptions and opinions. My own perspective on the rise of the seaside resorts has been challenged, Regency figures have emerged from obscurity and I have questions on the history of mixed-race individuals that I did not have before. At the heart of my choosing this topic is that I have squirrelled away manuscript references to disenfranchised people; I have a large file of incidental details compiled over some three decades. Until recently there has been a considerable lack of public interest and I did not have the foresight to anticipate the current movement. I hope the time is now right for this book.

I have struggled to define the long shadow that trans-Atlantic slavery has cast. I recently found a German news report of 1940 had linked slavery with the British navy's interception and boarding of the *Altmark* in neutral waters. The *Berline Börsen Zeitung* wrote 'In exactly the same manner behaved those Englishmen who laid the foundations of British wealth – the Drakes and Raleghs and Hawkins – slave dealers, silver ship-robbers and pirates'.[1]

This history had reverberations then and continues to this day. Throughout the writing of this book I have been mindful that this history cannot be separated from the wider study of empire and its impact on modern race relations.

Devon's Last Slave-Owners has been written from a British perspective but my childhood was spent in North America and makes me attentive to additional views and outlooks. I had my first brush with British race relations on the morning of my arrival in 1973: the breakfast table had a jar of Robertson's marmalade with a 'golly', a version of American Black rag dolls. Shortly afterwards I was taken aback by a brand of shoe polish and an episode of *The Black and White Minstrel Show*. Most surprising of all was the subsequent realisation that amongst the middle classes the British Empire was not discussed socially. It was commonly said at the time that money, sex, religion and politics should be avoided in polite conversation but no one admitted that colonialism was also taboo. I later wrongly assumed that it would figure largely in my undergraduate studies in London. Decades later public reticence continues although there appears to be a growing realisation that Britain needs to understand its past in order to effectively grasp modern prejudice. Increasingly historical studies are being led by the study of empire and of Britain's place in the world.

We have to untangle the complicated history of slavery if we hope to comprehend the fuller story of overt colonialism, one of the most important driving forces in British history, next to democracy, industrialisation or religion, from the sixteenth through to the twentieth centuries. I hope that in Devon the research in this book will be a useful step towards acquiring a reasoned and rational understanding of what seems to be both unreasonable and irrational history. But there are many modern perils and complications.

Preface

A generation ago the author of *Slavery, history and the historians* while noting that 'our understanding of slavery has gained enormously from the cut and thrust of the historians' debates' asked 'how is a wider audience to tune in to the multiplicity of voices which have spoken so eloquently on the history of slavery?'[2]

The public discourse has been transformed and is no longer merely charged territory. It has suddenly become not just adversarial but socially divisive and, in some cases, toxic. Fourteen years ago, when I wrote *Devon and the Slave Trade*, public discussions could be heated but remained respectful. The death in the United States of George Floyd on 25 May 2020 recharged the issue of race relations on both sides of the Atlantic; as with Brexit, elements in British society increasingly voice sharply contrasting and fixed views of the past. As opinion is paraded as historical fact, actual history is sacrificed. An unrestrained vehemence is driven by social media which in 2007 was still in its infancy. We have become accustomed to keyboard trolls using anonymity to spout ignorance and hatred. But history and the wider issues that are raised are too important to surrender to intimidation and censorship.

There are distinct differences in the slavery narratives of the United States and the United Kingdom; enslavement in America is history which took place within the country whereas in Britain it has been largely perceived as a history which concerns other places. Many Black Americans are the descendants of those who lived enslaved in America. In contrast the majority of the Black population in the United Kingdom are more likely to be twentieth-century immigrants, or the children of immigrants, whose enslaved ancestors lived in the Caribbean. Others are descended from African migrants whose ancestors may have been free. In the United States the history of the Confederacy casts a long and divisive shadow and remains a rallying point for White supremacists. In contrast, the defining element on this side of the Atlantic is the Empire which has a history complicated by the slavery legislation of 1807 and 1833. These two structures, with which enslavement is connected, had different lifetimes: the Confederacy was defeated in 1865 while the British Empire continued, it could be argued, until 1997 when Hong Kong was handed over to China. There are still, however, fourteen largely forgotten British Overseas Territories six of which are in the West Indies. More than four generations have passed since the American Confederacy but for the older generation in Britain empire remains living history.

In the United Kingdom Professor Margot Finn, as president of the Royal Historical Society, recently suggested the historical debate has become part of the wider 'cultural war' which for many years has engulfed the United States.[3] In the last year there has emerged a group of Parliamentarians (Common Sense) and the History Matters Project from Policy Exchange, an influential think tank. Those with opposite perspectives are interest groups, activists and campaigners. Should the past be celebrated or should it be reckoned with and atoned for? The aim of these rival ideologies is to fashion and control the narrative of national identity. Divisions have been heightened further by the impact of recent scholarship on race and empire which has contributed to a consensus amongst historians that university teaching needs to be reassessed. One element of this 'war' has been the National Trust's recent report on colonialism and historic slavery which became divisive amongst its members, volunteers and the public.

The fevered nature surrounding this topic tests historians whose dedication to impartiality and evidence has long been recognised as the basis for research, analysis and writing. The ethics of a historian, as set out by the Royal Historical Society in 2020, involve not only behaving with integrity 'through developing an awareness of one's own biases [and] disclosing qualifications to arguments' but in avoiding misrepresenting the past in 'concealing, falsifying or perverting historical records, but rather aiming for accuracy, fairness and rigour in their work and professional lives'.

My intention with this study is to examine Devon's role in emancipation and define slave-ownership at that time but there are particular problems for those who work on topographical areas outside leading population centres. In respect to Devon, the lack of detailed research has contributed to public views becoming polarised and exaggerated: some assume there were no slavery connections while others have extrapolated from studies of other parts of Britain and overstate Devon's role. There is disappointment that the level of involvement either approaches or does not match the wealthier and more industrialised parts of the country. Elements of history have become inconvenient. One side seeks recognition of the enormity of the enslavement of millions of Africans while the other prefers to discuss abolition, White slavery in North Africa or Africans' participation in enslaving fellow Africans. Only convenient history matters. Factual evidence inevitably disappoints if not infuriates those with entrenched views.

There are occasional suggestions that there is or has been a conspiracy to suppress the 'truth', that this history has been deliberately hidden or kept secret. The sad reality is that many important topics remain un-researched because Devon's history is reliant upon volunteers. It is not surprising then that topics such as prejudice remain unexplored: there are no published historical studies regarding, for instance, gender, physical disabilities, ageism, Romany Gypsies, Showmen or the LGBT+ community. I fully recognise that while many were enslaved because of their ethnicity there were many other men and women who were likewise the victims of prejudice. The most extreme example is of those men who were convicted of having engaged in same-sex relations; they, irrespective of skin colour, were murdered by the state until 1861. I am keen not to diminish the history of this or any other form of oppression but they fall outside the perimeters of this study. I have recently explored some of these topics in respect to Exeter, in *Not One of Us*, but a county study has not yet been possible.

This study also does not reference Trans-African slavery or that across colonial South Asia nor the wider history in its various forms in other cultures and continents. Once again, this is beyond the scope of this work as well as of the knowledge of the author.

While a lack of published research for Devon could be viewed as a form of collective amnesia, it should be questioned whether the history of enslavement, plantation-owning and trade in slave-produced goods may be neglected because it was less prevalent than in the leading parts of the country such as London, Bristol and Liverpool. Moreover, future research will be impeded by a continuing hostile environment. I hope that this book will help fill the void and that it will introduce the basic historical framework from which opinions can be formed. It might bridge gaps not only in historical knowledge but in social attitudes.

The last few years have seen a rapid reappraisal of linguistic terms and it is easy to cause offence without intending to, particularly when it comes to the misunderstanding of historical meanings. This book was written when a national furore erupted over a proposal to remove road signs which described Bideford as the 'Little White Town'. New versions now contextualise the term's origins from the popular Victorian novel *Westward Ho!*, they now read 'Charles Kingsley's Little White Town'. It was feared that visitors would not appreciate that in 1855 the author referred in his book to the colour of the buildings ('the white houses piled up the hill-side')[4] rather than making a racial association.

The subjective nature of language also presents difficulties. I have attempted to keep the text readable in varying words or terms but have favoured those which are currently deemed socially sensitive. It has been my aim not to soften terminology and thus disguise the inhumanity of enslavement, while also seeking not to lessen the dignity of individuals.

While words or terms fall in and out of use, their interpretation is crucial if we aim to understand the past. This is particularly true of the complex racial hierarchies which had terms with precise meanings. These defined the racial, cultural and legal position of an individual in contrast to the modern custom of self-identification which gives a precedence of choice over biological ancestry. For instance, on 1 October 1836 the *Exeter & Plymouth Gazette* reported that a nurseryman had developed a variety of dahlia which was described as being 'almost black and immensely large'. He named it 'Sambo', a term which then defined an individual with three grandparents who were Black and one who was White. It has been several generations since the term was socially acceptable but it is necessary to understand its historic meaning and use: it was one of many used to define the ancestry of interracial individuals. This book draws this term's meaning from historical documents and discusses others which are equally unacceptable today. All readers should find the words unacceptable and some may be offended by them.

Capitalisation has been used in respect to groups in racial, ethnic or cultural terms (e.g. Asian, Black, Coloured, Hispanic, Native American and White). While the ongoing reassessment of the use of capital letters in respect to white and black has provoked diverse views, I have chosen to follow the convention of the National Association of Black Journalists not to use 'white' and 'Black' because it indicates the former is the default race. Hence, I have capitalised both.

I have generally used specific terms such as Jamaican, Barbadian or Antiguan rather than 'slave' or 'enslaved person' but in respect to the last two I have given preference to the latter in part because it is fresher to a modern reader but occasionally have also deployed 'slave' in order to retain the harshness which it implies. I have generally extended this in reference to slavery in the Maghreb where most White Devonians were enslaved. 'Enslaver' and 'slaveholder' have been preferred to 'slave-owner' but the latter term has been used in this book's title in order not to diminish its severity. 'Estate-owner' and 'estate' have been used in preference to 'planter' and 'plantation' but the latter has been used occasionally because it more clearly defines a colonial landed estate. North Americans will be unaware that within a British context 'plantation' does not have the American cultural overtones but generally referred to a parcel of planted woodland or even to other colonial types of settlements. One exception may be the derivation of the Regency name 'Plantation Terrace' in Dawlish.[5]

While debate continues to rage over the use of these terms, in the same way as that regarding capitalisation, I fully recognise that as language continues to evolve modern conventions will be superseded by future sensibilities.

Words and terms quoted from historical sources have not been altered. I have deployed an extensive use of quotation from contemporary documents in an attempt to inform and give a flavour of the period but it needs to be recognised that these texts were written from privileged perspectives, and often ignored the implications of the background and source of wealth of the people being discussed, as well as often displaying prejudice against both enslaved and free people. I hope that readers will recognise the relevance of these materials without my having to repeat or emphasise in each instance the context in which they should be considered.

I am conscious that this book, despite being more than one hundred thousand words in length, is incomplete: no doubt additional former slave-owners connected with Devon in 1834 remain to be identified. Some of them will be short-term residents who were less likely to be noted in records. In 1830, for instance, a letter was sent to an Exeter newspaper from an anonymous former 'slave proprietor'. He, or she, then lived in Bishopsteignton but I have been unable to name her or him.[6] Three years later another former West Indian likewise wrote from Ilfracombe: his identity also remains a mystery.[7]

The images included in this volume cover diverse themes and subjects but some historical illustrations share unpleasant overtones of some written sources. These will hopefully not cause offence.

There are two notable gaps in original documents: no Colleton family papers have been identified nor are there documents relating to the Rolle's endeavours in Florida and the Bahamas. All 43 boxes of the latter family's papers have been examined although it is possible some documentary evidence has been overlooked given the collection remains unlisted despite it having been deposited in the Devon Heritage Centre as long ago as 1988.

I would like to express my appreciation to the individual collectors as well as to the trustees of the Art Institute Chicago, Birmingham Museums Trust, J. Paul Getty Museum, Library of Congress, Metropolitan Museum of Art, Museum of

▶ 1. Emancipation Day, 1834, as depicted by Alexander Rippingale in an mezzotint by David Lucas, 1834. It was entitled 'To the Friends of Negro Emancipation' with longer text 'a glorious and happy era, on the first of August, bursts upon the western world. England strikes his manacles from the slave, and bids the bond go free'. The current reappraisal of historical images has led to the Victoria & Albert Museum highlighting the text as 'offensive and discriminatory' and the National Maritime Museum has also cited the 'historical and offensive terms'. Neither the British Museum or the National Gallery of Jamaica have (yet) given similar warnings about the copies in their custody.

New Zealand, National Gallery of Art (Washington), National Museum of African American History & Culture, Rijksmuseum, Yale Center for British Art and Yale University Art Galley for permission to reproduce their images.

I am grateful to friends and colleagues who have provided guidance, support and help. A book of this kind draws on research carried on for many years and among my many debts will be some I have overlooked. I apologise to anyone I have omitted. I would like to thank Elly Babbedge, Professor Jeff Bolster, Professor Julia Crick, Jill Drysdale, Professor Margot Finn, Derek Gore, Professor Candice Goucher, Professor Colin Jones, Professor Maryanne Kowaleski, Rachel Lang, Dr Richard Lobdell, Keith McClelland, Peter Maunder, Professor Malyn Newitt, Alexander Paget, Dr Tim Rees, Dr Philip Salmon, Professor Mark Stoyle, Dr Andrew Thrush, Phil Trotter, Dr Anne Ulentin, Diane Walker, Tricia Whiteway, Michael A. Williams and Rob Wilson-North for their help which has taken many different forms. Tony Cole was very generous with sharing details of his family history and Ann Brown was very helpful in regards to the Catherine Elizabeth Hyndman Trust. I owe a debt to many library, archive and museum staff and volunteers including Kirsty McGill (Bedfordshire Archives Service), Linda Spurdie (Birmingham Museums Trust), Miles Robert (British Library), Jane Muskett (Chetham's Library), Adam Tuck (The College of Arms), Sophy Newton and Ann Smith (Cotesbach Archive), Roz Hickman and Trevor Waddington (Fairlynch Museum), Margaret Williams & Jennifer Breedy (Jamaica Archives & Records Department), Caroline Stanford (Landmark Trust), C. Esther N. Henry (National Archives of Antigua and Barbuda), Ayla Amon (National Museum of African American History and Culture), Naomi Ayre (North Devon Athenaeum), Gary Knaggs (North Devon Record Office), Maria Smit and Caroline Wittop Koning (Rijksmuseum), Bruce Wilkinson (John Rylands Library), John McClure (Virginia Museum of History & Culture), Helen Taylor (Wiltshire & Swindon History Centre) and Edward Town (Yale Center for British Art). I am grateful to Professor Jonathan Barry, Sue Jackson, Richard O'Neil and Dr Stephen Roberts for their helpful comments on the text. Any and all residual errors remain, of course, my own. I owe a particular debt to Keith Stevens for his continued encouragement and help. Finally, I would like to thank Lord Devon for his foreword and all those at Devon County Council for their support of this book.

While my interest in this topic is professional, I appreciate for others this is personal history. Some readers will be the descendants of slaveholders and others will have enslaved ancestors. One of the legacies of slavery is the enduring racism against Black men and women. This shared history will be felt and understood differently by each individual. I have endeavoured to assemble a basic historical framework as others seek to understand themselves and their identity in the world. All history matters.

Taddyforde, Exeter
August 2021

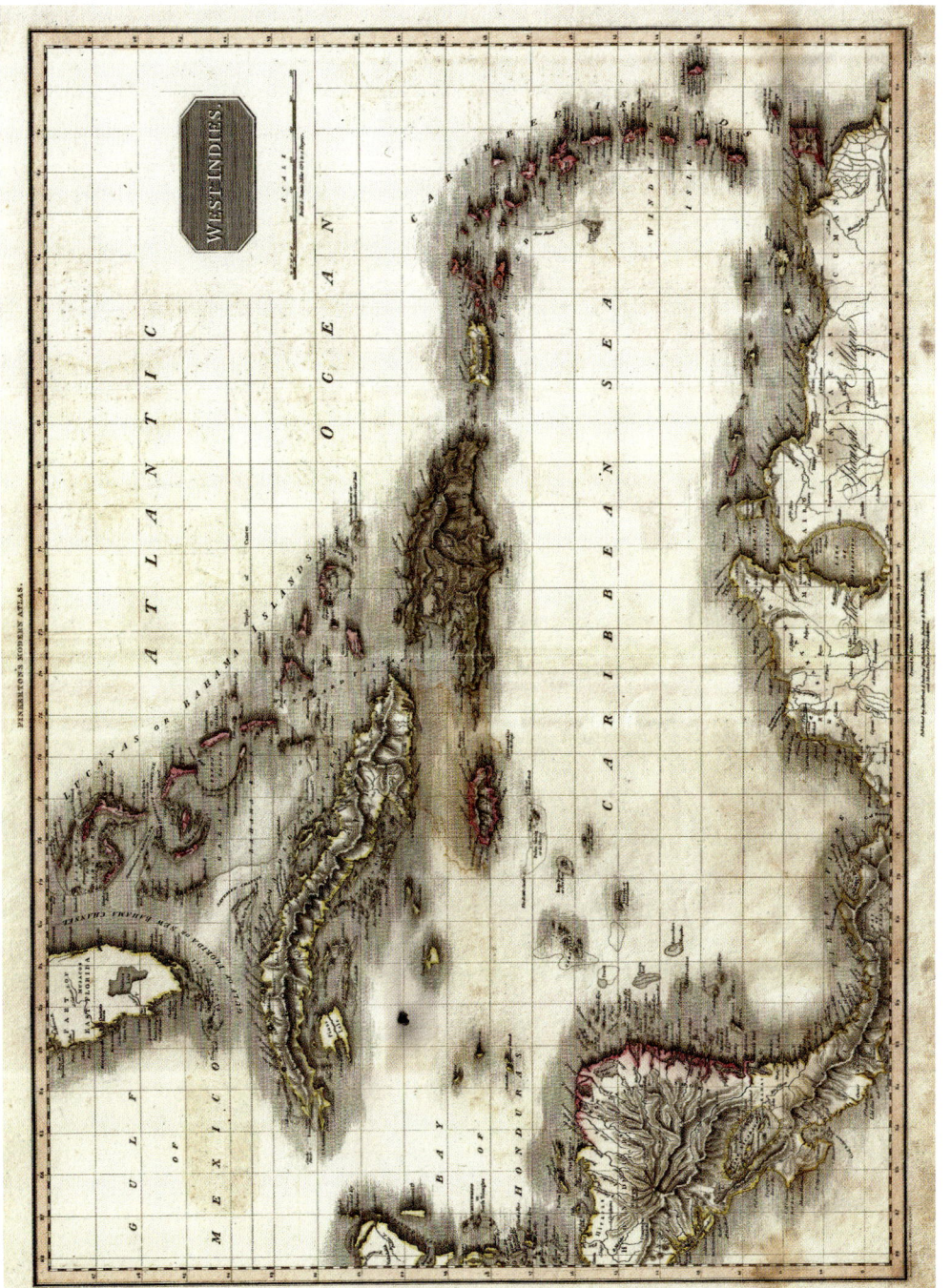

The West Indies as drawn by John Pinkerton, c1818

Conventions

Original spelling has been retained in quotations from North American writers. Each citing of individual compensation awards is followed by the modern equivalent in round brackets. These have been calculated using the historic money converter provided by The National Archives. An equal portion has been assumed for shared compensation awards.

Tables

1.	Plantations named after Devon places	67
2.	Population of British slave colonies in which there were Devon estate owners, 1830	68
3.	Ages of slaves in Demerara and Essequibo, 1832	77
4.	Location of births of residents in Devon's parishes with lowest populations, 1841 & 1851	130
5.	Location of births of residents in three resorts, 1841 & 1851	131
6.	Residents of Devon born in the West Indies and Mauritius, 1851–1871	132
7.	Slave-owners who had personal slavery compensation awards while resident in Devon on 1 August 1834	140
8.	Slave-owners who had personal slavery compensation awards while resident in Devon, 1835–1841	141
9.	Devon-born slave owners who had compensation, 1834	174
10.	George Beare's enslaved people, 1834	175
11.	Thomas Davy's enslaved people, 1817	180

Foreword

Todd Gray is to be thanked for providing a revealing and admirably detailed insight into slave ownership in Devon at the date of emancipation. Taking raw data from the compensation paid to those with proprietary interests in enslaved persons in 1834, Dr Gray has added his rare knowledge of county records and a sensitive and sophisticated approach to complex history. The outcome is a bold and groundbreaking account of the county's relationship with slavery that will be valuable to academic historians and interested readers alike for years to come.

As Dr Gray recognises, this work does not provide all the answers to Devon's long and complex association with empire and the distinct but related iniquity of slavery. The county that was so instrumental in Britain's early overseas expansions – home of Drake, Gilbert and Raleigh and departure point for the *Mayflower* – became by 1834 a quiet, bucolic retirement community for former imperial administrators, putting their feet up in quiet coastal resort towns. Todd Gray couples a forensic analysis of those imperialist's slave holding interests with fascinating biography and challenging historical analysis – and prompts many further lines of research. I hope this work encourages others to pursue this field of inquiry, as Devon will benefit immeasurably from understanding fully the consequences of its fabled maritime heritage, as well as a better appreciation of the Irish Plantations (acquired by families such as my own) and their role as precursors to Plantations across the Atlantic.

The past 18 months of coronavirus pandemic have been a dismal time. But to the extent lockdown forced Todd Gray to his study to generate this seminal work, we can be thankful and consider this as a silver lining to a desperately dark time. I hope it provides a ray of inspiration to others to consider our complex past afresh and with new eyes.

Charles Courtenay, 19th Earl of Devon

Introduction

This book asks one question, to what extent did Devonians own enslaved people on 31 July 1834?

At first glance, the history seems clear-cut given Devon's richest man, who was one of the few resident aristocrats, was a slave-owner and the county's Anglican bishop also had compensation for freeing enslaved people that day. However, the relationship of both individuals to slavery was more complex than it appears. Many of Devon's slaveholders, as will be seen, were not wealthy and the majority were resident in the county for short periods. Their life stories show they were born across the globe, came from a variety of social backgrounds, resided mainly in one type of Devon community and owned from one individual to many hundreds.

The enquiry in itself may seem straightforward, even rather limited, but no county has a study of slavery. Local studies in general are less common than national perspectives and consequently regional variations in the pattern and character of slave-ownership remain largely unknown. The difficulties are compounded by Devon being unrepresentative of England. In 1834 it had a low population, faltering economy and little industrialisation in comparison with the capital, the Midlands and the North. Within a generation the driving economic forces of Exeter and Plymouth had faded: the former lost its cloth industry and the navy and privateering had peaked in the latter. Slave voyages had never been economically significant and the trade in slave-produced goods had diminished in the mid eighteenth century. These factors also made Devon different to London, Liverpool or Bristol, the places most studied for their slavery connections.

Ownership was merely one of the ways in which individuals were associated with slavery. In its widest sense, it could be assumed that any consumer of slave-produced goods, including sugar, rum, coffee and cotton, directly benefitted from enslavement. In 1834 this would have defined some 16,564,138 people, the entire population of the country.[8] This study initially focuses on the most limited definition, those Devonians who personally received compensation for the loss of their enslaved workers in 1834, but then discusses other individuals who had financial and legal relationships with

◀ 2. Among these Devonians in costume at the Bachelors' Ball at Exeter in 1835 were Mrs D'Urban and Mrs Porter whose West Indian slaves underpinned their families' wealth. In contrast, slavery did not contribute to the Hungarian dress 'brilliant with diamonds' which was worn by Lady Rolle. Her husband's Bahamian estates had lost money.

slavery estates. The detailed nature of the documentation allows the exploration of this wide range of individuals.

Devon's historiography of enslavement studies

Nearly four hundred years ago the author of our first printed county history observed Devon was known through the tales of 'heroes' such as John Hawkins rather than from published histories. A Victorian recalled that Thomas Westcote had written that the annals of Devon had:

> 'long lain in obscurity, illustrated only by the valiant actions of the worthy heroes thereof, and not by the quills of the natives who are such as dare rather to adventure in their travels by sea and land, to discover new worlds, to find them and to conquer and people kingdoms therein, than to encounter the squint eye of envy or black heart of malice, by treading the ridged, untrodden, uncouth path, by which I have undertaken to guide you, which promiseth neither reward nor regard but scornful back-biting and scandalous detraction'.[9]

Two generations later Reverend John Prince noted exploration, privateering and colonisation in the West Indies in relation to Sir John Berry, Sir Francis Drake, Sir Thomas Gates, Sir John Hawkins, Captain John Oxenham and Sir Walter Ralegh but ignored forced labour. He wrote that Hawkins' coat of arms was:

> 'a demi-Moor in his proper colour, bound in a cord ... this seems to signify as if he had taken prisoner some roytelet [a little king] or chief person among the Moors'.[10]

His description appears at first glance to be at odds with the modern understanding that the heraldry glorified slaving. However, the original patent of 1565 described it as 'a demi-Moor in his proper colour, bound in a cord as bond and captive, with annulets on his arms and ears gold'. This was, as Prince also repeated, 'in token of his victory against the Moors'. The original patent noted the arms were granted for Hawkins' 'high and commendable service' in 'un-haunted parts' of Africa and America.[11]

More than a century later a description of a second local coat of arms is also of interest. In the next history of Devon,[12] written at the turn of the nineteenth century by the Lysons brothers, there are two references to slavery but both relate to North Africans enslaving Christians. In one passage the authors described the heraldry of Sir Edward Pellew, 1st Viscount Exmouth. His armorial supporters included:

> 'a figure designed to represent a Christian slave, naked from the waist upwards, holding in his dexter hand a cross, and in his sinister hand his fetters broken'.

▶ 3. Coat of Arms of Sir John Hawkins, 1565, with a young Black girl wearing a gold earing and with what appears at first sight to be gold jewellery.

of their arivall as it were, & moreo[...]

T

was graunte[...]
eight, arrived[...]
necessaries a[...]
warlike m[...]
hundreth m[...]
saide Ta[...]
whereof [...]
and coragious [...]
his greate pre[...]
golde a Sca[...]
Armes by w[...]
do ratifie confi[...]
and they it to vse [...]
witnes whereof [...]
annexed this Se[...]
and in the yth ye[...]

Introduction

This device referred to Pellew's bombardment of Algiers in 1816 in which he released more than a thousand European slaves including amongst them Devonians.[13]

This enslavement is of particular relevance because more Devonians were taken than those from other English counties. It has been estimated that at least one million White Europeans were enslaved. They could obtain their liberty by conversion to Islam or through paying a ransom organised by friends, family or state or church officials.[14] Enslaved Africans could in theory purchase their freedom and this was achieved mostly with the profits made from selling garden produce from allotments. A difference between the two groups is that White Europeans returned to a state of freedom whereas in the West Indies former slaves became free but continued to live in societies which regarded them as inherently inferior.

It is noteworthy that these historians did not discuss slavery more widely. Ironically, Americans confined at Dartmoor Prison during the War of 1812 compared it with their previous incarceration in North Africa:

> 'The food and the lodgings were in every respect superior among the Mohammedans than among these boasting Christians and their general treatment infinitely more humane; some of our companions had been prisoners among the Barbary powers and they describe them as vastly more considerate than the English'.[15]

Subsequent Devon historians acknowledged slaving but ignored plantations.[16] In 1831, when abolition was sweeping the country, Reverend Thomas Moore commented on Hawkins:

> 'In the year 1562 his extended views of trade suggested to his mind a plan which appeared to be the commencement of the African slave-trade by English adventurers – a trade so disgraceful to human nature, by the obvious iniquity of its principle and the atrocious barbarities inseparable from the practice of it. If, however, in more advanced periods of knowledge and civilisation, the great profits resulting from this inhuman traffic have blinded the understandings, and hardened the hearts of those who have been engaged in it, and rendered them insensible to its cruelty and injustice, it is nothing wonderful that the minds of the more respectable adventurers, at the time of which we are speaking, did not revolt at is commencement, when these Negroes were generally considered as little better than beasts of prey'.[17]

Moore concluded:

> 'Just as such exploits are now altogether reprobated, and honourable as it is to the English nation that they are at length rendered illegal, they seem to have conducted greatly to the reputation of those by whom they were perpetrated in that age of heroism. For Captain

◄ 4. Detail of an unfettered White slave from Algiers, part of Admiral Pellew's coat of arms, in the Church of St James, Christow.

John Hawkins bore the badge of these achievements in a crest of arms, granted him by patent, consisting of a *demi-moor in his proper colour bound with a cord*, a symbol, as it has been observed, worthy of the traffic! It would have been more significant could the label have been added *Am I not a man and a brother?*'[18]

Later Devon writers and historians also confined themselves to slaving. For example, in 1907 the author of *My Devonshire Book; in the land of junket and cream* referred to Hawkins having 'laid the foundation of our slave trade in the West Indies' by sailing to West Africa for 'black birds'.[19]

This avoidance of forced labour plantations may not necessarily be an act of social forgetting. During the last four and half centuries eight men have written county histories of Devon and few displayed interest in overseas land-ownership of any form. They have ignored plantations in sixteenth-century Ireland, where the Courtenay family of Powderham Castle held 85,000 acres from 1591,[20] or in Newfoundland where Devonians owned fish plantations from the seventeenth to the nineteenth centuries. There has been a similar lack of interest in former colonies in Africa, Asia or Australasia despite the importance of South Africa, India, Hong Kong, Australia and New Zealand. Histories have generally limited themselves to examining individuals, institutions and events within the geographical bounds of Devon. The main exceptions are Plymouth Plantation or Roanoke which have been celebrated for generations.

A century ago, in 1920, the history of a local slaving voyage, that of the *Daniel & Henry*, was first published[21] but it was not until 2007 that a collection of Devon-related slaving documents appeared.[22] That year a transatlantic slavery exhibition at Plymouth Museum revealed the lack of research into the city's past or that of the county.[23]

The only Devon historian to have written at length upon the West Indies also made three points in regard to the general study of history. In 1870 J. A. Froude, one of the most distinguished, popular and controversial historians the county has produced, said in his presidential address to members of the Devonshire Association that history:

'depends on exact knowledge, on the same minute, impartial, discriminating observation and analysis of particulars which is equally the basis of science'.

Second, he noted that historians had to deal with:

'combinations of reality and human thought which it is his business to analyse and separate into their component parts. So far as he can distinguish successfully he is a historian of truth, so far as he fails he is the historian of opinion and tradition'.

5. Dartington-born James Anthony Froude, 1868, twenty years before his travels in the Caribbean. ▶

Third, he outlined the responsibility of the historian:

'At present our sole duty is to study and set down with as much impartiality as our frailties will allow us, the truth as we can really discern it, imagining nothing, inventing nothing, concealing nothing, condemning nothing, save the breach of those moral laws which have been acknowledged sacred by universal consent and sympathising with all varieties of thought by which good men have allowed their actions to be guided'.

Froude's body of work demonstrates a sharp partisan quality but his critics went so far as to suggest 'Froude's disease' was his inability to 'make an accurate statement about any matter'.[24]

However, the principal reason Froude's comments are relevant to this study is because of *The English in the West Indies,* a book he wrote five decades after emancipation in 1888. In this travelogue Froude often discarded the use of evidence for personal opinion. Much of his commentary, including his doubts over the freeing of the enslaved and views on racial differences, sharply diverges from modern thinking on race, enslavement and colonialism. For instance he wrote:

'In no part of the globe is there any peasantry whose every want is so completely satisfied as Her Majesty's black subjects in these West Indian islands … If happiness is the be all and end all of life, and those who have most of it have most completely attained the object of their being, the *nigger* who now basks among the ruins of the West Indian plantations is the supremest specimen of present humanity'.[25]

The book was heavily criticised in the West Indies and shortly afterwards a Trinidadian published *Froudacity: West Indian Fables by James Anthony Froude.*[26] The authors offered contradictory visions of the future of the West Indies arising from emancipation.

Writing enslavement history

This book has been written amidst this hodgepodge of publication and attempts to understand one strand of history. The county's earliest public notice of African slavery could date to 1642 when a militiaman was described on his tombstone as 'not like a fool or a fettered slave'.[27] It could be assumed that Devonians were then aware of 'fettered' people, that is human beings held in chains, other than just those enslaved men who had returned from North Africa.

There is a substantial legacy of literature written by enslavers and abolitionists in the late eighteenth and early nineteenth centuries. Its use by modern historians and the examination of documentary evidence has resulted in a considerable understanding of Britain's role in transatlantic slavery. In the last fifty years a multitude of studies have outlined Europe's invasion of the Americas and its voracious appetite

Introduction

for natural commodities. West Africa contributed the lion's share of the workforce needed to make colonisation viable and Britain came to lead in the transportation of millions to a lifetime in servitude.

As useful and necessary as these studies are, this volume is possible only because other sources make it feasible to study areas of Britain: the emancipation legislation of 1833 generated a treasure trove of information. Reports were printed at the time and are now available online through the Centre for the Study of the Legacies of British Slavery.[28]

These papers recorded financial settlements made to slaveholders when their enslaved workforce became apprentices on 1 August 1834. This allows an analysis of ownership in each of Britain's twenty-one colonies as well as of individuals living in Devon when they claimed compensation. Their histories form the body of this study.

More problematic is the criterion for determining who was a Devonian and defining others' ties to Devon. Some former slave-owners moved to or visited the county after they were compensated. It is impossible to definitively list them given their residency varied from a few weeks to several decades. Three lives, those of Robert Houstoun, William Brooks King and James Rowe, demonstrate how complicated local associations were.

General Sir Robert Houstoun, or 'Black Dick' as he was known, was part of a large group of enslavers who lived abroad. The British Empire defined Houstoun's life. He received compensation while living in Scotland and moved to Devon twenty-six years later, possibly for his health as he died within a year. He was born in Scotland and his wife, Frances Follett, was the daughter of a Topsham naval captain. Houstoun was a general in the East India Company and many of his children were born in India. The end of his life came in 1862 at Thornton in Torquay where he resided with his wife, a footman and a lady's maid.[29] In 1836 Houstoun had acted as the executor of two estates in Grenada which had 154 enslaved persons. He also owned Belmont Estate through his father, a West Indian merchant. He received £5,024 8s 11d (in today's money £340,636.84) for 194 individuals.[30] His qualification for being a Devonian was his year's residence in Torbay. The Belmont Estate today specialises in cocoa.

In contrast to Houstoun, William Brooks King was associated with one colony, Jamaica, where he was born in about 1787. King emigrated to England after emancipation, possibly in 1837, and lived in retirement in West Teignmouth from 1838 until his death twenty-six years later. King may have migrated to be near his only child who in 1834 married Rhys Davis Powell, the 'cursed' owner of Craig Y Nos Castle in Wales. Sixteen years earlier, in 1818 when she was a small child, Sarah King had left Jamaica with her maternal grandparents, Adam and Sarah Dolmage, and settled at Beaufort House near Bath. Two years earlier her mother had died in childbirth and shortly afterwards her father remarried.[31]

King was Dolmage's attorney in Jamaica. In 1833 a visitor to that island described attorneys as:

'fat, sleek, well-fed, demure-featured gentlemen with a good deal of what the Irish people call cuteness about the mouth, lurking especially about its angles but not sufficient to predominate over a hilarious expression of the eye in which fun and frankness of disposition is mingled with shrewdness'.[32]

King had overseen the sale of Dolmage's coffee plantation in 1825 and both men were in the Jamaican civil service. Events in 1827, in addition to Sarah's marriage, suggest King had additional reasons for relocating: his household furnishings were sold in Kingston, a notice was placed in a Jamaican newspaper announcing the death of an illegitimate infant daughter and King was dismissed from his employment in the admiralty court because, it was publicly explained in a newspaper, he had 'gone off'.[33]

Nevertheless, he returned to Jamaica and later visited New York with his wife. A friend provided him with a character reference which described him as 'an honourable upright man' while his:

'lady is of a very old family in this island being the daughter of the late Reverend M. Campbell, rector of St Andrews, and sister of the present rector. She is agreeable, kind-hearted and genteel. I would not have ventured to request your notice of them had they not both been in every respect unexceptionable'.[34]

He was in Jamaica in 1835 and 1836 when he submitted two compensation claims of £1,179 10s 7d (£79,973.61) for 62 Jamaicans some of whom were on the Union Hill estate. King also acted as an executor or trustee for two other estates. His own awards would have helped him purchase The Hennons in 1838. This was advertised as a 'Gothic villa of high pretension… in the pure taste of the Elizabethan school'. There were ten acres of grounds and the house was designed by Samuel Alexander Greig, a Devon architect. It was later noted as:

'a large and handsome mansion, in the Elizabethan style, built by Richard Eaton, Esquire, but purchased by its present owner and occupant, William B. King, Esquire, in 1838. The lodge and stables are in the same style as the mansion, and the grounds command extensive and beautiful views of sea and land, and are laid out with great taste. In the dining room are some fine paintings by eminent artists, and in the drawing room is a richly carved mantel-piece which is much admired.'[35]

King had recently returned to London and travelled down to Exeter only a month before the house sale. His 'intimate friend', Herbert Jarrett James, was then living nearby in Dawlish.[36] Whereas Houstoun appears to have been an invalid, King was more representative of the West Indian estate-owners who enjoyed long retirements in Devon after collecting emancipation awards.

Thirdly, Reverend James John Rowe's associations demonstrates another degree of complication in untangling connections with slave ownership. In 1841 and 1851 his household comprised a number of individuals who had compensation awards. Rowe was born in East Down in North Devon in 1796 and was a cleric at Kentisbury (1837-41), St Mary Arches in Exeter (1841-66) and Morchard Bishop (1866-84). It was recalled at his death:

> 'A glance at his fine manly form was sufficient to reveal his early training was for the army before he entered the church. As *aide-de-camp* to one of the generals in the Peninsular War he was engaged in eight battles and was marching with his regiment to the battlefield when Waterloo was won'.[37]

Rowe's obituarist particularly praised his character:

> 'The deceased was a noble specimen of one of Devon's fine old English gentlemen and was justly revered and loved by his parishioners generally. The high example which he set of a pure and temperate life has not ceased to have effect since the infirmities of age precluded him from actively ministering to the spiritual needs of his flock.'[38]

No reference was made to Jamaica or slavery. His paternal family had been resident there in the early 1700s but returned to Great Torrington before Rowe's birth.

He had, through his wife, a share in the Old England estate. Rowe had married Elizabeth Williams Johnson in 1823 and in 1836, when resident in Somerset, claimed £158 1s 4d (£10,717.13) and another £148 17s 3d (£10,093.07) for a second estate. This was for nineteen Jamaicans some of whom were on the Old England Estate. The latter amount was also given to his wife's two aunts, Elizabeth James neé Williams and Ann Williams, who later lived with them in Exeter. All three women were Jamaican-born. Elizabeth Williams had married Hugh James, a Kingston medical doctor, in 1794 and in his will he left her his 'mountain plantation'.[39] She received £657 17s 1d (£44,603.37) for 20 individuals in one estate and possibly had other awards. James died in 1854 at Rowe's home in Mont Le Grand in Exeter and had been blind for at least three years. Her unmarried sister Ann received £148 17s 3d (£10,093.07) for six people on two other plantations.

Mrs Rowe is typical of the women whose slavery connections are obscured by awards having been made to their husbands. In another instance John Reed and his son John Groscort Reed held estates in Demerara and received compensation as awardees, executors or trustees of the astounding sum of £34,685 6s 2d (£2,351,709). Their widows lived together at 2 Hill's Court Crescent in Exeter in the 1850s and 1860s. Mary Reed, the elder of the two women, was noted in the census not as a former slaveholder but rather as 'a proprietor of railway stocks'. Lucretia Reed, another family member, had married Edmund Haynes who also retired to Exeter. Lucy Haynes lived at 4, Hill's Court Crescent and was another Barbadian.[40] Likewise, a similar household of West Indian women at Torquay at this same time included former slave-owners: Susannah Christian Cobham received £66 6d (£4,476.58) for 5 individuals in Barbados as part of the family's larger investment in slave plantations.[41] Welsh-born Elizabeth Farquharson's connections were also obscured by her husband's compensation of £877 13s 2d (£59,506.38) for 48 Jamaicans on the Hazel Grove estate. William Tatham Farquharson married in Wales, moved to Jamaica and his widow was living in Plymouth by 1851 when she was listed simply as a fundholder in South Devon Place before later moving to Napier Terrace in Mutley Plain.[42] These lives outline different connections to slave ownership and hint at a much wider and complicated history.

Gaps in the literature

There are few surviving plantation financial accounts, deeds or leases relating to Devon to augment compensation records but the greatest gap is the lack of any first hand accounts by any enslaved person. In 1854 a journalist interviewed Dahlia Graham, who had been enslaved in Senegal, and reported that she was not only 'somewhat' eloquent about her accommodation in Exeter's workhouse but also 'very grateful' and 'exceedingly happy'. She was 'rejoiceful':

> 'in her present happy position. Such are the mutations of sublunary things! Dahlia, kidnapped in Africa, endured the horrors of the middle passage, was sold into bondage in our colonies, and now at the patriarchal age of 93, she has a mansion to live in, gardens to live in, and the lieges of the Queen of England to minister to her wants! Fortunate Dahlia. How different an end to that which would, probably, have awaited her in her own country!'

However, we do not have her own words, merely those supplied for her.[43]

In *Twenty-eight years a slave* Reverend Thomas Lewis Johnson recounted his experiences in the 1880s and 1890s spent lecturing across Devon and living at South View, the home of H. O. Serpell, a Plymouth biscuit manufacturer, at Mannamead, the affluent Victorian neighbourhood. Johnson had been freed in Virginia after the American Civil War and was later an evangelist in Africa before visiting England. He wrote about his novelty in Devon as a Black man.[44]

Some writers have incorporated enslavement in their writing. In 1856 Charles Kingsley imagined the views of a crewmember of Hawkins. In *Westward Ho!* he composed what he thought would have been a Bideford sailor's justification for enslaving Africans:

> 'The negroes are of the children of Ham, who are cursed and reprobate, as scripture declares, and their blackness testifies, being Satan's own livery, among whom therefore there can be none of the elect, wherefore the elect are not required to treat them as brethren'.

▶ 6. Rose Hall, by Hakewill, 1825. The house was owned by John Rose Palmer, built in about 1775 and 'considered as the best in Jamaica'. Hakewill added, 'it is placed at a delightful elevation and commands a very extensive sea view. Its general appearance has much of the character of a handsome Italian villa.'

Another character, Sir Richard Grenville, rebuked him.[45] The biblical story of Noah's cursing of his son's descendants into perpetual servitude had been embellished with a racial slant in the sixteenth century and was still current three centuries later.[46]

Rebecca Anne Palmer, who lived in Sidmouth in the early 1800s, was the inspiration for Annie Palmer, the White Witch of Rose Hall, her Jamaican Great House in Montego Bay. The early-twentieth century novel of this 'woman of sinister beauty' includes ghosts, voodou, apparitions from hell, debauchery, unnatural cruelty, sadism, revenge and the murder of her husbands. It was summarised for tourists in the 1990s as:

> 'Dead for more than a century, Annie Palmer still stirs memories of her reign as mistress of Rose Hall Great House. Cursed by slaves as a white witch, Annie turned a magnificent plantation into a hell-house of atrocities. Countless slaves fell prey to her torture, while all three of her husbands met death at her hands.'[47]

A Jamaican prime minister cited the legend as a treasure in the island's history despite the details being factually incorrect. Nearly all of the specifics are hard to corroborate such as that she rode in male attire while in pursuit of runaway slaves but her death by strangulation in Jamaica runs counter to her actual death in Sidmouth.[48]

The King's Beard was published in 1952 and imagines events of Drake's raid on Cadiz as narrated by an Exeter man. It includes the liberation of Spanish galley slaves. There is little other literary evidence[49] with one exception being a story published in 1789 about a 'negro boy'. This was published in several national collections of amusing anecdotes. It was related that:

> 'A vessel lately in the Guinea trade, having arrived at Exeter, a Negro boy, the captain's servant, called Pompey, being on shore one Sunday about noon, observing several people resorting to a baker's for pies which had been left [to be baked] in the morning, and upon each person throwing a half penny upon the counter for the baking, which he considered as the purchase money. He returned on board exclaiming *Massa Massa, give me one halfpenny and I will bring you one great big pie*! His master not understanding what he meant, but willing to humour his intentions, complied with his request: he hastened to the baker's, threw down his money and the woman asking *which was his*? eyeing the whole group, he picked out the largest exclaiming *dis a my pie, dis a my pie*, the woman helping it on his head he repaired with the prize to his messmates who were not a little gratified with an unexpected repast, procured by untutored simplicity, at the expense of some person's hunger.'[50]

It is likely that this was a piece of creative writing but even so it raises questions as to whether Pompey, if he existed, was free or enslaved let alone how unusual it would have been then to see a Black boy in Devon. Other questions arise on the background to Devon's involvement in slavery including how commonplace it was for vessels in the African trade to visit Devon.

But the principal enquiry of this volume is identifying those Devonians who owned enslaved people in the slave colonies. This is addressed in the following pages in two parts. Part One comprises an introductory chapter which examines racial groups in the slave colonies and their terminology in relation to Devon. Chapter Two looks at the county's wider and longer associations with slavery. Two following chapters discuss the nature of the colonies and of Devon in 1834. These four chapters provide the background to the principal part of this book which forms Part Two, two chapters which analyse those individuals who directly benefited from enslavement through ownership.

Part One: Slavery & Devon, 1562–1834

Devon lost its lead in Elizabethan slaving to become by 1834 a back-water in slave ownership. This may have been the consequence of its economic position within the country but further research is needed to explore the extent to which Stuart and Georgian Devonians owned slave estates or traded in commodities, particularly tobacco, produced by forced labour.

One consequence of Devon's general embrace of exploration in the sixteenth and seventeenth centuries was the presence of small numbers of immigrants from Africa, the Americas and Asia. They lived in towns and villages across Devon and had uncertain degrees of freedom. By 1834 race had developed a meaning and significance that it had not had in 1562. An important tool in grasping liberty, which depended partly upon ethnicity, is understanding historical terminology. It also helps in comprehending the evolving nature of generations of slave ownership.

◀ 7. Dawlish in 1837 as depicted by John White Abbott. His view of E. P. Gore's Library and Public Rooms, established by 1811, illustrates the appeal of Devon's new seaside resorts to former slave-holders. The *Exeter Flying Post* reported on 15 December 1814 that the building comprised a billiard room, library, reading room and a dwelling house.

1.

2.

3.

4.

1

Slavery and the language of race

'Died in London, Thomas Porter of Rockbeare House near this city, a gentleman of high respectability, whose death is sincerely regretted by all who had the pleasure of his acquaintance', death notice, 1815

Ethnicity mostly determined freedom but some Blacks were free as were many of mixed European and African descent. In Barbados seventeenth-century legislation had distinguished two types of workers; it recognised those with freedom as 'Christian servants' while the enslaved were 'Negroes', a 'heathenish, brutish and uncertain dangerous pride of people'. The important distinction is that those with freedom were not described in racial terms as White but by their religion while those who had African ancestry were classed by their ethnicity and not termed slaves.[51]

Devon society was, like the rest of the country, broadly divided into class groups determined by culture and wealth, whereas the West Indies had four 'great classes' of race according to one observer in 1806. They comprised of 'European Whites'; 'Creole or native Whites'; 'Creoles of mixed blood and free native Blacks'; 'Negroes in a state of slavery'.

In addition, he noted there were smaller groups of Jews, Indigenous Americans and North American exiles from the Revolutionary War. Jewish men were given the rights of the Whites except they were ineligible to vote and could not serve as legislators or magistrates.[52]

West Indian slave societies were more complex than he suggested. It is essential to understand the language used in order to grasp the history Devon shares with the West Indies given some enslavers' siblings were multiracial and some men and women of mixed ethnicity themselves were enslaved persons. In one instance an anonymous

◀ 8. 'Creole Negroes' drawn by Isaac Mendes Belisaro for *Sketches of Character*, 1837–8. Figures noted include 1, a street vendor of sausages, and 2, a 'field Negro with his Kilmarnock cap' who also wore a blue checked shirt, Oznaburgh trousers and dark blue woollen cloak. The author was commended for his 'faithful delineations of people whose habits, manners and costume bear the stamp of originality and in which changes are being daily effected by the rapid strides of civilization ... steering clear of caricature'.

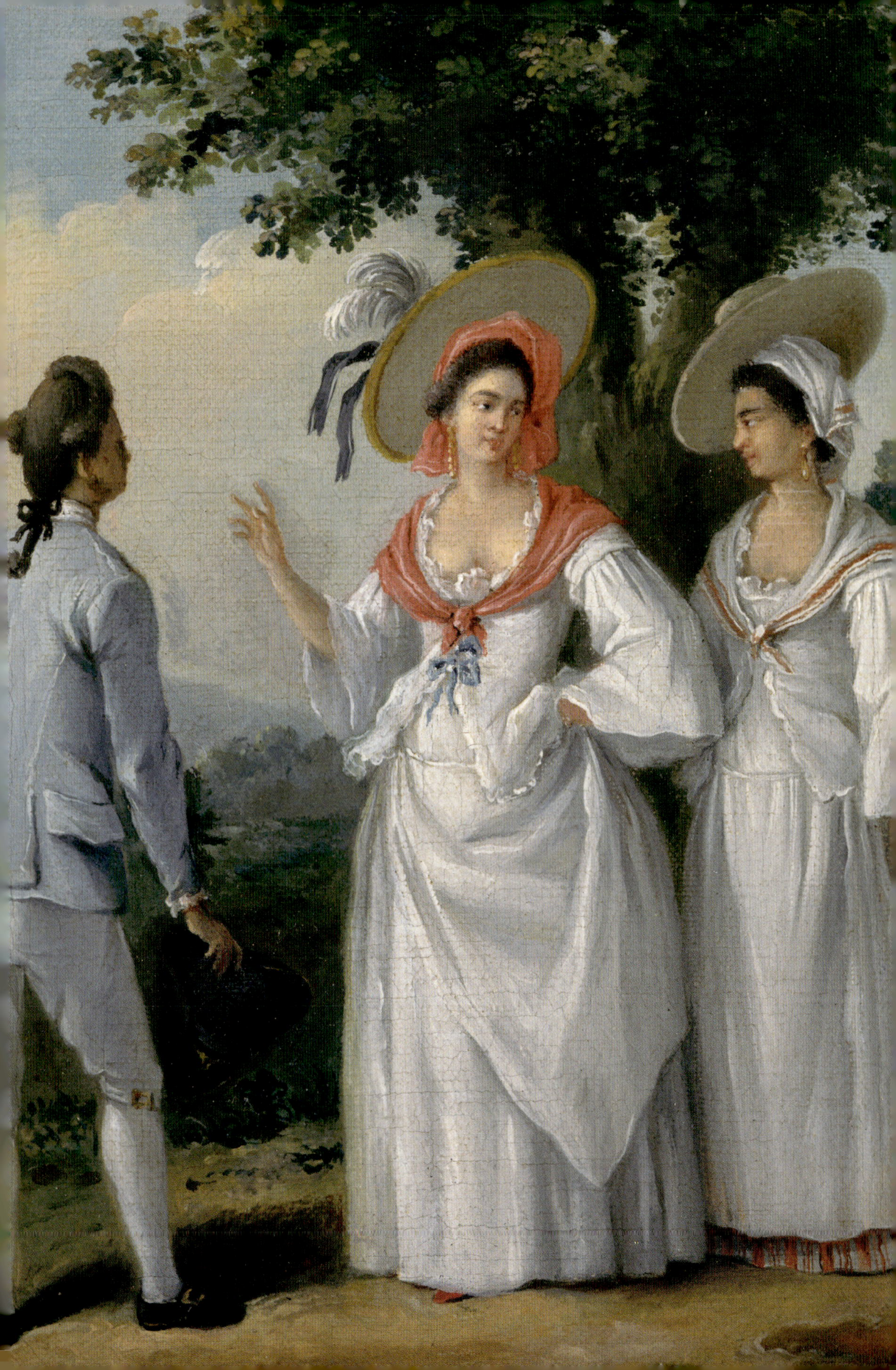

Devon owner referred to her half sister as being 'half caste' and a 'Mustee'.[53] She and other West Indian estate-owners lived in a rigid social hierarchy for which there was a complicated lexicon.

TERMINOLOGY

Some two dozen racial terms were commonly used in the slave colonies including African, Black, Brown, buckra, Coloured, Creole, man (or woman) of colour, European, half-caste, mixed blood, mongrel, Mulatto, Mustee, Musteefino, Negress, Negro, nigger, piccaninny, Quadroon, sable, Sambo, White and White Negro. It is noticeable that many are used today only to cause offence.

Devonians also employed a wide range of terminology. In the 1560s the word 'slave' was used by John Sparke, a Devonian, to describe the Africans taken by John Hawkins in England's earliest expeditions across the Atlantic. He also referred to them as 'Negroes' and 'merchandise'. 'Slave' was also in use by 1571 in Exeter where it was cited in defamation cases. It did not denote an individual as property but rather used to allege a man was a rascal or rogue who had lost his free will. It was uttered alongside a string of abusive terms such as when one man said to another 'thou art a whore-monger, whore-master and whore-mongering slave and thou were found abed with Joan Follet' and in a separate instance it was used by one man calling another 'a drinking beast, a drinking slave and a drunkard'. Other instances involved sex or alcohol including 'thou art a cuckoldly slave and thy wife meaning the said Margaret Tucker is a whore and a base whore', 'thy bastardly slave', 'thy whoreson slave', 'knave and slave' and 'a drunken rogue, a drunken slave and a common drunkard'. Perhaps the most unusual instance was recorded in 1569 in North Huish where one man said to another 'what a slave art thou to sit upon thy tail when that thou dost talk with thy better'.[54]

Other terms can also mislead. Some men and women described as 'dark' in Devon in the late 1600s had poor eyesight, possibly cataracts. This was different from the pejorative term 'darky' which was used in relation to skin colour in Devon from at least the 1800s.[55] One report, at Exeter in 1840, shows its scornful sense: an inebriated 'darkie' was brought into the city's courtroom and described as 'a ragged and wild-looking West Indian', having 'a woolly head' and called both 'Snowball' and 'Blackey'. The reporter referred to the whiteness of his eyes and teeth. The accused man himself used racist language, in perhaps an early instance of reclaiming a term, when he told the court 'me no fear de white massa, he give poor nigger someting to buy little bit o brade'.[56] In neighbouring Cornwall a 'darkey' defined a water house from the Cornish words *dour* (water) and *chy* (a house) but this use has not been found in Devon. 'Blackey' was also used in Devon in a similar manner to 'darky' at this time.[57]

Other easily misunderstood local terms in the years immediately preceding emancipation include The Black Dwarf, the name applied to James Tucker, an Exeter

◀ 9. 'Free West Indian Creoles in Elegant Dress', c1780, by Agostino Brunias.

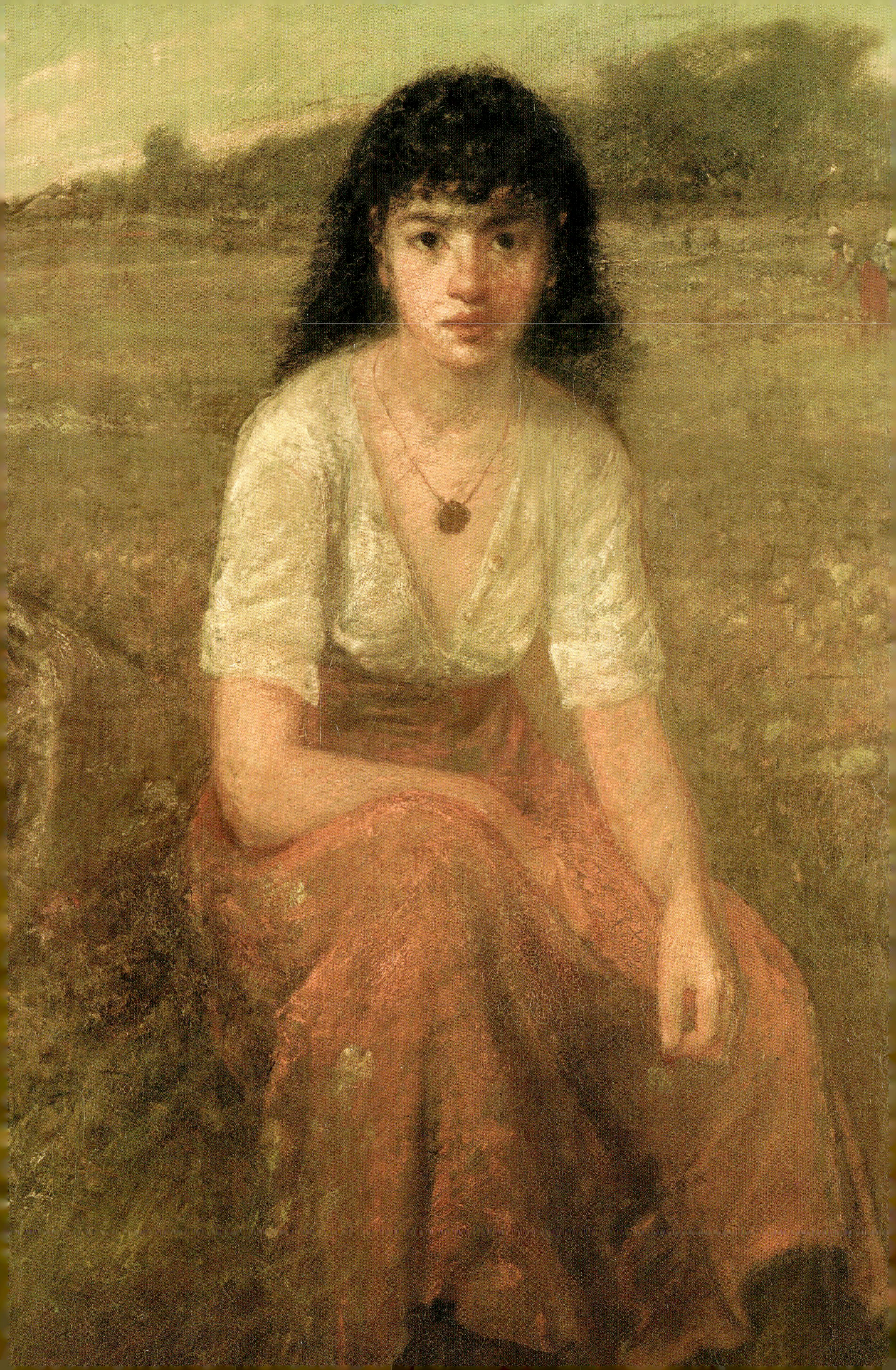

pamphlet seller, while 'The Black Man', also of Exeter, referred to the wooden statue of St Peter on the corner of North and High Streets.[58]

Caucasians

Nearly every slave-owner resident in Devon was Caucasian. As the ruling population in the West Indies they used the fewest terms to describe themselves. They were nearly always only noted as White but could be identified by their place of birth: White immigrants from Europe were termed Europeans whereas White men and women born in the West Indies were called Creoles (as were those of other races).

One visitor was surprised that White men in the West Indies assumed a sense of parity with one another. He observed a 'conscious equality' in which:

> 'the poorest White person seems to consider himself nearly on a level with the richest, and, emboldened by this idea, approaches his employer with extended hand, and a freedom, which, in the countries of Europe, is seldom displayed by men in the lower orders of life towards their superiors. It is not difficult to trace the origin of this principle. It arises, without doubt, from the pre-eminence and distinction which are necessarily attached even to the complexion of a White man, in a country where the complexion, generally speaking, distinguishes freedom from slavery. Of the two great classes of people in most of these colonies, the Black outnumber the Whites in the proportion of seven to one. A sense of common safety therefore unites the latter in closer ties than are necessary among men who are differently situated, so the same circumstance necessarily gives birth among them to reciprocal dependence and respect'.[59]

A later writer echoed this sentiment; Alison Carmichael was told in 1833 that in the late 1700s White men and women in the lower rank were 'admitted and invited to the best society'. This ceased once there was a sufficient number of the higher class to create a viable separate group.[60] The seventeenth-century White population would have included indentured or transported men and women such as Richard Tilly, an Exeter baker who chose banishment to Jamaica in preference to execution.[61]

A second term, 'buckra', was used by non-Whites to describe White men in the Caribbean. It may not have been used in Devon.

The term 'White Negro' was barely recorded. In 1833 a West Indian writer noted this defined members of the underclass of White men who, unable to find a White woman, were forced to:

> 'get a Negro, probably belonging to the estate they are employed upon, to live with them until they gradually forget their country and their early instructions and become, as the expression is, almost a White Negro'.[62]

◀ 10. 'The Quadroon' by George Fuller, 1880.

This differed from an English use of the term: in 1830 an Exeter fair exhibited 'White Negroes or White Black boys'. It was claimed that their parents were 'Black Africans' and that the children were 'amiable savages' and 'well-behaved barbarians'. In fact they were Circassians, natives of the North Caucasus who were known for their white skin.[63]

Blacks

The colonies' largest population, those of African descent, had the widest range of terminology. The English borrowed 'Negro', 'Negress', and 'nigger' from other European languages (Latin *niger*, French *nègre*, Dutch *neger*, Portuguese and Spanish *negro*). These terms described men and women with either dark, brown or black skin but in some European cultures it also included Amerindians and was used to define non-Whites.[64]

The terms 'negro' and 'nigger' were used in Devon before England established West Indian colonies in the 1620s. Barnstaple's parish clerk used them interchangeably in seven entries in his church register of baptisms, marriages and burials in the late 1500s and early 1600s. These terms generally accompanied the word servant. His counterparts in Colyton (1619), Hatherleigh (1606–1613) and Plymouth (1593–) independently used the same terms although 'black' and 'blackamoor' (used at East Allington in 1577 and St Mary Major Exeter in 1631) were more prevalent and perhaps transposable.[65] The latter term may have been initially limited to describing North Africans but it could be applied to all Africans at an early date such as when Sir Walter Ralegh noted in 1614 'the Negroes which we call the Black moors'. In Devon 'Moors' most commonly referred to North African Muslims who were also known as 'Turks' because of the political association between North Africa and the Ottoman Empire. They lived in the Maghreb (Morocco, Algeria, Libya and Tunisia), otherwise the Barbary coast, which furthered the religious division with people in the sub-Saharan south.[66]

In 1570 Nicholas Wichalse, a former mayor of Barnstaple, also used the word 'nigger' to describe a household member, otherwise only named as 'Anthony', who appears to have been a contracted servant. A bequest of five pounds was made on condition he remained in the service of Wichalse's widow Mary 'otherwise if she mind not to keep him to give him five marks [£3 7s 6d] and let him depart'.[67] Fifteen years earlier five Africans (noted in accounts printed at that time as either 'blackamoors' or 'Negroes') were brought from West Africa to Plymouth. It is unclear if they were forcibly taken. They may have been intended to subsequently act as intermediaries in trading voyages.[68] In 1567 another group of West Africans were taken to Plymouth and then transported to the West Indies by Hawkins on his third voyage.[69]

The uncertainties around Anthony's freedom is mirrored by that accorded to a second group of foreigners: the county had a handful of American natives in

11. 'Portrait of a young woman with a kerchief' by Wenceslaus Hollar, 1645. ▶

W. Hollar fecit
Antverpiæ Aº 1645

Bideford ('Ralegh', 1588–9), Stoke Gabriel ('Adrian', 1599) and Plymouth ('Giffard and Gorge', 1602) as well as another five at Plymouth in 1605. Few details are available regarding their circumstances; they have occasionally been noted as having been 'kidnapped' but enslaved would be a more accurate term. Some were named after Sir Walter Ralegh, Sir Adrian Gilbert and Sir Ferdinando Gorges in association with explorations led by those men in Virginia and New England. They, like the Africans in 1555, were brought to England as possible translators for subsequent trade and colonisation. A century earlier, in 1531, William Hawkins Senior had taken a Brazilian chief to Plymouth and then to London where he was presented to Henry VIII.[70]

An early Devonian use of the word 'nigger' was recorded in Barnstaple: in 1635 a judge heard a case of defamation in which one man had suggested to another 'go into Spain and dance with the niggers with bells about thy heels' by which he meant that the other man had 'lived incontinently with niggers in Spain'. There had been a 'great falling out' in which a string of abusive terms were exchanged.[71]

In nineteenth-century Devon the word had two other meanings. One sense was as a term of abuse to describe a rogue or rascal. Its pronunciation was recorded at Hartland: there it had a short *e* as in 'negger' or 'neggar'.[72] The term was also used from at least 1835 in relation to sawfly caterpillars (*Athalia spinarum* ssp. spinarum) along with 'the black army' and 'black palmers'.[73] In contrast, in neighbouring Cornwall fishermen used it to describe a sea cucumber also known as the 'cotton spinner'.[74] Both of the latter terms described creatures which were both black in colour and pests. Devon's most enduring use of the word began in 1939 with Agatha Christie's novel which was later renamed *And Then There Were None*. Two generations earlier the Victorian childhood rhyme had Devon in the lyrics.

The word 'black' also had meanings which differed from modern usage. Individuals so described at their baptisms show the term indicated a wide geographical area: there was an 'Indian black servant' at Ashprington in 1687 and an 'American Indian or black' at Instow in 1791. While there was an 'East Indian of colour' at Bideford in 1811, there were also two 'Asiatick blacks' who married at Exmouth in 1797. They were probably from India given the witnesses, including Jane and Mary Ducarel of The Manor House, had family connections there: their mother was Sharaf un nissa Khanum, daughter of the Rajah of Purnia.[75]

Leonard French of Totnes was also described as black but for a different reason. In 1586 it was noted this forty-four-year-old soldier had died in Spain and he was described as having been 'of stature tall and grosse and of a blackish complexion … had a black beard and the hair of his head black and his grain marvellous black'. Another description repeated he was 'a tall man of black complexion'. The meaning may have been like that used about Charles II who was known as the 'black boy'.[76]

The uncertainty about the use of 'black' is shown in a reference to James Black (Jacobus Black) at Dartmouth. Black was a servant of a local man, Thomas Gale, and was noted as coming from 'Indea', which was probably somewhere in Asia or even Africa. He may be the first recorded Black man in Devon; he was cited in a tax assessment of 24 July 1484, eight years before Columbus first voyaged to the 'West'

Indies and more than a generation before any Devonian was known to have visited Africa.[77]

The word could also be considered slanderous such as when in the 1630s an Ottery St Mary woman was called a 'black whore', a Kentisbeare woman was called a 'broad-faced whore and a black-faced whore' and an Exeter woman was told 'thou art a whore, a black-mouthed whore, a drunkard, a drunken sow and a drunken beast'. A woman of Bishopsteignton had similar abuse: she was told 'thou art a whore, a balled whore, a stewed whore, a black-mouthed whore and a scale-faced whore'. In another case, of 1619 in Exeter, a woman was also called an 'arrant whore and black whore' while in 1635 a Totnes woman heard she was 'a whore and a base black whore'. Likewise, in 1640 a Crediton woman was called either a 'base black muddy whore' or a 'base pockey black whore'. These terms hint at meanings other than skin colour.[78]

It is uncertain how interchangeable these terms were. In some instances black may have been used to describe the darkest skin colour and such variations were problematic in describing those of mixed race. Also, the West Indian awareness of the racial distinctions between West Africans does not appear to have been prevalent in Devon. This is in contrast to voyages made in the 1530s when Devonians first learned of the variety of West African cultures.[79]

Mixed European and African descent

Individuals with both European and African lineage made up the second largest section of West Indian society and they used terms which had developed over hundreds of years. They were, in the words of one historian in 1972, 'the children of White and free Colored, of White and slave, free Colored and slave, and free Colored and free Colored'. Their origins were described as 'diffuse'.[80]

Portuguese colonists began fathering children in Africa in the late 1400s[81] and not surprisingly the practice was continued by Europeans in the West Indies. In 1791 one writer explained that White Caribbean settlers refrained from marrying because they anticipated a quick return to England. He wrote that they:

> 'in the meantime content themselves with the company of a Mulatto or Negro mistress who brings them a spurious race of children, the maintenance of whom, together with the extravagance of their sable mothers, soon dissipates the first savings of their keeper's hard-earned wealth.'[82]

West Indian writers were more frank than their English counterparts in describing society. In 1837 two writers not only noted interracial unions but observed 'that form of licentiousness which appears among the higher classes in every slaveholding country' involved both married and unmarried men. They explained that:

> 'Men with large families kept one or more mistresses without any effect at concealment. We were told of an *Honourable* gentleman who had his English wife and two concubines, a Colored and a Black one.'[83]

In 1830 a St Kitts colonist wrote openly about his sexual attraction to interracial women. He enthused:

> 'After the white fair ones, the brown dark ones do attract my notice, of whom there is a numerous and beautiful collection in this island. Their charms have persuaded one or two of my countrymen to join them in the holy state of wedlock; which they seem to have a great notion is the best possible *luck* ever invented, and by no means so easy to force as a mere liaison *d'amour*. There are others however who differ in opinion, but as I have never heard their arguments, I will not pretend to give *le pourquoi et let parceque*.'[84]

Some unmarried White men were open about their families:

> 'the children of these connections usually sat with the mothers at the father's table, though when the gentlemen had company, neither mothers nor children made their appearance. To such conduct no disgrace was attached, nor was any shame felt by any party.'[85]

Even so, another writer observed that interracial children did not have their fathers' social standing[86] even when free. Male children were generally employed as tradesmen rather than as field labourers and female children, distinguished by the title 'Miss', were often domestic servants.[87] They also occupied a distinct class in being:

> 'a people neither African nor European, but more properly West Indian. This class – the middle class – is already very large and intelligent and is rapidly increasing. It is composed of small landed proprietors, of business men, clerks in public and private establishments, editors, tradesmen and mechanics. Shut out from the Whites on the one hand, who will not admit them to their society, and from the Blacks on the other, to whom they are immeasurably superior, they nevertheless are constantly receiving accessions from the ranks of both'.[88]

In 1828 the speaker of the Jamaica Assembly explained his aversion to mixed-race and Black Jamaicans.

> 'You hate a Jew much, a Unitarian a little more than a Jew and a Roman Catholic you both hate and fear. We West Indians have no repugnance to sit with a Jew but we dislike the contact and the smell of a Negro. We think little of the religious doubts of the Unitarians but we have been used from infancy to keep Mulatto men at a distance. We do not puzzle ourselves much about the mummeries of popery but on the other hand we love the pure blood of an Englishman better than the mixed stream that flows in the veins of the other descendants of the Negro'.[89]

For others the exclusion of multi-ethnic people was thought to be based on illegitimacy rather than race. It was suggested that this was a particular concern of White women.

'It is not to be wondered at that they should be unwilling to invite the Colored people to their social parties, seeing they might not infrequently be subjected to the embarrassment of introducing to their White wives a Colored mistress or an *illegitimate* daughter. This also explains the special prejudice which the *ladies* of a higher class feel toward those among whom are their guilty rivals in a husband's affections, and those whose every feature tells the story of a husband's unfaithfulness.'[90]

A number of observers noted that White women in the West Indies, unlike their counterparts in England, rarely had unions with Black men ('a thing so very odious in the opinion of Creole White women in general, that the most profligate of them would shudder at the bare idea of submitting to it, and there is hardly to be produced an instance of the kind in the West Indies') as White men did with Black women. They also commented that interracial women preferred White men with the result that mixed-race men were forced to partner Black women.

Those of mixed European and African descent were in six ranks which were similar to those of the Spanish and Portuguese.

Mulatto	½ White, ½ Black (Black mother & White father)
Sambo	¼ White, ¾ Black (Mulatto mother & Black father)
Quadroon	¾ White, ¼ Black (Mulatto mother & White father)
Mustee	7/8 White, 1/8 Black (Quadroon mother & White father)
Musteefino	15/16 White, 1/16 Black (Mustee mother & White father)
White	31/32 White (Musteefino mother & White father)

After six generations a child who was 1/32 Black was legally considered White.[91]

The wider terminology can be confusing. In the West Indies 'Coloureds' referred to those also described as 'of mixed blood'[92] but the term man or woman 'of colour' could, in Devon at least, signify polyethnic heritage as well as anyone who was not White. For instance, in 1842 Abraham Bocas appeared in Exeter Guildhall on a complaint of robbery. He accused the landlord of stealing five sovereigns from him in the Pestle & Mortar in the West Quarter. Bocas was:

'a man of colour attired in a very incongruous way – a portion of a frock and pair of trousers of common printed linen peeping from under the skirts of a dirty and much worn great coat, his thick and clumsy shoes terminating the singular effect, whilst the swarthy hue of his complexion became the more conspicuous by its contrast with the white handkerchief tied turban fashion around his head'.

It transpired that he spoke Hindustani and that he was a Muslim. He swore his oath on a copy of the Koran and Reverend Elijah Toynes, a former missionary in India, acted as a translator. Bocas was also noted as a Black man and a foreigner. This curious episode, in which the court decided in Bocas' favour, highlights the difficulties in language. Amongst the witnesses was one Sarah Jackson who was described pointedly as 'an interesting young woman with a child in her arms'.[93]

Likewise, in 1864 a 'man of colour' named Allah, who was also described as a 'Negro', may or may not have been of African descent. His circumstances, in which he was charged by the Society for the Prevention of Cruelty to Animals, do not reveal his ethnicity. The court heard he was part of a travelling show at Barnstaple:

> 'A young rabbit was given him and he immediately bit it behind the head, and began to suck the blood. He tore it to pieces and ate part of it. The rabbit was a tame one, about half grown.'

Allah did not speak English and his employer explained that he did not think 'there was any harm in what he had done as the nigger fed chiefly on bullock's lights, and ate nothing but raw meat.' It was suggested that he had been expelled from Teignmouth for the same behaviour but Allah disputed this by claiming it was 'another nigger' who ate live rats.[94]

INTERRACIAL CHILDREN OF DEVONIAN SLAVEHOLDERS

Devonians apparently knew it was not uncommon for West Indian White enslavers to father children with enslaved women or others of African descent. In 1844 a journalist assumed that the Bahamians who bore Lord Rolle's surname were his descendants but he never crossed the Atlantic:

> 'The Rolles appear to have had plenty of piccaninnies in the olden time as we read a long list of names – Kitty Rolle, Sukey Rolle, Peggy Rolle, Damon Rolle, Malachi Rolle, Pompey Rolle, Cuffin Rolle, etc.'[95]

Rolle was unfairly ridiculed but there were interracial children in Devon including the son of John Stedman, the author of *The narrative of a five years expedition against the revolted Negroes of Surinam*. Stedman retired to Tiverton and his son was educated at Blundells.[96]

The Alphington Ponies were probably Devon's most visible interracial individuals in 1834. These twin sisters were the granddaughters of Sir Patrick Blake, owner of a number of West Indian forced-labour plantations. In 1776 he returned to England from St Kitts and Montserrat with two daughters whom he had fathered with enslaved women. One, Barbara, subsequently married Andrew Durnford and lived in Alphington and Torquay with her twin daughters. The Durnford sisters were prominent because they dressed alike and promenaded in unison through the streets arm-in-arm.[97]

In 1835 the local daughter of a slaveholder wrote anonymously as 'V' of her West Indian memories. She reminisced about Anda, a nineteen-year-old 'half-caste Mustee girl' who was:

'of incomparable symmetry, she deserved a far different fate! Though uneducated and by nature superstitious, yet her mind, had it been only cultivated, would have proved of no inferior grade. But alas, my sister, *for such she was*! And alas, my father, for blame rests with thee! And though a legal marriage entitled me to the estate which your adventurous spirit gained, yet can I not forget that there lived one whose name can never be mentioned in conjunction with mine, without in some degree infecting it, and casting a foul blot upon thine otherwise fair frame.'

Anda died before her sister could bring her to England to share her inheritance.[98]

William McCaul shared his inheritance with mixed-race siblings. He moved from St Vincent to London by the spring of 1827 and shortly afterwards arrived in Ilfracombe: he was there in November for his marriage and three children were born there in 1828, 1833 and 1834. He lived at Coronation Terrace and died there at the age of 48 in 1834.[99]

McCaul's father James bequeathed him property in Calliaqua in St Vincent and gave £1,000 to two 'Mulatto' children as well as an annuity to a 'Mulatto' woman from Carriacou. It is probable that they were William's siblings. McCaul Senior had two other stipulations. He left an annuity of forty pounds, a house and his freedom to his servant Frank, who was listed in 1822 as a twenty-six-year-old Negro house servant who had been 'brought from Britain'. He also gave William 'the service of a Negro woman named Mary together with her daughter Peggy and her sons Jerry and Paul during his life and they are afterwards to be made free'. A slave register shows that this took place between 1 January 1825 and 31 December 1827; the manumissions of Peggy and Paul, described as 'mongrels', were listed at about the time he arrived in Ilfracombe. McCaul signed their freedoms in London on 19 May 1827. Mary was then aged about fifty, her daughter Peggy was twenty and her son Paul was eighteen. A second son, Jerry, also previously recorded as a 'mongrel', died in 1824.[100]

In 1833 Hubert Whitlock of Heavitree married Emily Cornish of North Huish near Totnes and shortly afterwards they sailed to their estate in Demerara. Mrs Whitlock may not have been aware that her husband already had a family in Demerara. He was one of the three sons of George Whitlock who also lived in the colony. Brother William had died there aged 24 in 1827 and Hubert had purchased a plantation with younger brother Edward. Hubert and Emily had a son born in 1834, Hubert died the following year and Emily returned with her son to Devon. By 1841 she was living at The Strand in Topsham and ten years later the census enumerator found her at 2 Park Place in St Sidwell parish, Exeter.

George Whitlock, a surgeon, lived in Ottery St Mary up to at least 1814 and by 1819 moved to 1 Salutary Mount in Heavitree. He had eight sons, six of whom lived to adulthood. One became a surgeon, two had careers in India and the remaining three sons chose life in Demerara. The year 1835 was notable for the Whitlock family: father George died in Heavitree on 8 January, Edward married in Demerara in March, Hubert died in Demerara on 7 September and the emancipation claim was made on 7 December.[101]

In 1830 Hubert and Edward jointly purchased the estate with a third party, Walter

Urquhart, possibly a carpenter. Edward, the surviving brother, received £600 18s 7d (£40,743.78) for 13 individuals. Hubert bequeathed his part of the Kinderen estate to seven women and girls in Demerara. On 12 October 1834 he wrote that he felt 'duty bound' to give the plantation, along with its livestock and human property, to 'the Coloured woman Maria Shepperd and her children Maria, Rebecca, and Sarah and Barbara (twins) and to Mary and Jane my children by the Black woman Clarissa Styles'.[102]

INTERRACIAL SLAVEHOLDERS

Mixed-race men and women also owned slaves and one writer claimed enslaved West Indians themselves owned other individuals.[103] Ann Furse of Kingsnympton benefited from slavery through two husbands. In 1827, at Bristol, she married Donald McMillan, an attorney, who in 1835 claimed £2,230 12s 6d (£151,239.27) for 84 individuals on the Perseverance Estate in Grenada. Shortly after his death she married Edward Connett, another attorney who had been living in Starcross. He had also been working in Grenada on the sale of various plantations and left her £500 when he died fourteen months after their marriage.[104] McMillan was noted as 'an old and respectable inhabitant' whose death was 'much regretted' and has recently been identified as a 'free Coloured'.[105] In 1819 he acted for the Nutmeg Grove Plantation in Tobago which had, amongst others, a slave named Dartmouth.[106] Three other mixed-race enslavers lived in Devon.

James Lee Brodbelt, Plymouth

Brodbelt, a Plymouth medical doctor, had a shared compensation claim for two plantations. He was Jamaican, as were his parents and grandparents, and had a notable career in England, including Devon, as well as in the United States. Brodbelt was born in 1803 and came to Britain where he, and his brother Thomas, were awarded medical degrees at the University of Edinburgh in 1824.[107] He married two years later in Woolwich and moved to St Helier in Jersey where his daughter, Charlotte Jersey Brodbelt, was born in 1827. By 1832 he was in Plymouth during the cholera crisis. The borough later presented him with a silver snuff box, along with other 37 other medical men, as a token of the 'gratitude of his fellow townsmen for his humane attention of the poor during the awful visitation of malignant cholera at Plymouth'. Brodbelt was registered as a voter in Plymouth at least until 1845 but his place of abode remained Jersey. He also owned property in London. In 1848 Brodbelt and his wife sailed to the United States and settled in Ohio where Brodbelt Lane in Columbus was named after him.[108]

Brodbelt's two grandfathers were medical men. His maternal grandfather was Hon. James Lee who served on the council of Jamaica and died while voyaging to England

▶ 12. 'Two West Indian Women of Color, a child holding the hand of one and attendant Black Servant', c1780, by Agostino Brunias.

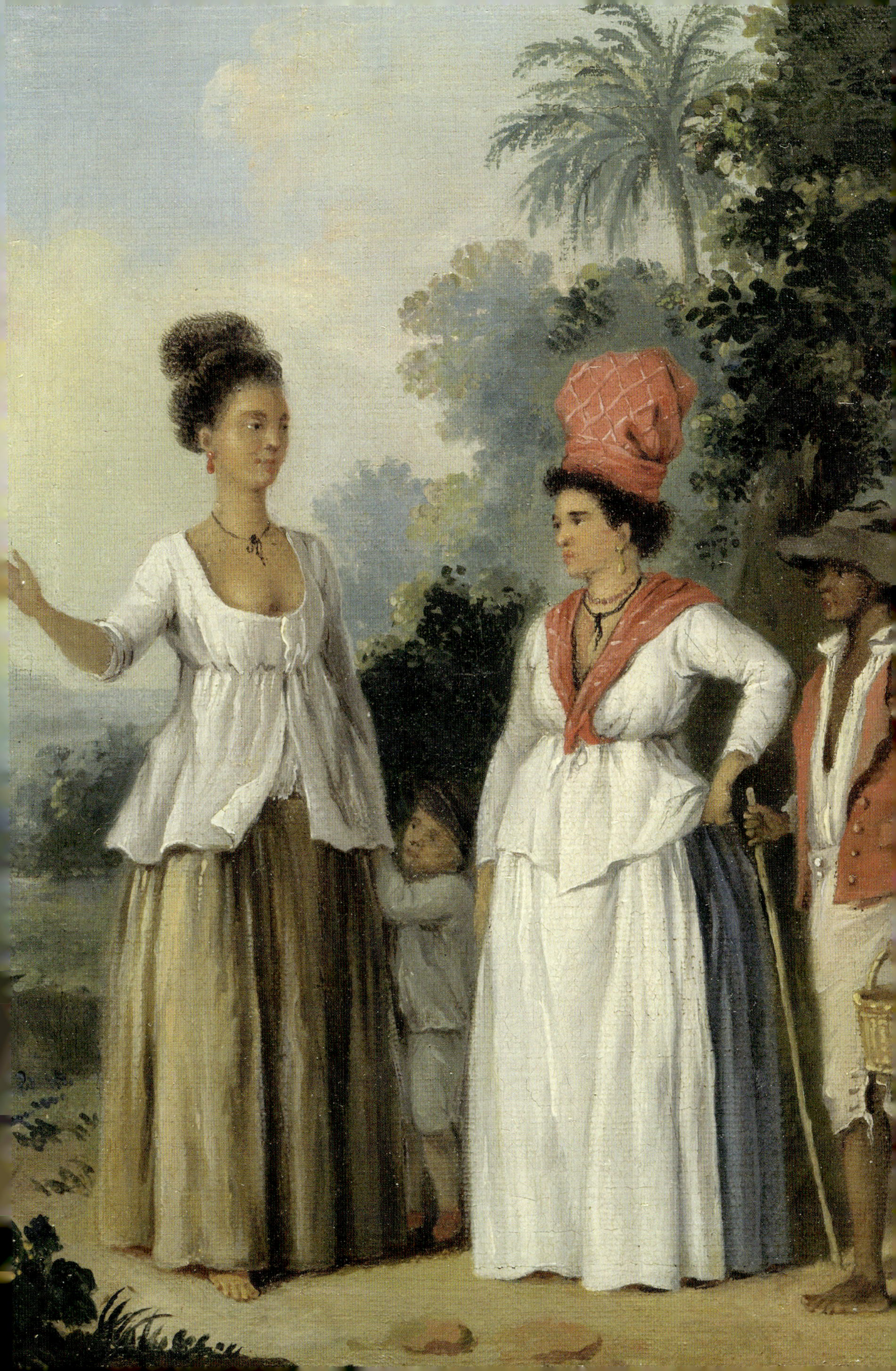

in 1821. In his will Lee stipulated that substantial land holdings on the island were to be shared between his 'faithful' Eliza Gardener Johnson, a free Black woman, and Jemima Johnson Lee. Moreover, three illegitimate children of the latter woman, Eliza Lee Brodbelt, James Lee Brodbelt and Thomas Lee Brodbelt, were to have bequests. The children's baptism record noted their mother as a 'free Mulatto'. James Lee Brodbelt, being one quarter black, would have been termed a Quadroon.[109]

His paternal grandfather, Dr Francis Rigby Brodbelt, was born and died in Jamaica. In his will he requested that, in order to please Dr James Lee, his widow was to grant freedom to Bella alias Eliza Johnston, 'a Negro woman slave, her property'. His widow was promised compensation of either two hundred pounds or three new enslaved people. Brodbelt's wife was Anne Gardner Brodbelt née Penoyre, the writer who in the late 1790s lived for some time in Chudleigh.[110]

Brodbelt also studied medicine at Edinburgh. His estate in 1827 was worth in excess of £120,000. Three years earlier he added Stallard Penoyre to his surname because of an inheritance clause in the will of his godfather, Thomas Stallard Penoyre.[111] Brodbelt, who had substantial properties in Hereford and Somerset, also provided for his three children. There were other siblings, including Anna Maria Brodbelt, who were not included in the bequests.[112]

Brodbelt was unsuccessful in one claim and shared two others; in total he received £112 6s 6d (£7,615.78) for 16 enslaved Jamaicans. In 1822 his slave Mingo Orgill, 'a Negro boy', died from the wheels of a wagon having passed over him.[113]

Mary Haverfield née Ross, Great Torrington

Mary Ross, who was one sixteenth Black, was identified in her father Robert's will of 1820 as one of his five illegitimate children. Ross owned several plantations and made bequests of fifty Jamaican pounds to his 'reputed' children William Ross, James Ross and Elizabeth Ross, 'a free Mulatto'. He bequeathed the same amount to Elizabeth Upton Swarbeck, the mother of his other reputed children, Samuel Ross and Mary Ross.[114]

In 1818 twenty-year-old Mary Ross married Commander Robert Tunstall Haverfield in Kew. He was the son of the head gardener and she had a dowry of £8,000 (£542,410.40) secured on the Palmer Hut and Bybrook estates. A third of Ross' residuary estate was also bequeathed to her. Robert Ross, then of Henrietta Street in Cavendish Square, London, stipulated that his son William, who was living with Haverfield in Bideford, was to receive a further £15,000. Ross was a magistrate and owned 260 Jamaicans in 1836.[115] It is unclear how the bride and groom met given that Mary Ross had been raised in Jamaica. Her father had visited England in 1815 and it was perhaps then that arrangements had been made.

Mary Ross' mother, Elizabeth Upton Swarbeck, was the daughter of John Swarbeck and Mary Upton, and described as a 'free Mulatto'. Mary and Robert Tunstall Haverfield lived in Bideford and then at Beam, a mansion on the River Torridge outside Great Torrington, sometime after 1818.[116] They appear to have left in 1830. The property was owned by Lord Rolle and described in 1789 as 'a most lovely and sequestered spot'.[117] By 1838 the couple were at Bridge Street in Bideford and it was in that port that their children were born. A son, Robert Ross, was born in 1818 and educated at a private school in Great Torrington and at the Bideford Grammar School. It was intended that he attend Cambridge but Mrs Haverfield's income dropped from £1,500 per year to less than £300. This was blamed on emancipation. It was claimed that 'very little she ever saw of the compensation money voted by Parliament to the planters'. Mrs Haverfield paid for her son's passage to Australia where he became a newspaper proprietor.[118]

Why they chose North Devon remains uncertain. Great Torrington was a backwater compared to Bideford, then the major port in North Devon and one with historic ties to the West Indies. In 1813, some five years earlier than their arrival in Bideford, an advertisement was placed in a local newspaper in which 'M. H.' advertised 'A woman of colour would be glad to attend a lady going to Jamaica in the next fleet'.[119] Commander Haverfield died in 1839 and by 1851 his widow had returned to Great Torrington. She lived in South Street and died two years later.[120]

The two women with whom Ross had children were identified in his will. Elizabeth Upton Swarbeck was probably the individual noted as Miss Betsy Swarbeck in the *Royal Gazette of Jamaica* in 1827. She was described as a person of colour living in Spanish Town, then the capital of Jamaica, who owned a runaway slave named Ellen, 'a Creole woman, 5 feet 3½ inches, some of her upper front teeth are lost'.[121] Some of Ross' enslaved people were advertised in the same newspaper. In 1814 two had absconded. One was Charles, a Creole who stood at five feet one inch tall and had RR, presumably for Robert Ross, branded on his left shoulder. Likewise that year, another runaway was George, a Mandingo who was five feet eight inches tall. He had the same brand.[122]

Margaret Taylor, Dawlish

Taylor was Jamaican-born and came to Devon in 1830. Little is known about her other than the details she revealed in a letter dated 10 November 1835. She wrote as 'a person of colour late of Kingston Jamaica but now residing at Dawlish' who had come to England as an attendant to a lady 'with whom she has ever since resided'. This may have been Hannah Barnes or Jane Caroline James, both of whom had also lived previously in Jamaica before moving to Dawlish.

Taylor wrote 'on your petitioner leaving Jamaica she was possessed in fee of a domestic Negro woman slave named Margaret Taylor Bennett domiciled in the city and parish of Kingston, which slave was duly registered by your petitioner as owner'. Moreover, Taylor was 'in a state of great poverty and became possessed of the said slave by purchase from the savings alone of her own industry'. She added that she had not claimed 'in consequence of your petitioner's secluded situation and from utter ignorance of the course to be pursued.' She received £23 9s 1d (£1,590.22) for the loss of Bennett.[123]

In 1829 Taylor had previously owned two individuals. Bennett, then recorded as a thirteen-year-old 'Creole Negro', also owned Princess alias Mary Linda, noted as a fifty-year-old Negro born in Africa. In 1817 she had owned Belle, a twenty-one-year-old described as an 'African Negro', and three years later she also owned Belle's year-old daughter Jeanette.[124]

CHARACTER

Few terms were used to describe slave-owners. They themselves used oblique words such as proprietor or planter. By the 1820s the public mood had turned against slavery but there was a public reticence to discuss enslavers. It might be reasonably inferred that some slaveholders attempted to obscure their associations. The lack of written references to them compounds the difficulty in imagining how individuals justified owning others. One question we often ask is what kind of people were they? A Tiverton abolitionist argued that slavery debased the owners by making them proud, cruel and oppressive.[125] This was certainly the case with Devon's most famous slave-owner, Annie Palmer, who is remembered more vividly in Jamaica than any other Devonian. In 1929 her life formed the basis of a novel and Johnny Cash composed a ballad in her honour in 1973. Palmer remains a striking part of contemporary Jamaica culture and is popularly recalled as a sadistic, depraved murderer who practiced voodou. The real woman appears to have led a quiet life in Sidmouth.[126]

Some owners expressed moral qualms such in 1807 when an Englishman travelled to Jamaica to see his newly-inherited plantation. Matthew Lewis stayed the first night at an inn and wrote in his journal:

> 'a remarkably clean-looking Negro lad presented himself with some water and a towel. I concluded him to belong to the inn and on my returning the towel, as he found that I took no notice of him, he at length ventured to introduce himself by saying *Massa not know me, me your slave*! and really the sound made me feel a pang at the heart. The lad appeared all gaiety and good humour, and his whole countenance expressed anxiety to recommend himself to my notice but the word *slave* seemed to imply that although he did feel pleasure then in serving me, if he had detested me he must have served me still. I really felt quite humiliated at the moment and was tempted to tell him *Do not say that again, say that you are my Negro but do not call yourself my slave*'.[127]

But both men fully understood he was Lewis' legal property despite the uneasiness felt by at least one of the two.

There is little evidence that Devon slave-owners were held accountable in public. They were ridiculed as a group in 1827 when a writer referred to them as 'drones',[128] that is a parasite which benefits from the labour of others, but such attacks were unusual. One exception was Sir Alexander Cray Grant who was born near Kingsbridge but was otherwise unconnected to Devon. He was mocked as a slaveholder during the hustings for two Cambridge parliamentary elections. A flag displayed Grant flogging a Black woman. A journalist claimed:

13. Shackles, pre 1860. ▶

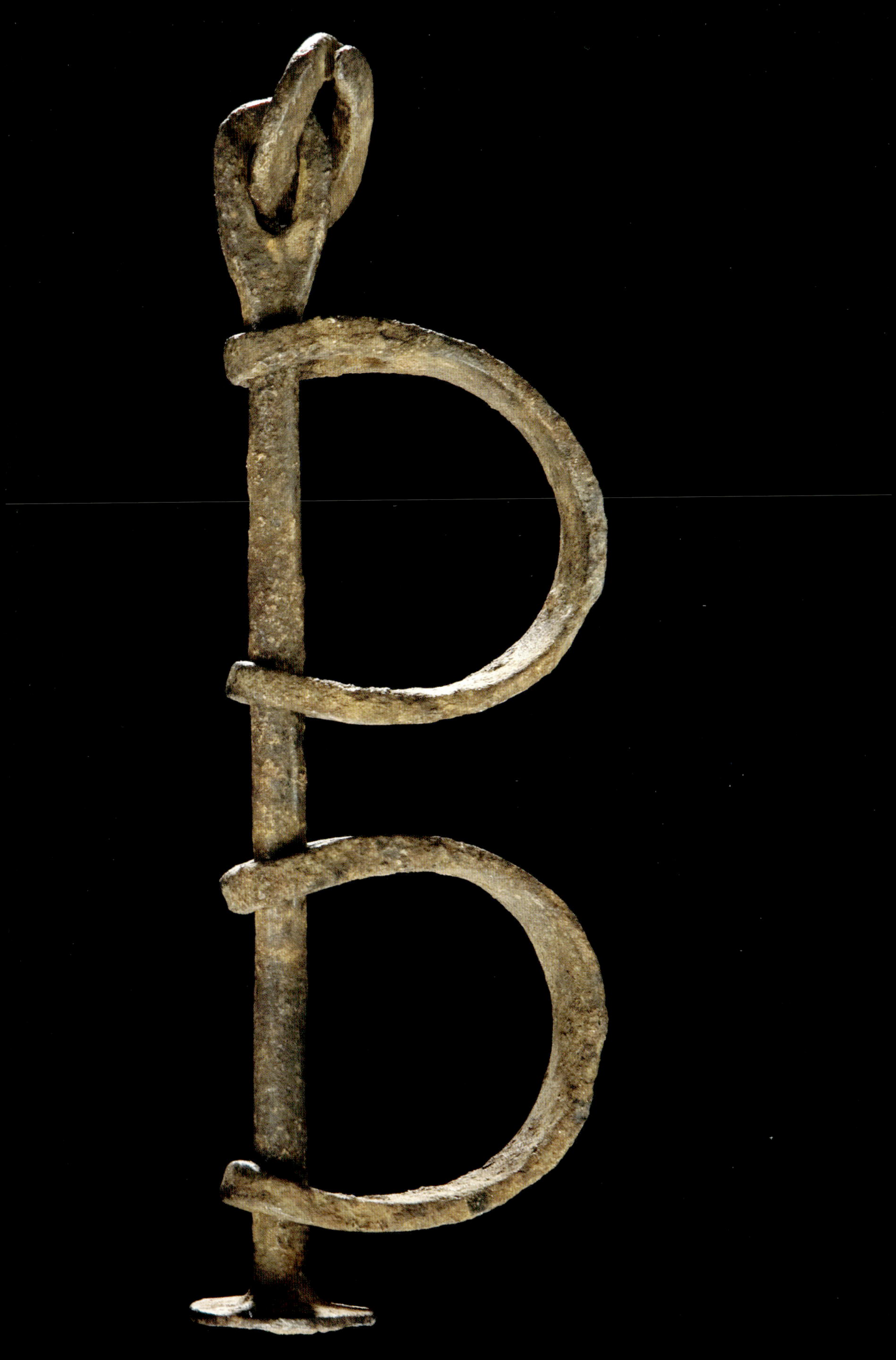

'he had in his day cut the flesh from the backs of half the Black women in the West Indies'.

He was also named as a slave-owner, slave-driver and slave-trader. The comments resulted in the threat of a duel but was settled in court: it was decided that Grant was incorrectly named as a slave-trader but was apparently rightly called not just a slave-owner but slave-driver.[129]

Another exception was Lord Rolle who was mocked on a number of occasions including in 1838 when it was noted he had a weekly income of £2,000 but still 'went with his money bag to the treasury' for compensation of £4,333 6s 9d (£293,805.92).[130] In another rare example, in 1841 one of the Porter brothers from Rockbeare was scorned during the parliamentary election. It was alleged he had intimidated voters and was dismissed as 'but the other day he was a great slave-owner, till the people of this country bought his individuals and now he sells dear sugar'.[131]

Obituaries

It was expected that obituarists praised the character of the dead. For instance, Mary Willis, the Antiguan-born widow of a London merchant, who died in 1810 at Exmouth aged 84, had a glowing obituary. She lived in Hampshire and Bath but retired to Devon. A journalist wrote she was:

> 'a widow lady of exemplary benevolence, liberality and piety, without ostentation. She survived, but a few weeks, the loss of her only daughter, Mrs Mary Cure, also a widow lady, late of Bath, after having lived together fifty-four years, and giving to the world a lively example of the *beauty of holiness* so that it might be truly said they were lovely in their lives and in their deaths they were not divided. In them were united the most pleasing cheerfulness and urbanity of manners, to the strictest attention to all duties of sincere religion. The remains of Mrs Willis, were, this morning, interred in the same grave with those of her daughter, in the cathedral church of this city.'[132]

A memorial stone in Exeter Cathedral bears the inscription:

> 'Mother and daughter, widows, formerly of Bath, whose piety, real goodness of heart and beneficence have (we trust) through the mercies of an almighty saviour, erected to their memories a monument more lasting than all earthly records'.[133]

She and her daughter died twenty-four years before compensation would have been paid. Her will provides an additional insight into her character: neither woman had a natural heir and Mrs Willis wrote to Lydia Sutton of Norfolk that:

> 'I consulted with my daughter and granted her the approbation to settle our property upon such of our friends were thought most worthy and had children, and for whom we had the most sincere affection and we had none equal to yourself and family'.

Willis specified the bequest included:

'Negroes and other individuals, horses, mules, and cattle to the same plantations belonging with the offspring and increase of such Negroes and other individuals and cattle'.[134]

The obituary of John Foster Barham Junior, who benefited from forced labour estates although he himself did not own individuals, was also fulsome. Barham lived in Exeter by 1816 and had been a partner in the London firm Plummer, Barham & Plummer which had West Indian mercantile interests. His father was a Jamaican slave-owner but in 1789 bequeathed his son a legacy of £10,000 (£767,611) instead of a share in the plantation. Amongst his slaves in 1817 was a man named Exeter.[135]

It was announced in July 1822 that Barham was moving from Exeter to the continent. His home, 4 Jeffery's Row on the north side of Sidwell Street, was an eight bedroom house with two parlours and a walled garden which measured 180 feet in length and 24 feet in width. There were also two greenhouses and a two-storey summer house.[136] Barham died four months later. His obituary was effusive but incomplete:

'a gentleman eminent for his classical attainments, and who united, to an acute and solid judgment, a delightful native ingeniousness and simplicity of heart, which, during the course of a long life, in all his intercourse with society, guided him in the difficult paths of high honour, and Christian rectitude. Besides an attention to general literature, the importance of the subject directed his studies to theology; and the delight which he received from excursions amidst the beautiful valleys of the county, was always united with an attention to this object; and the works of Eickhorn, the great German critic, in general accompanied him, with a selection from other writers. With a mind so ardent, so vigorous in important pursuits, the lighter works of imagination became as a relaxation, a source of high delight but his sensibility to the poetical beauties of our great writers, can alone be felt by those who had the happiness to enjoy his society, and to listen to his readings.'[137]

Rockbeare's John Payne was also praised for his exemplary character. He worked as a plantation manager in Demerara and died there in 1837 aged twenty-six. He had been there for some eight years and managed a number of large estates. His younger brother, Frederick, was also in Demerara and died at the same age.[138] Payne was:

'a young man of a very amiable disposition, to the most unblemished integrity he added much firmness of purpose and suavity of manner'.[139]

Another obituarist was even more expressive of the warmth of his personality.

'The deceased was the son of Mr John Payne, of Ford House, Rockbeare; he had been in the island about eight years, and from excellence of his talents, and his great worth and integrity, had obtained the entire confidence of many of the non-resident gentry to whom he was agent. He had the management of several large estates in his immediate neighbourhood, and such was the fidelity of his nature, that matters of the greatest trust and responsibility were entrusted to his care with the most unbounded confidence. In private life he was a kind hearted young man, and the affectionate disposition which always breathed through and animated his letters to home, as well as the general warmth of heart which he displayed on all occasions, have rendered doubly poignant the shaft which has deprived his bereaved and sorrowing relatives of one whose return they had anticipated at no distant day, with feelings of the brightest hope'.[140]

Each obituary, and those of every other Devon slaveholder, failed to mention slavery.

Anglican clergy

It seems particularly incongruous that a clergyman could sanction slavery but some 150 Church of England clerics received compensation awards, about one per cent of all Anglican clergymen. At least seventeen in Devon financially benefited from forced labour. These men may have taken notice of their bishop: Henry Phillpotts, whose brother owned individuals, had not supported emancipation until it came into force in 1838. In contrast, a predecessor, Frederick Keppel, ordained 'a Black' in 1766.[141]

Butterleigh's rector from 1824 to 1830, John Thomas Grant, inherited a share in a Demerara plantation but died before the emancipation act.[142] Another cleric at Oakford, Reverend James Parkin, acted as a trustee for a Cornish friend's son, John Price, who had inherited the Worthy Park estate in Jamaica. In the 1840s Plymstock was connected to slavery through its Jamaican-born curate, Reverend Edward Francis Coke. His father and grandfather were both slave-owners. One estate had 71 Jamaicans for whom they claimed compensation of £1,299 2d (£88,074.45).

Another cleric was Reverend Henry Nembhard who came to North Devon in the 1850s. He was born in Jamaica in 1795, trained in England and lived in London. At his leaving Bideford to become rector at nearby Instow the parishioners thanked him for his unwearied Christian labours. He moved to West Putford[143] and died in 1876. No mention was made in local newspapers of the 48 Jamaicans, some of whom lived on Hounslow Estate, for whom he received £961 2s 10d (£65,166.65) in 1837. This money had come at an unusual, and revealing, period in Nembhard's life. He had entered Trinity College, Cambridge, in 1818 but a relation, not long after Nembhard's death, recounted:

'Henry Nembhard became very wild and extravagant at college. He was refused by Miss Rowe on this account, and taking her refusal to heart he disappeared about the time of his father's death, and for some fifteen years none of the family knew what had become

14. Diorama of the waterfront of Paramaribo, South America, 1820. ▶

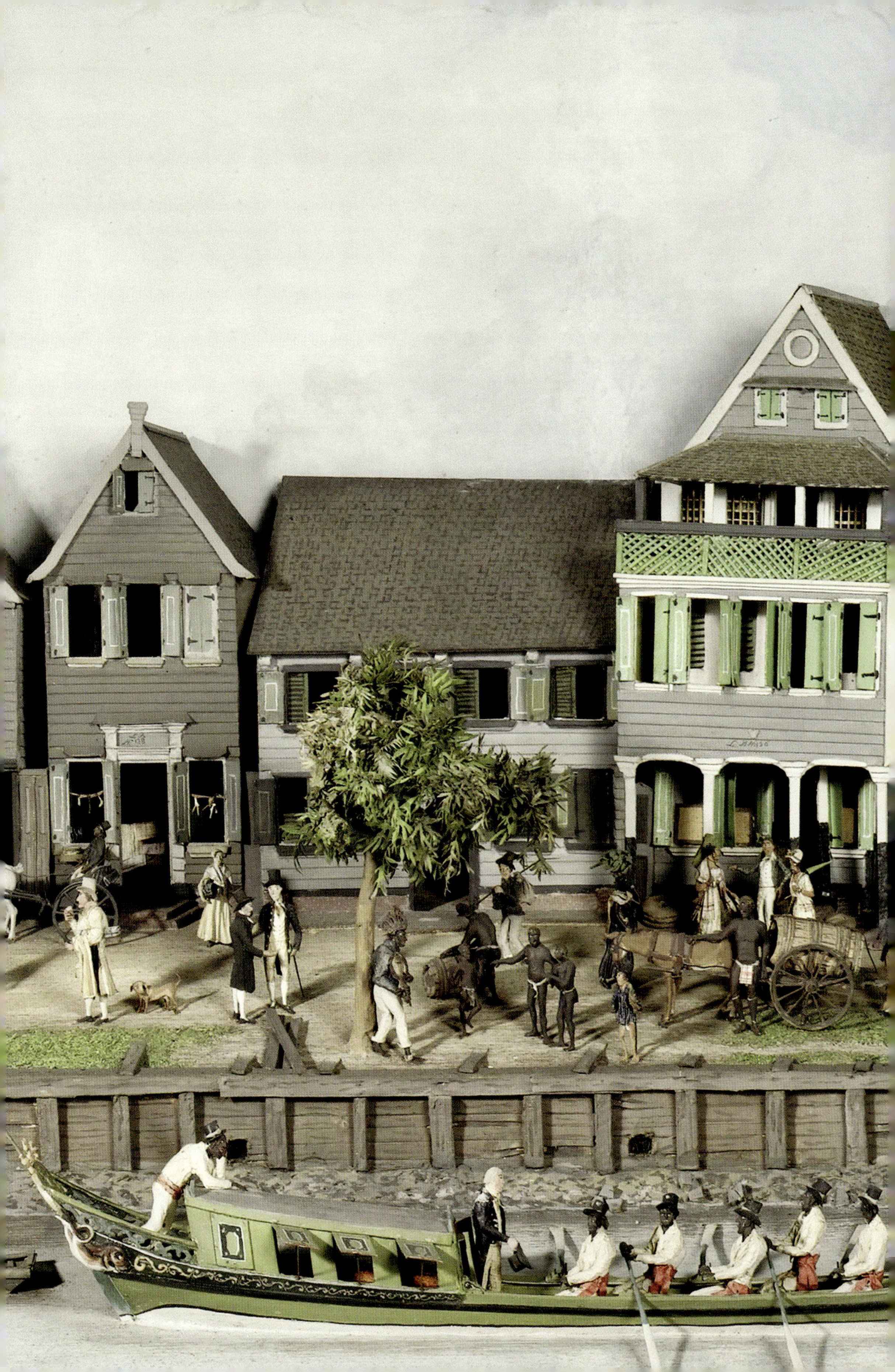

of him. In 1838 his sister-in-law Elizabeth Nembhard née Brooks, while making a short tour in the north of France, accidentally found him imprisoned for debt in a French town where she stopped to change horses. She paid his debt, a very small one, brought him to England, and reconciled him to Miss Rowe who in spite of her refusal had been faithful to him. They were married, and Henry, who by this time had quite sobered down, took Holy Orders. He died greatly respected and beloved.'[144]

Nembhard married in 1842 and may have moved to North Devon because his wife had been born in East Down.

Another slave-owning clergyman was Somerset-born George Trevelyan who served as the vicar of Stogumber for fifty years and was the domestic chaplain of Harriet Hay, Countess of Errol and illegitimate daughter of William IV. On 30 March 1851 and 7 April 1861 the census enumerators found that Trevelyan, despite being paid as a cleric in Somerset, was living more than a hundred miles away in Oxfordshire. His obituary in 1871 noted that 'for some time' he had been a Colyton resident; by 1866 Trevelyan lived in Fore Street with his wife Frances and a number of indoor servants. He had inherited shares in six plantations (including Tempe, Simon, Requin, Sagesse and Beausejour Estates) in Grenada for which he received, with four other family members, £5,417 17s 10d (£367,340.10) in emancipation compensation. He died aged 76 and his devotion to his faith was demonstrated by his funeral's theatrics: it was said that Colyton 'swarmed' with locals eager to see a High Church procession.[145] What is not recorded is any mention, let alone justification, for his ownership of 1,004 human beings.

For thirty-two years Reverend William Godfrey Pollard Burton was the rector of St Thomas in the Vale in Jamaica and after his death in 1847 his widow Elizabeth and their family moved to Tiverton. Their nine children had been born in Jamaica. By 1851 Mrs Burton was working as a schoolmistress and her household included three Jamaican nieces. In 1835 she and her husband had received £728 13s 7d (£49,405.49) for 34 enslaved Jamaicans some of whom were on the Wakey Hill estate.[146]

In addition to these enslavers, Reverend Humphrey Senhouse Pinder, rector of Bratton Fleming for thirty-six years, was bequeathed £2,000 (£135,602.60) from estates in Barbados owned by his father. The latter had received £4,307 4s 4d (£292,034.89) in compensation for 204 individuals. Pinder spent his last years in Exeter where he died at 3 Southernhay West in 1888.[147] Another Barbadian was Mary Ann Barton whose Exeter-born husband Reverend Henry Charles Benyon Barton was the rector of West Ogwell in 1851. Her family had owned 195 Barbadians and received £4,326 12s 9d (£293,351.65) in compensation.

Eight remaining clergymen (John Campbell Fisher, Walter Stevenson Halliday, Hinds Howell, James John Rowe, John James Scott, John Swete, Charles Waymouth, James King Went) are noted in the following pages. No comments on the justification of slavery appear to have been made by any slave-owning Devon cleric.

2

From slavery to emancipation

'Having heard all of this, you may choose to look the other way but you can never again say that you did not know', William Wilberforce, House of Commons, 12 May 1789

Devon's enslavement of Africans lasted nearly three hundred years although there was increasing opposition in the late 1700s as Devonians, like their fellow countrymen, responded to national and international events, influences and pressures. In 1788 a visitor described Cold Spring, a Jamaican plantation owned by the family of Elizabeth Wallen who later died in Exeter. He gushed:

'A person visiting Cold Spring for the first time almost conceives himself transported to a distant part of the world, the air and face of the country so widely differing from that of the regions he has left. Even the birds are all strangers to him. Among others peculiar to these lofty regions is a species of the swallow, the plumage of which varies in colour like the neck of a drake and there is a very fine songbird called the fish eye, of a blackish brown, with a white ring round the neck.'[148]

More than a generation later, in 1832, 'Humanitas', a Plymothian writing under a *nom de plume*, also enthused:

'It is a pleasing sight to pass over the estates at the busiest seasons, the scenes are beautifully picturesque. In the distance we view the lofty mountains which surround the savannahs or plains, these are enlivened by the numerous dark figures of the Negroes at work as the eye passes over the rich cane field, whose broad green blade waves gracefully to the last, are exposed to our view, the thickly curled heads of these children of never-ending slavery. The females are distinguished by the graceful fold of a coloured cotton kerchief drawn tight round the head, turban fashion, with a knot in front'.

However, he or she added:

> 'The pleasing contemplation is soon destroyed, a sudden and painful thought rushes on the mind, as the loud lash of the driver harshly grates upon the ear, whose sound reverberates through the mountains, and we feel, and know they are slaves, and this within the British dominion. Englishmen, do you not blush at the thought?'[149]

EUROPEANS AND AFRICAN SLAVERY

Devon's early relationship to slavery is unlike those of other counties. In 1573 Francis Drake took the lead in England's exploration of the world, in 1583 it was Sir Humphrey Gilbert, another Devonian, who established the first colony at Newfoundland and it was his brother, Sir Walter Ralegh, who was sanctioned by the crown to establish American colonies along the eastern seaboard and as far south as the Caribbean. This took place three generations after the Spanish and Portuguese had explored and settled the more lucrative southerly parts of the Americas. English colonisation developed alongside the French, Dutch, Danish and Swedes, fellow latecomers.

Europeans, beginning with Columbus' four voyages in the West Indies from 1492 to 1504, searched for highly lucrative commodities such as bullion, precious stones, pearls and dye woods. Initially Spain appropriated Indigenous people as its workforce and even used them in Europe: as early as 1494 the first enslaved people transported across the Atlantic were men and women seized by Columbus and brought to Spain for sale.

The Spaniards found the pool of potential American labour insufficient and turned to Africa to make up the difference. By 1502 Africans began to be taken across the Atlantic (from Spain) to supplement the Indigenous workforce. From the early 1400s Portugal and Spain had been slaving on the western seaboard of Africa; men and women were sent to Madeira, the Canaries and the Iberian peninsula. This was part of a general enslavement of non-Christians which included not just Jews and Muslims but 'cannibals' in the West Indies and African 'heathens'.[150]

Devon was also unlike other parts of England in that it first sent enslaved Africans across the Atlantic. In the 1560s it helped develop the Spanish and Portuguese slave colonies when Sir John Hawkins organised three voyages. A generation earlier his father had traded on the same African coast. These enterprises, in what was called nearly a century ago 'a trade in human flesh and blood',[151] had crucial support from London and Spanish merchants and initiated what would become a major part of British mercantile activity. Devon subsequently failed to maintain its lead and eventually contributed only 0.25 per cent of all recorded slaving voyages from Britain. Plymouth's involvement in the eighteenth century has been described by one historian as minute and sporadic. There were some 29 Devon slaving voyages out of the estimated 12,000 that left Britain. The number of individuals transported on Devon's ships, of the total number of the estimated 16,000,000 individuals who were enslaved, was also proportionately small, some 0.03 per cent of the total number.[152]

Devon's comparative lack of interest in slaving may be contrasted with the earliest and most long-lasting involvement the county had with a colony. From the early 1500s it was focused on Newfoundland where the economy was unsuited to slavery. Devonians developed fishing plantations but these utilised free labour in the form of thousands of Westcountry men. Devon was involved in the island through to the early 1800s.

Devon was also heavily immersed in plantations in Ireland: from the 1550s the crown had confiscated Irish-owned land and colonised the country with English settlers. The most notable connection was Sir Walter Ralegh's involvement in the Munster Plantation in southern Ireland but the longest lasting link was that of the Courtenay family of Devon: in 1591 Sir William was granted an estate which increased to more than 85,000 acres and part of it was retained by his descendants until 1908.[153]

There was no British demand for enslaved people in the Americas until it established colonies on the North American seaboard. Hence, the first recorded instance of the British use of African slaves took place in 1619 when a Dutch ship seized some twenty men and women at sea, landed in Virginia and sold them to the colonists. Over the following 188 years millions of Africans were forcibly taken to British colonies in the Americas. There were other individuals enslaved in South Africa and in colonies along the Indian Ocean.[154]

EARLIER SLAVEHOLDERS

It is not yet known how many Devonians owned slave estates either as absentee owners or as migrants in the West Indies in the generations before emancipation. Some individuals and families can be identified but it has not been determined how proportionate they were with the rest of the country.

The Colleton family

John Colleton, his daughter Louisa Carolina Colleton and grand-daughter Sophia Louisa Graves were prominent members of one of Devon's best known slave-owning families.

Sir John Colleton (1608–66) was the first of his family to be involved in American colonisation: his Devon home was in Exeter and in 1663 he became one of the eight Lord Proprietors of South Carolina, North Carolina and Georgia, the leading colonisers of those American states. Four were peers and the remainder were knights. Five generations later the Colleton family lived mainly in America but also owned a Devon mansion at Exmouth where the Withycombe Raleigh parish register shows baptisms for Andrew Hector Harris and Elizabeth Marchant described as 'blacks' who belonged to the family in 1748. There was also a baptism in 1731 and a burial four years later of William, 'an Indian servant' of the family. The family is remembered in Exmouth largely for the introduction of Magnolia grandifloras from the Carolinas.[155]

1700

John's descendant John (1738–1777) retained the large estate in South Carolina which then had two large mansions named Fairlawn and Exmouth. He married Ann Fulford in 1759, they lived together in America until 1767 but three years later they divorced following the birth of John Fulford, her illegitimate son. They had one child, Louisa Carolina Colleton, who was born in 1763. Her middle name was taken from her birthplace. She subsequently inherited the family estate of more than 12,000 acres including Exeter Plantation.

Louisa was raised in South Carolina until the outbreak of the American Revolution when, in 1777 at the age of 14, she was sent to England. Shortly afterwards she was an orphan and spent several years with her maternal family at Great Fulford. Louisa later detailed the life of a West Indian heiress coming of age in Devon:

> 'At length the hour, the important hour, arrived which gave the heiress the uncontrolled command of her splendid fortune both in the Old and New World. It would be a waste, my dear children, both of your time and of mine, to enumerate how many sought to win the hand they deemed so wealthy; an heiress is ever the object of attraction however destitute of merit either mental or personal. The very cause that renders her an heiress leaves her an isolated being and assuredly the mark for interest or envy to aim at. She is fortunate if she had understanding enough to resist being the dupe of the insidious flattery she will receive.'[156]

After the war, in 1785, Louisa, sailed across the Atlantic to assess her inheritance. She first visited the Bahamas part of which was retained by her family. However, the British government had seized the islands and while there she learned land grants had been made to compensate American loyalists such as the Rolle family who had lost their settlement in Florida.

Louisa next visited South Carolina and found her land had been wasted, the main house burnt and her enslaved people dispersed. Her reaction was:

> 'whilst contemplating the place of my nativity, my attendants informed me that the hunted deer often took shelter amidst the ruins. From which I then turned heart-struck at finding that desolation brooded where plenty formerly had revelled in her gayest mood.'

Ruins of the brick house were still visible as late as 1842.[157]

Not only were her American estates ravaged by war but her English ones were raided to pay for their return. Some six thousand acres of the South Carolina estate were later sold by the family but they retained substantial holdings until 1839.[158] Rear Admiral Graves continued to seek redress from Parliament for the family's interests in the Bahamas.[159]

◀ 15. The Exeter Plantation, built in 1726 by Hugh Butler, the husband of Anne Colleton, on land leased by Sir John Colleton. The photograph was taken in 1938.

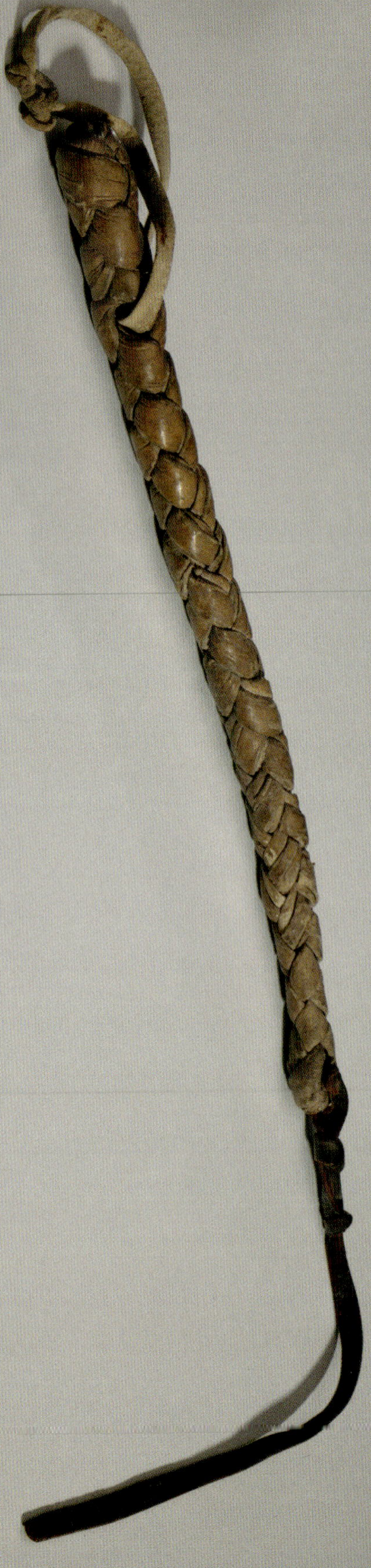

Louisa's sense of entitlement was reflected in her description of herself as 'Baroness of Fairlawn, Landgravine of Colleton and Sovereign Proprietress of the Isles of Bahama'. An indication of her attitudes can be found in her description of medical care she received when four years old and when her life 'was despaired of' by European doctors. Her nurses:

> 'recollecting that there was an African on the barony said to be well-skilled in magic and herbs, entreated my parents to permit him to be called in, to which they readily consented.'

As a White family they were outnumbered by the enslaved who had brought with them their own medical traditions. Her parents, in treating their sick child, had to negotiate the clash between African and European practices. Louisa wrote that her parents:

> 'although they had no confidence in his magic, they were well aware that the African doctors were well skilled in medicinal herbs and judicious in their use of them, by which they effected the cures they made, though they ascribed their success to their skill with magic, thus establishing their influence with unbounded sway over the minds of the credulous; for superstition enchains the ignorant throughout the world.'

The African was on watch in the nursery throughout one evening and spoke with Sir John in the morning. He believed that the spirit of Louisa's grandmother, along with those of her dead siblings, were attempting to take Louisa into the afterlife. He advised placing a bible under her pillow and prepared a plant-based juice to abate her fever and drive away spirits. The four-year-old child recovered.

Louisa commented on three men and women whom she termed 'attendants'. One maid named Bath accompanied her across the Atlantic. On her return to South Carolina Louisa met 'a Negro sailor belonging to me' named Hamman. He had been employed by her father as a navigator and was the second slave that she acknowledged as having saved her life. The ship's captain risked the lives of his passengers when he misunderstood his navigational coordinates. She credited Hamman with saying to the captain:

> 'I have been used to this coast from a boy and commanded one of my master's schooners, which was more than as big again as this, ever since I have been a man. I know nothing of your charts but I know your course is wrong, and if you persevere in it, you will be dashed on the breakers of St Augustine. I don't fear for myself, I can swim. But my mistress and my daughter Tachina are on board and they will be lost.'

◀ 16. Slave whip owned by a British abolitionist, late eighteenth century.

The captain subsequently charged Louisa for Hamman's passage and he was indignant when he heard.

> 'What? exclaimed he, pay for me? and he clapped his hands together vehemently, as if I was a land lubber, *me* who am a pilot on the coast, *me* who saved his life and his vessel from being lost and brought him safe to port and he charge for my passage?'

Louisa tried to soothe his pride with money but he responded 'No!, I was born and bred up on your lands. It was my duty to save you.' In another passage Louisa suggests that Hamman spoke differently from how she had recorded. She wrote he used 'the Negro patois'. When he said 'lili missi, lili, for nothing him have heart big mo no to much' he meant, 'in plain English', to say 'a great heart in a little body'. It is likely she translated other passages.[160]

Louisa married in 1787 Rear Admiral Richard Graves.[161] Some five years later they rebuilt Hembury Fort, a substantial country house in Buckerell erected by his uncle, Admiral Samuel Graves. Louisa was, in her own words, a striking woman. She and her husband were captured in 1801 while returning to England from a second visit to South Carolina. They were taken to Spain and at Madrid she became an object of attraction 'as they had heard of the extraordinary length of my hair, and were curious to ascertain the truth of the report'. French, Italian and Spanish women 'bowed and with the utmost politeness took the comb out of my hair which they shook around me in order to gratify their curiosity'.

She explained:

> 'My hair at this time was above seven feet long English measure and so thick that when shook around me I was as completely concealed as if wrapped in a mantle. The colour of my hair was a black auburn and very fine with a slight wave in it. On these occasions my husband or the Ambassadress at whose house it was thus displayed, always gathered it up, winding it round my head in a Grecian coil.'[162]

The family is remembered in Exeter through Colleton Crescent. Louisa recalled that she developed the land previously known as The Friars:

> 'I laid the foundation stone of the centre house of Colleton Crescent on the 3rd September, 1802, amidst a numerous concourse of spectators. General Simcoe, who was then general of the western district, handed me down the platform where the architect with the plan and the master mason with his attendants and implements for building awaited me. The band of the Inniskillin Regiment of Horse attended on the occasion, ready to strike up *God Save the King* the moment I appeared, which they continued playing till I drew off my glove and laid my hand on the stone, the signal for the music to cease. While I addressed the architect, after having laid the foundation stone, under which was deposited a box containing coins of gold, silver and copper, I presented a purse of gold to be distributed amongst the workmen on this occasion. The purse was emblematical.'[163]

Six months before The Friars had been cleared of its cloth racks; the city's cloth industry was withering and land was being utilised for building homes for retirees. Louisa died in 1822.[164]

In 1813 one of the Graves' daughters, Sophia Louisa Graves, married Tristram Radcliffe, the owner of the Exeter estate in Jamaica. The couple sailed to the West Indies where Radcliffe died eleven years later. It was then noted that 'from his amiable disposition [he] acquired the friendship of a number of respectable inhabitants who deeply deplore his untimely loss'.[165] Sophia remarried six years later, in 1830, but this was another short marriage: it lasted six years. Her second husband, Baron Maximilian August von Ketelhodt, submitted on her behalf a successful compensation claim of £137 9s 5d (£9,320.70) for 5 Jamaicans. His second claim for the Exeter Estate failed; £3,695 11s 2d (£250,563.66) was awarded to a Liverpool merchant who had financially underpinned the estate.

Some lesser known late Georgian slave-owners

Devon's other known enslavers were less prominent figures. They included John Pool Baker, a Jamaican who in 1802 acquired the Grove Place estate from the Bealey family of Exeter. Two decades later Elizabeth Wilkinson, an unmarried woman, received an annuity based on the estate's profits. This is revealed in Baker's will of 1825 in a bequest of two hundred and fifty pounds. He referred to Miss Wilkinson as a spinster lately of Exeter 'who now resides with me' in London. The couple had a son, John Pool Wilkinson Baker, who was born in London in 1802 and who inherited the plantation.[166]

Likewise, John Sayers owned a plantation in Demerara which was sold upon his death in 1808. He was resident in Totnes when he made his will the year before although he appears to have been born in Ireland and was resident in London thereafter. Similarly, Robert Hilton Angwin, who was probably born in Jamaica, owned an estate there which he sold in 1829. He died four years later. On three occasions he voyaged between the West Indies and his Torquay residence, Hampton House. Another Jamaican is Grace Cosens, a widow who owned enslaved people when she died in Exeter in 1821. Her connections with Devon have yet to be established.[167]

Lyon family, Kenton

The Lyon family are also of interest. In 1780 Edmund Pusey Lyon inherited two thirds of his father's estate, including a Jamaican plantation which the latter hoped his son 'would have more grace and goodness than to sell anything I have so dearly earned'. However, it appears the land was subsequently sold with the consequence that there was a financial benefit but not a direct ownership of plantations.[168] Lyon was an attorney and worked in Jamaica and England as Agent General for Jamaica from 1803 until 1812 when ill health forced his retirement.[169] In 1805 a meeting of the West India Planters and Merchants thanked him for his zeal, diligence and ability in arguing against abolition.[170] In 1806 and 1807 a petition passed through parliament on the society's behalf in which Lyon argued 'that the trade to Africa for labourers has been for a great number of years sanctioned, approved and encouraged by royal charters and proclamations and by repeated acts of the British legislature'. Moreover, he urged that 'they should continue to obtain supplies of Negroes from Africa'.[171]

Lyon was raised in Jamaica but in 1802 was in England for his marriage to a sister of Sir John Duntze, a leading Devon merchant. They lived in Kenbury House in Exminster and Staplake Mount in Kenton. The latter was described shortly before Lyon took possession as a brick-built villa, covered with painted stucco, set in fifty acres of land in which was situated an octagon pavilion built for summer parties. He also erected Hoopern House in the district of Pennsylvania in Exeter which shortly after his death was described as having an entrance hall, dining room, drawing room, morning room and book room on the ground floor. There were five best bedrooms upstairs as well as three dressing rooms.[172] It would appear that Lyon was not short of money.

Lyon became a magistrate and deputy lieutenant for Devon and died of 'gout of the stomach' in 1831 at Staplake but his monument noted him as living at Hoopern. His obituarist failed to notice his endeavours to promote slavery nor the benefits that it brought him. He was described as:

'an enlightened and active magistrate, we have, in taking passing notes of magisterial and county business, long been in the habit of bringing his name before the public, and the acknowledged estimation in which his talents were held, and his public labours received, afford the best panegyric his character, and the most fitting commentary on the man. But he is gone; and our nagging pen will no more attempt the task of following the words of wisdom and experience which fell from his lips. He is gone at a time when talents such as his were more than ever in request and he concluded a life of usefulness and labour, perseveringly continued at a crisis amidst personal sufferings which would have made others shrink under their heaviness, when perhaps the public could least spare him. But *fiat* of the Almighty has summoned him away, and he has entered his rest.'[173]

Nibbs family, Washfield

From 1772 the Nibbs family lived at Beauchamp House, a country house set within fifteen acres of grounds at Washfield near Tiverton. It was described in 1810:

'The house consists of a dining room, 36 feet by 19 feet, a good drawing room, hall and breakfast room, five good bed rooms, besides servants' rooms and all necessary and convenient offices'.[174]

James Langford Nibbs was born in Antigua where the family had owned plantations since the seventeenth century. He emigrated to England and inherited the Haddons (or Weekes) estate in 1750 through his brother in law John Weekes (who had inherited it from his first wife Rebecca Haddon). The estate was subsequently placed in trust as part of the arrangements made for his son's marriage to a wealthy first cousin. His other son, James Langford Junior, who has been described as a wastrel, brought himself into debt through gambling and this eventually led to his being disinherited. His father noted in his will of 1792 that his imprudence had reduced him to 'straights'. Nibbs took his son to Antigua with the hope it would curb his gambling. Jane Austen's father acted as one of the marriage settlement trustees and it has been noted that there are substantial similarities between the Nibbs' family history and a sub-plot in *Mansfield Park*.[175]

Ogilvie family, Totnes
Isabella Ogilvie's mother was at the centre of one of the great sensations of the late eighteenth century. Clementina Perry Ogilvie of Bath was the heiress to the Jamaican estates of her uncle George. Although described as 'amiable, modest and obliging, timid and not forward', at the age of fourteen and eleven months she eloped to Gretna Green with Richard Vining Perry, a twenty-six-year-old Bristol apothecary. 'The Bristol Elopement' of 1791 drew the attention of Thomas Rowlandson amongst others. She died in 1813 and only three years later her Totnes-born daughter, the eldest of her siblings, died in the town aged only twenty-six. She left her share in the Jamaican estates to her sisters.[176]

Stephen Oakeley Attlay of Teignmouth
Attlay inherited the Prospect estate in Jamaica from his father and held it from the 1780s. He was an absentee owner and resided in Knightsbridge but from 1830 was in Teignmouth living at Mare Platt House and later at East Cliff House. He assigned his compensation money of £2,809 10s 1d (£190,488.03) to the mortgagees in 1836; a local banker, Robert Jordan, was owed £1,000. In 1837 Attlay's home in Teignmouth and his possessions were sold through public auction. He died the following year.[177]

William Bremner of Plymouth
Dr William Bremner was born in 1773 on the island of Dominica where he owned Aberdeen, a coffee plantation. He came to Plymouth in 1827 and died the following year. Bremner built No. 2, Bedford Terrace which his widow sold the following year. It comprised:

> 'an entrance lobby, front parlour 16 feet by 14 feet 4 ins., back parlour 13 feet 6 ins. communicating with the former by handsome folding doors, and forming when open an excellent room of 31 feet by 29 feet 6 ins. On the first floor is a drawing room of 21 feet 10 ins. by 14 feet 6 ins. and best bedroom behind. On the second floor are three excellent bedrooms and three good servants' rooms, with a large closet over. The front kitchen is large, and fitted with grates, smoke jack, pantries, and every other convenience; the back

BOARDI[NG]
SCHO[OL]
FOR
YOUNG [LADIES]

kitchen a cooking apparatus, oven, furnace, &c. The premises are well supplied with spring water.

The house has been recently built by the proprietor in the most substantial manner, and finished in the first style, with marble chimney pieces and cornices of the best description, water closets, etc. and is altogether suited for the reception of a genteel family.

In the area, in front, there are very convenient wine and coal cellars; behind, a curtilage, with pantry, small garden, two-stalled stable, coach house, and hay loft. In front of the house a small flower garden; also a large walled garden well stocked with choice fruit trees, vegetables, etc. The prospects from the house are commanding and picturesque, embracing the Sound, Mount Edgcumbe, Devonport, Hamoaze, and the surrounding country to the extent of many miles.'[178]

The property illustrates the style of living enjoyed by some slave-owners.

John Ellis Junior of Mamhead

As lavish if not more so was the lifestyle of a family who lived for a short period at Mamhead. John Ellis resided there in the early 1800s. In 1810 he inherited from his Jamaican-born father interests in half a dozen plantations including Newry. The family's status is indicated by his sister having been presented to the queen that year. It was noted in the press:

'This young lady was dressed with peculiar taste and elegance in white and silver. The dress was exactly suited to the youthful and interesting form of the fair wearer'.

Ellis died in Paris in 1832 and the compensation awards were subsequently given mostly to men, other than the family members, who had moved from Devon.[179]

John Reeder of Fremington

In 1772 Reeder established an iron-making and brass casting foundry in Morant Bay in Jamaica. He shares his name with a better-known man who killed 'Three Fingered Jack', otherwise Jack Mansong, a leader of insurrectionist Jamaicans at this time. Some of the foundry's workers were enslaved and were owned by Reeder.[180]

Reeder appears to have been a North Devonian. He returned to England in the late 1780s and by 1797 owned a four-bedroom dwelling in the village of Bickington in Fremington outside of Barnstaple. During these years Reeder was occasionally in London and moved to Bates Hotel in the Adelphi where he died in 1798. At this time his sister, Elizabeth Nicholas, was residing three miles away at Pill House in

◀ 17. Rowlandson's view of the Bristol elopement, 1792.

Barnstaple. Any other ties he might have had with Devon have not yet been found[181] with the exception of the Rolle family of Stevenstone.

The Reeder family had various connections with the Rolles. Their association appears to have originated with the previous generation: it was later claimed that John Reeder's father had been 'sincerely attached' to Denys Rolle and his family. They may have been connected through Rolle's settlements in Florida and the Bahamas. The second generation continued some familiarity: Reeder was in contact with Rolle's son John and his sister lived in a dower house owned by Elizabeth Rolle née Chichester. On a number of occasions Reeder's daughter wrote to John Rolle seeking financial help for herself and employment for her son. By this date Rolle had already lobbied William Pitt for a position in India for Reeder's son and sought a pension for Reeder.[182]

Something of Reeder's character comes through in two letters with the Webber family of Buckland in Braunton. Twenty-four-year-old John Incledon Webber had sailed to Jamaica in 1783 and while there met Reeder. Webber wrote to his father Philip:

> 'I had an opportunity making some acquaintance with the gentlemen of the island particularly with Sir Thomas Champneys, a Somersetshire man, and Mr Reeder, one of our part of the world, found me out, from whom I received every mark of esteem and friendship, took me to his home in the country, treated me with the greatest hospitality, in fact I was as one of the family both with him and Sir Thomas, they live very near each other and a Mr Beckford (not a son of Mrs Baker but a very distant relation – he is member of the Assembly). From those gentlemen I met with every mark of friendship and civility particularly from Mr Reeder and his amiable wife. In short I am at a loss for words to describe their friendship and hospitality'.[183]

Webber was serving in the Royal Navy and six years later collapsed in ill health on his return from another West Indian voyage. He was placed in a strait-jacket for his own safety and it was Reeder, presumably then in Fremington, who travelled to Gosport to collect and return him to his family in Braunton.[184] Webber had sailed along the African coast on a anti-slaving patrol and he died in Barbados four years later.[185]

According to Reeder's married daughter, Eliza Crosse, the foundry originated when her father met Mr Bailey, a West Indian proprietor. Crosse wrote that her father:

> 'being of an enterprising character determined to accompany him to Jamaica. Not long after his arrival, there was a meeting of the House of Assembly to take into consideration the great disadvantage the planters were under from being obliged to send to England for all their materials for the manufacture of sugar etc. A plan was proposed to erect a building on the island but where to find an individual equal to the task was the difficulty. Mr Bailey said a young man was with him who had some money and a most active mind, he would propose it to him. On his doing so, my father said he was quite ignorant of such a business, neither had he sufficient money. On meeting they proposed to advance him £3,000 currency on bond.'

Reeder himself stated that he arrived in Jamaica in about 1760.[186]

The foundry was built in 1772[187] and Reeder later claimed it made an annual profit of £4,000 [£344,418]. In 1780 he left Jamaica on medical advice and when he returned he:

> 'found all his works dismantled, his reverberating furnaces demolished, some of the materials buried, such of the stock as might be of use to the [French] enemy (who were there assembled in great force at Cumberland Harbour) carried on board His Majesty's ships and all the rest of his works irrecoverably dismantled and destroyed by order of the governor lest they fall into the enemy's hands'.

Reeder failed to resurrect the foundry and from 1783 he began a three-year residence in the Spanish Main where he sold Jamaican iron. He was awarded £3,000 as compensation but Reeder spent the rest of his life attempting to recover his full losses of £22,000 (£1,491,628.60).[188]

In 1787 Reeder conveyed the foundry, its land and enslaved people to a group of largely London-based merchants.[189] Four years later, in 1791, the buildings, contents and land were auctioned and the sale details confirm Reeder had developed a considerable operation. There were three main buildings with the largest being a framed house 66 feet long, 38 feet wide and 12 feet high. It had a 'strong double roof' with about 6,000 pantiles. A second building was nearly as large: it was 65 feet in length, 33 feet in width and 8 feet high. The walls were fourteen inches thick. A third stone building adjoined the latter; it was 63 feet long and 47 feet wide. The 'framing and roof' were made 'of the best hard timber'.

The machinery was described as being:

> 'Two mill stones
> A large parcel of wooden models for casting iron work
> A machine for cleaning cotton
> A parcel of carpenters' tools
> Four forges containing about 3,000 bricks each and two forges containing about 20,000
> A parcel of the very best hard wood of large dimensions very suitable for mill work
> Spars and rigging for a shallop
> A large quantity of old iron and iron work
> Four shafts for a water wheel
> A large crane strongly bound with iron
> Four pair wheels for a waggon, three feet diameter
> A large cooper's anvil'
> There were also some fifty acres of land for sale along with a lease 'of the house and offices on the hill'.[190]

During its short operation the foundry employed as many as 276 'slaves, Maroons and free Coloureds'. Reeder commented that they were:

'perfect in every branch of the iron manufactory so far as relates to casting and turning mill cases, cannon, iron boilers etc. and in weighing iron anchors, mill gudgeons, axles, etc.'.

This phrase has led historians to theorise that the foundry was reliant on their 'African metallurgical expertise' and that the workers' skills were 'legendary'.[191] This originated more than thirty years ago when it was postulated:

'there was a range of interactions between African and European technologies within which the Africans contributed considerable skills and expertise and demonstrates that technology transfer was an inevitable consequence of the Atlantic slave trade'.[192]

It has been suggested that their expertise 'drew from a rich iron-making tradition' in Africa rather than from England.[193] Historians have embraced this notion of an African knowledge transference to the West Indies; one has echoed that Reeder's workers 'introduced African metallurgical technology' to Jamaica and another that they were 'apparently selected for their metal-working skills'.[194]

Reeder family correspondence at the Devon Heritage Centre provides another explanation: the workers' expertise came through training provided by colonists. Reeder's daughter explained:

'My father sent to England to procure artificers such as were necessary under whom his Negroes worked to become in course of time sufficiently acquainted with the business to dismiss all the White men but him and a perfect foundry was established, where not only sugar utensils were made but cannon manufactured'.

Reeder referred to them when in 1781 he found that:

'In consequence of the dismantling my foundry I have lost the capital, the most valuable of my Negroes are dead (for the instruction of whom sixty White artificers had been engaged from 100 to £50 per annum) from my being under the necessity to employ them in husbandry, despondency ensued. Trades Negroes consider themselves of rank superior to others and cannot brook the disgrace of being employed in the cultivation of lands.'[195]

In 1772 Reeder had owned forty men and women who he described as 'Negroes and other slaves'.[196]

Some of the British men can be identified: five died between 1779 and 1783. They were described as being a foundry-man, blacksmith, foundry head manager, carpenter and coppersmith. A sixth man died on the voyage to Jamaica.[197] In 1779 John Jeremiah, another indentured servant, absconded from the foundry. Reeder placed an advertisement in *The Jamaica Mercury and Kingston Weekly Advertiser.*

'As he was procured from England at a considerable expense, and his place cannot be easily supplied with another, Mr Reeder will be much obliged by any gentleman securing him and acquainting him thereof. He knows no reason for his absenting himself but the want of *Bristol cheese*. Whoever employs him, or carries him off the island, may depend on being prosecuted.'[198]

Reeder was thinking of another indentured servant when he wrote following his foundry's dismantling that:

'his machinery for making bar iron hath been totally useless to him since and will remain so until proper people are procured from England, to put it in order. That one [man] hath been engaged at the expense of a hundred and forty pounds but who died soon after his arrival, without ['completing it' crossed through] having effected anything.'[199]

Reeder would appear to qualify his comment on the 'perfect' skills of the workers and these can be appraised alongside the results of archaeological investigations in the early 1990s which indicated that the foundry was built in a manner similar to other English establishments rather than with those in Africa.[200]

Charles Waymouth of Dawlish

Twenty-four-year-old Reverend Waymouth died in 1832, a year after his mother bequeathed her interest in a St Kitts estate but before the emancipation act came into effect. His mother was the daughter of a London insurance broker and his father was an Exeter merchant. They lived in Dawlish from at least 1797 and at Newhouse in Mamhead from 1805 to 1814. His siblings also died in their twenties.[201]

On 18 April 1831 Waymouth was appointed curate of Cadeleigh. He died the following year, two years after his marriage and a year after his mother's death. She owned sixty-four Kittians including three eight-year-old boys who were part of the Grass Gang and three ten-year-old boys who were field workers.[202] Waymouth was the successor at Cadeleigh to Reverend Stephen Oakeley Attlay Junior, another slave-owner whose father resided at Teignmouth.

Among those individuals for whom further research is needed is Sir Manesseh Masseh Lopes of Maristow House in Roborough in West Devon. He was best known for having been found guilty by Parliament of political bribery and corruption. It has long been questioned whether Lopes was a Jamaican plantation owner. At his death in 1831 he left a fortune of £800,000 (£54,241,040).[203]

Some individuals benefited from slavery, notably merchants who sold slave-produced goods, without having personally owned enslaved people. They include Nathaniel Elliot, a West Indies merchant, who moved from London to Exeter by 1808 by which time he had purchased land in the South Hams at West Alvington as well as a house in the parish of St Sidwell in Exeter. He died three years later.[204]

Likewise, James Richards was a Bristol sugar refiner in partnership with his second wife's brother and nephew, George Gibbs Senior and Junior from Topsham. Richards died aged 80 at Ilfracombe in 1829. His widow Elizabeth, who was born in Topsham, was 'as deaf as a post and uses a trumpet'. She continued to live in Ilfracombe until her death at the age of 90 in 1840.[205]

ABOLITION AND EMANCIPATION

Iberians moral qualms about early African slaving repeatedly resurfaced through the sixteenth century with debates on the propriety of enslaving fellow human beings. Some argued that only non-Christians or individuals captured in armed conflict could be enslaved but various churchmen questioned all forms of slavery. In Britain abolitionists began campaigning in the 1750s and finally succeeded in 1807 in ending the transport of enslaved people across the Atlantic.

Abolition meetings were held across Devon in the late 1700s and petitions were sent to Parliament although North Devon was slower in coming forward than the rest of the county. Plymouth excelled itself when in 1788 a group of Plymothians published a print of the *Brookes*. It became one of the most successful images of abolition. Devonians continued to be active into and through the nineteenth century.[206]

In the hustings at Devonport in 1832 a flag bore the most famous abolition motto 'Am I not a man and a brother' with Erasmus' line beneath 'he who allows oppression shares the crime'.[207] There are few other references to the former phrase being used in Devon but it must have had a strong resonance as it was remembered many years later. In 1865 James White, noted as a 'man of colour', was arrested in Teignmouth for invading a constable's private apartment with the intention of sleeping there. He implored him 'Am I not a man and a brother?' The phrase was also adopted by Devonians in relation to other forms of discrimination.[208]

Thousands of Devonians signed abolition petitions and among the leaders was John Prideaux, a Plymothian who was a member of the Society of Friends. He was given a stirring tribute upon his death in 1859.

> 'The cause of the enslaved and oppressed African race he warmly and earnestly espoused, promoting, to the utmost of his power, every plan tending to their relief. These feelings had grown with him from childhood, his father having been one of the first members of the Anti-Slavery Committee in Plymouth set on foot by Thomas Clarkson. It was characteristic of him that, not content with feeling for the slave, or even labouring from his deliverance from bondage, he for many years scrupulously abstained from the products of slave labour, whenever a substitute for them could be obtained'.[209]

Abolition was led by the Dissenters, most notably the Unitarians, Methodists and Society of Friends. At a meeting in Exeter in 1834 it was observed that ladies with the 'bonnet of drab' were most prevalent. The abolitionists were concerned not

18. Akin to taking the knee, copper token inscribed 'Am I not a man and a brother?', c1796. ▶

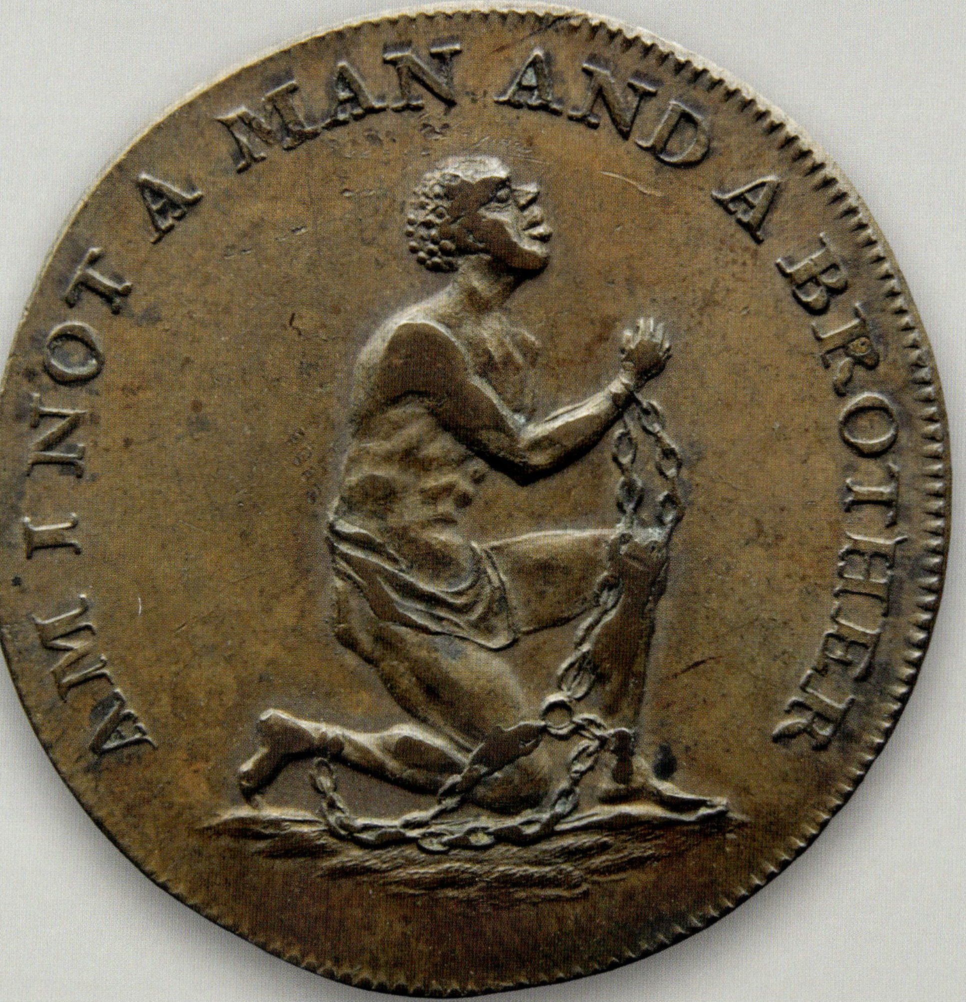
AM I NOT A MAN AND A BROTHER

merely with transatlantic slavery but slavery in its widest sense including that across Africa.[210]

There were three main ways in which Devonians were informed about slavery in the generations following 1807. Firstly, some individuals had first-hand experiences through travel in North America and the West and East Indies. Some disseminated their impressions. Secondly, printed literature was commonplace: not only were there dozens of books, tracts and pamphlets but local newspapers printed relevant news stories, editorials and letters. Finally, there were public meetings and rallies which often drew large audiences.[211]

Every Devon meeting supported abolition; not one was held to back slavery although pro-slavery attendees occasionally attempted to water down resolutions. For instance, at a raucous meeting in Ilfracombe in 1830 Albany Saville, a former Member of Parliament for Okehampton, argued that despite his ignorance of the West Indies he felt that given 'slavery having been permitted by the wisdom of the all Bountiful Creator to be the lot of some of our fellow creatures' they, as 'beasts of burden', received only reasonable treatment from their owners and Devonians should not interfere in their lives. Those attending the meeting disagreed.[212] Likewise, in Barnstaple George Mellis argued against immediate compensation; his argument was that it would take generations to civilise enslaved people.[213]

At Exeter in 1833 Joseph Sparkes, a local merchant, said 'he had no doubt that those who lived 40 years hence, would wonder how such a question could have required discussion at all in a Christian country'.[214] Nevertheless, he and many others worked from 1823 as the Devon & Exeter Anti-Slavery Committee. Other societies, including religious ones such as the Central African Mission, were also active. For nearly two hundred and fifty years Devonians, like the rest of England, have campaigned to end slavery in the Americas as well as in Africa, Asia and latterly Britain itself.[215]

Devon audiences also listened to formerly enslaved men such as John Brown who escaped from the American South and in 1850 travelled to Redruth to see a Cornish miner he had met in Detroit. Two years later Brown lectured on his life to audiences in Exeter, Plymouth and Tiverton and later wrote *Slave Life in Georgia*.[216] Amongst others who spoke in Devon whilst on national lecture tours were Lewis Smith and Reverend William Johnstone.[217]

This second phase of campaigning led in 1833 to Parliament passing the next landmark piece of legislation: on 28 August 'An Act for the Abolition of Slavery throughout the British Colonies; for promoting the Industry of the manumitted Slaves; and for compensating the Persons hitherto entitled to the Services of such Slaves' received Royal Assent. It took effect on 1 August 1834 and applied to all British colonies with the exception of Sri Lanka, St Helena and the territories controlled by the East India Company in India, South East Asia and China.

The act compensated owners for the loss of their forced labour. Compensation was set at £20,000,000 (£1,356,026,000) and was paid by Parliament. Enslaved children under the age of six were given their freedom but adults had a lengthy period in which they continued to be tied to their former masters: the legislation established apprenticeships, in which enslaved people were required to continue to work for their former owners. It was organised in two stages, domestic servants served four years to 1 August 1838 while field workers worked for wages for a further six years until 1 August 1840. Legislatures in some colonies shortened the period of service.

Some voices noted the Act was unjust because the enslaved received no recompense. A Methodist preacher from Devon commented:

> 'It was called *compensation* money! But to whom? Not to the Negroes who had been robbed of the just reward of their own labours; but, to their so-called owners, as if they had been victimised on the altars of national justice.'[218]

Emancipation came at a time in which Roman Catholics and Jews were seeking equality with Christians and, most importantly, when the Great Reform Act was passed. In 1832 this expanded the electoral base, reformed the constituencies and changed the makeup of the House of Commons. Thus, the Emancipation Bill passed its third reading in July 1833. Devon's twenty-two representatives appear to have all voted in favour.

Emancipation was celebrated on 1 August 1834 in North Devon by the Dissenters who opened their chapels 'for thanksgiving to Almighty God for the emancipation of our fellow creatures from slavery'. A celebratory bazaar was held that day in Exeter and amongst the banners were 'The Glorious First of August'.[219]

A Devonian resident in the West Indies in the Emancipation period was clear in his estimation of what had been achieved. James Bickford from Modbury wrote:

> 'A clear and broad road was created for all classes to respectable professions, intermarriages and the acquirement of material comforts without prejudice or distinction'.[220]

While further work is needed to determine whether Devon's level of investment in earlier slave-plantations was comparable to other parts of the country it is certain that the process of abolition was furthered by the public's clear understanding of the brutality of life in the slave colonies.

3

The slave colonies in 1834

'The blacks dislike the browns, the browns look down upon the blacks and the whites have no love for either', Richard Robert Madden, Jamaica, 30 May 1834

The slave colonies not only supplied Britain with exotic products but they also imported British manufactured goods, boosted the nation's maritime infrastructure and yielded high custom revenues to the government. There were economic fluctuations with profits greatest in the 1700s as plantations became less economically viable in the early 1800s.[221]

Devonians owned enslaved people in most of the colonies. In 1828 a West Indian contemplated the character of West Indian society:

'Everything we saw reminded us that we were in a land of slavery, and though in an English colony, that liberty, the glory and boast of Englishmen, was here denied to thousands of our fellow men, differing from us, it is true, in colour and intelligence, but still our fellow men. Every Briton, on first setting foot on West Indian soil must, on this subject, experience sensations nearly allied to those of sorrow, sympathy and regret'.[222]

Devonians who visited the West Indies encountered a society which was markedly different to that which they would have been familiar. Each colony had its own racial mixture of Indigenous people, ruling Europeans, enslaved Africans and free people of mixed race.

On the Europeans arrival in the West Indies and Mauritius in the 1490s they found an array of Indigenous people with distinct languages and cultures. By 1834 there remained populations of varying sizes in Antigua, British Guiana, Dominica, Mauritius, St Vincent, Tobago and Trinidad but not in the Bahamas, Barbados, Grenada, Jamaica, Nevis or St Kitts.[223]

In 1834 many Europeans, who were in the minority, were non-British settlers from Denmark, France, the Low Countries, Portugal, Spain and Sweden. One writer separated them into two classes. In the higher echelon were planters, principal merchants and civil servants while the lower comprised tradesmen, overseers and shopkeepers. Descendants of poor Irish and Scottish settlers were known in Barbados as Redlegs. In the early 1800s other free immigrants were recruited from Europe and the United States as well as from Africa, South Asia and China.[224]

Enslaved people made up the greatest part of the population. Some had arrived before Atlantic transportation ended in 1807 and were listed as 'Africans' in emancipation documents. In some lists they were noted as Mandingos (from Senegal) Coromantees (Ghana), Passams or Whydaws (Benin), Igbo (Nigeria and Guinea), Kongos (Congo, Angola and Gabon) and Angolas (Angola).[225]

A third group, the second largest, comprised interracial individuals, mostly of European and African ancestry, who were born in the West Indies and known as Creoles. This term also included other people born in the Caribbean. Mixed-race people were also known as 'people of colour' or 'Coloureds'.[226] In 1807 one writer, in favour of slavery, described society in Demerara.

> 'When a European arrives in the West Indies, and gets settled or set down for any length of time, he finds it necessary to provide himself with a housekeeper or mistress. The choice he has an opportunity of making is various, a Black, a Tawny, a Mulatto or a Mestee; one of which can be purchased for £100 or £150, fully competent to fulfil all the duties of her station. Some of them are so much educated as to be able to read and write. … They embrace all the duties of a wife except presiding at table. So far decorum is maintained and a distinction made. They employ themselves in needle work and other domestic affairs. Their usefulness in preserving the arts and diffusing the habits of cleanliness is felt and allowed by all, there being a lack of civilised European women. If a young progeny of Coloured children is brought forth, these are emancipated and mostly sent by those fathers who can afford it, at the age of three or four years, to be educated in England'.[227]

Dutch men had established, before the English arrived in Demerara, a similar practice amongst Indigenous women.[228]

The names of some enslaved people indicate Devon ties but before discussing these, we should note that the practice of name-giving was complicated by the different traditions inherited from Europe and Africa. Names had either African or European origins and some individuals had several names. In some instances an individual was known to an owner by one name but they themselves sometimes used another called a 'plantation name'. Subsequent owners could also assign new names.

In West Africa individuals used a variety of names. In contrast, the English practice followed by slaveholders was that a first name was fixed at baptism and a surname was taken from the paternal line or at marriage from the husband. Nicknames were casual. The introduction of the European practice of Christian baptism for enslaved Africans or their descendants formalised first and second names which in some cases were determined by owners.[229]

Some enslaved people were named after thirteen urban areas in Devon. These were Barnstaple (in Jamaica), Bideford (Jamaica), Budleigh (Jamaica), Dartmouth

(Jamaica, St Kitts, St Vincent, Tobago), Devonport (Barbados), Exeter (Barbados, British Guiana, Jamaica, St Kitts, St Vincent, Tobago), Exmouth (Grenada, Jamaica), Sidmouth (Grenada), Tavistock (Jamaica), Tiverton (British Guiana, Jamaica), Topsham (Jamaica) and Totnes (Jamaica, St Vincent). The most popular Devonian first name was Plymouth; these men lived in Antigua, the Bahamas, Barbados, Grenada, Jamaica, Nevis, St Kitts, Tobago and the Virgin Islands. Others called Devon lived in Jamaica and this continues as a personal name mostly in the United States and the Caribbean. There were many more with the more cumbersome name 'Devonshire': they were in Antigua, the Bahamas, Barbados, Grenada, Honduras, Jamaica and St Kitts. Exon (the Latin form of Exeter) and Plymouth were used as surnames in Jamaica. Barbadians and Jamaicans were also named Tamar. More popular were some place names from neighbouring counties which included Bridgwater, Bristol, Chard, Cornwall, Dorchester, Falmouth, Minehead, Penzance, Somerset, Taunton and Weymouth.[230]

It is difficult to find a Devon connection with individuals given many had several owners over their lifetimes.[231] Some plantations had a number of men with place names for their first name: 'Biddeford' was owned by Henry Cerf who also owned Aberdeen, Bristol, London, York, Windsor, Dublin, Scotland and Kent. Likewise, Henry Shirley owned two Jamaican males called Barnstaple, one was aged 12 and the other 80, but he also owned Bedford, Deptford, England, Fife, Greenwich, Gloucester, Liverpool, Port Royal and York.[232]

One firm connection lies with James Davy who owned men called Topsham and Devonshire in 1817. Both were born in Africa. That year Davy christened these men along with some of his other Jamaicans for whom he gave new names. Prince, for instance, became Edward Davy and Dick's new name was Richard Davy. Other men were renamed: Cudjoe became Joseph Davy, Thomas became Thomas Davy and William became William Davy. Some women were also given new first names as well as the surname Davy: Caroline had been Mintas, Elizabeth (Princess), Hannah (Boxey), Helen (Lucretia), Isabella (Thisbe), Louisa (Mimba), Rosa (Bella) and Ruth (Alice).[233] Their owner had lived at Countess Wear outside Topsham and established coffee plantations in Jamaica. His son James Lewis Davy was later awarded compensation of £2,156 11s 1d (£146,217.18) for the loss of 106 individuals on the Heavitree and [Countess] Wear plantations.

In contrast, the census in 1841 shows that no White people in England were given Devon place names as a first name with the exception of Exeter Latter, a fifteen-year-old agricultural labourer who was born in Sussex. While such names were considered inappropriate for the White population, other names popular amongst enslaved people can be found in Devon. In 1841 one such name was Scipio, derived from Latin meaning a staff or walking stick. Scipio Cock was a Winkleigh farmer, Scipio Copper was a Mariansleigh agricultural labourer and Scipio Luxton a Cullompton cordwainer. Each was fifty years old and had been born in Devon. Earlier instances included men in Churston Ferrers and Werrington.[234] Both of the latter were Black but at an earlier date the name was given to Devonians such as Scipio Luxton of Broadwoodkelly in the early 1600s. It was used in Devon at least a generation earlier and in a number of instances passed from father to son.[235]

Classical names were among those given to West Indian enslaved people; this included Adonis, Caesar, Nero and Pompey for men and Juno, Minerva and Venus for women. Of these male names only Caesar was used in Devon in 1841: father and son Caesar Hodder lived in Topsham. Minerva was the name of a ten-year-old-girl born in Devon who lived in Stoke Damerel in 1841. There were also no individuals in Devon recorded that year with such 'slave' names as Prince or Princess. Nor were any Devonians given a day of the week as their first name; West African children were sometimes named after the day or time of their births and Devonians owned individuals with these names.

In comparison, a few individuals resident in England in 1841 used Devon places for surnames: Mary Bideford lived in Middlesex, Robert Sidmouth lived in Hertfordshire and there were families with the surnames Devonport and Exeter in the North West and South East of England. A family of seven with the surname Topsham lived in Kingsteignton.[236]

Some plantation names were derived from Devon. Five in Jamaica and British Guiana were named either Devon, Devon Pen, Devon Plantation or Devonshire Castle. Eighteen others took their names from places within the county.[237]

Table 1

Plantations named after Devon places.

Place in Devon	Colony
Barnstaple	Jamaica
Bideford	Jamaica
(Countess) Wear	Jamaica
Exeter	Jamaica (5)
Exmouth	British Guiana (2)
Heavitree	Jamaica
Plymouth	Montserrat
Town of Plymouth	Tobago
Saltram	Barbados, Jamaica
Topsham	Jamaica
Torrington Castle	Jamaica

There were also two Mount Edgcumbe estates in Jamaica as well as Edgcumbe in Barbados which may have been named after the mansion formerly part of Devon. Further research might identify those who first chose these names in the generations before emancipation.

THE WEST INDIES

The slave colonies differ in their histories and populations which are outlined in Table 2.

Table 2

Population of British slave colonies in which there were Devon estate owners, 1830.[238]

	White	Slaves	Interracial	Total
Antigua	1,187	29,600	5,513	36,300
Bahamas	5,007	9,503	2,520	17,030
Barbados	14,812	82,026	5,312	102,150
British Guiana	3,701	88,666	8,235	100,600
Dominica	703	14,706	3,591	19,000
Grenada	701	23,884	3,806	28,400
Jamaica	18,903	319,074	40,703	378,050
Mauritius	unknown	64,331	unknown	unknown
Nevis	453	9,194	1,403	11,050
St Kitts	1,498	19,094	2,808	23,400
St Vincent	1,400	23,100	3,500	28,000
Tobago	453	12,551	1,146	14,150
Trinidad	3,323	22,757	15,985	42,065
Others	7,929	40,344	11,608	49,883
Total	54,772	748,327	102,980	842,748

West Indian travel accounts written by British visitors outline their characters. A striking example was penned in 1833 by R. R. Madden, a special magistrate. He discussed the islands in terms of their femininity. Madden suggested Barbados was like a plain, elderly Dutch spinster ('flat, stale, dull and unprofitable') whereas the sweet and sombre features of St Vincent were akin to 'a lovely Creole damsel luxuriating in repose whose smiles are like *the setting glories of a happier day*'. Grenada, praised for the 'stately splendour of her mountain scenery', was like a 'Spanish senora of gorgeous loveliness whose sun-bright eyes and noble air are bills at sight on the beholder's admiration'.[239] Madden also provided compelling insights into the nature of colonial slave societies as did other writers such as Richard Bickell who compared the conditions of West Indians with those of the English poor. He commented that all Devonians would reject the food provided to the enslaved as 'hardly fit for human and rational beings'.[240] These accounts help in understanding the characters and differences of the colonies.

19. 'Digging or rather hoeing the cane holes', 1823, in Antigua by William A. V. Clark. ▶

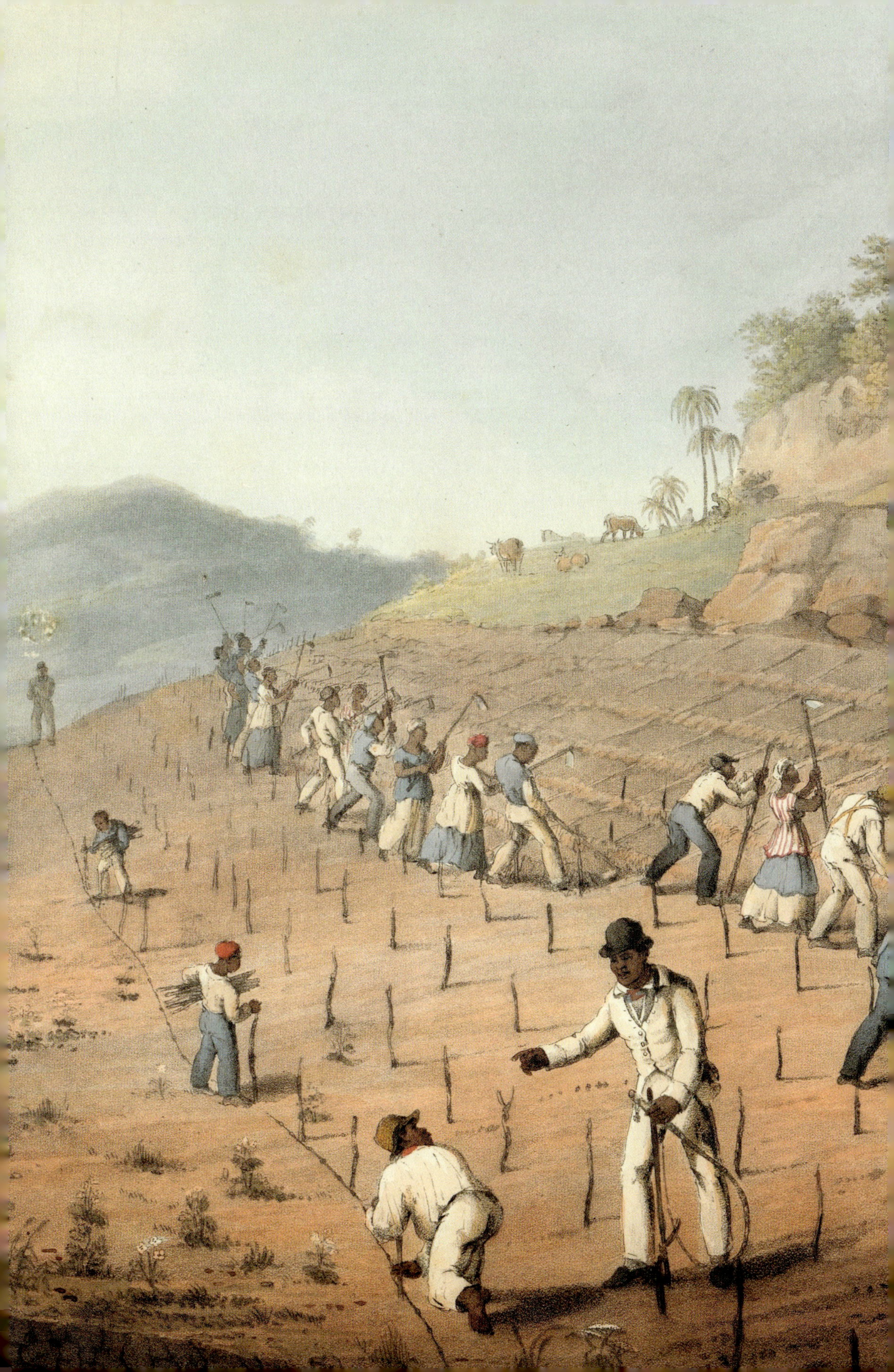

Antigua

Antigua and Barbuda were first colonised by the English in 1632 and remained a British colony until independence in 1981. Antigua is 21 kilometres (12 miles) in width and in area some 281 square kilometres (110 square miles). Barbuda is approximately half its size. In 1825 a visitor thought that Antiguan plantation houses were the best-appointed in the West Indies. He wrote:

> 'many of them are very old mansions, and constructed upon a more spacious and substantial plan than is generally deemed expedient in these days of mortgages. A small park or lawn is commonly enclosed round the house, and the sugar works, which however picturesque at a distance, are a very disagreeable appendage at hand, are so well concealed by trees and bushes that in many cases their existence would not be suspected by a person within the principal building'.[241]

In 1834 the ethnic mix was composed of a small number of Indigenous people as well as immigrants from Britain, Ireland in the mid 1600s and from Africa shortly afterwards. Portuguese settlers came from 1846 onwards and Middle Eastern immigrants arrived in the late 1800s. In 1836 only a third of the formerly enslaved population were non-Christian.[242] Table 2 shows Antigua was neither in the highest or lowest groups of populations of the slave colonies.

John Hyde Doyle of Exmouth was the only Devon resident to receive compensation: he had £1,704 11d (£115,536.52) for 102 Antiguans on the Body Ponds estate. In addition, Lyons Walrond of Broadhembury would have received compensation were it not for pre-existing financial obligations. There were 29,600 enslaved people in Antigua in 1831 and the government subsequently paid £424,391 to the estate-owners for 29,003 slaves. Sugar was the dominant commodity produced by forced labour.[243]

Others had Devon connections prior to the awards including Baijer Otto Baijer, George Beare who was a senior customs official in Antigua and Reverend John Swete, the writer of the Picturesque in Devon. In 1781 he inherited an estate and another in Jamaica from his aunt.[244] Another Georgian family active in Antigua had been resident in Washfield: the Nibbs family owned several estates. Others include Elizabeth Caroline Batt of Lawell House in Chudleigh who sought in 1817 to retain her Antiguan inheritance from her grandparents Henrietta and George Byam.[245] In respect to trade, the vibrancy of the cloth industry in Devon prompted two sons of a Tiverton dyer to investigate exporting dyes from Antigua in 1748.[246]

Antigua and Bermuda were the first colonies to rid themselves of slavery: on 1 August 1834 the estate-owners immediately released their workforce from the apprenticeship scheme. An Antiguan informed an Exonian that day 'What a day this is! In our little island thirty thousand beings who lay down last night slaves, have risen this morning free from their former masters'.[247]

The first of August was recalled by another as 'the bright day of liberty'. Frances Lanaghan Flannigan wrote:

'The 1st of August fell upon a Friday and after enjoying themselves upon the following day with their friends, and joining in the ordinances of God upon the Sabbath, the greater part of the Negroes returned to their agricultural and other employments on the Monday morning with the utmost decorum and good temper.'

She concluded, with no mention that they had been in the state of slavery, that:

'Defective as the Negro character may be, their behaviour at that eventful period of their lives must elicit praise from the lips of all, and prove a lasting theme of gratification to the friends of liberty.'[248]

Sixteen years later an American visitor agreed:

'Her rulers were wise in their generation. They foresaw that, with the substitution of free labor for slave labor, much had to be learnt and much to be unlearnt; that the success of the new system could only be determined by time and experience; and that an early start in the race was a point to be gained – not to be neglected. And so it undoubtedly was. Antigua has never had any cause to regret the independent course that she then thought proper to pursue'.[249]

Visitors reported Antigua became more prosperous after emancipation. The governor was asked if anyone wanted to reinstate slavery and he replied 'no, not one'.[250] There was, in the estimation of a traveller in 1837, 'an accumulation of talent, intelligence and refinement greater perhaps than in any English colony excepting Jamaica'. He also regarded Antigua to be 'the morning star of our nation'.[251]

The Bahamas

This collection of some 700 isles, reefs and keys, the most northerly of the islands Devonians held enslaved people, was a British colony from 1717 until full independence in 1973. The area is some 10,010 square kilometres (3,865 square miles). There were an estimated 40,000 Lucaynas in 1492 but the islands were deserted by 1650 when English settlers began colonisation. The Spanish had obliterated the Indigenous population through warfare, enslavement, disease and emigration.[252]

John, 1st Baron Rolle, was the only slaveholder resident in Devon to receive compensation. He had owned 377 individuals in the Bahamas for which he received £4,333 6s 9d (£293,805.92). In 1826 the islands' population was recorded as 4,588 White, 2,259 'free, Coloured' and 9,186 slaves.[253] Four years later the estate-owners received compensation payments totalling £128,340 7s 5¾d.[254]

The islands have been regarded as having a non-plantation society but for a short period cotton was a successful crop. After some fifteen years, by 1800, production had collapsed and in its wake estates practiced diversified agriculture particularly in producing foodstuffs for self-sufficiency and sale in local markets. The exception was salt-production for export.[255]

The Rolle family owned land on Great Exuma from 1783 until 1838. It may have been because of their influence that a Devon curate officiated there from 1797.[256] Five years previously it was claimed that Denys Rolle was the only landowner who insisted that his enslaved people were given religious instruction. A cleric wrote in 1792:

> 'I have given little instruction to Negroes, excepting that at a plantation in Cat Island for two nights I gave extemporary discourses to about 20 Negroes and one night to Mr Denys Rolle's Negroes on this island. The Negroes seemed to be attentive and serious. Mr Denys Rolle (the Member of Parliament's father) has given orders to his agent on this island to have family worship daily among his Negroes. The present agent every evening gives them family worship and likewise says somewhat to them concerning a heaven and a hell.'

The writer, a clergyman, also commented upon the enslaved in a manner partly reminiscent of slaveholders:

> 'I acquired an aversion to the enslaving of Negroes which still continues with me, though a good deal abated from observing that in the colonies where I have been, as Virginia and these islands, the Negroes are tolerably well treated. I am persuaded that the bulk of the colonial Negroes are happier than the Negroes in Africa, especially in this respect that the former have as good a share of understanding as Whites alike, illiterate as they, whereas the faculty of reason seems to be almost dormant in the Negroes newly imported from Africa. On the other hand I look upon the Colonial Negroes as far from being so happy as the labourers in Britain because they are not free and have little sense of religion and morality'.[257]

A generation after emancipation a report noted Rolle's settlements: at Steventon (named after Rolle's home of Stevenstone in Devon) 'the people are in middling circumstances, some poor and some comfortable' while in Rolletown 'they are industrious and comfortable'.[258] The Rolle history reveals his enslaved people had an unusual degree of independence including in refusing to relocate to Trinidad in 1825. They were also distinguished by continually acting in solidarity when dealing with Rolle's overseers in the years preceding and during the emancipation process. This, along with the financial losses suffered by Rolle, led to their early freedom as well as acquisition of land.

In 1876 a visitor noted of Rolletown:

> 'The people here, as in all the Exuma settlements, are the emancipated slaves of Lord Rolle and Mrs Adderley, who own the island in about equal shares. This is one of Lord Rolle's places but he has made it over to his former slaves. They are living pretty much as in slavery times; the only difference being that they are free (i.e. lazy) and cultivate their own land. The big Buckra (white man) house is in ruins'.[259]

Few other Devonians played a significant part in the history of the colony with the exceptions of General George Monck and Sir John Colleton, and later his son Peter, who were active from 1670 in their capacities as two of the eight Lord Proprietors who oversaw the development of the Bahamas as well as Georgia, North Carolina and South Carolina.[260] There was another connection: in 1834 *The vision and other poems in blank verse* was jointly published in Exeter and London. It was written by John Boyd, 'a man of colour' from the Bahamas.[261]

Barbados

This island, known as Little England, was first settled in 1625 and continued in British control until full independence in 1966. Barbados, some 34 kilometres in length (21 miles) and 23 in width (14 miles), is in area 432 square kilometres (167 square miles). The first impressions of a visitor in 1837 was that the island was small and low-lying and yet highly populated and under intense cultivation.[262] The principal commodities were sugar, rum and cotton.[263] A visitor in 1825 visited a slave's dwelling:

> 'The hut is a cottage thatched with palm branches and divided into two rooms; one is the chamber of the parents, the other the common hall with a table, chairs and a broad bench with back to it for the children to sleep on at night. Some huts are larger and smarter than this. Jack *something or other*, the driver on the Society's estate, has two large four post beds, looking glasses and framed pictures. Jack is a good-natured fellow, offered me some wine and hath begotten twelve children or more'.[264]

Barbados was England's first slave society. The Indigenous population had been enslaved by the Iberians, died of imported disease or fled before the English began colonising. Irish and Scottish immigrants, many indentured, arrived in the seventeenth century and were followed by Jewish settlers from Brazil and enslaved Africans. In the late nineteenth and early twentieth centuries further immigration took place from Europe and South Asia. In 1676 the Assembly of Barbados passed legislation which forbid further immigration of the Indigenous population of New England for slavery. During the first generation contract workers undertook much of the labour but by the Restoration a plantation society emerged with Africans forming a majority. The English estate owners discarded the labour structures they knew back home and embraced the systems which had been practiced by the Iberians in the Americas for more than a century.[265]

In 1829 the population was classified in terms of freedom (14,959 White, 3,119 free Coloured, 2,027 free Black) or enslavement (81,902). British immigrants included many of Irish or Scottish descent, who in 1834 were termed Barbadians and of whom Richard Montgomery Martin, a British civil servant and a founding member of the Statistical Society of London (1834) and of the Colonial Society (1837), wrote they were 'a numerous class between the great planters and the people of colour'. Moreover:

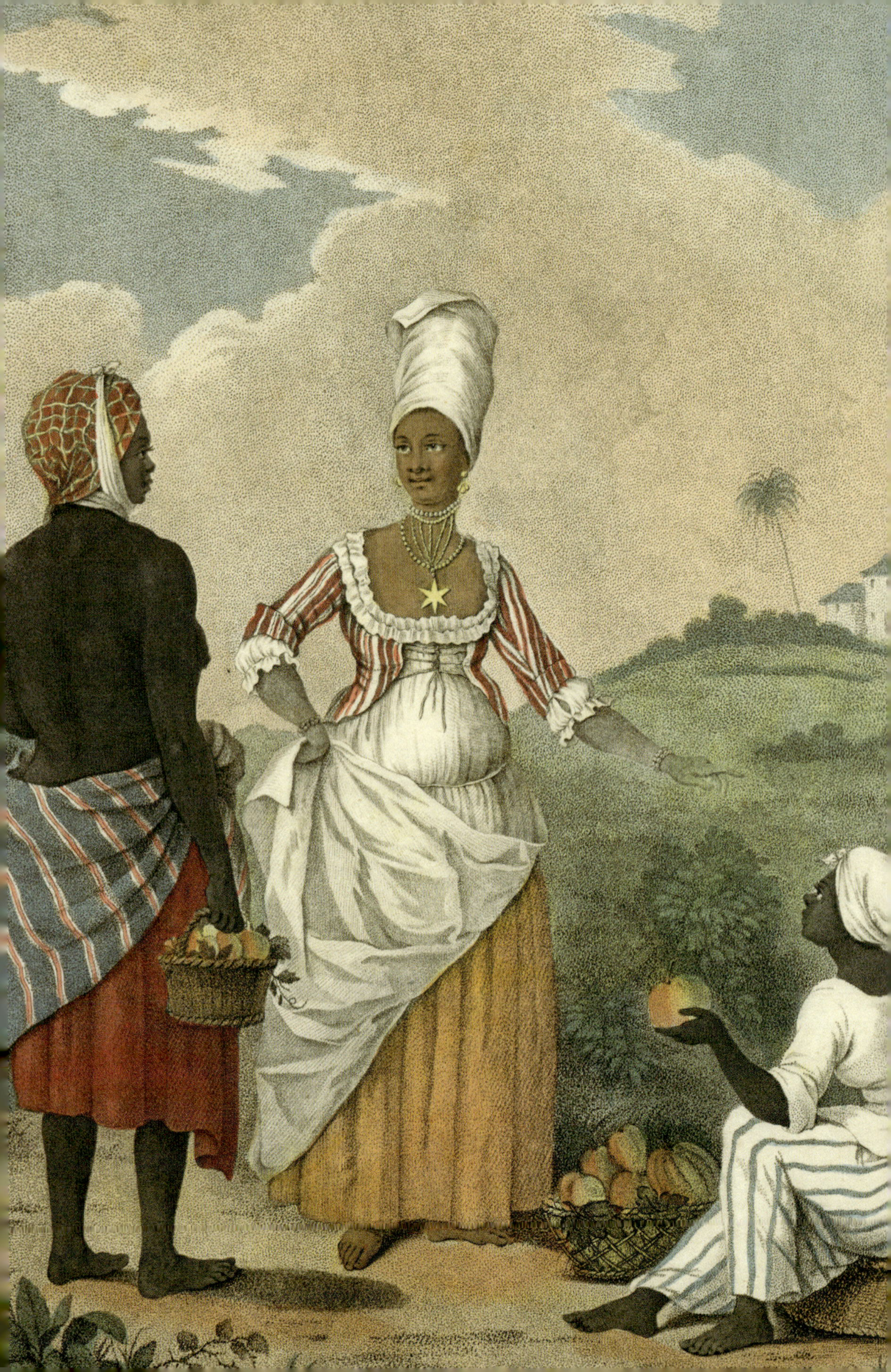

'many of them are descended from the original settlers and have no precise knowledge when their ancestors first arrived. They accordingly regard this island as their nation and only abode, and do not, like the planters or the Negroes, look back to the scenes of their infancy as their better home'.[266]

Three years later a planter described these poor Whites, some eight thousand in number, as 'the most degraded, vicious and abandoned people in the island who were very far below the Negroes'. Moreover, he regarded them as drunken, licentious, poverty-stricken 'ragamuffins' and a 'body of the most squalid and miserable human beings'.[267] Nevertheless, these men and women, known as Red Shanks, considered themselves superior to enslaved people although some stole and begged alms of wealthier Blacks. Their ancestors had been imported to fulfil a legal requirement that a planter had one White person for every sixty enslaved people.[268]

Emancipation was preceded in 1816 by a rebellion in which some 20,000 enslaved people took part. Ten years later the island's legislature passed the Consolidated Slave Law which granted property rights, the ability to give evidence in court cases and a reduction in manumission fees. It also granted the right for White people to kill enslaved people during revolts. Six enslavers (William Bovell of Plymouth, Sarah Oxley Cadogan at Exeter, Edmund Haynes of Exeter, Hinds Howell of Washfield, Emanuel Lousada of Sidmouth, Henry George Windsor of Budleigh Salterton) were at least partly resident in Devon when they received compensation for 1,180 individuals, the third highest number owned by Devonians at that time in any colony. In total the estate-owners received compensation awards of £1,714,561 (£116,249,464.73) for 83,225 individuals.[269]

Barbados was one of the principal slave islands and Devonians John Colleton and Thomas Modyford were involved in its early development. Some other connections are less obvious. For instance, in 1851 the rector of Cadbury had as a lodger his aunt, Susan R. Yearwood, whose father Seale had owned more than a hundred Barbadians. She had owned in her own right at least four individuals.[270]

Emancipation Day, 1st August 1834, was so quiet in Barbados that, according to one planter, a stranger would not have noticed a difference but three years later observers concluded that the apprenticeship period was not as successful as had it had been for Antigua.[271]

Demerara (British Guiana)

Guyana, on the north coast of South America, was a British colony from 1831 until independence in 1966. It comprised three territories (Berbice, Essequibo and Demerara) over which Britain had disputed sovereignty with the Dutch and French since the seventeenth century. This is the most southerly of the colonies in

◀ 20. 'The Barbadoes Mulatto Girl', 1779, by Agostino Brunias.

which Devonians owned enslaved people in 1834 and the county had considerable connections.

Guyana, the only former British colony in South America, is in area some 215,000 square kilometres (83,000 square miles). There was no local legislature because the three territories were a Crown Colony. A number of groups of Indigenous people lived alongside colonists from the Low Countries and Britain in the seventeenth century. Enslaved Africans were brought by the Dutch from 1640 and there was substantial immigration from Portugal (from 1835), India (from 1838) and China (from 1853). Guyana has one of the highest percentages of people of Indian descent: 39.3 per cent are descended from Asian immigrants.[272]

An early writer described the colonists in unflattering language. Edward Bancroft wrote in 1769:

> 'The White inhabitants of this colony are Dutch, English, French, Swiss and Germans but chiefly the two former. Many of these are unfortunate persons, whom the unavoidable accidents of life, or frowns of fortune, have induced to seek an asylum in distant countries, where their industry is often so amply rewarded, that they are enabled to return with opulence and credit, and bless those accidents which reduced them to the necessity of abandoning their homes and which they once esteemed the greatest misfortune'.[273]

He may have been thinking of men like the five slaveholders (James Hackett, Henry and Thomas Porter, John and Thomas Teschemaker) who were in Devon in the 1830s when they received compensation for 1,622 individuals, the highest number of enslaved people Devonians owned at that time in any colony. Catherine Hyndman nearly received a substantial award for her father's plantations but died, in Torquay, shortly before the compensation was paid. Hyndman had recently been orphaned and her connection at that time with Torquay is uncertain. Her brother established in her memory Miss Catherine Elizabeth Hyndman's Bounty to the Church of England. For nearly two centuries the money from coerced labour has enabled grants to build and refurbish Anglican churches.[274]

The estates were laid out differently in British Guiana than those in other colonies: they were in uniform rectangular patterns along the seaside or rivers. The fertile land had been reclaimed from the rain forest. Many were below sea level and had walls or dykes as protection against inundation.[275] In 1832 there were 65,517 enslaved individuals, of whom 34,349 were male and 31,168 were female.[276] A few years later the estate-owners received compensation totalling £4,281,032 (£290,259,534.94) for 84,075 enslaved people in British Guiana.[277] Their ages were calculated in 1832.

Table 3

Ages of slaves in Demerara and Essequibo, 1832.[278]

Males aged under three	1,974
Females aged under three	2,112
Three to five	2,744
Five to ten	5,401
Ten to sixteen	6,115
Males over sixteen to thirty	8,008
Females over sixteen to thirty	8,005
Over thirty to forty	8,345
Forty to fifty	13,585
Fifty to sixty	7,149
Sixty to seventy	1,613
Seventy to eighty	363
Eighty to ninety	40
Ninety to 100	7
Over 100	2
Ages unknown	24
Total	65,487

The colony's main products, produced by forced labour, were sugar, rum, coffee and cotton.[279]

In 1837 Robert Montgomery Martin observed that Dutch planters had taken Indigenous women as housekeepers ('broomstick relations') whereas:

> 'the taste of the English seems to be directed in a darker channel … those who live in immediate contact with us are so degraded by the practice of all our vices without any encouragement to copy our virtues that a humane mind is disgusted at the picture. To such, how bitter must be the reflection, though undoubtedly true, that this horrible state of abandonment is entirely caused by our criminal and hard-hearted neglect of the first duties of humanity. The Dutch were angels [compared] to us'.[280]

Perhaps Devon's most significant role in Demerara was through the Porter family which initiated cotton growing in the late 1700s. There were allied families such as the Sloane family of Rockbeare who in the early 1800s held at least four estates in Demerara including Friendship, John, Paradise and Pomeroon. John Plantation was purchased for £5,000 in 1813 and within three years it had a workforce of 107

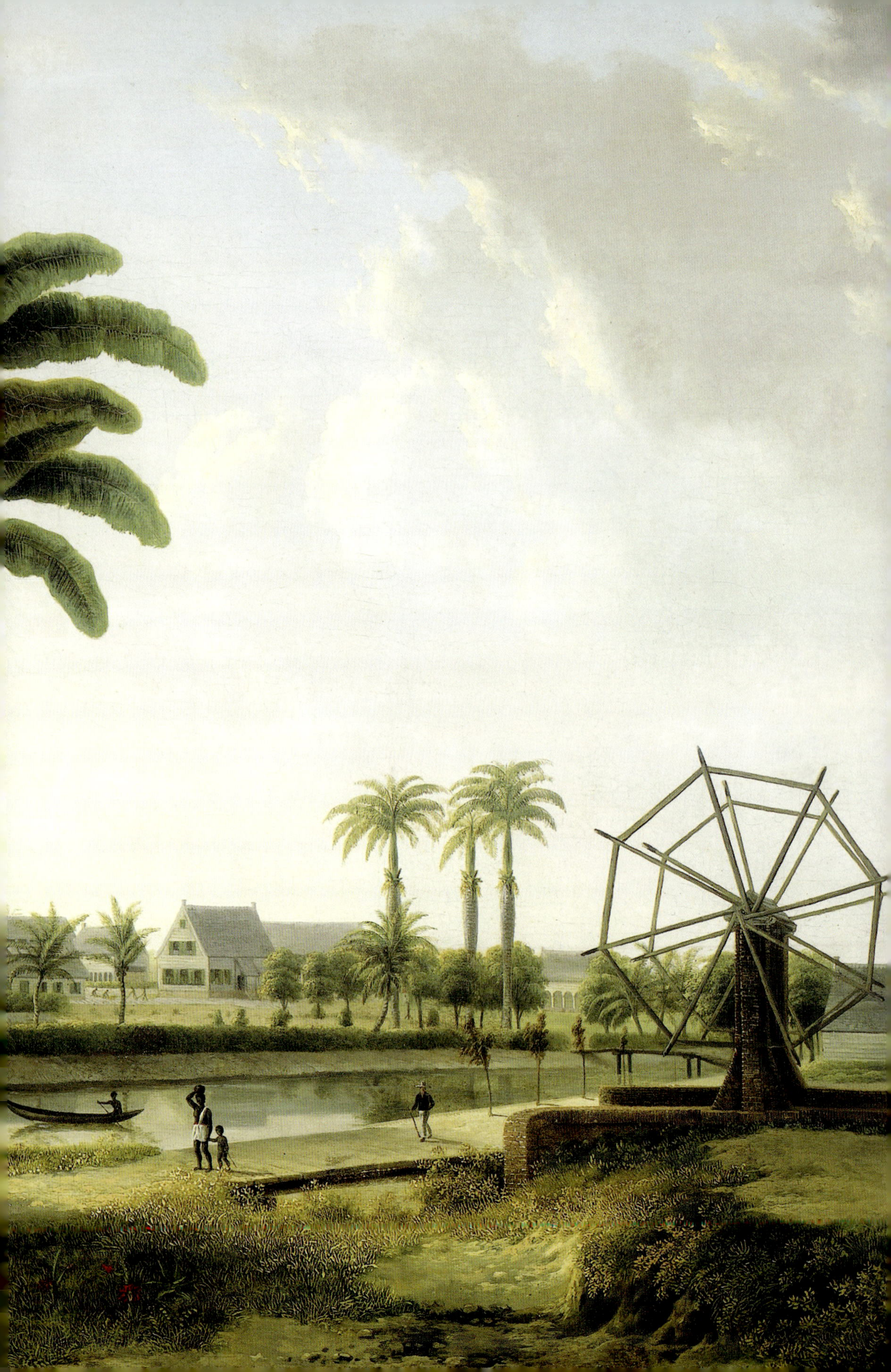

individuals. Mrs Ann Sloane was the sister-in-law and neighbour of Thomas Porter and he loaned her £5,381 10s against the Friendship Plantation.[281]

Another connection lay with Josephine Haley who in 1843 died voyaging from Demerara to England. She had been living, possibly as a visitor, at Dix's Field in Exeter and was the daughter of John Daniel Haley, a Demerara plantation owner. In 1835 compensation totalling £1,239 13s (£84,049.88) was paid for the loss of 69 individuals. The family had been born in the colony but were of Dutch ancestry. Josephine had an equal share with three illegitimate siblings. The race of the mother, Caroline Kragelius, is not specified in the documents nor are those of three children, Agnes Theresa, Dirk Horatio and Arabella Caroline Constantia, for whom it was recorded their father had great affection. Haley set up a trust for 10,000 guilders to be paid to his children from this union.[282]

Some individuals in Devon had indirect links such as Miss Ealsworthy, formerly of Chulmleigh, who in 1828 married the rector of St Swithan's church in Demerara.[283] Also, in 1868 Sir William Henry Holmes, a leading civil servant in Demerara, died in Plymouth where he had been resident for four weeks. His family had been living at 13 Clowance Street but it is not known if they had any particular Devon connections.[284]

Dominica

Britain colonised the island from 1761 and Dominica remained largely in its control through to 1805 when it became a colony. It is 47 kilometres (29 miles) in length and 26 kilometres (16 miles) in width. In area it stands at 750 square kilometres (289.5 square miles). The island's population of Indigenous people was supplemented by Africans and European immigrants who had British, French, Spanish or Italian ancestry. There were also American Loyalists.[285] In 1832 there were 791 White people, 4,077 'free Blacks' (and mixed race people) and 14,387 enslaved people. At emancipation the island's 14,266 enslaved individuals brought the estate-owners awards of £277,737 (£18,830,929.66). At Sidmouth Henry Stuart claimed for one individual on the New Hampshire estate. He was the only Dominican slave-owner resident in Devon. The principal exports at this time were sugar, coffee, rum and molasses.[286]

A visitor described the housing of the enslaved:

'The Negro houses are cottages neatly thatched with palm or plantain leaves. Some have floors of wood and are well furnished with a bed, cooking utensils, etc. but this depends on the station and industry of the occupiers'.[287]

In 1831 the island's assembly passed the Brown Privilege Bill which gave rights to free people of colour including representation on the legislature.[288]

◀ 21. View of a coffee plantation in Surinam, by Willem de Klerk, nineteenth century.

In 1825 a visitor found one plantation a rural idyll. He enthused:

'The situation was a clean terrace jutting out from the breast of the mountain which rose to a great height above it. Palm trees stood around, coffee bushes flourished upon the declivities, and cascades of water burst through the close vegetation on the ground too precipitous to be planted. Below lay the valley, the silver waterfall gleamed through an avenue in the hills and magnificent piles of rock, sometimes black and bare, sometimes green with countless traceries of creepers, formed the scene right opposite. As I have said before, planters are not poetical but, my heart! if I possessed this place, methinks while young morning blushed or high noon slept, or gentle dewy evening made nature think and pause, I would stroll upon my terrace or sit … and forget the world of strife and penury and pain, till I lapsed into a citizen of the other world of peace and plenty and joy!'[289]

The writer did not comment on the forced labour which made this paradise possible.

In 1840 a visitor commented upon the change in Dominica since emancipation. He wrote:

'the trifling unsettlement which took place at the date of full freedom soon subsided and they are working in a quiet inoffensive manner on the estates of their former masters.'

Various civil servants confirmed 'they continue to conduct themselves with every propriety', 'their general conduct is orderly and industrious' and 'their conduct is orderly, quiet and peaceable'.[290]

Grenada

Grenada was a British colony from 1763 (except for an interlude of French rule from 1779 to 1783), a crown colony from 1877 and independent from 1974. There was an insurrection, with French assistance, from 1795 to 1796. The island, 21 kilometres (13 miles) in length and 12 kilometres in width (7.5 miles), is in area some 348.5 square kilometres (134.6 square miles). The Indigenous people had been killed or migrated to other islands largely by 1654 and were replaced by French, English and Scottish settlers alongside enslaved Africans. One governor commented in 1776 that the population was 'a strange discordant mass of heterogeneous animals … easily irritated to do mischief, but seldom to be roused to do good'.[291] Later migration included free workers from Malta (1839), Portugal (from 1846), Africa (1849) and South Asia (from 1856).[292]

Mary D'Urban of Topsham, Alexander Hamilton Hamilton of Topsham, Donald McMillan of Starcross and Henry Stuart of Sidmouth were in Devon when they received their compensation for 407 individuals. Another owner, Robert Houstoun, later moved to Torquay from Scotland. He arrived in 1861 and died there a year later. Houstoun had owned 194 Grenadians. The estate-owners received in total £615,6/1 (£41,743,294.17) for 23,729 slaves. The principal exports were sugar, rum, cocoa, molasses, cotton and coffee.[293] It was the impression of a visitor in 1825 that 'the prejudice of colour is fainter in this colony that in almost any other'. Moreover, he wrote:

> 'the free Coloured man has every privilege of the White, although there never has been, and at present it is not to be wished that there should be, an instance of any of that rank sitting in the Assembly. In the actual state of their average improvement it is quite sufficient that they are esteemed free in every sense and are treated with justice and respect'.[294]

Earlier Devonians who were involved in Grenada include Peter Walker, an attorney who moved from the island to Burlescombe near Tiverton in 1780. He owned a Grenadian plantation and two enslaved people, named Gift and Leveille, and subsequently emigrated to India.[295] In 1802 Sarah Bishop, of Exeter, married Samuel Gibbes, the owner of two estates in Barbados who also was the Receiver General of the island. She does not appear to have had subsequent associations with Devon.[296] As discussed elsewhere, in the late 1700s John Reeder of Fremington improved the manufacturing process of making sugar and rum.[297]

Seven months before emancipation one English visitor thought the enslaved were orderly, industrious and eager for their freedom. However, an Exeter man received a letter from a Grenada planter written within days of emancipation who wrote:

> 'there has been a general strike of work, the Negroes loitering away their time in perfect idleness and quarrelling among themselves. We have offered higher wages than we can afford to give since the alteration in the bounty, which is a severe blow on our interests and must seriously depress prices and our canes are suffering from want of weeding, and other plantation operations are getting very backward. The Negroes claim their houses and gardens as their own and I believe, till they can be convinced to the contrary, there will be very little done'.[298]

Following emancipation local authorities brought in free Chinese workers to correct a labour shortage. By 1860 there were at least three hundred Chinese on the island and they were given free medical care and reasonable accommodation. There were supplemented by labourers from India, Malta and Madeira as well as liberated formerly enslaved people from Africa.[299]

After emancipation, in 1859, a visitor to St George, the island's capital, found:

> 'The streets are overgrown with weeds, the houses look as though something much less formidable than a hurricane would level them with the ground, and there is evidence everywhere of former splendour and of money lavished, thoughtlessly lavished, I should say, under the mistaken impression that these islands would one day form a great West Indian Empire. Whenever I visit a West India city I am not so much surprised at its present condition as at the traces it bears of the exaggerated and visionary hopes of its early inhabitants'.

He noted however that wealth was much more evenly distributed and that near the ruins of a great house were humbler dwellings which had been improved and multiplied as had villages.[300]
*19

Jamaica

Although Columbus was the first European to explore the island in 1494, Spanish interest subsequently petered out and from 1655 it was colonised by Britain. It remained a British colony until independence in 1962. It is the third largest island in the Caribbean with some 10,990 square kilometres (4,420 square miles). In length it is some 248 kilometres (154 miles) and in width 84 (52 miles). Jamaica owes its name to its Indigenous people. Two years after emancipation Robert Montgomery Martin commented on the earlier genocide by the Europeans.

> 'It is a melancholy reflection that the original inhabitants of Jamaica, to the amount probably of several hundred thousand, were destroyed by the European colonists within fifty years after their settling on its shores; had they been preserved, as sound policy as well as humanity would have dictated – and of which the island of Ceylon with its million of Coloured inhabitants afford us an excellent illustration – the deadly curse of slavery (double cursed to the enslaved and the enslaver) would have been avoided and an incalculable amount of human misery avoided'.[301]

In 1509 the Spanish supplemented the Indigenous population with enslaved Africans. When, in 1655, the Spanish were expelled enslaved people escaped into interior regions and mixed with the Indigenous people: their descendants became known as the Maroons, the 'wild' or 'untamed'. White indentured servants formed the main part of the workforce in the initial years but British colonists diversified the racial mix of the island with Africans and then South Asians (from 1838), free Africans (from 1841) and Chinese (1860).

On the eve of emancipation one visitor observed a multiplicity of creeds, languages and interests. He found English, Irish and Scottish residents ('amalgamate well enough together'), native Creoles ('the defects of the Creole character are more than counter-balanced by its virtues'), French immigrants from St Domingo ('a very respectable, industrial class of people'), Spanish settlers from 'The Main' ('the connexions and descendants of those who formerly carried on a flourishing trade'), Jews (some were respectable and honourable but the rest were 'neither remarkable for their meekness in prosperity or their moderation in the possession of power as masters'), the free mixed-race population (the tendency of the colonial laws was 'to degrade the brown man in his own estimation, to debase him in the eyes of the white community and to deprive the state of the services of one who might have been looked to … for protection

22. Watercolour entitled 'Negro man in straw hat', 1808–1815, in Jamaica by William Berryman. ▶

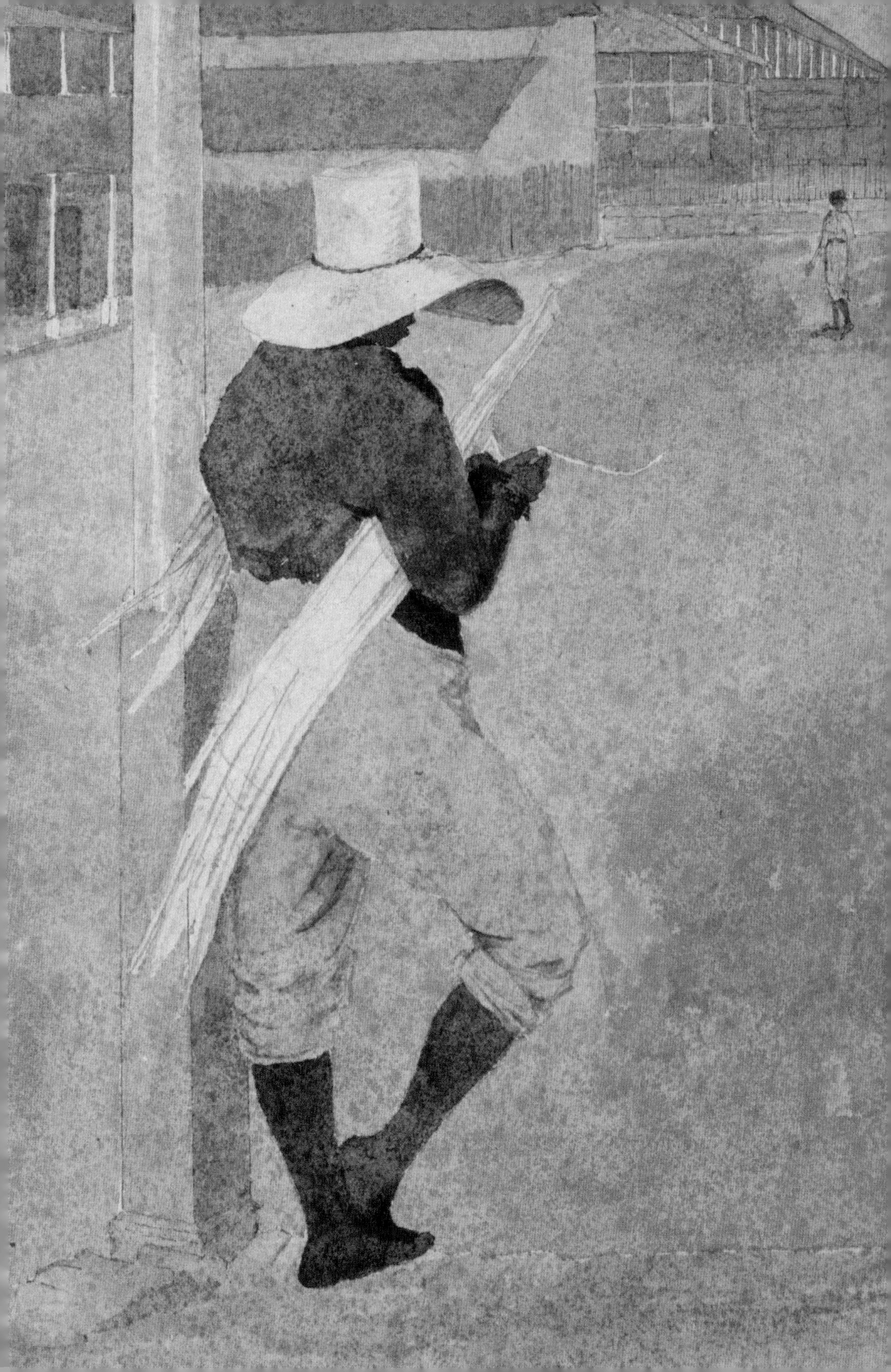

from the Negro') and the enslaved ('the voice of the million is against his possessing one high-minded sentiment of honour, humanity or gratitude'). He later noted that emancipation had passed 'without the slightest disorder'.[302]

Four enslavers were in Devon when they received slavery compensation. Thomas Davy of Ottery St Mary, John Dicker Inglett Fortescue of Buckland Filleigh, Henry Adolphus Hawkins in Bideford and Thomas Rossiter of Tiverton owned in total 258 Jamaicans. At emancipation there were 311,455 enslaved Jamaicans and the planters received a total of £6,121,446 (£415,041,996.68) in compensation.[303] The leading exports produced at this time were sugar, rum and coffee.[304] Nearly twenty years before emancipation one slave-owner described the homes of his workers:

> 'The Negro houses are composed of wattles on the outside, with rafters of sweet wood and are well plastered within and whitewashed; they consist of two chambers, one for cooking and the other for sleeping, and are in general well furnished with chairs, tables, etc. and I saw none without a four post bedstead and plenty of bed clothes'.[305]

Robert Montgomery Martin also detailed Jamaica's social hierarchy. He surmised that the White population, which included English, Irish, Scottish, French, German and Portuguese settlers, were in two classes. The higher had two components: it comprised principal merchants, chief estate-owners and government officials while below them were tradesmen, overseers and shopkeepers. This last group were mainly Jewish. Martin looked upon the Europeans with distinct partiality:

> 'Hospitality and urbanity distinguish the Europeans in Jamaica, as in all our other colonies, but their means are now sadly disproportioned to their generous hearts. A high independence of character has ever characterised the British residents in Jamaica'.

Martin perceived there was a second group which comprised mixed-race people who were Creoles or 'free people of colour'. The remainder of society were Maroons and the majority of the enslaved people, who were born in Africa, he termed Negroes.[306]

Jamaica's economy declined after emancipation. One American visitor in 1860 observed:

> 'I know of no country in the world where prosperity, wealth and a commanding position have been so strangely subverted and destroyed as they have been in Jamaica within the brief space of sixty years'.

Moreover, he wrote:

> 'I know of no country in the world where so little trouble has been taken to investigate the causes of this decline or to remedy the evils that have depressed the colony.'[307]

He dismissed the estate-owners in attributing 'this widespread ruin' solely to emancipation. William Sewell argued that the problems lay with the colonists themselves. Some seventeen thousand workers were brought into Jamaica, from China, Africa, India and the United States, in the decades that followed emancipation but the island remained poorer than during the early 1800s.[308] Two generations after emancipation one writer concluded that country labourers had remained 'economic slaves'.[309]

Nevis

This island was settled by English colonists from 1623 and was a British colony from 1670 until it became fully independent, with St Kitts, in 1983. Nevis is about 11 kilometres (7 miles) in diameter and in area 93 square kilometres (36 square miles). A narrow strait separates it from the larger island of St Kitts. The Indigenous population was forced from the island in 1640 and by 1834 there were French, English, Irish, German and African migrants who were later supplemented by free workers from South Asia (from 1874), Madeira (from 1847) and Lebanon (c1880).

In 1825 a visitor regarded Nevis as the most captivating of any in the West Indies. Henry Nelson Coleridge enthused:

> 'From the south and west is seems to be nothing but a single cone rising with the most graceful curve out of the sea and piercing a fleecy mass of clouds which sleeps for ever round its summit. It is green as heart can conceive, perfectly cultivate, and enlivened with many old planters' house of a superior style and churches peeping out in the most picturesque situations imaginable'.[310]

Frances Dent, a naval wife in Plymouth, was the only estate owner with Devonian associations who received compensation. The 8,792 enslaved people in Nevis brought the estate-owners £149,611 (£10,143,820.29) in compensation.[311]

There were earlier Devon connections with Nevis. Lady Nelson, who retired to Exmouth, was born on the island while Rear Admiral George Tobin, whose father was a Nevis plantation owner from Bristol, was born in Salisbury, had a naval career and moved to Teignmouth in his mid forties. He died there at the age of seventy in 1838. In 1814, the year after Tobin moved to Teignmouth, former Admiralty Judge John Abel Ward died in the resort. He had also owned an estate in Nevis and in his will made particular mention of 'John and Thomas Martin, sons of my Negro slave Suckay Gillis, and Frankey Bass my female Negro and her progeny'.[312] In 1798 Elizabeth Willesford, the daughter of the Tavistock School Headmaster, married a Somerset man and the couple subsequently moved to Nevis.[313] In 1805 Robert Paul of Exeter died in Nevis but his history there has not been determined.[314] Mary Scarborough, a Colyton widow, inherited Scarborough plantation in 1809 and sold it before emancipation. Her son John had been born in Nevis.[315]

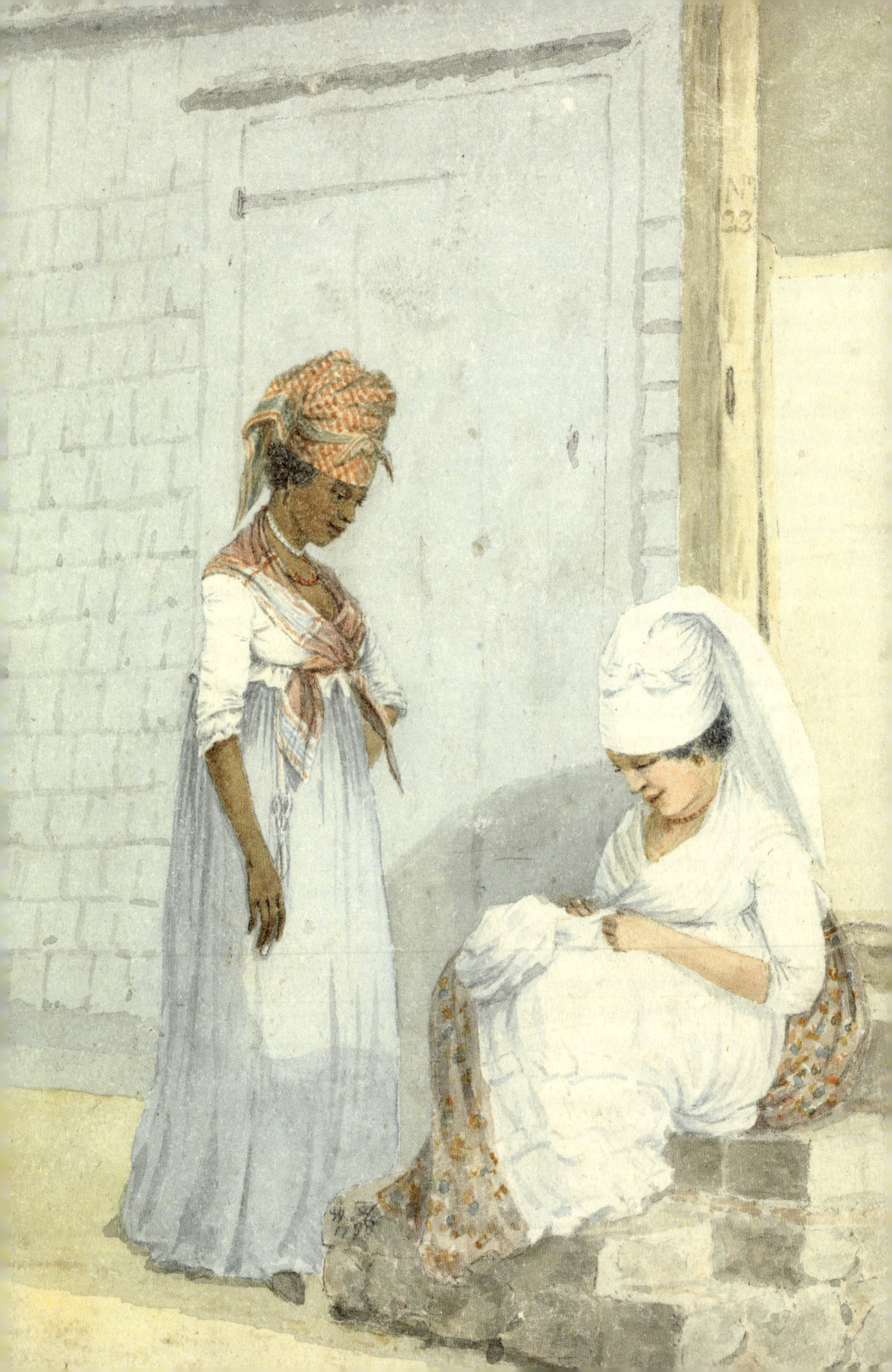
No
23

St Kitts (Christopher)

In 1493 Columbus was the first European to explore the island and named it after the saint with whom he shared his name. England's settlement of St Christopher (later shortened to St Kitts) began in 1623, it became a British colony in 1713 and gained independence, with Nevis, in 1983. St Kitts is 29 kilometres (18 miles) in length and 8 kilometres (5 miles) in width. In area the island is some 168 square kilometres (65 square miles). The Indigenous population was largely removed by 1640 and supplanted by French and English colonists. Enslaved Africans had been brought from the 1620s.

In 1834 17,514 slaves brought the estate-owners compensation of £293,331 (£19,888,223.13). Two slaveholders were resident in Devon when they received compensation: George Stanley Cary of Follaton and Sir William Templer Pole of Shute owned 389 individuals, 2.2 per cent of St Kitts' emancipated Kittians. Sugar was the principal commodity and the population decreased following emancipation.[316]

In October 1834 the editor of the *Exeter & Plymouth Gazette* received a letter by an unidentified slave-owner, possibly Cary or Pole, whose estate manager had written seventeen days after emancipation.

'The Negroes refused to work after the 1st of August, the labourers upon almost every estate were absent, and declared that they would not work without wages. The Governor proclaimed martial law, and all the militia have been doing constant duty to the present day. Many of the ringleaders were apprehended and severely punished and all the rest of them have returned to work, and are now labouring very orderly. I am happy to say that they committed no acts of violence, and I am inclined to think that the prompt steps that were taken prevented them from doing so.

We had information that they intended burning down the works on the different estates on the Island, but fortunately we had a great deal of rain at the time, which was much in our favour. I think that what has taken place will do a great deal of good in the end: the Negroes are so much alarmed, that I have not seen them work so well since I have known the Island – all are now work and quiet.

If the Government will support us, so as to carry the laws into effect, we may yet do tolerably well for the next six years. The work of all the estates in the Island has been very much retarded. The present regulation for working the labourers is *nine hours per day*, for five days in each week, and they have Saturday to themselves, so that if have them at work on Saturdays we shall have that extra expense to pay; but as their hours are short, I am in hopes that we may get a good deal done in the time they are obliged to work for us. The weather has been most favourable lately, from rains, which will assist the next crop very much.'[317]

A few months later another letter in a different newspaper appeared: it was written by a local man's brother who lived in St Kitts. He had a different view:

◀ 23. Seamstress in St Kitts, c1795, by William Kay.

> 'The Negroes are working remarkably well, most of the planters say they get more work done now than under the old system. They have all Saturday to themselves. On that day they come to our *Emancipation Shop* (as they term it) and spend much of the money they have earned during the week chiefly on *finery*'.[318]

In 1825 a visitor commented on race relations. It was his opinion that:

> 'I have reason to say that there is no colony, with perhaps the exception of Grenada, where the free-Coloured people are treated with so much justice as in St Kitts. There are instances here of respectable White and Coloured persons intermarrying which is a conquest over the last and most natural of all prejudices'.[319]

On 1 August 1834 Lord Romney released his enslaved Kittians from apprenticeship. Antigua had granted this privilege and their counterparts in St Kitts demonstrated and then rioted. Public order was restored by the end of the month and the apprenticeships, except those for Romney, continued for another four to six years. After emancipation the workforce was increased by immigrants from Ireland, Britain, the United States, Portugal, India and Africa.[320] In 1840 a minister compared the island with his last visit in 1826 and suggested 'the change for the better in the dress, demeanour and welfare of the people is prodigious'.[321]

St Vincent

The island derives its name from Columbus having first seen it on that saint's day in 1498. Over the subsequent three centuries it had a mixed history of French and British settlement until it officially became a British colony in 1763. It gained independence in 1979. The island, with the northern two-thirds of the Grenadines, is in area some 369 square kilometres (142 square miles). St Vincent is 29 kilometres (18 miles) in length and 18 kilometres (11 miles) in width. On account of its mountains, one of its nicknames was the 'West Indian Switzerland'.[322] In about 1675 shipwrecked enslaved Africans were rescued by the island's Indigenous people and their descendants, known as Black Caribs, subsequently shared the island with French and English colonists. In 1838 a Devonian visited the 'Red Caribs' and when he left he felt 'an agony of regretful sorrow and shame which has never wholly left me since'. The island's ethnic mix was diversified with additional Africans and free labour from Portugal (1845–8) and South Asia (from 1861).[323]

In 1820 a visitor found St Vincent 'captivating' when she first arrived:

> 'I saw a succession of small valleys, covered with canes and pasturage, intermingled with slight elevations in the fore-ground, upon which here and there a dwelling house could be distinguished, while the prospect was terminated by mountain heaped upon mountain, in that wild confusion that told of those awful convulsions of nature to which these tropical regions have been subject'.[324]

Mrs Alison Carmichael, an estate owner's wife, was a promoter of slavery and after her residence suggested it was 'the land of real kindness and hospitality'. Perhaps not surprisingly, it was also her opinion that enslaved people in the West Indies led better lives than the working class in Britain.[325]

John George Cox was living in South Molton when he claimed his compensation for two individuals in St Vincent. In total the colony's 22,786 enslaved people brought £579,300 (£39,277,293.09) in compensation.[326] Visitors in the 1820s were shocked at the sight of chained men and women cleaning the streets. One asked 'what is to be expected from a man who has once been pointed at and hooted by his fellow slaves? Does such a punishment soften his heart or improve his morals? On the contrary does it not make him callous and shameless?'[327]

While housing differed in the West Indian colonies, one planted in 1782 described it in St Vincent:

> 'the Negro houses are of no fixed dimensions; some are very large and some very small, according to the fancy or ability of the Negroes, who are however generally assisted by their masters with posts and main timbers, and occasionally supplied with boards. Thus the village is irregular, some houses boarded, some of them stone and part boards, and most of them wattled or thatched'.[328]

A Devon minister was on the island during emancipation and described his first service. He observed the:

> 'motley appearance of the congregation: diversity of complexional shades, naked feet of the Blacks, red cotton tied headgear, fantastic hats, with and without brims, together with a few of the Whites and better-to-do coloured of the congregation dressed up in beautiful muslin or very light silks, presented the most curious audience I ever expected to see'.[329]

The principal commodities were sugar, rum, molasses, coffee, cocoa and cotton. By 1851 the population had increased in twenty years from 27,000 to 30,000. A labour shortage was blamed for the decline in sugar production following emancipation but a commentator argued in 1861 that the real causes were a lack of capital and the indebtedness of proprietors. He also noted that production by the large landowners had fallen while that of the new smallholders had increased; the small proprietors 'created by a system of freedom are enjoying unexampled prosperity'.[330]

Tobago

The island became a British colony in 1763 and, despite twice being lost to the French, it remained under British control until independence, with Trinidad, in 1962. In 1638 the corporation of Exeter was invited by the Earl of Pembroke to colonise Tobago: it was suggested that more than 120 local men and women could be sent by the city to create a plantation which would produce dyes, ginger and sugar.[331] The island is

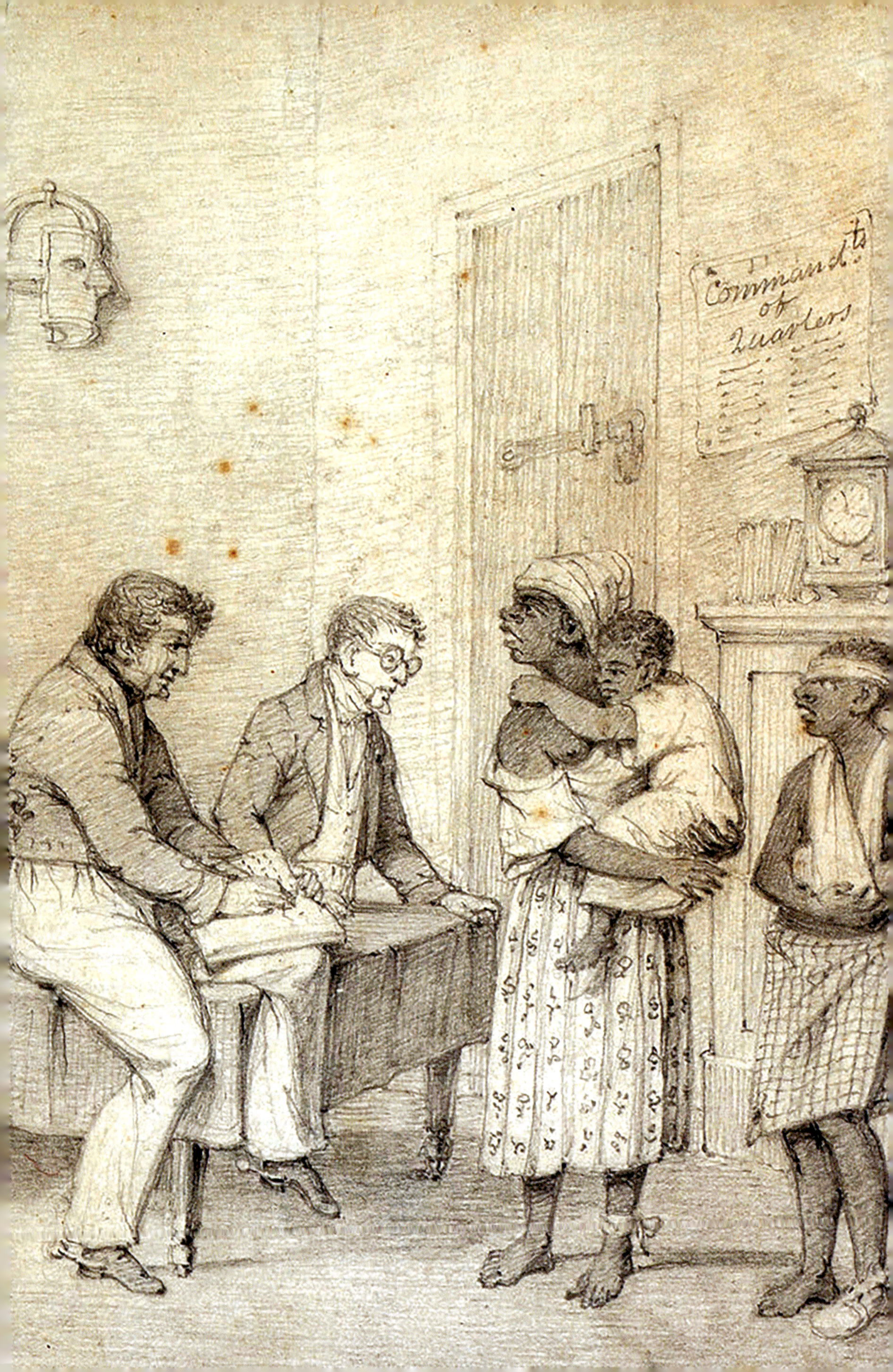
Commandts of Quarters

some 298 square kilometres (115 square miles). Tobago is 41 kilometres (25.5 miles) in length and 12 kilometres (7.5 miles) in width. Later immigration came from China (from 1806), Portugal (1834), South Asia (from 1845) and Africa (1851).[332]

In 1792 an owner described the enslaved peoples' housing as:

> 'built of boards, uniform throughout the estate, are about 26 feet long by 14 feet wide, consisting each of two apartments, besides a portico or covered walk with a seat in front, off which a closet at the end is taken from the portico to form a small kitchen or storeroom. The roof is of shingles'.[333]

The principal exports were sugar, molasses and rum. Sugar production fell after emancipation and capital flowed from Tobago to Trinidad, only forty miles distant.[334]

Caroline Robley, Anne Toby and Isaac Toby were the only owners of enslaved people during emancipation who were resident in Devon at some point. The island's 11,592 enslaved people brought the estate-owners £233,367 (£15,822,585.98) in compensation.[335]

Devon had earlier connections with Tobago including with Sir William Young, governor from 1807 to 1815. His son, Sir William Lawrence Young, was born at Sidmouth in 1806 but subsequently lived in Buckinghamshire. A grand-daughter married Ulric Theodore Hemmington of Woodbury Lodge in 1818. Young appears to have been as vaguely associated with Sidmouth as he was with the Caribbean of which he wrote in 1835 that he was 'not being connected at present with the West India interest'.[336] Another Devon link is with William Sloane who owned estates in Tobago and died in Exeter in 1797.[337] Alexander Lamb, a barrister, also owned two plantations in Tobago as well as at least three houses in Totnes. He died on his voyage to England having left 'for the benefit of his health'. In 1835 Lamb owned eleven enslaved people in Tobago and another five in Grenada.[338]

Trinidad

The island, the second largest of the British West Indies colonies, had mixed European settlement until it became a British colony in 1797. It became independent in 1962 and is now a twin island republic with Tobago.

Trinidad is some 4,768 square kilometres (1,841 square miles) with an average length of 80 kilometres (50 miles) and width of 59 kilometres (37 miles). 'Bold and majestic as it rose from the ocean' was the description given in 1819 by one visitor sailing to the island.[339] There was no local legislature as the island was a Crown Colony. The Indigenous population was supplemented by Spanish, French and British immigrants alongside enslaved Africans. Later migration occurred of free labour, including former slaves, not only from America and West Africa (1815) but from China (1806), France and Germany (1839), India (1844), Portugal (1846) and Syria

◀ 24. Pencil sketch of Trinidad entitled 'Protector of slaves office'. The figures to the left are noted as the Assistant Protector and the Translator, 1833, by Richard Bridgens.

and Lebanon (1904).[340] Thirty-five per cent of Trinidad's population have (Asian) Indian descent which is the highest proportion in the Caribbean: only Guyana and Surinam have higher percentages.[341]

In 1810 the British government did not grant voting rights to free interracial men because they outnumbered the White population. Multi-ethnic people also paid additional taxes on public entertainments and had a curfew of 9.30pm but were charged less for passports and some medical care.[342] John Scott, of Lympstone, was sent as a Special Magistrate to Trinidad in 1837. His diary lays bare the tensions on the eve of emancipation between the enslaved and those who had owned them.[343]

William Bovell at Plymouth may have been in Devon when he received Trinidad compensation money. Alexander Scott Broomfield was another owner of Trinidadians who later moved to Devon as did Maria Strickland. The island's population of 20,428 enslaved people brought the estate-owners £1,021,858 (£69,283,300.82) compensation.

In the 1820s a plantation owner described the workers' accommodation on her estate. There were:

> 'two rows of wattled mud cottages, white-washed and thatched with cane tops, very similar in external appearance to the cottages all over Devonshire, only they have no such chimneys as are common in England'.[344] It was in 1825 that Lord Rolle attempted to move his enslaved workers from his estate in the Bahamas to Trinidad. The government refused to grant permission and the Bahamians also rejected the plan.[345]

Full emancipation was granted a year earlier, on 1 August 1838, rather than 1839 as was stipulated in the legislation. This was partly the result of a deep dissatisfaction felt by the partly-emancipated former slaves who, on 1 August 1834, marched to the governor and demanded their full freedom. They also threatened to strike.

The island's principal exports were sugar, coffee and cocoa while of lesser importance were molasses, rum and cotton.[346] Trinidad was considered under-developed in comparison with other West Indian colonies and the government sought to increase the population and work force by introducing eighteen thousand free migrants from China and India as well as others from Portugal, France, Canada and the United States. Public funds supplemented travel costs.[347] The economic disruption, brought by the ending of slave voyages in 1807 and emancipation in 1834, was responsible for a later petition from a group of Mandingos in Trinidad who wanted to return to Africa.[348]

Nearly a generation after emancipation, in 1860, one visitor observed that the capital city, Port-of-Spain, was exceedingly prosperous as was the countryside, with its 280 sugar estates, which he found exhibited 'equal enterprise and progress'.[349] He also noted that the majority of the population was:

25. Pencil sketch of Trinidad entitled 'Preparing for the field', c1838, by Richard Bridgens. ▶

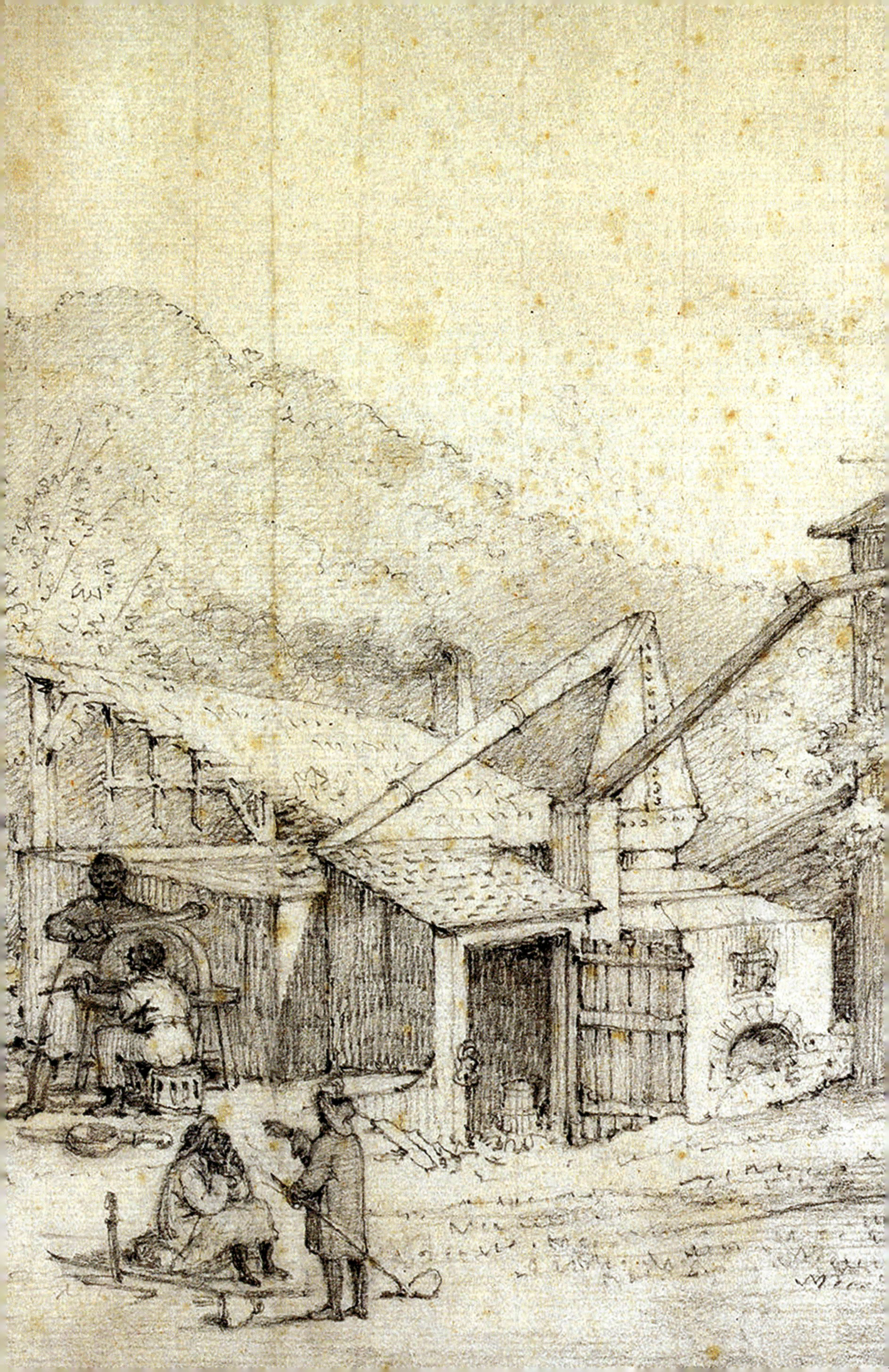

'Negroes and half-castes. They include Creoles of this and other islands, brought here in the days of slavery and since, native Africans imported as free labourers from Sierra Leone, Africans taken from captured slavers and a few hundred liberated slaves who emigrated to this island about sixteen years ago from the United States. Many of these people are nearly, and some perfectly White, and the census, probably from the fear of giving offense, does not classify the population according to color'.

A minority remained on their former owners' estates after emancipation but the majority became proprietors of their own land holdings.[350]

THE INDIAN OCEAN

By 1833 the British Empire stretched across the Indian Ocean from South Africa in the west to Australia in the east. In between were the East India Company's territories of India, Ceylon (Sri Lanka) and Mauritius.

Mauritius

This island, formerly known as the Isle of France, became a British colony in 1810 and continued until independence in 1968. The Cape of Good Hope was the nearest British slave colony. The island is some 2,040 square kilometres (790 square miles). There was no local legislature as this was a Crown Colony.

In contrast with the colonies of the West Indies, the enslaved people in Mauritius had been kidnapped, particularly from 1723 by the French, from Madagascar or from Mozambique and the eastern coast of Africa. The relative proximity of Mauritius to Africa led some enslaved people to attempt to return to their homes. After 1807 more slaves were brought to Mauritius via the Seychelles. One observer in 1775 was horrified by what he saw:

> 'They are landed with a rag round their loins. The men are ranged on one side and on the other the women with their infants who cling for fear to their mothers. The inhabitants, having examined them as he would a horse, buys what are for his purpose. Brothers, sisters, friends, lovers, are torn asunder and bidding each other a long farewell, are driven weeping to the plantations they are bought for.'

They mostly produced sugar, with some coffee and spices, which competed with that produced in the West Indies.[351]

A visitor from India noted in 1835 that enslaved people born in Mauritius were, like their counterparts in the West Indies, known as Creoles. He observed a social distinction between them.

> 'The Creole Negroes, who are infinitely superior in intelligence, address and aptitude for the luxuries and tastes of civilisation to the other branches of the sable family, regard

the unsophisticated amusements of the continent born *noirs* with the most supercilious contempt'.[352]

He also discovered a deep division between the White population and those of mixed race. This he attributed partly to the 'stain of illegitimacy' but more so in regards to the simple fact that a father or grandfather had been a slave.[353]

Thomas Drane moved to Devon in the same year in which he received compensation for 206 of the 68,613 individuals for which £2,112,632 (£143,239,196.02) was paid by the British government.[354] The average worth of each individual was calculated at £69 14s 3d and emancipation began on 1 February 1835, a year after the West Indies.[355] Drane's share was £6,868 8s 1d (£465,686.73).

The island was visited three years before emancipation by James Holman, an Exonian known as the Blind Traveller. It was his opinion that the earlier French colonists had not treated their workforce as well as the English estate-owners:

> 'the sooner that all the French planters are succeeded by English ones, the sooner will the island become more productive and valuable. The people of colour will also derive advantage from the change, as the English are less prejudiced against their association, than are the present landowners, who testify the greatest scorn towards them, and refuse to admit them into habits of intercourse, no matter how slightly their blood may be tainted. As education progresses, and a liberal feeling spreads, there can however be no doubt that the British planters will overleap these narrow bonds and that equality of intellect, station and moral dignity, will be considered a sufficient claim to companionship among all free people, not matter what be the hue that it has pleased heaven to make their faces.'[356]

There had been a revolt in 1832 and the editor of a Plymouth newspaper wrote:

> 'how frantic the minds of the Whites are become and [we] may gather from thence the probability of desperate measures being adopted which may produce the evil we dread, *viz*, an explosion of hatred, nursed by years of oppression and stimulated by the fiercest and most ungovernable passions'.[357]

Open disagreements between the estate-owners and the English government resulted in three years of difficult relations and after emancipation those formerly in coerced labour largely discontinued working in the sugar plantations. One consequence was the introduction of cheaper labour from India. For generations visitors had been confronted with a wide variety of Africans but in the late 1840s they were augmented by the Indian migrants who were given fixed-term contracts and known as 'coolies'. This attempt to regulate labour was derided in Parliament where it was said the Indians were indolent, mendicants, runaways, vagrants, thieves, vagabonds, filthy, diseased, dissolute, immoral and disgusting. In contrast, a missionary found them hard-working and living frugally in order to send money home to their families.[358]

Devon's absence of compensation awards for the remaining colonies (Anguilla, Bermuda, Cape of Good Hope, the Caymans, Honduras, Montserrat, St Lucia and the Virgin Islands) does not preclude earlier activity. For instance, Captain Duncan Campbell, a Scot, was a settler in South Africa in the 1820s and 1830s. He later chose to retire to Exmouth where in 1841 he lived on the Strand with his wife Mary and Nancy Zoolah, a ten-year-old who was later described as a 'Mulatto' born in South Africa. By the time she was seventeen she was living in the St Thomas Workhouse where she had an illegitimate child. No evidence has been found to identity Miss Zoolah's father nor that of her son James.[359]

26. Exmouth in 1840 as painted by Henrietta Maria Crompton from the west side of the River Exe.

4

Devon in 1834

'Sam was at an evening party a week ago where there were a hundred and twenty people but they don't walk about the parade and show themselves as one might expect. We know only the Herrings and Mrs and the Miss Polands and Sir John Kean. Mrs and Miss Weekes and Mr and Mrs James have called upon us', Elizabeth Barrett Browning at Sidmouth, 1832

Slave-owners mainly lived in a handful of carefully selected areas of Devon: in 1834 those places which had been economically dynamic were sharply declining while previously marginal communities suddenly became centres of investment and development. Devon's economic ties with the West Indies were, by 1834, weak: only one port, Bideford, had a reputation as once having had significant trade with the West Indies. In 1808 a suggestion was made to increase commercial ties: John Robley, a West Indian merchant whose wife later died in Tiverton, argued for exporting Devon pilchards to the West Indies.[360] The scheme, which would have competed with North American cod and Scottish herring, was not pursued. In the early 1600s Devon fishermen had a part in the export of salted cod for enslaved people in the Caribbean.[361]

On 30 May 1831 Devon's population stood at 493,908, 2.9 per cent of the national total of 16,564,138.[362] Although the third largest county in England in terms of its landmass, Devon was becoming one of the least populated parts of the country as London, the Midlands and the Industrial North rapidly expanded. Devon had become a backwater and was better known for its history than for its present. Economic decline and stagnation were producing the old world charm which would be appreciated by later generations.

By 1834 the county's greatest export, woollen cloth, had fallen by the wayside. For centuries Exeter had been the funnel through which much of Devon's woollen cloth had been finished and exported. In the late 1700s production collapsed as war closed markets, the East India Company bypassed Exeter and other cloth-producing centres of England supplanted Devon. Scattered pockets of production in places such as Cullompton, Harberton and Buckfastleigh were important locally but Devon was no longer the country's leading cloth producer. Plymouth had declined following the defeat of Napoleon in 1815. The naval base at Devonport had driven the local economy from the early eighteenth century but greater Plymouth became economically lethargic. In the south-eastern corner of Devon the production of Axminster carpets ceased: the factory burned down in 1828 and shortly afterwards the company was declared bankrupt. In 1834 urban Devon lacked the dynamism of recent generations.

There were some bright spots. Mechanised lace had transformed Tiverton in the early 1800s and it also revitalised Barnstaple. Copper mining was increasingly important in and around Tavistock as were exports of ball-clay from Teignmouth. Even so, the loss of the cloth industry was a body blow to Devon's market towns.[363]

Rural Devon was also in a weak state. Corn prices had collapsed following peace in 1815 as had agricultural sales to the army and navy. The countryside became depopulated as the population moved to urban areas, other parts of England, the colonies and the United States.

Commerce was also hindered by poor communications. Three years earlier Exeter's councillors rectified economic decline by expanding the quay: their decision not to invest in a railway resulted in bankruptcy. The railway finally reached Exeter in 1844. By 1834 it had been several generations since Devon's merchants had re-exported high numbers of 'plantation goods' to other parts of Britain and there is little indication that the West Indies were of any substantial consequence to the economy of Devon.[364]

While much of Devon was experiencing economic stagnation there were two areas which were markedly different: the north and south coasts were dotted with new fashionable resorts. It was these communities that drew many retired slaveholders. The milder weather, particularly along the south coast were particularly attractive to former residents of the West and East Indies. Some individuals continually changed their place of residence and lived in a number of different resorts and towns.

Some slaveholders brought servants, some of whom were probably formerly enslaved, from the colonies to Devon. This included two women from Demerara with the Walcott household in Budleigh Salterton, one or two Jamaicans with the James family at Dawlish, a male servant, possibly a Barbadian, with Ward Cadogan at Topsham, another male servant with Admiral Barton in Exeter, two Black servants and an 'Indian' servant with the Colleton family at Exmouth and two Asian Indians with the Ducarell household also in Exmouth.

The West Indians were part of a large racial mix. Other servants included Peter Rose, an Indian, who lived with Lieut. Colonel James Brunton at Headon Cottage on Topsham Road near Exeter. He and his wife may have chosen Topsham because it was her birthplace but coincidently Brunton was also acquainted with Josias Du Pré Porcher, an East India Company official who purchased nearby Winslade House in 1810.[365] That year Brunton, a Scot who had been employed by the East India Company, died at Dawlish.[366]

His household effects included books on India, 'several elegant vases and various other curious china and glass' and a 'fashionable panelled gig with travelling trunks and seat behind for a servant'.[367] The latter was presumably for Rose. Brunton's executor struggled to settle Rose's future. He was ill with tuberculosis of which a correspondent informed Brunton's brother it was 'a complaint to which I have observed the natives of India are frequently liable on residing in this country'.

Two weeks after Brunton's death Rose wrote:

> 'It is no use for me to stay in this country. I am but a poor servant and far from home and [in] a strange country there's nobody to partake to me now my poor master is gone'.

Brunton had made a legacy of one thousand pagodas each to two daughters 'born to me previous to my marriage by a country-born half-caste woman' in India and to several other servants but not to Rose.[368] His subsequent history has not yet been found although a man noted as 'Peter Rose, servant' arrived in Bombay in 1837.[369]

COASTAL RESORTS

Most former enslavers drawn to Devon resided in nine resorts and to some extent created a community of West Indian plantation owners. They included Elizabeth Barrett Browning and her family who spent nearly three years in Sidmouth. From 1832 to 1835, when the emancipation legislation was passed, she privately commented upon the effect on slave-owners.

> 'The West Indians are irreparably ruined if the Bill passes. Papa says that in the case of its passing, nobody in his senses would think of even attempting the culture of sugar, and that they had better hang weights to the sides of the island of Jamaica and sink it at once. Don't you think certain heads might be found heavy enough for the purpose? No insinuation, I assure you, against the administration, in spite of the dagger in their right hands.'

Shortly afterwards she refined her views:

> 'Of course you know that the late Bill has ruined the West Indians. That is settled. The consternation here is very great. Nevertheless I am glad, and always shall be, that the Negroes are – virtually – free!'

The family appears to have known few of their peers in Sidmouth, who numbered at least one hundred and twenty, but it was her view that 'many more known-faces and listened-to voices' were in the resort than she later had in London. Among their few Sidmouth acquaintances were Mr and Mrs Herring:

> 'Of whom Papa is slightly acquainted, have called upon us, and shown us many kind attentions. They are West India people, not very polished, but certainly very good-natured.'

Among the handful of others she met were four members of the James household at Helens Cottage. They subsequently received substantial compensation for the loss of their Jamaican slaves as did Browning's father, Edward Barrett Moulton Barrett who had an award of £12,453 8s 2d (£844,357.27). It has been speculated that Elizabeth Barrett Browning believed she was mixed-race.[370]

Budleigh Salterton

This south coast resort developed in the late 1700s shortly after nearby Exmouth. In 1805 it was described as:

> 'Rising fast to eminence as a watering place. A pleasant row of houses have been lately built and are in general much occupied. From this coast in the least stormy weather the appearance of the sea is awfully boisterous; it has a very steep shore covered with round stones. The bathing is very fine and luxurious for those who are fond of a rough sea, a tremendous surf, rolling billows, etc. You are told there is no bathing equal to Budleigh'.[371]

In 1830 it was noted that 'nothing of consequence is connected with this place as regards trade'. A year later the population of the parish of East Budleigh, which then included Budleigh Salterton, was 2,044.[372] The resort had Devon's highest number of slave-owners resident on Emancipation Day in 1834: these four men (John Campbell, Nicholas Russell Garner, Henry George Windsor and probably John Tharp Clarke) comprised 0.2 per cent of the population.

Before emancipation Budleigh Salterton had attracted William Wylly, a prominent American Loyalist in the West Indies. He had moved to the Bahamas where he became the Attorney General in 1797. Wylly converted to Methodism and became 'a paternalistic humanitarian in respect to the slaves'. Other slaveholders in the Bahamas regarded him as an agent of abolition and a long-standing dispute became known as 'The Wylly Affair'. He was eventually arrested in regards to offending the Assembly of the Bahamas, was accosted by a member and horsewhipped in public. From 1822 Wylly served as the Chief Justice of St Vincent. He emigrated to England in the summer of 1827 and died at Budleigh Salterton in January 1828.[373] Other local men who had slave connections include Henry Baston who inherited the Cedar Valley estate in Jamaica following his uncle's death, Captain Thomas Cowan, in 1836. He had been born in Tamworth but subsequently lived in Minehead in Somerset and at 10 South Promenade and Woodbeer Villa in East Budleigh. He died in a lodging house at 16 Eaton Place in the parish of St Sidwell in Exeter in 1892. The slaves had been sold before Baston inherited the estate and the compensation money was claimed (unsuccessfully) by his uncle.[374]

An enslaved man living in Jamaica in 1823 was named Budleigh. His owner, Elizabeth Marshall, was born in the South Hams.[375]

Dawlish

By 1834 this resort had been developing for a generation and the comments from visitors illustrate the appeal it had to West Indian retirees. In 1787 one lady who visited observed:

> 'Dawlish was not then what it is now. It was no watering place but a small rural village, pastoral indeed but without other pretension either to beauty or to picturesque effect. It consisted of a straggling line of small houses, mostly thatched and many whitewashed cottages, interspersed with little gardens, extending irregularly from the sides of a shallow brook.'[376]

In 1800 another traveller commented it had grown from a marshy vale to 'perhaps the most pleasing and elegant of any of the accustomed watering places in this county'.[377] Another visitor disagreed. Reverend Richard Warner thought it inferior to Teignmouth because:

> 'every method which bad taste could suggest to rob the village of its native simplicity has been adopted such as a long line of uniform modern houses in front of the wild indomitable sea. Gothick structures of mud and cottages costly and superb have nothing to entitle them to the name but their thatched coverings.'

Moreover, he felt it was nothing like a South Devon seaside village but instead conveyed the idea of a resort near London where the 'bucks' of Cheapside and Whitechapel went in the summer to 'wash and be clean'.[378]

Visitors continued to arrive. In 1810 one reported that Dawlish was:

> 'a new bathing place built within five or six years, and may poetically be compared to Venus rising out of the sea. The buildings extend along three sides of a square, fronting an open beach. The houses are of stone, neat and modern built, a good gravel walk is made round an enclosure, in the middle of which is a fine plot of grass, ornamented with shrubs and beautified with a running stream of water.'[379]

That same year a different traveller had another perspective. He wrote that its sheltered nature:

> 'renders its air suitable to the valetudinarians of whom numbers of all sorts were daily to be seen seeking that without which life is not worth the holding – health. Originally the people who composed the list of visitors were of this denomination but of late years numbers attracted by the romantic spot of Dawlish come for their enjoyment and pleasure'.[380]

Dawlish 5 Miles fm Teignmouth the Rocks called stones

Fourteen years later, in 1824, another commentator also noted that Dawlish originally had a different clientele. He observed that:

> 'from a small fishing cove has within a few years risen into a state of comparative elegance and extent. At first it was resorted to by those who wished for more retirement than they could enjoy at well-frequented places but by degrees, its pure salubrious air, the conveniences it afforded for bathing, and its natural beauties, pointed it out as an eligible summer retreat'.[381]

Dawlish continued to grow through the 1820s and another's observations in 1830 show why it was then attractive to former colonials. He thought that it:

> 'occupies a delightful spot, in a valley, having the sea on the east and on the other sides high and pleasant grounds. But a very few years since, Dawlish was an inconsiderable fishing cove but has now become a watering place of considerable reputation and appears in a state of progressive improvement. For the accommodation of visitors a handsome row of buildings has been erected along the strand and public rooms opened, comprising elegant apartments for reading and refreshments, and ball and billiard rooms. They are situated to command a fine view of the channel and lead to the public esplanade.'[382]

By 1831 the population had risen to 3,151. Two slaveholders (Hannah Barnes and Margaret Taylor) were living in Dawlish on Emancipation Day in 1834 and while they comprised 0.06 per cent of the resort's population, they made up a higher proportion of the 58 resident members of nobility, gentry and clergymen.[383] Others linked to slavery include George Cole, John Dicker Inglett Fortescue, Jane Caroline James, Maria Strickland and Mary Waymouth.

Exmouth

Exmouth was Devon's first seaside resort. This would have surprised one late sixteenth-century writer who surmised that it was 'known for nothing but the bare name and the fisher huts there'.[384] A century and a half later it was a very different place. In 1759 an Exonian wrote:

> 'here many of the gentry of Exeter much resort in summer for the benefit of fine fresh air and here is a conveniency made for safely and privately bathing in the seawater, of late much used and found beneficial'.[385]

By 1778 Exmouth was firmly established and an elderly American visitor commented:

◄ 27. Dawlish by Henrietta Maria Crompton, 1840.

'This is a bathing town lying as its name denotes at the mouth of river Exe, round about it lie flats to a great extent … I was told 375 strangers have been numbered here at one time'.[386]

The annual number of visitors was soon in the thousands. In 1810 a young male traveller observed:

'I cannot say I was much pleased with Exmouth as a watering place. There is a good row of red brick houses on a hill and cliff close to the town, having a grass plot & walk in front, near the edge of the cliff at the mouth of the river. Here the company which frequent Exmouth are accustomed to promenade in summer evenings. There we accordingly walked till dusk, desiring to see and, if possible, form an estimate of the rank and fashion of the visitants. We did not however see anything very remarkable for either elegance or beauty. There are several machines for bathing which is said to be pretty good, but not equal to Sidmouth. A great part of the town is very poor, the streets narrow and paved with sharp pebbles, but I conjecture modern improvement and the rage for watering places has greatly changed the appearance of Exmouth within these few years. There are certainly many very good houses adjoining some built in rows, others on the banks of the river near the town. And there is a tolerable good square …'[387]

Others felt differently. In 1830 it had a glowing description in a directory:

'It is situated on the seashore between the cliffs which open as it were on purpose to receive it and was formerly an inconsiderable fishing town but is become one of the most flourishing watering places in the kingdom, affording every accommodation and convenience to its visitors. The houses on the Beacon are very commodious, commanding an extensive and varied prospect, exhibiting on the right a magnificent and most delightful land view, on the left a vast expanse of sea and in front the broad and rapid estuary of the Exe. The beach, which is of fine sand, and gradually sloping to the water, is extensive, and forms an enchanting walk when the sea is calm. The cliff fields and the rock walk are very pleasant, besides these there is on the Beacon a delightful terrace made at the expense of Lord Rolle who also embellished the cliffs with plantations. The soil around Exmouth is dry and the temperature of the air so mild that winter seldom begins till after Christmas and then it is of short duration. The climate here is considered to be something like that of Pisa in Italy in befriending weak lungs.'[388]

The population then stood at 4,192. Thomas Hall was the only slave-owner resident in Exmouth on Emancipation Day in 1834: he was 0.02 per cent of the resort's population and one of 70 resident members of the nobility, gentry and clergy.[389] The resort attracted retirees, some shortly before they died, who had been connected with slavery including not just famous individuals such as Lady Nelson but lesser-known men and women like Catherine Addison, Mary D'Urban, Admiral Sir Manley Dixon, Reverend Fisher, Clifton Wintringham Loscombe, John Prettejohn, Maria Strickland, John and Thomas Teschemaker, Alice Ann Welch and Mary Willis.

Two slaves were named Exmouth. One was an infant 'Mulatto' born in Jamaica. His mother was known as Little Fanny and both were owned by Richard Watt.[390] Another boy with the resort's name, a twelve-year-old from Carriacou, a Grenadine island, was owned in 1829 by William Urquhart.[391] He was probably the seventeen-year-old of that name, owned by George McClean in 1834, who died that year on Grenada.[392] No associations between these owners and the resort of Exmouth have been found.

Ilfracombe

This North Devon resort developed a few years after those on the south coast. A visitor in 1787 observed:

> 'the town is little more than one street till you come to the quay, but it is of considerable length. As you descend a bold and rocky cliff rises directly in your view and forms the grandest background to the ships that lie in the harbour and the buildings which surround it that can be imagined. … From a little cove in the Bristol Channel about one hundred and fifty yards wide, and about twice that depth, a low and narrow valley extends a considerable way inland, edging a little away from the direction of the coast. It is sheltered from the storms that vex this shore by a high and uneven ledge of rocks, which though covered with earth in many parts, yet here and there their craggy tops appear high above it. The town is ranged on the opposite side of the valley, every part of which is finely defended from the sea by the ledge, which always higher than the houses, gradually rises to a very respectable hill …'[393]

Two years later another visitor was told that trade consisted largely of importing Welsh coal and exporting Cornish tin and copper to Wales. Other commodities were herring, rope and cordage.[394]

Change came by the late 1790s. A visitor in 1797 thought the situation was 'truly romantic' while another three years later concluded Ilfracombe was extensive, irregular in shape and 'extremely singular in appearance'.[395] By 1822 it was noted as 'an agreeable summer residence' which was 'of late years been much frequented as a bathing place'.[396] In 1840 a memorial stone, presumably erected to advertise local health benefits, was placed outside the parish church to commemorate four men and women, all centenarians, who died in Ilfracombe at the ages of 100, 102, 103 and 107.[397]

In 1810 Ilfracombe was filled to capacity with fashionable visitors and one traveller was acutely aware of differences between them and local people. She wrote:

> 'Anyone about to write a novel of character should come down to Ilfracombe, where many most amusing and original traits are awaiting a chronicler. Such a set of oddities as would be found among the natives surely cannot be assembled in any other place.'[398]

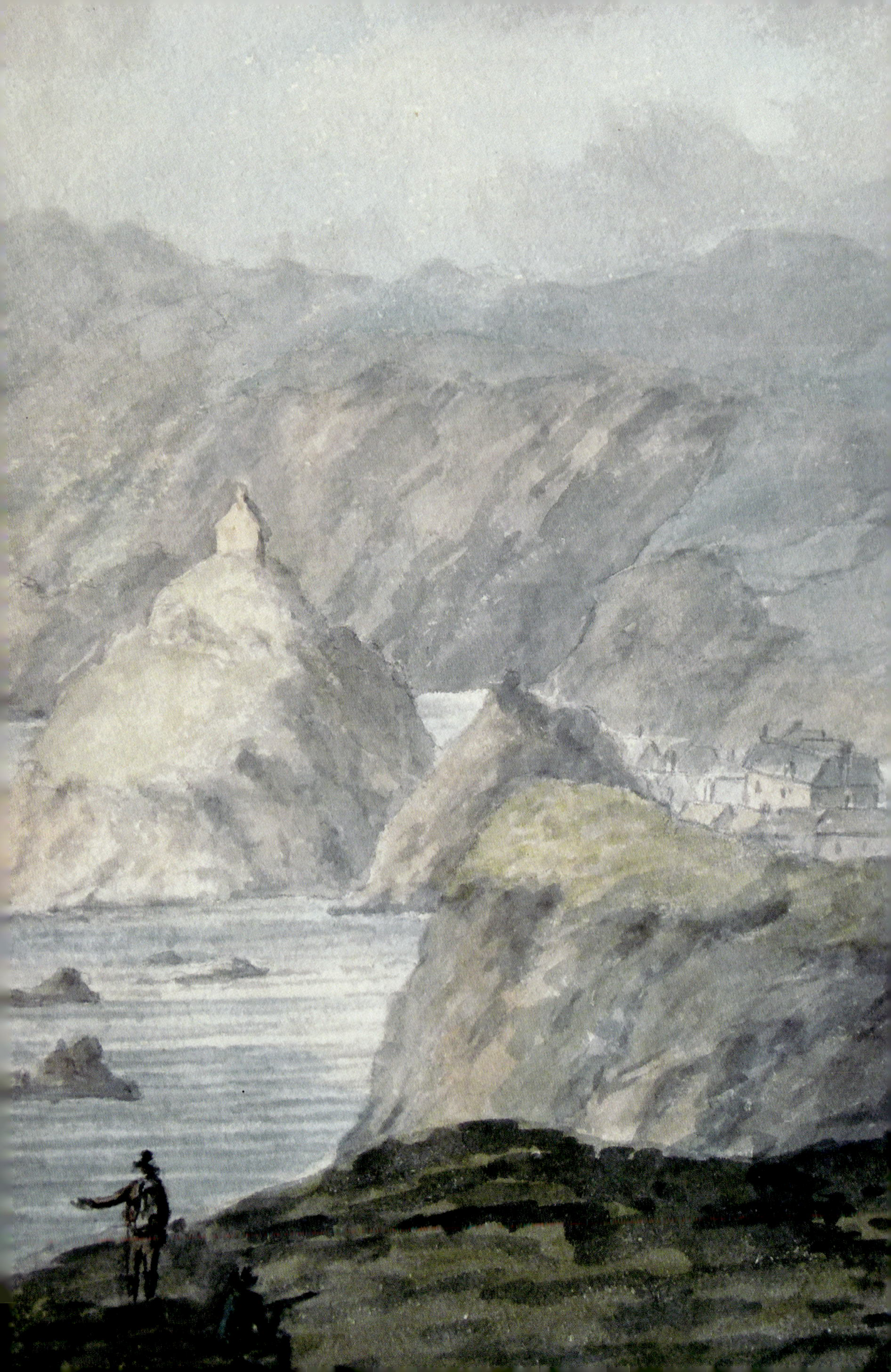

That same year another visitor observed that the lodging houses were mainly owned by retired captains of small trading vessels and that they supplemented their incomes by renting rooms. He also commented:

> 'There is not much to be seen at this seaport town, which is of considerable extent and a good deal of trade is carried on especially to and from Ireland. The harbour was full of vessels and a scene of some bustle seemed to pervade the place. The houses are mostly whitened which gives an air of neatness to the town which it does not really possess, the ascent into it is very steep and we were obliged to drag the carriage even through the streets which in places are very narrow'.[399]

Ilfracombe's population increased to 3,201 by 1831. John Teschemaker was the only slave-owner resident on Emancipation Day in 1834; he was 0.03 per cent of the population but a much higher portion of the 25 members of resident gentry and clergy. The resort attracted a number of former slave-owners such as Dr Jesse Foot who had owned six Jamaicans in 1817. He appears to have sold them before he moved to Devon by 1830 and died in Ilfracombe twenty years later.[400] A former speaker of the Barbadian assembly died in Ilfracombe in 1868; Sir John Thomas and his family had been occasional visitors but it is unclear if he had owned slaves. Other short-term residents included George Tuckett and William McCaul who was in the resort in 1833 when his daughter was born. Elizabeth Bryan née Rodon later moved to Ilfracombe to be with her daughter and in 1851 Mary Dazell travelled from Cheltenham to visit her daughter when the census enumerator called on the 30th of March.[401]

Perhaps Ilfracombe's most enduring connection with slavery lies with Rapparee Cove of which it has been claimed since 1879 that the remains of shipwrecked Black slaves have been found on the beach and in neighbouring fields. The *London* was wrecked in 1796 on its voyage from St Kitts but a connection with any skeletons of as many as fifty French prisoners is still uncertain.[402]

Lynton

Lynton also developed after its south coast counterparts. Visitors' comments outline its progress. In 1787 one dismissed it as 'situated in a little hollow just within the hill that rises steep from the sea and is but an indifferent village of poor thatched houses'. Two years later another thought improved access and better accommodation would transform Lynton into one of England's most popular resorts.[403] In 1797 yet another traveller commented that the 'little sequestered village of Lynmouth' was 'rivalled in situation by few places even of the opposite more celebrated shore'.[404] A generation later another tourist was equally impressed. He wrote that he and his party:

> 'took up our quarters at the inn called the Valley of Rocks. Some good ale, a mutton chop and Tenby oysters from the opposite coast of Wales, soon made us forget the fatigue and

◀ 28. Ilfracombe by Henrietta Maria Crompton, 1840.

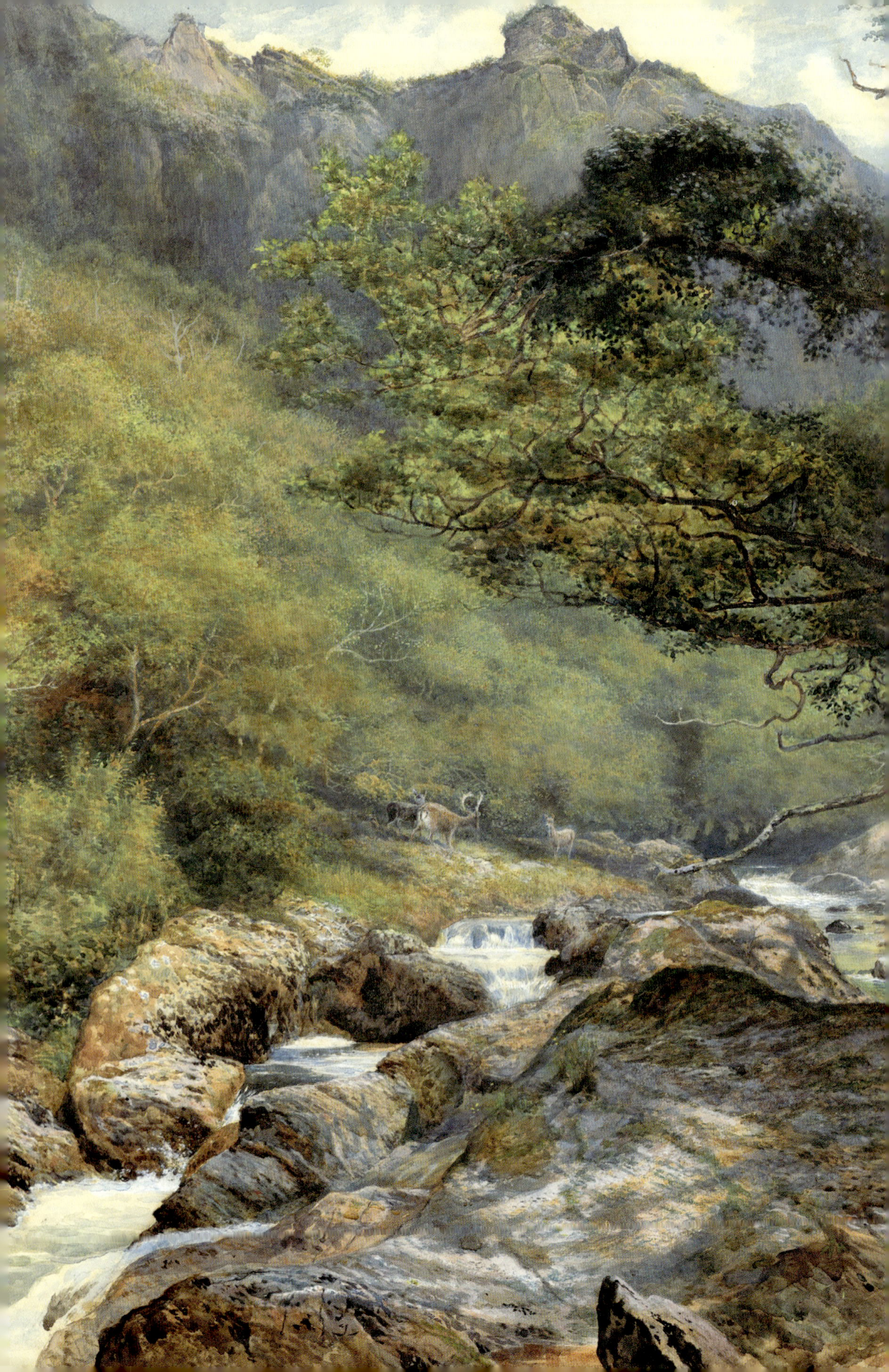

labour of the day. We slept sound and were on foot soon after six the next morning… a most astonishing romantic place… the place itself for wildness and grandeur of scenery beggars all description.'[405]

In 1831 the population stood at 792 and its visitors included Reverend Halliday who built Glenthorne at nearby Countisbury. He was the only resident slave-owner on Emancipation Day in 1834; Halliday was 0.1 per cent of the population. The resort later counted two former slave-owners, Alice Welch and Reverend John James Scott of Combe Park, as residents.

Sidmouth

In 1834 Sidmouth proudly distinguished itself in Devon for having hosted a member of the Royal family: the sojourn in 1819 of Edward, Duke of Kent, with his daughter Victoria at Woolbrook Cottage was one of the boasts of the new resort. In 1798 Sidmouth's entry in *The Universal Gazetteer* had merely noted 'it is a small fishing town but was pretty considerable before its harbour was choked up'.[406] By 1810 it was called by one Somerset visitor 'the Brighton of the West' but he also thought it was 'Taunton Removed'. He observed:

> 'The situation of Sidmouth is altogether inviting though the town has not much in itself to recommend [it]. It is the salubrity of its climate and the gaiety to be found here that attracts visitors, besides being surrounded by a beautiful country. It is astonishing to think what a multitude of people flock thither in search of pleasure or in other words dissipation, a few old men, gouty and infirm, the remains of a worn-out constitution sometimes are to be seen crawling along seeking that which when they had got, they took no care of, and hoping that the genial air of Sidmouth might enable them to add a few years more to those which they had so dissipated away'.[407]

Sidmouth developed as a principal seaside resort despite the railway not arriving until 1874 but in some respects its character remains much as it was in 1834. This extends even to its cliffs. In 1833 one resident commented:

> 'After a great deal of wet weather, or indeed after an excessive drought in summer, I have seen many tons of earth and stones come from the cliffs into the sea with a noise like thunder and then the natives will run with open mouths and open eyes and say *There's been a roozement*.'[408]

Former enslavers were among the wealthy retirees who lived out their last years in Sidmouth. In 1824 a guide noted 'the ornamental cottages of this place, particularly Lord Gwydir's, Miss Floyd's, Baruch Lousada's, etc. are much admired'.[409] Some of

◀ 29. 'On the East Lyn', by William Henry Millais, c1865.

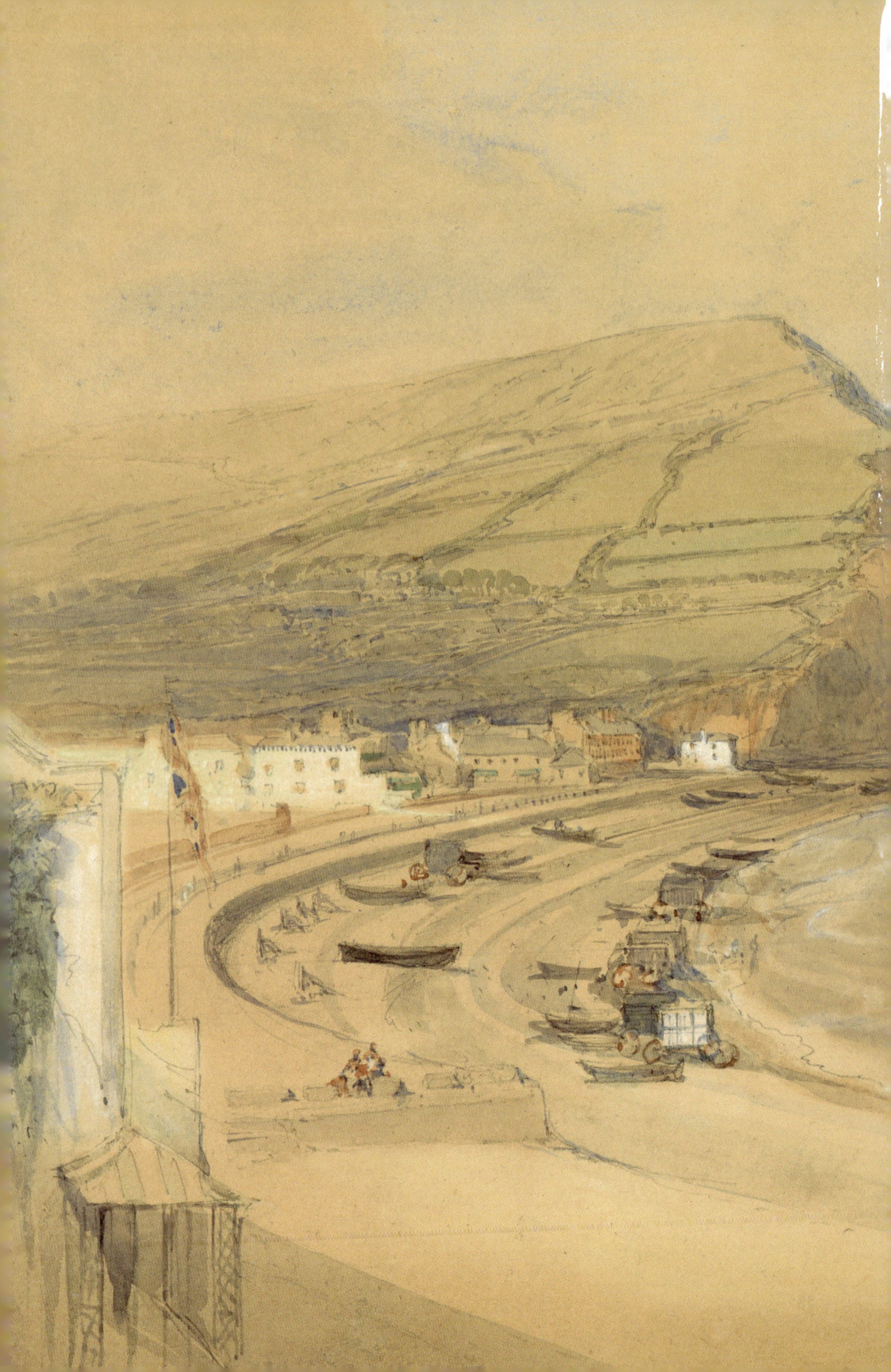

the best known of these new homes were occupied by slave-owners. Powys, one of the town's most prestigious properties, was inhabited from 1851 by Major General Sir Henry Floyd whose wife Mary had three Jamaican estates as part of her marriage settlement. His aunt, Miss Elizabeth Powys Floyd, had built Powys sometime around 1820. It was described in 1826:

> 'on the upper part of a sloping field, now converted into a spacious lawn and shrubberies, Mr [sic] Powys Floyd has lately completed a villa in the cottage style, occupying a large extent of ground: the rooms, which are uncommonly large and lofty, are all on the ground floor, the conservatory occupying the centre of the building. It is called Powys Cottage.'[410]

Miss Floyd died in 1830 and left the bungalow to her nephew Henry who lived the following years in Italy and Belgium.[411] This 'much admired residence' was occupied by a niece, Miss Ridout, who was given a life interest. When her cousin Henry retired his family moved to Sidmouth, first living at Bedford House but subsequently at Powys, with some of their eleven children as well as with half a dozen or so servants. The family continued to reside in the resort until the mid 1870s.[412]

Other notable homes owned by slaveholders include Witheby which Miss Floyd built between 1800 and 1810, Helens was occupied by the James family, Cotmaton by Henry Stuart and Peak House was owned by the Lousada family. Another family member, Moses Gutteres, lived at various prominent houses (Helens, Belle Vue and Belmont) from the early 1802s onwards.[413]

In 1832 Elizabeth Barrett Browning described the growth of Sidmouth:

> 'It is scarcely possible, at least it seems so to me, to do otherwise than admire the beauty of the country. It is the very land of green lanes and pretty thatched cottages. I don't mean the kind of cottages which are generally thatched, with pigsties and cabbages and dirty children, but thatched cottages with verandas and shrubberies and sounds from the harp or piano coming through the windows. When you stand upon any of the hills which stand round Sidmouth, the whole valley seems to be thickly wooded down to the very verge of the sea and these pretty villas to be springing from the ground almost as thickly and quite as naturally as the trees themselves. There are certainly many more houses out of the town than in it and they all stand apart, yet near, hiding in their own shrubberies or behind the green rows of elms which wall in the secluded lanes on either side.'[414]

Sidmouth's population rose to 3,126 by 1831. Two slaveholders were resident on Emancipation Day in 1834; Emanuel Lousada and Henry Stuart comprised 0.06 per cent of the population but a much higher portion of the 77 resident members of the nobility, gentry and clergy.[415] Amongst retirees with slavery connections, not all

◀ 30. The seafront at Sidmouth by David Roberts, 1845.

of whom received compensation awards, were Mary Bucknor Clark, George Cole, James Cunningham, Phillip Haughton James, Elizabeth Mary Mayne, Ann Clarke McClery and Rebecca Weekes. Not all were wealthy.

One West Indian was recorded as having been named Sidmouth, he was born in Grenada in 1821 and was owned by Cinderella Commissioning.[416] No connection has been found between the owner and the town of Sidmouth.

Starcross

In 1800 a traveller noted this 'charming village' on the west bank of the River Exe had an:

> 'inn we may rank among the most pleasant of the houses here, whose bow window presents a delightful prospect of the swelling Exe from the town of Topsham to its estuary'.[417]

By 1824 it had remained small but was a desirable place to live. It was:

> 'principally supported by its connection with the shipping and business of the port of Exeter, is nevertheless improving and becoming the resort of many families, convenience by the ease of its proximity to Exeter. It possesses a very fine terrace walk, together with views of all the rich scenery of the banks of the Exe.'[418]

Starcross had two residents associated with slavery in Edward Connett and John Anderson who lived at Warren House, halfway between Dawlish and Starcross.

Teignmouth

At the time of emancipation Teignmouth was said to have become 'a haunt of high society' and yet of all the new coastal resorts Teignmouth retained the greatest commercial activity. The town was divided into east and west sections:

> 'The eastern part of the town is the principal resort of company. Here the public rooms are situated – a neat building comprising tea, coffee, assembly and billiard rooms. There are also excellent cold, hot and vapour baths, good libraries and a neat theatre. A promenade and drive lead from the public rooms towards the south over an extensive flat called the Den. The view hence up the river is extremely beautiful, the ground gradually rising on each side into verdant hills, well cultivated and adorned with wood.
>
> The trade of Teignmouth consists chiefly in a commercial intercourse with Newfoundland and its local business is well supported by numerous visitors and a highly respectable resident gentry. The exportation of clay and granite, and the importation

31. A view of Teignmouth by Thomas Girtin, 1797–8, looking up the Teign estuary. ▶

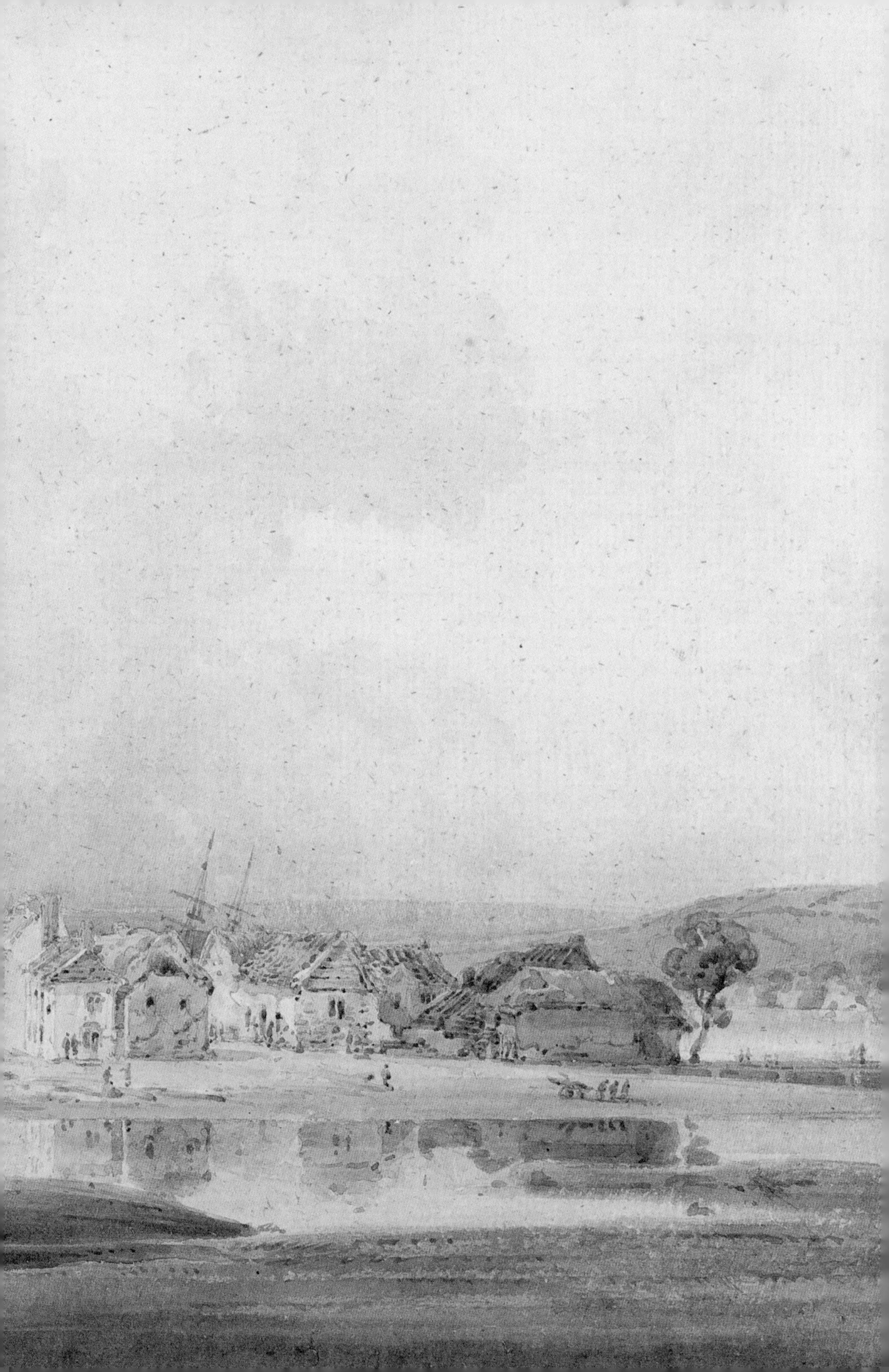

of coal are carried on principally in craft built here and at Shaldon, where are yards for launching vessels of 3 to 400 tons'.[419]

Like other South Devon resorts, tourism developed by the early 1770s. In 1778 an American visitor concluded that those of 'a higher rank' visited the resort in comparison with Sidmouth and that although the houses were irregularly built Teignmouth had a better appearance, its shops were well-filled and there was a 'face of success and industry'.[420]

The social life in 1800 was described by another visitor:

> 'I was much entertained with the acquaintance and informations of new society; the great variety of company, which assembled every fine evening, walking on the promenade, morning visits to the fish market and drawing the seine[net]s on the river, excursions at sea, and rides in the vicinity. Parties were frequently formed for these purposes and the variety of entertainment occupied my time agreeably'.[421]

It may have been the division of the town between trade and tourism that made one visitor blanch. Catherine Sleep wrote in 1835 that she was particularly horrified by the language she heard in Teignmouth. This was exemplified by a man painting her windows who began to curse just as his employer was convening a religious meeting. She explained to a friend, 'my weak nerves trembled so much I could scarcely attend to the meeting'.[422]

By 1831 the population had increased to 4,688 and the town had two resident slaveholders, Stephen Oakeley Attlay and John Panton Passley, on Emancipation Day in 1834. They comprised 0.04 per cent of the population but a higher portion of the 91 resident members of the nobility, gentry and clergy. The resort attracted former West Indian estate-owners including William Brooks King, Catherine Seaman, Edward Butler Taylor, George Tobin, James King Went and Martha Euphemia Wilson. Some lived in Teignmouth for a considerable period. In 1823 a fashionable fancy dress ball featured ten boys who served refreshments 'habited as Black slaves'. It is not known if any of the resort's slaveholders attended the event.[423]

Torquay

Torquay gradually became Devon's largest resort and attracted a number of former slave-owners. It developed later than many other resorts: a national gazetteer failed to mention tourism in its description of Tor Bay in 1775[424] but two generations later, in 1830, its appeal could not be ignored:

> 'The views round Torquay are delightfully romantic and picturesque, the buildings good and the accommodation for visitors equal to those of any other bathing place on the coast. Within these few years it has deservedly advanced in estimation as a watering place and baths of all kinds have been established for the service of the invalid … The business of this place is very limited: a little is done in the coasting and Newfoundland

trade but it is principally indebted for its prosperity to the number and respectability of individuals invited hither, from all parts, by the warmth and salubrity of the climate and the enchanting attractions of scenery presented at every point in its vicinage.'[425]

Five years later another writer acknowledged it had grown rapidly from 'little more than a collection of fishermen's huts' into a prosperous resort. The West Indians who moved to Torquay would have recognised his description:

'Its appearance to the stranger on his first entrance is of the most delightful kind; a pretty little basin of water, round it quays, handsome shops in its front, elegant terraces rising, perspective on the one hand, richly fertile woods on the other, classical villas peeping out from green shrubberies, and before you an expanse of ocean almost unbounded in its extent.'[426]

By 1831 the population had risen to 4,786 including Robert Hilton Angwin who moved from Jamaica having sold his plantation before emancipation. The remaining West Indian estate-owners relocated after emancipation including John Nelson Bond, Thomas Drane, Robert Houstoun, William Adlam O'Halloran, John Randall Phillips, Charles Schaw and Robert Semple. Some, such as Alexander Scott Broomfield, lived in Torbay for a short period: he died while on a visit. Others, including John Hooper Holder, lived in the resort for at least a decade. He retired to Torquay by 1841 and lived at The Castle in Lower Union Street with his wife and a general servant, lady's maid, footman, butler and housemaid. He subsequently moved to France.[427]

URBAN AREAS

A smaller number of men and women associated with slave owning moved to Devon's traditional urban areas.

Barnstaple

This ancient market town attracted at least three widows and a vicar who owned West Indians. Barnstaple gradually became more attractive to retirees. In 1759 it was noted that the haven:

'became so shallow that most of the trade removed to Bideford. Yet it has still some merchants and a good trade to America and to Ireland, from whence it is an established port for landing wool. And it imports more wine and other merchandize than Bideford, and is every whit as considerable. For though its rival cures more fish, yet Barnstaple drives a greater trade with the serge-makers of Tiverton and Exeter who send to buy wool, yarn, etc.

Tis pleasantly situated among hills in the form of a semi-circle to which the river is a diameter … It has also a paper mill. The streets are clean and well paved, and the houses built of stone.'[428]

Other writers confirm a character unlike those of the seaside resorts. A visitor in 1787 added:

'There is a considerable pottery of the common earthenware carried on at this place, as the manufacture was new to many of us, we stopped a while to observe this little creation as it rose under the hands of the workmen.'[429]

In 1790 another writer commented:

'It is more populous than Bideford but not better built and stands lower. It has two squares and an extensive walk adjoining the rivers Yeo and Taw, commanding a beautiful land and sea prospect as the tide washes its banks twice every day.'[430]

A generation later industry had been revamped:

'The woollen trade, formerly carried on here with considerable spirit, has of late been much reduced. The largest establishment in this branch now is conducted by Messrs Rennels & Company. Lace is made to a considerable extent. The principal houses in this trade are Mr J. Miller of Stoney Bridge Mill and Messrs Symons at Newport. The importations of this town consist of coals from Wales, timber from America, wines from Spain, etc. Its exportations comprise corn, oak bark, leather and coarse pottery. The malting trade is carried on here by a number of individuals and there are ship building yards in which are employed many hands. A silver lead mine is worked at Swimbridge.'

In 1822 the port was designated for the storage of West Indian rum. Customs payments were delayed through goods being placed in bonded warehouses.[431]

By 1799 it had also become attractive to incomers and in 1830 it was noted:

'Besides these sources of wealth, the pleasing character of the country around and the comparative cheapness of this part of England have added greatly to its inhabitants by inducing many independent families to settle here entirely. A circumstance that renders Barnstaple one of the genteel towns in North Devon, it boasts indeed of some marks of a Metropolis having a theatre, ladies' ball every Thursday, gentlemen's every Friday night, a musical society once a fortnight and a subscription news rooms.'

It had everything, one traveller noted, except for a decent pavement. This visitor objected to the 'little oval pebbles' with which its streets were paved 'being not only extremely unfavourable to the shoes but what is much worse, very injurious to the feet'.[432]

There were no slaveholders resident in Barnstaple on Emancipation Day despite the town and immediate area having a resident population of 137 members of the nobility, gentry and clergy. The population then stood at 6,840 and amongst the former slaveholders later attracted to Barnstaple were Mary Ann Barnett, Catherine Griffith, John James Scott and Elizabeth Vidal. They may have known Captain Thomas Stewart, a retired soldier from Barnstaple who in 1818 recalled his debt to an American Black woman who had shielded him when he escaped from a Philadelphia prison during the War of 1812.[433] Barnstaple also had what a loose connection with Thomas Huxtable. In 1838 the *North Devon Journal* reported the death in the West Indies of Thomas Huxtable, brother of Anthony Huxtable 'of this town'. The latter was a Bristol surgeon who later moved to Reading and who had uncertain family connections with Devon. His brother Thomas received compensation for two estates in Jamaica shortly before he died.[434]

Bideford

Three eighteenth-century descriptions and another of 1830 outline the changing fortunes of Bideford including the rare link made between the West Indies[435] and a Devon port.

In 1759 *The Grand Gazetteer* noted:

'Tis a clean, well-built populous place and has a street that fronts the river three quarters of a mile long, in which are a noble quay and custom house, where ships of great burthen load and unload in the very bosom of the town. There's another street of good length, almost as big as the High Street of Exeter, well built and inhabited by wealthy merchants. It being esteemed one of the great trading towns (taking one with another) in England, sending fleets every year to the West Indies, particularly Virginia and Newfoundland, and Ireland, from whence tis an established port, as well as Barnstaple, for landing wool. Forty or 50 ships of this port have been employed for fetching cod from Newfoundland and here is also a great export, particularly of herrings. Other ships are sent to Liverpool and Warrington to fetch rock salt, which is here dissolved by the sea water into brine, and then boiled up into a new salt which is justly called Salt upon Salt, and with this they cure their herrings'.[436]

In stark contrast, a visitor in 1787 found Bideford:

'like many more famous places has to boast its ancient splendour and to lament its present decay. So lately as the beginning of the present century it carried on a considerable trade to different parts of the world, and especially America but at present not more than 300 vessels in a year are cleared out of this port.'[437]

In 1794 the decline was again summarised:

'The town is pleasantly situated on both sides of the river [Torridge], about three parts lying on the slope of a pretty steep hill on the west wise and the remained at the bottom of a hill on the opposite side ... For about a century it enjoyed a very considerable

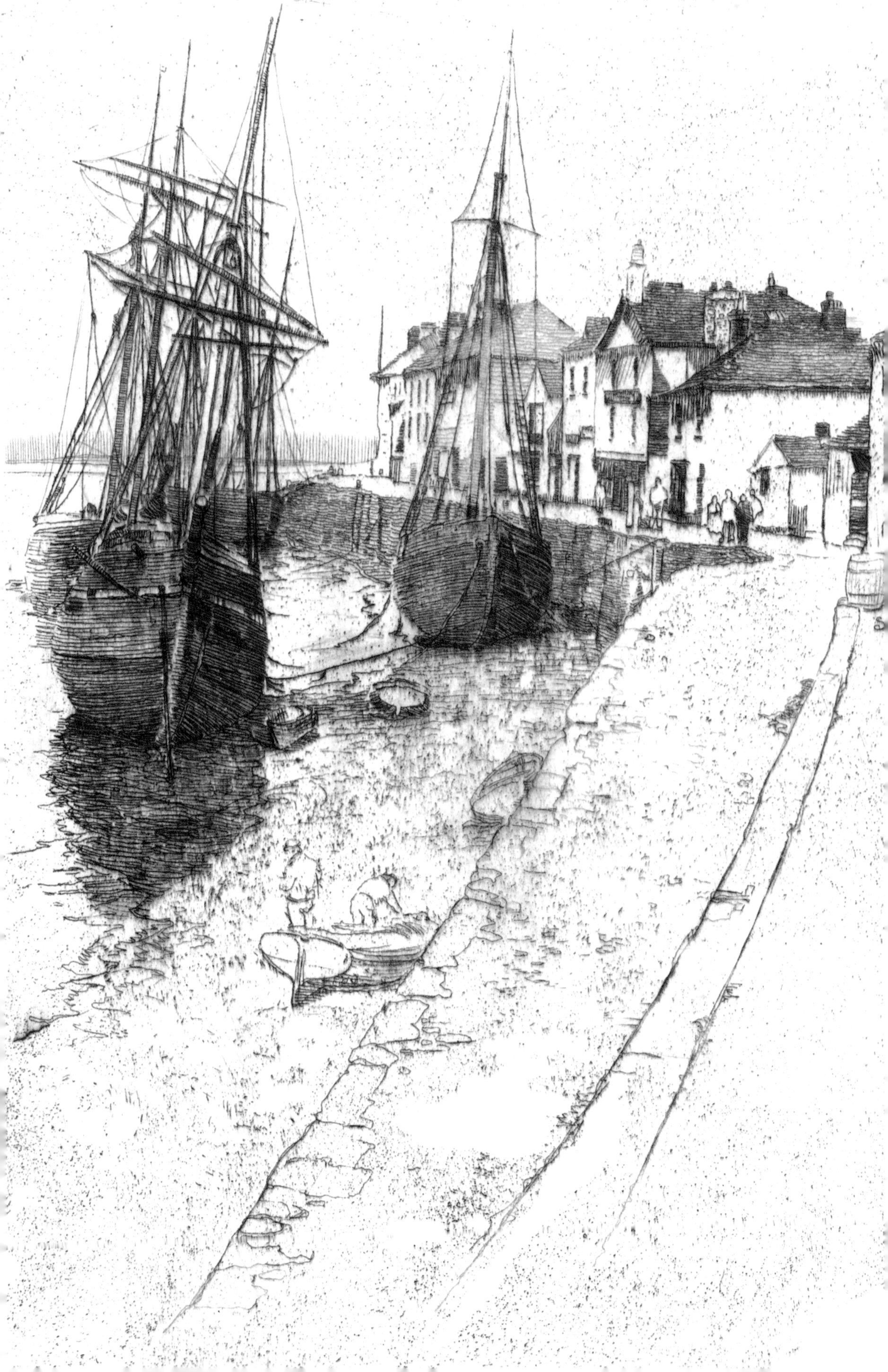

foreign trade, principally to Virginia and Newfoundland. Since 1760 its commercial consequence has been reduced very low but at present there is a good prospect of its rising again. Here is a very excellent quay, a noble river and every advantage necessary for carrying on an extensive and profitable foreign trade. Timber is exceedingly plenty and cheap, as also are labour and provisions of all kinds. Few towns in Devonshire are more healthy or equally pleasant … Large quantities of coarse earthenware are manufactured here, and carried to various parts of England and Wales. Many cargoes of oak bark are annually exported from hence to Ireland and Scotland … This town formerly exported large quantities of herrings to different parts of the Mediterranean but that trade entirely ceased many years ago.'[438]

A few years later another visitor dismissed it as large, wretched and dirty 'with all the filth, inconvenience and disagreeableness of a seaport and little of its bustle and animation'.[439]

By 1830 the port changed:

'there are now some large establishments here and the merchants are opulent and most respectable. Since the warehousing system has been extended to the port of Bideford, its trade has kept increasing and consists chiefly in importing timber from North America, general goods from Ireland and coals for the north west of the county, exporting oak bark, iron and other goods to Ireland, earthenware, tiles etc. to Guernsey and Jersey, linen and woollen goods, cordage, iron, provisions, naval stores etc. to the colonists in North America. The coasting trade in corn is to, and general goods from, London and Bristol; slates, china ware, iron castings, bar iron and limestone from Wales. The principal manufacture of the place is a peculiar kind of earthenware, viz. ovens, salting pans, pitchers and other coarse wares. There are in the neighbourhood some culm and mineral black paint mines. The former are becoming very productive having been worked but partially until lately for nearly two hundred years'.[440]

By 1831 the population stood at 4,846. There were no slaveholders resident in Bideford on Emancipation Day despite the town and immediate area having 50 resident members of the nobility, gentry and clergy. Earlier, in 1802, John Clevland of nearby Tapley, the MP for Barnstaple from 1766 to 1802, had invested in three plantations in Jamaica.[441] Some former slave-owners moved to Bideford for a short time including Catherine Griffith, Reverend Henry Nembhard and possibly Henry Adolphus Hawkins.[442] Mary Haverfield and her brother William Ross lived in the port as well as in nearby Great Torrington.

◀ 32. Appledore outside Bideford, by Sears Gallagher, undated.

Devonport

Plymouth Dock was created in 1690. In 1808 one visitor commented:

> 'the town of Dock is an infant of yesterday, compared with Plymouth. A century back it was a desolate common, without houses or inhabitants, a singular contrast to its present appearance, that of a handsome, regular town, with a population of at least 25,000 souls'.[443]

It was renamed Devonport in 1824. This royal dockyard is situated to the west of Plymouth and occupied some 71 acres in 1830. The population of the parish of Stoke Damerel, including Devonport, then stood at 34,893. Residents who had personal associations with slave-owning included Admiral Sir Manley Dixon, Sir William Henry Holmes, John Martell, Admiral George Rich and Admiral Houston Stewart. All but one were connected to the navy. Dixon was the only slaveholder resident on Emancipation Day in 1834 despite there being 231 resident members of the nobility, gentry and clergy.[444]

In 1810 a traveller enthused:

> 'The entrance was magnificent to a degree, on the left hand you have at one view beneath your feet the towns of Dock, Plymouth & Stonehouse. Mount Edgcumbe and the surrounding countryside, on the right the river covered with old men of war and hulks full of French prisoners. In the front the ocean itself, nothing of the kind I think can be finer'.

He commented further that Stonehouse not only had the best residences 'but there most of the genteel people live. In fact, it is a gay and cheerful place.'[445]

One man was named Devonport: he was a seven-year-old Barbadian in 1827 and was owned by Ann Barnes who was, in 1836, awarded compensation for four slaves.[446]

When the Reform Act was passed in 1832 an elaborate public procession in the Three Towns included, at the end, 'A friend of the Negro, with an appropriate banner, supported by two of that oppressed race'.[447]

Exeter

Devon's capital was a busy cloth manufacturing centre until the generation before emancipation. In 1759 the industry was in its heyday when Andrew Brice, in *The Grand Gazetteer*, wrote:

> 'All kinds of mechanic businesses are here more or less exercised, but those of the woollen manufacture, in its various branches, are vastly the most numerous, though not so much as 50 or 60 years past, when 8 out of 10 perhaps were combers, spinsters, weavers, etc. Yet not so inconsiderable trade is now carried on in woollen goods, particularly serge, insomuch that £10,000 of a Friday is, or has lately been bestowed in that one commodity'.[448]

Seventy years later, in 1830, it was noted that the foreign markets had 'failed' and that the industry was 'much reduced'. There was still a local demand for cloth but the city turned from manufacturing to attracting wealthy migrants.

> 'the cheapness and plentiful supply of its markets in comparison with other places, the agreeable walks and rides in the vicinity, the numerous and genteel society now formed in the city and neighbourhood, the respectable schools and public college for instruction, and places of divine worship for all denominations, together with the constant supply of amusements, the shorter distance from the sea and so many fashionable watering places, make Exeter, in point of residence, one of the most healthy and desirable in the kingdom'.[449]

The demise of cloth-making was accompanied by an increase in filth. In about 1811 one commentator noted:

> 'The mop, the pail and the scrubbing brush are never heard to be in motion and seldom seen. They never wet their floors and hardly condescend to disturb the industrious spider. I am sorry to say that I could almost compare the lower class to Hottentots. I afterwards found that I had here taken my leave of all regard to cleanliness. Well it might be called a virtue, for the want of it I could readily denominate a vice. Surely those authors, who generally praise the English for possessing the virtue of cleanliness, have never travelled in this part of the country'.[450]

Richard Collins was the only slaveholder resident in Exeter on Emancipation Day in 1834 although Rebecca Potter lived outside the city bounds in Heavitree and Eliza Abell resided in Alphington: together they comprised 0.01 per cent of the combined population of 31,369 but a higher portion of the nearly four hundred resident members of the nobility, gentry and clergy.[451] Others lived nearby in Topsham. It was Exeter's subsequent reputation as a salubrious and highly affordable residence that possibly drew former West Indian estate-owners. Some lived in the best addresses (Colleton Crescent, Southernhay, Mont Le Grand) while others either rented or inherited substantial houses (Bystock Terrace, Higher Summerlands, Duryard Lodge, Newport House, Northbrook House) and one boarded in lodging houses.

Great Torrington

The economy of this inland market town in North Devon was summarised in 1775 as 'a great trade is carried on to Ireland etc. and especially in stuffs [cloth]'.[452] In 1783 one visitor found it 'remarkable for nothing' but four years later another described the town's particular appeal:

> 'The principal show of Torrington is a view from the Bowling Green, as our business is to see what is to be seen we contrived to steal enough from the next morning to pay our tribute of admiration to this striking spot. By a crooked interesting walk, we

advanced most unexpectedly to the edge of a bank which appeared near two hundred [feet] perpendicular from whence you look down upon the Torridge winding through a fertile wooded vale immediately under your feet. About half a mile up the valley the river appears gliding out between two woody hills…'

He also found that Great Torrington had an unusual connection with the Caribbean.

'Our hair dresser stumped in on one leg, and curiosity naturally prompted us to enquire what was become of the other. A shark had taken a fancy to it in the West Indies last war. He was bathing in very shallow water when the animal seized him by the foot and dragged him some distance before he separated it and then the poor fellow was able to swim to the shore in this crippled state, before the fish thought of returning for the second morsel…'[453]

It was at this time that Denys Rolle obliterated the town's bowling green (which he owned) because of excessive gambling and coarse language. This was:

'on account of the reputed dissipation of the gentlemen of the town who were accustomed (it seems) now and then to game, and if fortune proved adverse, to execrate that fortune by words which were deemed not proper for gentlemen of character and decorum to make use of.'

The turf was dug up, the boundaries broken down and the summer house dismantled.[454] At the end of the eighteenth century the town's main employer was woollen cloth manufacturing.[455]

In 1831 the town's population stood at 3,093 and it was noted as:

'a small but respectable and prosperous market town … The manufactures of Torrington comprise gloves and coarse woollen goods, the former being the principal branch of trade. Lead is found in the neighbourhood but not in sufficient plenty to excite speculation. A canal, cut by Lord Rolle, through his own lands, communicates with Bideford and is an accommodation to the intercourse of the two towns'.[456]

Rolle, a slaveholder, rented a property to a former slave-owner, Mary Haverfield, and at least one local family, the Rowes, were West Indian estate owners.

However, there were no resident slaveholders in the town on Emancipation Day except Captain Haverfield at Beam and Lord Rolle lived nearby at Stevenstone. There were 32 other resident members of the nobility, gentry and clergy. Despite Great Torrington's apparent remoteness there was an earlier connection. Charles Hiern, a medical man, owned Jamaicans and had family in the town as well as at Barnstaple, Bideford, Okehampton and Bristol. In 1767 he returned to England and while in Epping Forest fell off his horse and died. His plans had been to retire to a small Devon farmhouse. In his will Hiern bequeathed his enslaved people to Judith Rowe, 'a free Mulatto woman'. Two years earlier he had an illegitimate daughter, Lucy, with Juliana [?sic] Rowe.[457]

Ottery St Mary

Ottery St Mary, which had a population of 3,849 in 1831, was economically less dynamic than its neighbours Cullompton and Honiton but in 1830 one observer admired its situation, views and church. He overlooked the late eighteenth-century serge factory which had been recently converted for silk production. Thomas Davy was the only slaveholder resident in the town on Emancipation Day. He was one of 22 resident members of the nobility, gentry and clergy in the town and immediate area. By 1851 Eliza Jopp, a Jamaican, was living in Paternoster Row. She shared the house with her brother John, a blind retired military man who had also been born in Jamaica. Jopp had received £69 19s 2d (£4,743.27) compensation for four Jamaicans.[458]

Plymouth

In 1775 the town was noted as developing:

> 'from a mere fishing town to become one of the biggest in the county and is one of the chief magazines in the kingdom, owing to its port, or rather two harbours, the safest in England and capable of containing 1,000 sail… This town has a good pilchard fishing, drives a considerable trade to the Straights [Gibraltar] and West Indies, and has a custom house…'[459]

A visitor in 1783 thought the situation of Plymouth was low, the pavements intolerable and its streets narrow, disagreeable and dirty. There was however, praise for the Hoe as a 'delightful promenade'.[460] A traveller staying at Dock in 1810 did not enjoy his visit to Plymouth. He had planned on a night at the theatre but:

> 'When we arrived, not liking altogether the look of the place which is a dirty nasty town, we made as much haste back [to Devonport] as possible with a bad idea of the town of Plymouth'.[461]

Twenty years later the port had expanded only to contract shortly afterwards: in 1830, following the end of the Napoleonic war in 1815, it was observed:

> 'Through the vast number of people that resorted here during the war, besides those that belonged to the army and navy, the town has increased greatly within the last 40 years. But since the termination of the war many of those have disappeared and the town affords a melancholy proof that peace has come without bringing to all parts of the country its usual blessings'.

The same writer also commented:

'The general appearance of Plymouth is not fully in unison with its importance, yet great improvements have been made and if these are not so extensive as might be wished, it is not that the inhabitants are not alive to the necessity of prosecuting works of public benefit but that their spirit has sustained a paralysation from the woeful depression of trade. It is to be hoped however that Plymouth may at no distant period find those resources within herself which shall be uninfluenced by national warfare and unimpaired by the presence of peace'.

He made no mention of overseas trade:

'The manufactures here are neither extensive nor numerous; the principal comprise rope, twine and sail cloth making, soaperies, tanneries and iron foundries. There are also ship-building yards, a tolerable trade in coals, corn and timber and a number of ships are employed in the coasting trade to and from London, Bristol, etc.'[462]

In 1831 the population of Plymouth's two main parishes stood at just over 31,000 with another 9,571 at Stonehouse. Not surprisingly, the former West Indian slaveholders who moved to Plymouth were nearly all connected to the navy. Edward Rodon Huggins's wife Emily was the only slaveholder resident in Plymouth on Emancipation Day.

Tiverton

William Camden wrote of Tiverton in the later sixteenth century that 'the woollen trade brings both gain and glory'.[463] For centuries cloth underpinned this market town. In 1790 it was summarised as:

'pleasantly situated at the confluence of two rivers, the Exe and Leman, and on that account was anciently called Twiford. A fine stream runs into it which waters every street … The town was formerly very considerable for making kerseys, but the trade now carried on here consists in the manufacture of serges, druggets, duroys, sagatees, diapers etc. in which the annual amount is now suppose to be about one hundred and fifty thousand pounds.'[464]

Twenty years later, in 1810, another writer provided a fuller view. He wrote:

'The four principal streets are commodious and form a quadrangle, enclosing an area of gardens in the centre of which is a bowling green perhaps the best and most frequented in the west of England. The other streets are not generally so wide, but none are so narrow as to incommode two or three persons walking abreast, on each side the stream of water running in the middle. The length of the town is nearly one mile and the breadth exactly three quarters of a mile. The two rivers afford plenty of fish in the proper season and greatly assist towards the well conducting of the several branches of the woollen trade as well as in driving a great number of mills for grinding corn. This town is noted for the greatest woollen manufactory in the county of Devon after Exeter and next to it of all the inlands ones in wealth if not in numbers of people'.[465]

Shortly afterwards there was a transformation. It was noted in 1830 that whereas in 1790 there were 700 cloth looms in daily use 'this branch of trade is now almost extinct'. Tiverton had refocused its industry:

> 'A few years ago a very large lace manufactory was established here. It is the staple trade of the town employing about 1,000 persons. The principal manufacturers are Messrs Heathcoat & Company.'[466]

The population neared 10,000. Some former enslavers, such as Anna Binney, Caroline Robley and William Tringham lived in Tiverton for brief periods in contrast to the Teschemaker brothers who were resident for more than a decade. Tiverton-born Thomas Rossiter was unusual as a Jamaican slave-owner who returned to his home town. He and Thomas Teschemaker were the only slaveholders resident in Tiverton on Emancipation Day: they comprised 0.02 per cent of the population but were a higher portion of the 52 members of the nobility, gentry and clergy resident in the town and immediate area.[467]

Three West Indians were named Tiverton. One of their owners, Anna Marshall, was a Devonian who later lived in Tiverton. She had owned Topsham and Tiverton who had been taken to Jamaica from Africa.[468] In 1823 Marshall's mother Elizabeth owned Tiverton and Totnes, the first a thirty-eight-year-old African and the second an eight-year-old Creole, in Jamaica.[469] In Berbice lived a 'yellowskin', a thirty-three-year-old African-born man called Tiverton. He was owned in 1822 by Samuel Hiles who also held 'Europe'.[470] In 1819 he may have been owned by George Munro.[471] Munro and Hiles do not appear to have had Tiverton connections.

It was not because of Tiverton's associations with the West Indian colonies in the 1830s that fifty years after emancipation it was the first parliamentary constituency in Devon to consider electing an Indian to Westminster. Nanda Lal Ghosh, a London solicitor, attempted to stand for the Liberal Party but it was subsequently claimed his pockets were not deep enough to win the Tiverton election. A Conservative-supporting newspaper had stated 'We have nothing to say against Mr Ghosh because of his colour. Under dusky skins there beat hearts as true and good as those of Englishmen'. One of his campaign issues was improving the working conditions of the field workers in India.[472]

Topsham

Topsham, the port of Exeter, came to mix commerce with gentility. In 1776 an elderly American visitor commented 'the town is much better built than Sidmouth, has some very good houses and almost all covered with slate or tile'.[473] In 1830 it was noted as being:

'Some years ago this was a very flourishing little place in its foreign and coasting trade but its welfare being much influenced by the prosperity or descension of the manufactures and exports of Exeter, it has consequently declined of late years. There is, however, still some good business done in the coal and timber trades, ship-building and rope, twine and sack making. There is also an extensive paper manufactory and a large foundry for chain cables, anchors, etc. belonging to Messrs Davy & Co. The principal object that will arrest the attention to the stranger here is the beautiful strand, which is justly admired for the extensive and varied views presented from it … The great number of gentry and opulent individuals resident in Topsham and its immediate vicinity is a great source of benefit to the home trade of the inhabitants and bestows upon the general appearance of the place and neighbourhood an aspect pleasing and respectable'.[474]

The transformation into a desirable residential area continued. In 1853 one writer noted:

'Of late there has arisen a desire, on the part of the inhabitants to render it attractive to strangers, who may prefer to take up their temporary abode at a little distance inland rather than on the coast; and many improvements have recently been made in consequence. Topsham is placed in a very pleasant situation – stretching for a mile or more along the east bank of the river, where it widens into the appearance of a lake, or an arm of the sea. The town consists of one main street, a mile in length, at the bottom of which is the quay. The older part is irregularly built, and the houses are mostly mean; but many houses of a better class have been erected within the last few years. These are so situated as to command very fine views of the estuary of the Exe, with the rich scenery of its banks, and the sea beyond. The Strand is well planted with elms, and would form an agreeable walk in itself but of course its value is greatly increased by the beautiful scenery which is beheld from it …

The churchyard affords wide and rich prospects, both up and down the river, and over the surrounding country. A good deal that is picturesque will be met with about the crazy-looking town itself, and some amusement will be found in watching the employments of the townsmen.'[475]

Two slaveholders, Alexander Hamilton Hamilton of The Retreat and Mrs D'Urban of Newport House, were resident on Emancipation Day. They comprised 0.06 per cent of the population of Topsham but were a higher portion of the 52 members of the gentry and clergy resident in the port. Former slaveholders came to live in some of the larger houses in and around the port such as Northbrook Lodge and Seabrook House as well as in the Strand.

Three enslaved people named Topsham were owned by the afore-named Anna Marshall, James Davy and Lauchlan McLean who, in 1836, had compensation for four Jamaicans. In 1817 his enslaved people included a forty-year-old man born in Africa who was given the name Topsham. He also owned Maryann Devonshire, an eight-year-old Creole.[476]

Totnes

This market town was summarised in 1775 as having a 'woollen manufactory but there are more gentlemen than tradesmen of note'.[477] In 1799 it was noted that the town 'boasts a situation perhaps unrivalled in point of beauty'.[478] The population in 1831 stood at 3,442. It was:

> 'principally of one good street, nearly three quarters of a mile in length, terminated on the east by the Dart, over which a superb bridge has been lately built, the river dividing Totnes from the suburb of Bridgetown. Craft of 60 tons burthen belong to the town, other vessels keep up a constant intercourse for the transportation of heavy goods from London, Liverpool and Plymouth, and boats continually ply on the river for the conveyance of goods and passengers from hence to Dartmouth, a distance of ten miles. The principal manufacture is woollen goods generally and serge; but the main trade of Totnes arises from extensive exports and imports, by which a populous and extensive district is supplied and supported.'[479]

The parish register recorded the baptism of John Peters, 'a Negro born in Demerary in the West Indies, an adult', in 1798 but there is no indication of his connection with Totnes. He may have been associated with several local families.[480]

The Cary family at Follaton House were the only slaveholders resident in Totnes on Emancipation Day. As a single individual George Stanley Cary was only 0.03 per cent of the general population but had higher status than nearly all of the 60 members of the nobility, gentry and clergy resident in the town and immediate area. Other Totnesians connected to slave-owning include a collection of residents of Weston House in Berry Pomeroy, including John Bent, Member of Parliament for the town in the 1820s. Another was Dr John Bush who was born in Martinique and lived at Bridgetown from 1837 (when he married Hannah Clarke of Highweek) until at least 1841. By 1844 he had returned to the West Indies and died in Berbice. Bush's father had owned Mary Hope's Estate in British Guiana.[481]

It may be indicative of Totnesian culture that a ceremony mocking emancipation was held in September 1834. A curious news story entitled 'More Slaves Emancipated' was printed in one newspaper.

> 'At a meeting of slave proprietors held at Totnes on Monday last, it was unanimously agreed to emancipate all those slaves who by their former tractable and obsequious conduct had rendered themselves deserving of that favour from their former masters. Twenty one were immediately introduced and had their manacles struck off at the time, on paying the small sum of four pounds fourteen shillings and sixpence, to be divided

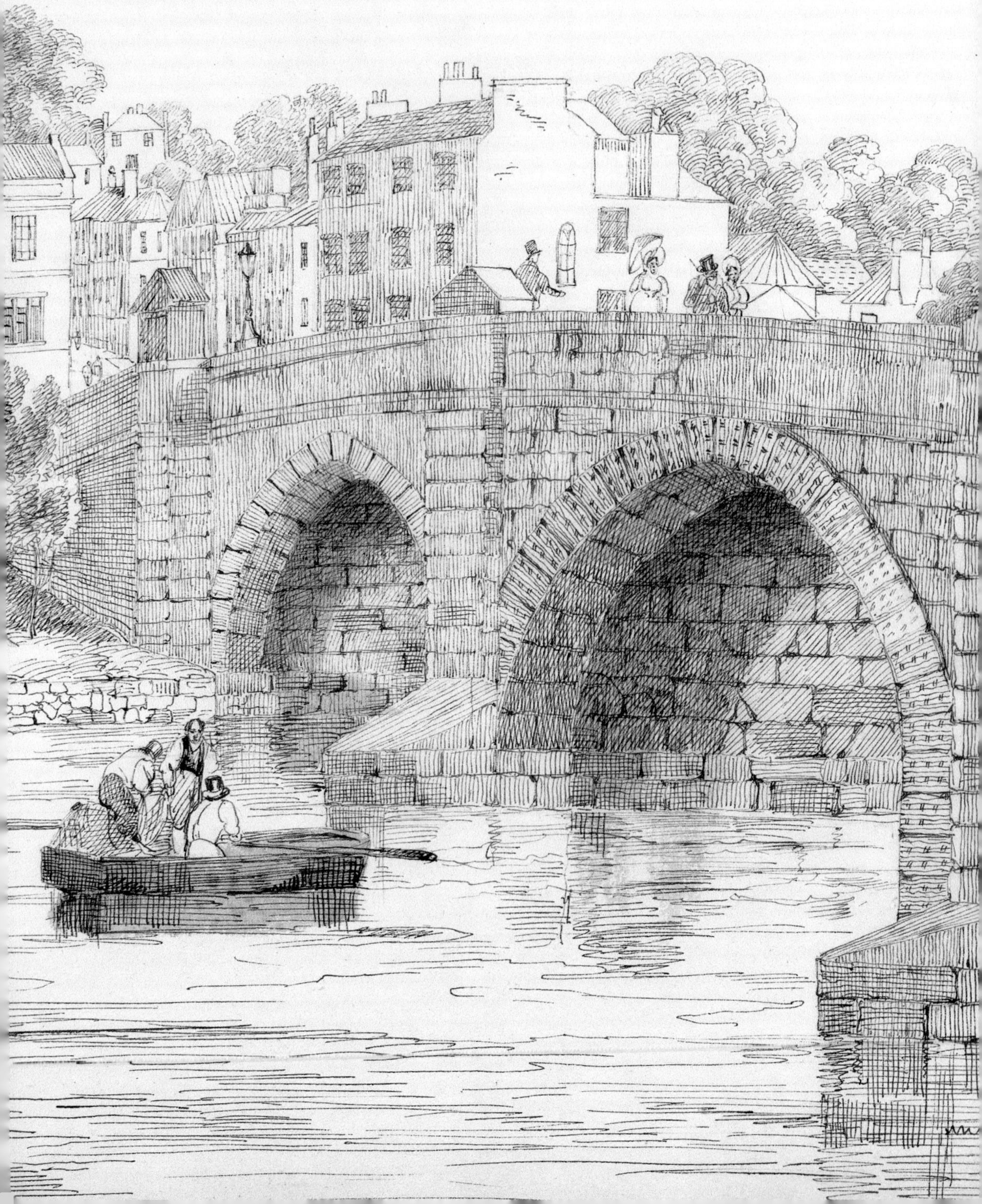

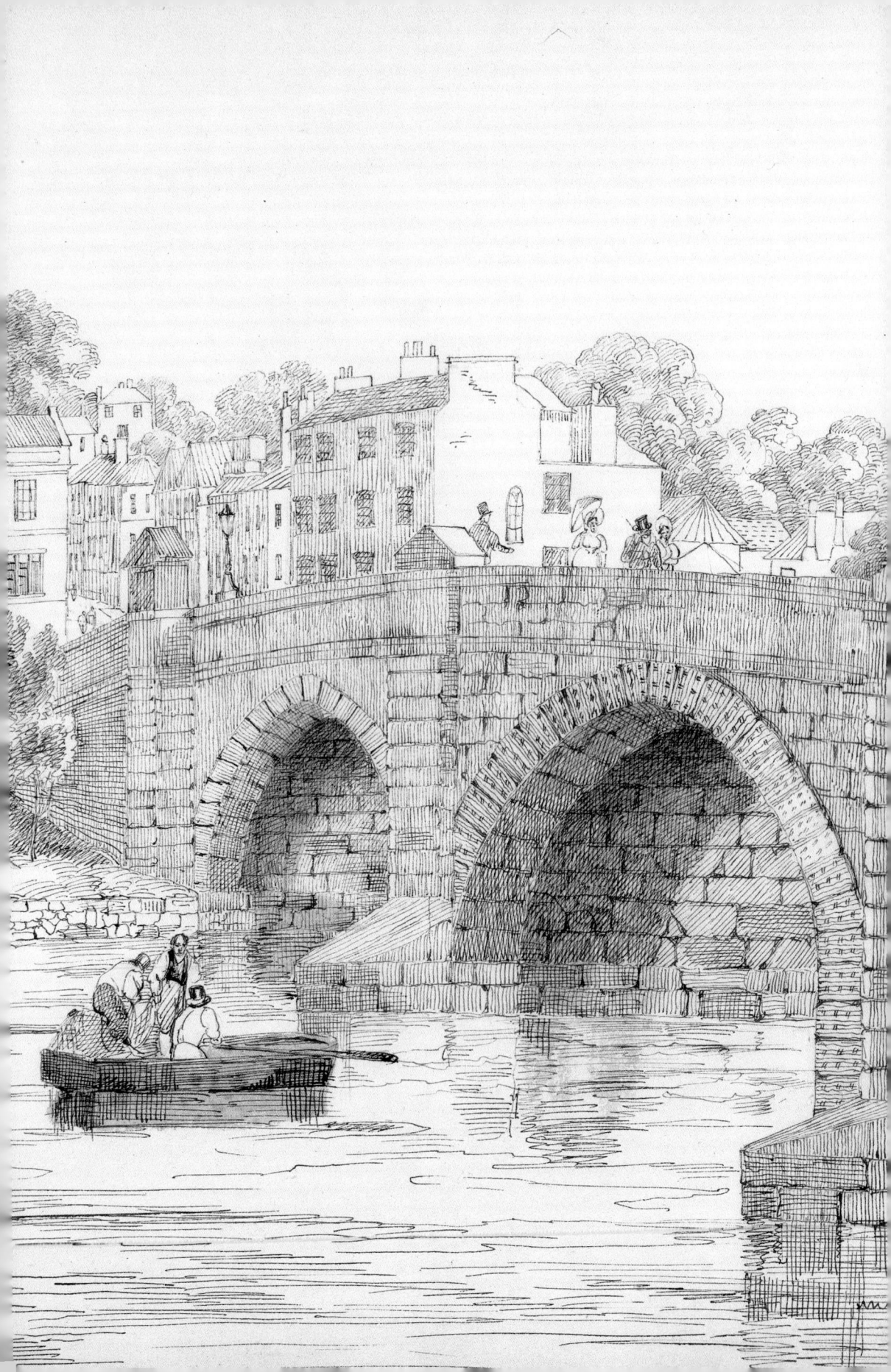

among the several drivers. Seven more of the second class are on trial, and if they prove submissive and obedient, they also will be emancipated the beginning of next week, on paying the drivers the aforesaid sum each.[482]

This may have been a lark, a piece of satire or a ceremony in the tradition of secret societies.

By 1834 the county's largest urban centres, Exeter and Plymouth, were far less prosperous than they had been a generation before and the countryside was losing its population as agriculture stagnated and declined. The dynamism in Devon was centred on its growing coastal resorts and among the migrants they attracted were former owners of slaves. While Devon-born slave-owners were at a minimum, the county found it had a new type of resident in former West Indian colonists and British absentee slave-owners who appreciated the warmer climate, fashionable houses and polite society found in coastal communities.

DEVON'S BLACK POPULATION

It is difficult to identify individual Black Devonians in the past and impossible to categorically ascertain their number but it is unlikely that it historically reached as high as 0.1 per cent of Devon's overall population.

The county did not have the mass migration that occurred elsewhere in the middle of the twentieth century but war in 1812 and 1939 temporarily brought large numbers of Black Americans to Devon. In both instances they were segregated from White Americans. Between 1813 and 1815 a thousand Black sailors were incarcerated in Dartmoor Prison. They included seventy-three men born in the West Indies, South America, the East Indies, Africa and Europe. Some were from Jamaica and Mauritius. They were led by Richard Craftus, otherwise known as King Dick or Big Dick, who stood at six foot three inches and was then in his mid twenties. Another prisoner was William Lane, a 'Mulatto' from Boston, who was an officer and allowed to live in private lodgings possibly in Ashburton.[483] Between 1942 and 1944 a second group of Black Americans lived across the county awaiting D-Day and some 83 mixed-race babies are known to have been born.[484]

Outside of these two periods of war, it would appear that the county has never had enough Black Devonians to be considered as a historical community but rather were isolated individuals scattered throughout the county. The highest number of foreign-born Victorian immigrants were most likely Irish, particularly in Exeter and Plymouth which had a combined population of several thousand Irish in 1851.[485]

◀ 33. Totnes from the Seymour Hotel in Bridgetown, by Sir Charles D'Oyly, 1838.

Ethnicity and sources: the census, parish registers and newspapers

No document required race to be recorded but census enumerators provided possible indications. In 1831 they did not note ethnicity or place of birth but in the following census, taken on 6 June 1841, they asked each individual whether he or she had been born in Devon or outside of it. A decade later, on 30 March 1851, enumerators noted where residents were specifically born. These answers are possible indicators of race and former enslavement.

Birth places recorded in Devon's smallest parishes in 1841 and 1851 indicate a low level of immigration of all kinds from outside the county to isolated places.[486]

Table 4

Location of births of residents in Devon's parishes with lowest populations, 1841 & 1851.

	1841 Devon	o	1851 Devon	UK	f
Buckland Tout Saints	55	1	47	1	0
Bittadon	57	1	65	2	0
Creacombe	58	0	34	1	0
Satterleigh	61	0	56	1	0
Honeychurch	69	0	59	0	0
Clannaborough	69	1	62	0	0
Shillingford St George	68	4	68	1	0
Ashbury	46	4	70	0	0
Cheldon	90	0	75	3	0

In 1841 individuals were recorded as having been born in Devon or elsewhere ('in Scotland, Ireland or Foreign Parts') but three residents were highlighted as having been born in the West Indies.[487] Table Four shows that ten years later there were declining population levels in six of these nine parishes. Table Five reveals a greater social mix in three resorts.

Table 5

Location of births of residents in three resorts, 1841 & 1851.

	1841 Devon		Other		Total
Dawlish	2,781	(86%)	437	(14%)	3,218
Ilfracombe	3,138	(86%)	525	(14%)	3,663
Sidmouth	2,806	(85%)	503	(15%)	3,309

	1851 Devon		Other		Total
Dawlish	2,976	(83%)	601	(17%)	3,577
Ilfracombe	3,161	(87%)	481	(13%)	3,642
Sidmouth	2,776	(81%)	668	(19%)	3,444

Table 6 shows that in the census of 1851 243 individuals in Devon were noted as having been born in the West Indies and Mauritius; this was 0.04 per cent of the county's total population of 567,098. They included former slaveholders who were listed mainly as annuitants, fundholders or land proprietors. A higher number were employed and 76 of the remainder were children including school boarders and three orphans in a Plymouth institution. It is not known how many were Black or formerly enslaved. The number of West Indians is minor compared to the 5,067 Irish immigrants listed in that census but similar to the 319 individuals who had been born in India.

Table 6

Residents of Devon born in the West Indies and Mauritius, 1851–1871.

	1851	1861	1871
Anguilla	0	0	0
Antigua	2	5	3
Bahamas	0	0	0
Barbados	27	22	10
Bermuda	49	33	77
British Guiana	8	9	10
Caymans	0	0	0
Dominica	4	1	0
Grenada	4	4	0
Honduras	1	2	2
Jamaica	110	97	97
Mauritius	5	23	27
Montserrat	1	1	0
Nevis	3	0	0
St Kitts	10	6	7
St Lucia	0	0	0
St Vincent	10	3	5
Tobago	2	0	0
Trinidad	7	4	9
Virgin Islands	0	1	0
Total	243	211	247
Devon total	567,098	584,373	600,814

The number of immigrants from the former slave colonies was 0.03 to 0.04 per cent of the county's population from 1851 to 1871.

Parish registers

While census data reveals places of birth, parish records occasionally noted ethnicity. Sixteen Black men and five women were recorded in Devon's parish registers from 1800 to 1834 as having been baptised, married or buried.[488]

Arlington

Thomas George Lawrence, 'a Negro servant of Thomas Hall, Esquire, so far delivered', baptism, 13 April 1805

Budleigh Salterton

Maria, aged 55, 'a black woman servant to Mr Walcot', baptism, 17 Feb. 1828
Nancy, aged 24, 'a black servant belonging to James Wolcot', baptism, 28 May 1828

Exmouth (Withycombe Raleigh)

John Worsely, 'an African Black belonging to the band in Denbigh Militia' and Mary Webber, marriage, 12 March 1801
William Surmanid Hicks, 29, 'an African American', baptism, 4 Oct. 1805
Mary Ann, 60, 'a black woman who came from the island of Christopher', baptism, 18 June 1809
Thomas Chaser, 35, 'an African by birth', baptism, 12 Sept. 1811

Heavitree

Ann Peel, 'a Negro woman', baptism, 17 March 1805

Lympstone

Joseph Cutting, 'a black man', baptism, 3 Jan. 1808
Richard Smyth, 'a black', baptism, 22 Aug. 1808
James Trim, 'a black man', baptism, 4 Aug. 1811

Morchard Bishop

Charles Southcott West, 'parents deceased, a Negro of Africa, servant to Mr Harris of Crediton', baptism, 13 Nov. 1815

Stoke Damerel

Thomas Barthurst, 20, 'of Wampo in the East Indies, a black man', marriage, 18 Oct. 1802
Charles Phoenix, 35, 'a black man', baptism, 23 Sept. 1803
John Williamson, 16, 'a black boy', baptism, 15 Nov. 1809
Charles Williams, 26, 'a black man, son of Charles and Grace Williams', baptism, 19 Feb. 1810
Charles Zeno, 16, 'a black boy', 13 April 1810

Stonehouse

Thomas Scott Mclean, 16, 'an African taken in infancy from the coast of Mozambique, sea boy on board HMS *Africa*', baptism, 13 Feb. 1835

Tiverton

Thomas Bretton, 'a native of Africa now resident in the town of Tiverton, servant', baptism, 21 July 1813

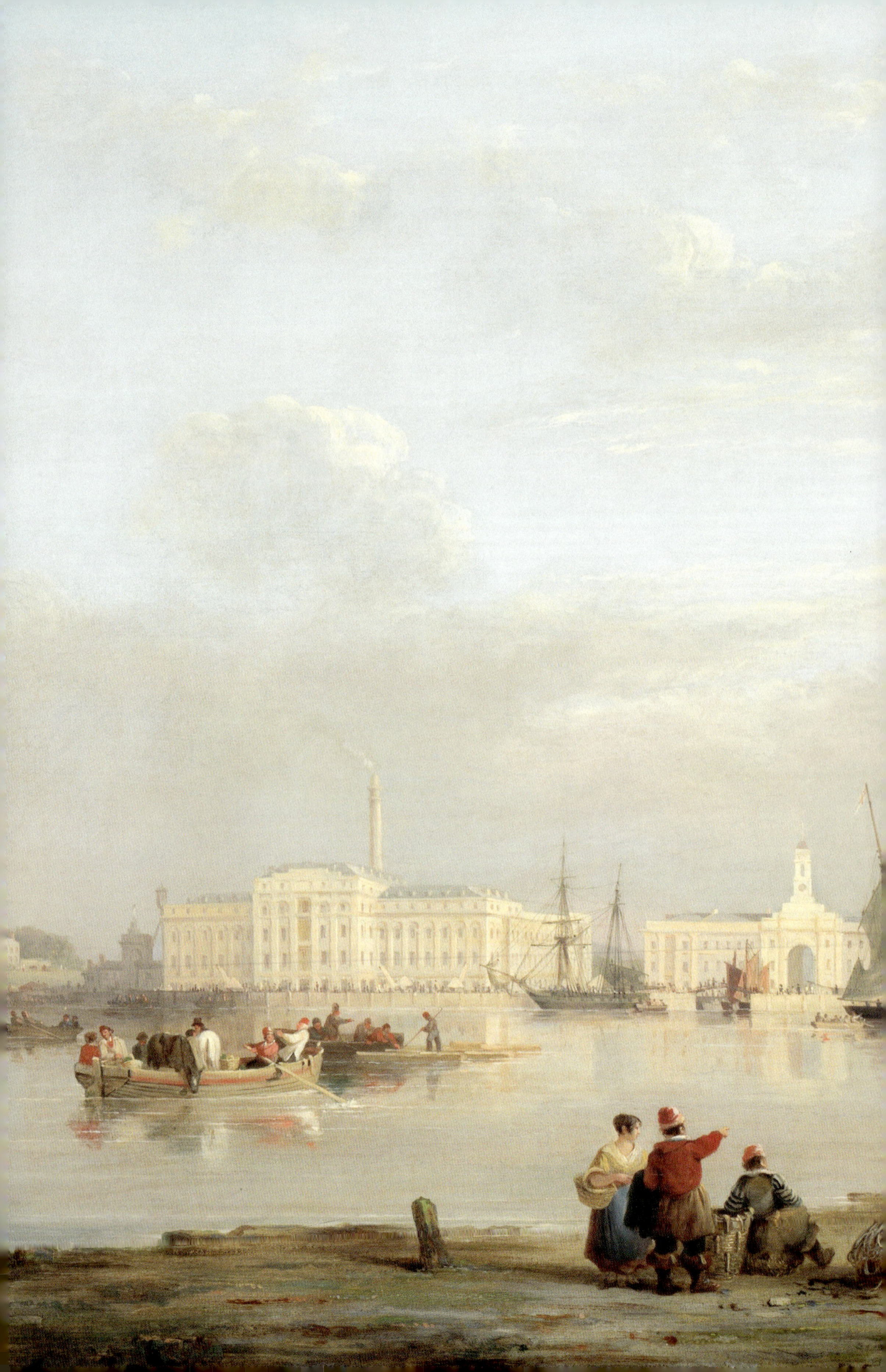

Topsham
John Williams, 'a Negro', burial, 13 Dec. 1805
Mary Williams, widow, 'a Negro woman', burial, 7 Jan. 1809

Two of these references pull James Percy Walcott out of obscurity. Walcott was born in Barbados in 1791 but subsequently lived in England, Demerara, South Africa and finally Australia where he died in 1872. In the 1820s he lived in Budleigh Salterton at Kersbrook, a substantial property with three sitting rooms and four bedrooms situated in an acre of land. In 1828 Walcott sold the property because he was 'going abroad'. He had owned Good Hope and St Christopher estates in Demerara. In 1828 the parish register noted Walcott's servants Maria and Nancy who presumably had been enslaved and travelled with him from the West Indies. They were baptised the year the family left England.[489]

News reports

More men and women of African descent can be found in news reports but they were referred to by journalists in various ways. Only occasionally were they called Black. In one instance at Bideford in 1827 a 'Black man', otherwise only identified as a 'man of colour', was reportedly found in bed with a Welsh woman.[490] The latter term was also used in 1827 to describe James Clements, a Jamaican who worked as a caricaturist in Plymouth's public houses as well as a servant to a local clergyman. His physical description was detailed: Clements was 'a most eccentric looking character dressed up in the style of a modern European dandy with braided coat and foraging cap with broad gold lace'.[491] In comparison, Henry Browne was 'a robust' man of colour when he was arrested in 1834 for begging in Exeter.

Journalists used other terms such as when Elizabeth Jackson was called 'a Mulatto woman'; she had allegedly used obscene language in a Plymouth street in 1860. Only occasionally were indicative nicknames recorded. In 1863 William Wonnacott, who was another 'Mulatto', was charged with being drunk and violent at the Blackamoor's Head in Exeter. His nickname was Curly Billy.[492]

Loaded language was used such as when in 1830 a woman in Exeter, Sarah Gander, was cited as 'a swarthy looking woman' while in another instance she was described as 'a Mulatto woman'. Her child was 'bronze looking' or 'a mahogany coloured piccaninny'.[493] Thomas Dartmouth Rice might be mistaken as another example. He was referred to as having 'all the appearance of a real American *nigger*' but was performing in blackface at Exeter in 1840.[494] The references to Black men and women indicates a transient and smaller population than in the large urban areas of the country but they also give the impression of a racial association with criminality.

◀ 34. The Victualling Office, Devonport, c.1835, by Nicholas Condy. The naval dock made Plymouth the most cosmopolitan part of Devon and with Stonehouse made Plymouth the county's greatest urban area.

Occasionally reports provide substantial details. In 1815 a newspaper advert identified William Easdon, a parish apprentice who absconded from his master, as 'a Mulatto, aged about 14 years, about 4 feet 7 inches high, wore away a dark brown coat and waistcoat, and leather breeches'.[495]

Likewise, in 1829 Charles Dunbar, a ninety-eight-year-old 'man of colour' in the employ of Vice Admiral Robert Barton, died in Exeter at 4 Dix's Field, 'the house of his master'. His death notice recorded that this 'faithful servant' had 'attached himself to the admiral by some conduct during an action in which they were both engaged'. His length of service, thirty-six years, suggests that he may have originally been enslaved. Barton had been stationed in the West Indies and saw notable action commanding the *Lapwing* in 1796 off St Kitts and Anguilla.[496]

There was another news story, seven years earlier, when in 1822 a journalist observed that he, at the age of 90 and described as 'a man of colour', was in a St Sidwell hair-dresser's shop being shaved alongside six other men who had a combined age of 571. Dunbar was the eldest.[497]

Of at least equal interest is the extraordinary history of Antonio de Benguela who also lived in Exeter. The first of two news reports, printed on 22 February 1834, noted a wedding in Cathedral Yard:

> 'This morning, at the parish church of St Mary Major, by Special Licence by the Reverend John Fisher Turner, Antonio de Benguela, a native of Benguela on the coast of Africa, to Miss Halfyard, daughter of Mr Halfyard of this city'.[498]

Four months later a second story appeared of a death:

> 'Suddenly, on Monday last, Mr Antonio de Benguela, a native of Benguela, on the coast of Africa, who was sent as a slave at six years of age to Rio de Janeiro in Brazil, where he was purchased by a niece of Francis Turner, Esquire of this city, and brought to this country by her as a present to Mrs Turner, who caused him to be christened and educated. He remained with Mr Turner a very faithful servant until the time of his decease. It was but very lately that he married a daughter of Mr Halfyard of his city – he was in the 27th year of his age'.[499]

De Benguela was baptised in St David's Church on 26 September 1817 as 'a young African' who was presumably then nine years old. Sixteen years later Mrs Sophia Turner died, in May 1833, and her death may have been the catalyst for de Benguela's marriage nine months afterwards. Her husband, Francis Turner, headed the household at 25 Southernhay. He died a wealthy merchant in 1838 and his estate included paintings by Titian, Pieter Brueghel and Nicolas Poussin.

Turner was the head of Francis Turner & Company, a firm which specialised in Portuguese merchandise. Turner was also a Vice-Consul of Portugal and in 1834 the country's royal flag hung from a window at his home. Benguela was then a Portuguese colony in Africa.[500]

In December 1816 John Turner, the nephew of Francis, died at Lisbon where he had

Part One: Slavery & Devon, 1562–1834

been born and where he had returned for health reasons. Turner was a merchant with interests in Rio de Janeiro. He had a glowing death notice ('the amiability of whose disposition and manners was the admiration of all his acquaintance, more particularly of his relatives and friends').[501] Presumably it was at this time that his widow returned to Exeter and brought de Benguela with her.

Ann Halfyard, who was to become Mrs de Benguela, had been born in Exeter and her father was Richard Halfyard, a yeoman from Whipton. Shortly after her husband's death, Mrs de Benguela gave birth to a daughter, Ann Halfyard de Benguela. She married at the age of 21, was childless and died in 1862. Mrs de Benguela lived longer; after the death of her husband she worked as a seamstress and lived mostly in Exeter until her death in 1875. No details have been found on how her marriage was viewed in Exeter nor on how her husband, as a former slave, was treated.

No mention was made in news reports of the existence of Antonio's brother, Fernando, who was baptised separately in 1828. Also a servant, he was then about twenty years old. He lived in the precinct of Bradninch, a small enclave on the southern edge of Rougemont Castle, and it appears that his master was George Turner, an attorney who was Francis Turner's nephew.[502]

Perhaps the last enslaved man in Devon was Moses Smith who was born in the American state of Georgia in about 1862. He lived in Barnstaple from 1883 until his death in 1917 and was continually referred to as a 'coloured man' and occasionally as a Black man. Smith was in court on charges of using obscene language, assault and theft. He married Fanny Gibbons, a Bideford-born woman, in Great Torrington in 1883 and they had three sons, one of whom was decorated in the Great War. Smith had been a well-known local boxer in his youth and worked as a fish hawker in Barnstaple.[503]

It is clear that Smith's ethnicity was at the heart of some public brawling. In 1904 after he had used obscene language and then questioned the parentage of another man's nineteen children, Smith's adversary told him he would not allow a white man to speak to him in that manner let alone a black one. He then called Smith a black monkey who responded 'where is my tail?'. Smith added that he could not help his colour and objected to being made the subject of 'such remarks'.[504]

Three years later a neighbour called Smith a black dog. Smith told the court not only was he not a dog but wanted to stop such remarks being made to him. His wife informed the judge that she had married a man, not a black dog.[505]

In addition to these enslaved men, Victorian Devon had a former White slave, Dame Florence Baker. She was probably Romanian and was purchased at a Bulgarian slave market by Sir Samuel White Baker, the African explorer. They married by 1865 and lived at Sandford Orleigh near Newton Abbot.[506]

SPANISH LAW

Part Two: Devon and slave-ownership, 1834

Thirty-four men and women living in Devon on Emancipation Day were recognised as the unencumbered owners of enslaved people and thus eligible to receive compensation. On 1 August 1834 their awards related to enslaved people in Antigua, the Bahamas, Barbados, British Guiana, Dominica, Grenada, Jamaica, Nevis, St Kitts, St Vincent, Tobago and Trinidad.[507]

These Devonians owned 4,957 individuals, some 0.8 per cent of the 636,358 men, women and children who were emancipated in these colonies,[508] and received awards of £138,634 18s 11d (£9,399,629.55) which was 1.8 per cent of the £7,741,824 given to all British absentee owners or 0.8 per cent of the £16,356,668 given to all slaveholders. The thirty-four Devon men and women were 0.1 per cent of the 34,407 slave-owners in Britain and across the empire who had compensation. In comparison, Devon had 3 per cent of the country's population.

They had on average £4,077 in compensation, the equivalent of nearly 56 years' wages for a skilled British tradesman. Three Devonians had exceptionally high awards and accounted for £70,829 5s 8d (£4,802,317.49) or 51 per cent of the county's payments. The average compensation of the remaining thirty-one Devonians was £2,187 (£148,281.44), the equivalent of 30 years' wages for a skilled tradesman. In comparison the average compensation payment given to all 37,407 slaveholders was £437 (£19,629.17). The size distribution is skewed by the high rate, of more than a fifth, of single-slave ownership in the West Indies and of a quarter in Mauritius.[509]

Only two were North Devon residents; Walter Halliday lived in Lynmouth and John Teschemaker was briefly a resident of Ilfracombe but he like his brother Thomas led a peripatetic lifestyle in that they also lived in Tiverton and Exmouth. The remainder lived in South Devon. Exeter and the surrounding area was a particular draw: Alphington, Bradninch, Clyst St Mary, Heavitree, Rockbeare, Topsham and the city itself attracted ten slaveholders. Twelve others chose the seaside resorts of Budleigh Salterton, Dawlish, Exmouth, Sidmouth and Teignmouth.[510]

A handful remained in or returned to where they were raised; five men were born and died at Bicton, Ottery St Mary, Shute, Tiverton and Totnes. Three followed their

◀ 35. Pencil sketch of Trinidad entitled 'Protector of slaves office', 1833, by Richard Bridgens. The figure to the right is captioned 'Protector of Slaves' and on the left is a Planter.

Table 7

Slave-owners who had personal slavery compensation awards while resident in Devon on 1 August 1834.

Unless specified, shared compensation awards have been calculated according to the number of awardees. The actual divisions may have differed. Some ages have been approximated.

Name	Birth	Age 1/8/34	Compensation	Enslaved number	Award date	Devon residence
E. Abell	?Jamaica	14	£287 16s 4d (£19,514.34)	17	1836	1830–41
S. O. Attlay	Yorkshire	74	£2,809 10s 1d (£190,488.03)	141	1836	c1823–38
H. Barnes	Bristol	68	£157 8s 9d (£10,674,47)	9	1836	c1834–7
J. L. Brodbelt	Jamaica	34	£112 6s 6d (£7,615.78)	16	1837-8	1832–48
W. G. Burn	India	44	£414 4s 3d (£28,084.15)	19	1836	c1814–52
J. Campbell	London	68	£2,004 11s 2d (£135,911.66)	102	1841	c1813–41
G. R Cary	London	52	£7,095 18s 5d (£481,112.66)	438	1835	lifetime
J. T. Clarke	Jamaica	40	£163 14s 9d (£11,101.62)	8	1836	1830–71
R. Collins	Unknown	82	£4,821 7s 7d (£326,895.78)	247	1836	lifetime
T. Davy	Devon	61	£1,101 3s 8d (£74,661.66)	59	1835	lifetime
M. Dixon	Canada	80	£271 14s 2d (£18,422.18)	23	1837	1830–7
J. H. Doyle	London	29	£1,704 11d (£115,536.52)	102	1836	c1832–61
M. E. D'Urban	Devon	31	£3,013 12s 7d (£204,327.98)	113	1836	lifetime
John Fisher	Unknown	77	£289 17s 9d (£19,654.75)	13	1835-6	1816–39
N. R. Garner	?Barbados	68	£1,119 10s 6d (£75,905.25)	56	1836	c1830–7
T. Hall	Jamaica	77	£9,495 1d (£643,773.63)	503	1836, 1838	1823–39
W. S. Halliday	India	41	£3,168 12s 8d (£214,837.46)	165	1836	1830–72
A. H. Hamilton	Scotland	51	£3,184 15s 3d (£215,931.04)	140	1835	1810–53
H. Howell	Barbados	26	£3,194 9s 7d (£216,589.84)	161	1836	1833–55
E. R. Huggins	Hampshire	45	£385 2d (£26,104.07)	23	1835-6	1830–42
E. Lousada	London	51	£1,268 9s (£86,002.56)	63	1836, 1838	1831–54
J. P. Passley	Jamaica	46	£1,503 8s 4d (£101,933.60)	80	1835	c1833–40
G. Pearse	Devon	34	£4,390 4s 3d (£297,662.11)	228	1836	lifetime
W. T. Pole	Devon	42	£2,648 8s 2d (£179,565.53)	170	1835	lifetime
H. Porter	Demerara	43	£35,960 14s 8d (£2,438,184.47)	709	1835	c1796–1857
T. Porter	Demerara	44	£19,295 8s (£1,308,253.20)	385	1835	c1796–1858
R. Potter	Jamaica	49	£135 19s 9d (£9,220.13)	8	1838	c1820--43
J. Rolle	Devon	77	£4,333 6s 9d (£293,805.92)	377	1836	lifetime
T. Rossiter	Devon	62	£1,064 9s 4d (£72,172.22)	55	1835	c1826–39
H. Stuart	Unknown	unk.	£1,935 9s 10d (£131,228.85)	71	1835	c1820–37
M. Taylor	Jamaica	unk.	£23 9s 1d (£1,590.22)	1	1837	c.1834–7
J. Teschemaker	Demerara	42	£5,293 6s 1d (£358,892.90)	106	1837	1833-67
T. Teschemaker	London	33	£15,668 3s (£1,062,320.94)	335	1835-7	1834-53
H. G. Windsor	Canada	50	£319 7s 6d (£21,654.04)	14	1836	1834

careers to Plymouth while one cleric served in three inland country parishes. Seven of the thirty-three spent their entire lives in the county whereas the remainder resided in Devon for an average of 24 years.

The thirty-four men and women were a portion of the individuals connected with enslavement. Table 8 shows that a further nine slaveholders, who included one with plantations in Mauritius, came to Devon in the following three years. They owned 2,173 individuals and received £46,571 14s 8d (£3,157,624.06) in compensation.

Altogether these forty-three owners held 7,130 individuals, 1.0 per cent of the 700,689 men, women and children who were emancipated in the thirteen colonies.[511] They owned on average 166 enslaved people.

Table 8

Slave-owners who had personal slavery compensation awards while resident in Devon, 1835 to 1841.

Unless specified, shared compensation awards have been calculated according to the number of awardees. The actual divisions may have differed. Some ages have been approximated.

D. Burke	Unknown	66	£26 5d (£1,764.25)	2	1835	c1836–7
J. Cunningham	Jamaica	54	£14,448 13s 5d (£979,638.67)	703	1836–7	c1835–52
T. Drane	London	40	£6,868 7s 1d (£465,682.34)	206	1837	1837–64
J. C. Fisher	Somerset	43	£6,571 9s 10d (£445,555.68)	359	1836	1835–55
H. A. Hawkins	Devon	44	£384 5s 2d (£26,053.21)	18	1836	1835–7
W. H. Heaven	Gloucestershire	35	£11,742 13s 2d (£796,167.50)	538	1835–6	1836–83
E. L. Hinds	Barbados	34	£46 12s 1d (£3,159.82)	2	1836	1836–7
P. H. James	Jamaica	39	£6,419 17s 5d (£435,275.59)	342	1836–7	1836–73
J. Martell	?Jamaica	38	£63 16s 1d (£4,326.01)	3	1835	1835–48

Thirty-nine of the forty-three were men. Eight were born in Devon, six in London, six in the rest of the country and twenty in the colonies. Their average age was forty-nine. In total these forty-three men and women received £185,206 13s 7d (£12,557,253.62).[512]

The smaller group of 34 slave-owners comprised 0.007 per cent of the county's population and the larger group of 43 made up 0.009 per cent. At this time Devon had higher numbers of individuals working in most occupations, including specialised ones such as auctioneers or straw hat makers, but a better comparison might be with the number of the upper classes; 2,952 were listed in Devon in 1830. Several of Devon's 34 slaveholders had either the income or status to be regarded in this element of society but the remainder comprised, at most, 0.9 per cent of their peers.[513]

The 43 men and women were supplemented, as will be seen in the following pages, by a greater number of individuals who also had personal financial associations with plantations. The bigger picture shows the complex nature of the slave economies which stretched across the Atlantic.

Two stages followed the early eighteenth century period of prosperity of the slave estates: from 1775 to 1815 many passed through inheritance from colonists to English residents. Nearly all of these 43 Devonians acquired their estates in this way. Secondly, from 1815 to 1834 an economic collapse caused many plantations to be underpinned by creditors. About ten of the Devonians acquired their plantations through personal endeavours including refinancing.[514]

In addition to being direct owners, there were many other ways in which individuals received compensation for their loss of enslaved people. Understanding how Devon was connected to slavery requires untangling the financial arrangements under which the plantations were organised in 1834.

The Rolle family

The most striking example of slave-ownership for Devon concerns the Rolle family. In 1836 they received compensation of £4,333 6s 9d (£293,805.92) for 377 Bahamians. This was at the end of a seventy-year involvement and theirs was the most remarkable history for any Devon family; it comprises an extraordinary back story, the county's best-known enslaved person, the granting and expectation of partial liberty, the early freeing of the apprentices and the enduring gift of the estate to them.

The family's ownership of enslaved people took place over two generations, firstly with Denys Rolle who was later described as 'a great botanist, great traveller, great walker and great talker'.[515] He was, as will be seen, an uncommon man who led a singular life dominated for nearly two decades by colonisation.

Rolle was the third son and eventual heir of John Rolle of Bicton and Stevenstone. To these two mansions he added others including Beam and Hudscott. Rolle married in 1750 and had eight children born between 1751 and 1762. In 1764 he left his family behind in England in order to establish a colony in Florida. Rolle remained there for much of the 1760s and the settlement would dominate his thoughts for the following nineteen years. He has been described as 'Plutarchian' while another writer thought he had 'broad but visionary ideas'. Rolle himself wrote that he intended to establish 'an ideal society' and others have amplified this to describe the colony as Utopia and even Xanadu.[516]

Rolle was granted nearly 80,000 acres with the stipulation that he would colonise it with White Protestants. He left England onboard *The Two Friends* with fourteen men and women and began the difficult process of establishing Rollestown, his colony which was also called Charlotta or Charlotia. Subsequent recruits increased the population to some 300 White colonists. They came in a piecemeal fashion: in 1765 thirty-seven French colonists arrived and the following year two hundred families followed them from New Providence. However, it proved challenging to attract and keep settlers despite extensive recruitment. Even before Rolle left England it was reported in newspapers that he had arranged for gentlemen, artificers and families to set out from Bristol and that other families would follow from Barnstaple and

Bideford in the autumn. Two hundred Devon families duly emigrated. Rolle paid their transport.[517] They were joined in 1767 by 93 German migrants, known as Palatines, who sailed from Plymouth.[518]

Some writers summarised Rolle's workforce as comprising one hundred families but an early commentator, in 1791, dismissed them as 'a bad choice of citizens'.[519] One group of sixty were disparagingly noted as 'shoe blacks, chimney sweepers, sink boys, tinkers and tailors, bunters, cinder wenches, whores and pickpockets'. The colony's governor wrote they 'left England because they were idle and starving and will not easily be prevailed upon to work in America'. However, Rolle has recently been remembered as creating 'an asylum for unfortunates, a place where the underprivileged might be rehabilitated and started on useful, self-supporting lives'.[520]

In 1818 a traveller simplified the colony's history and embellished it with a sensational emphasis. He speculated that Rolle had:

> 'formed it for the singular and romantic purpose of affording an asylum to the penitent prostitutes of our country. Hither numbers were brought but whether the zeal of the founder subsided or the penitence of his Magdalens ceased, I know not. But certain it is they have left no other remembrance than the story of their settlement. We cannot but believe that the intentions of Mr Denys Rolle were formed and executed in the spirit of philanthropy. But that there was a species of folly and infatuation in the choice of the objects of his bounty, daily observation demonstrates. Did he propose to found a colony of Amazons?'

He surmised that the actual intention was intermarriage with the Indigenous people.[521] This skewed view of Rolle's aims was repeated in 1837 when it was suggested that he had brought 'nearly three hundred miserable females who were picked up about the purlieus of London. His object was to reform them and make of them good members of society. They all died in a few years'.[522] A Florida guidebook, written in 1922, was one of many to dismiss the settlement as a 'short-lived colony of derelicts from London streets'.[523]

A Victorian novel, *The Power of Woman*, featured Rolle's colonists in the same vein:

> 'Why don't you go up the St Johns to Rollestown? They say there's a minister there. One of Lord Rolle's imported London queans might take pity on you. I'm told they're marrying them to Indians now'.

At this Jack Penman laughs.

> 'By Jove, Cutter, there's a chance for *you*. They say my lord reformed them all before he shipped them to Florida, though every lady of 'em has beaten hemp in English Bridewell'.
> 'But you will have to hurry Isaiah,' giggles Stork. 'There are only six wenches left now, the rest have died. Would you like to hear what I shall write about your suggested spouse in my history of Florida: *Lord Rolle, a philanthropic nobleman, selected from the purlieus*

of London the three hundred most abandoned women in Whitechapel and shipped them to Florida, to improve the virtue of the Indians, likewise of Mr Isaiah Cutter'.[524]

Each of these writers overlooked the more familiar history of Black slavery: by 1767 Rolle had 22 enslaved people and their number increased to 150 by 1779. At this time they lived in huts situated in a square before the mansion house. Rollestown came to an abrupt end in 1783 when the British government gave Florida to Spain and the settlement was abandoned. Rolle retained his 140 slaves who were then redeployed in his subsequent plantation.[525]

Initially Rolle had reservations about using Black slaves in Florida; he preferred White colonists but his hesitation was not prompted by a disbelief in slavery. In fact, he thought Africans were better off in British colonies than under what he considered to be the harsher rule of their own leaders.[526]

The number of the enslaved grew up to 1783. In 1780 Rolle purchased 57 enslaved people from another estate owner: they included six girls (Bell, Dinah, Jeaney, Aga, Peggy and Lucy) and eight boys (Pompey, Ned, Joe, Bob, Hugh, Damon, Isaac and Turpen).[527] His slaves on one site were recorded in 1783. There were 96 working men and women (including a tar burner, a carpenter, a gardener, a 'squarer', two carters, eight sawyers, four coopers, a driver, 44 turpentine and field labourers, a midwife and thirty one young men and women), 32 boys and girls employed in light labour and 11 men and women unable to work. They produced turpentine, rice, maize, rye and indigo and tended cattle, sheep and pigs. In a good year the citrus orchards produced 1,000 gallons of orange juice.[528]

Detailed calculations were made of the potential productivity of the Higher Plantation in Rolleville: he itemized the profits each enslaved worker contributed in cultivating 24,000 acres of rice, 4,000 acres of maize, 6,000 acres of pasture and 42,000 acres of pine for making turpentine.[529] Rolle may have been endeavouring to provide opportunities for impoverished White workers but his Utopia was dependent upon Black enslavement.

Rolle sought compensation of £24,365 (£1,651,978.67) for the loss of Rollestown and Chichester Plantation and received a lump sum along with a land grant in the Bahamas which the British government aimed to revitalise by bringing in Loyalists from the Carolinas, Georgia and Florida. In the last months of 1783 Rolle founded two settlements, Rolleville and Rolletown, at opposite ends of the island of Great Exuma. He subsequently increased his holdings to 5,000 acres. His plantation boat was named *The Devonshire*.[530]

On the eve of the move to Florida Rolle became apprehensive that his enslaved people would abscond and promised two men 'partial enfranchisement'. This was to encourage the remainder to remain faithful. Rolle had deployed this practice in the colony's early years. In 1769 he wrote that there had to be a safe proportion of White colonists to the slaves who were 'dangerous necessaries in other provinces and in the

▶ 36. Detail of Great Exuma showing plots 4 and 5, of 1,200 acres, and plots 93 and 96, of 775 acres, which belonged to Denys Rolle, drawn by Josiah Tattnall, 1792.

eral

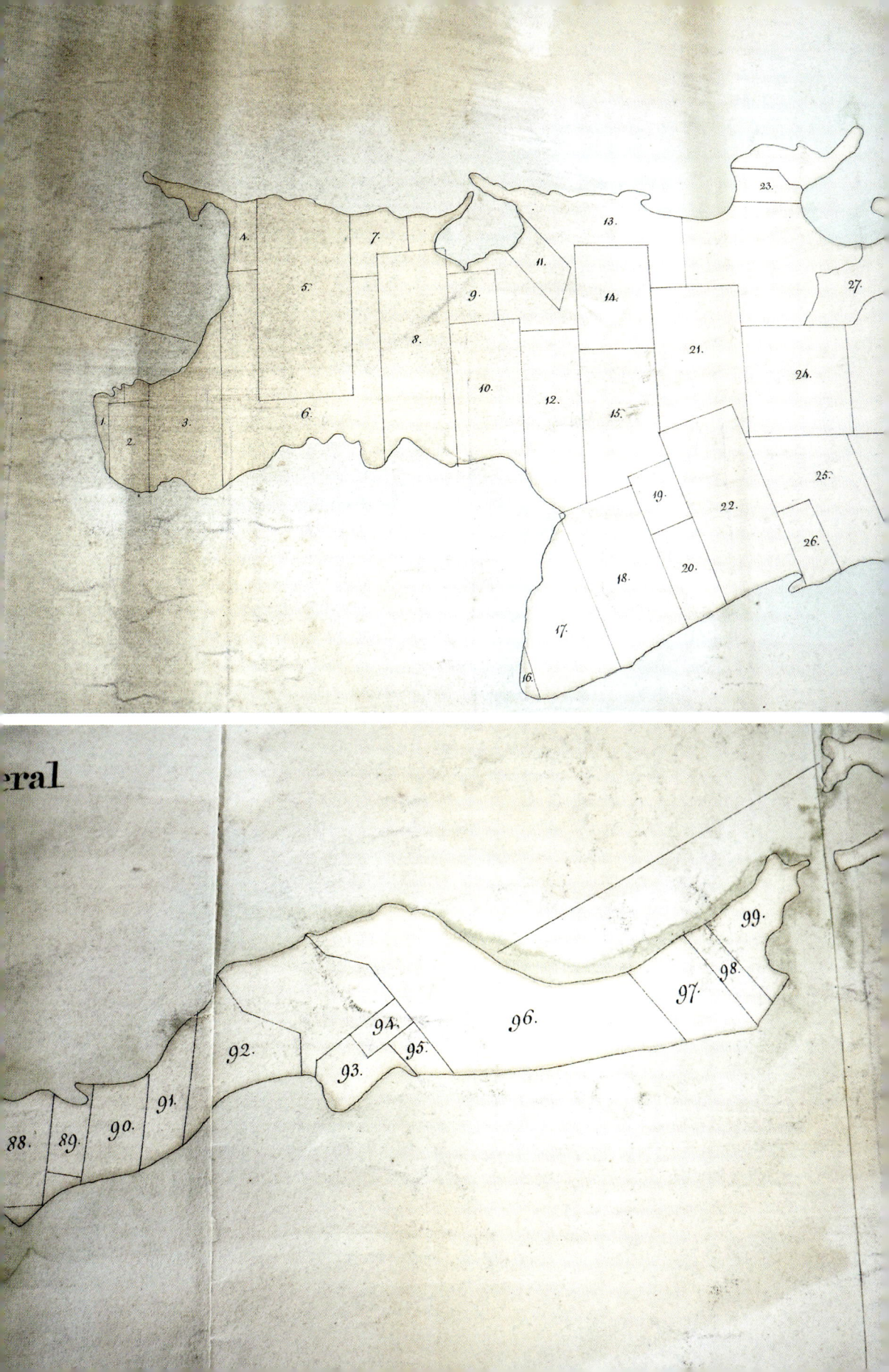

West India islands'. In order for them to 'be converted into useful and safe assistants' he encouraged an:

> 'expectation of liberty as the reward of fidelity which will be given them under certain regulations after a considerable servitude, and of which an example of two who have served longest will be given this year to show the others the happy prospect of British freedom which they are entitled to indeed by birth in their own country but have been deprived of it and enslaved for ever, to serve the greed, the avarice and luxury of the wanton lords of mankind'.[531]

At least ten enslaved people died in transport due to a shortage of water; in 1783 they sailed in the *Peace and Plenty* to the Bahamas but the vessel was delayed by calm and contradictory winds.[532] On 1 November 1785 a survey of the workers at Exuma revealed there were 96 men, women and children. Another 69 were either dead or missing.[533]

Rolle had a difficult financial start to his new Bahamian operation. In about 1791 Rolle explained to King George III at Weymouth that his second crop of cotton was captured, two hurricanes damaged his settlement and his enslaved workers were on short provisions until he was able to circumvent the American trade embargo.[534]

Little more is known of their history until 1794 when a new overseer, George Divine, signed a 'kindness' agreement to work under Benjamin Lord. The undertaking was necessary, it was noted, because newly-arrived English overseers were 'more severe on the slaves' than Creoles or longstanding European residents. Divine undertook:

> 'not on any pretence whatever to inflict any kind of punishment on the Negroes without previously acquainting said Mr Lord therewith the nature of the offence and his orders thereon obtained for such punishment.'[535]

A substantial owner of land and a Member of Parliament for Barnstaple from 1761 to 1774, Rolle was also known for his eccentricities. He sailed steerage on his first voyage to Florida and reportedly slept under a row boat. It was reported in the first years of the colony that he:

> 'constantly continues with settlers, eats very oft as they eat, and drinks as they drink, and lies down very quietly on a bear-skin and takes his repose, which endears him greatly to them'.[536]

Rolle had a passion for natural history with a love of botany and gardening. In 1759 and 1761 he won gold medals from the Society for the Encouragement of Arts, Manufactures and Commerce for planting Scots Pines and Oak trees in Devon.[537] Rolle established a botanical garden 'near' Exmouth, possibly at Bicton, and imported

37. Detail of the statue of John, Lord Rolle, by E. B. Stephens, 1843. ▶

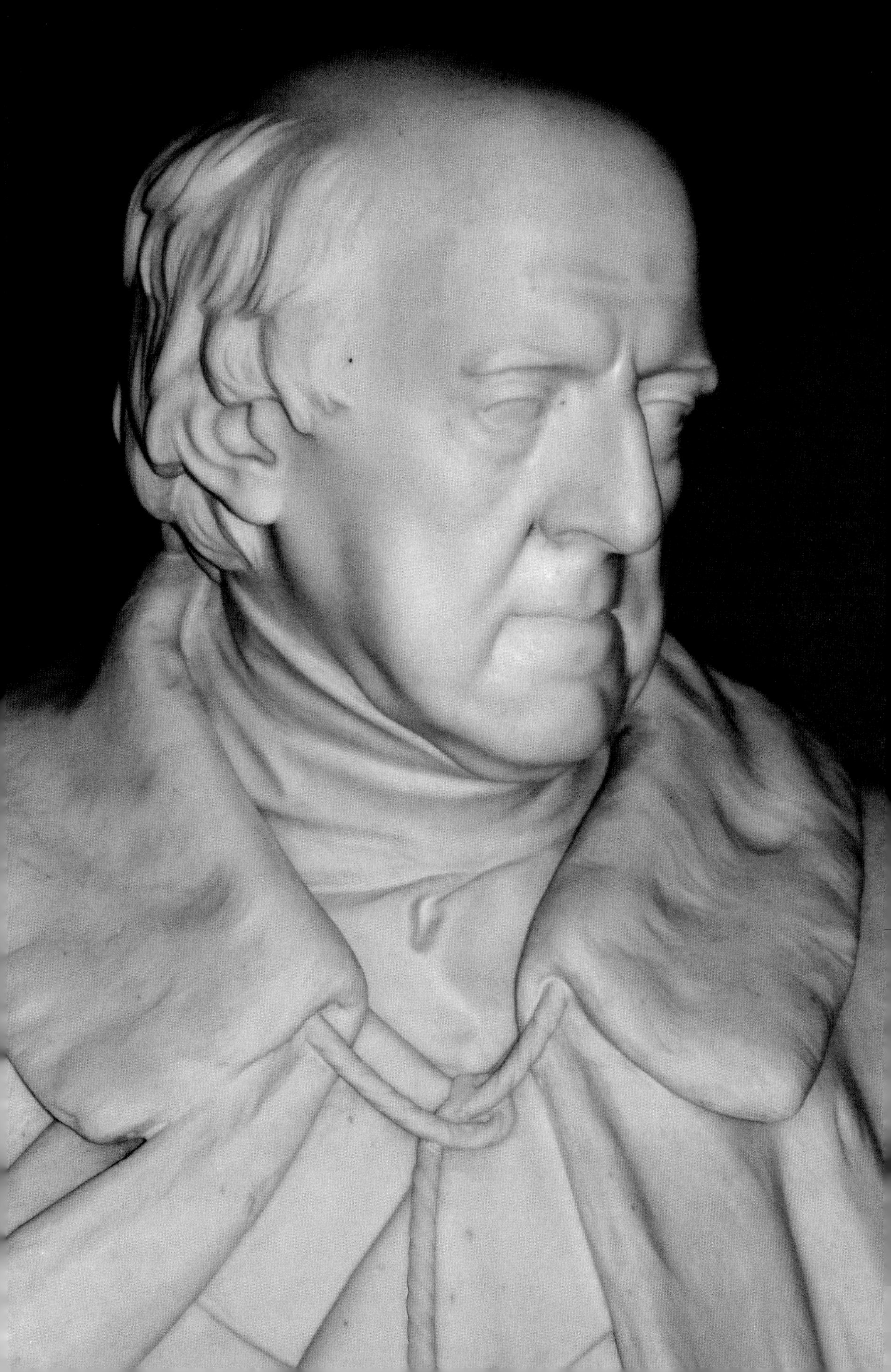

a ship-load of mould from Hounslow in order to grow heathers. He engaged in manual labour: one commentator noted in Florida he had 'a positive delight in the hard tasks of the field labourer'.[538] It was said of him in Devon that Rolle was:

> 'the richest man in Devonshire and yet nothing pleased him more than to do a labourer's work. He would set out early in the morning, bag of provisions and spade on his shoulder, dressed like a peasant and work as hard as any day labourer on his estate.'[539]

Rolle claimed an unusual affinity with animals and recounted stories of attachments formed by stray cats, dogs and horses as well as wild bears, birds and snakes. He died in 1797 whilst on a favourite eight mile walk between his seats of Stevenstone and Hudscott. An obituarist termed him 'a man who lived to God and for the benefit of his fellow-creatures'.[540]

The Great Exhuma estate was inherited by Denys' son John, 1st Baron Rolle, who became known in Devon from 1827 for the Rolle Canal which linked Great Torrington with Bideford but became nationally known on two occasions.

Firstly, in 1784 he was the principal character in *The Rolliad*, a satirical epic poem. In it he was ridiculed for his ancestors, one was 'counted the fattest man of his day' and another 'died of a terrible dysentery', and one passage alleged 'somewhere in the back settlements of America there is now actually existing an illegitimate branch of little Rolles':

> 'Though wide should spread thy spurious race around,
> In other worlds, which must not yet be found,
> While they with savages in forests roam
> Deserted, far from their paternal home.
> A mightier savage in thy wilds Ex-Moor,
> Their well-born brother shall his fate deplore.'

He was mocked for his attempts to be ennobled, which finally occurred in 1796, but the satirical thrust centred on Rolle's support for William Pitt the Younger.[541]

Secondly, Rolle was famous for an accident at the coronation of Queen Victoria in 1838: he tripped and *rolled* down the steps to the throne.

Rolle, like his father, was active in Parliament where his political opponents called him 'Mr Rigmarolle'. One commentator noted:

> 'nature had denied him all pretention to grace or elegance. Neither was his understanding more cultivated than his manners refined. He reminded me always of a Devonshire rustic but he possessed plain common sense, a manly mind and the faculty of stating his ideas in a few strong words'.[542]

He represented the County of Devon from 1780 to 1796. In 1796 he commented to a friend 'the Bill for the Abolition of the Slaves will pass our House, but will meet with greater opposition in the other'.[543] It may have been in aid of John Rolle becoming one of the Members of Parliament to represent Devon that his father Denys spent £1,700 (£130,493.87) in 1790.[544] A contemporary observed the bribery that year which in Exeter had its own term:

> 'The pernicious practice of *quilling* then commenced, and was continued with very few intervals until the month of June following, attended with an enormous expense to the candidates and with more injury than benefit to the electors.'[545]

Rolle did not visit his Bahamian estate but was an absentee owner. He employed an attorney in Nassau and an agent in Great Exhuma. In 1825 Rolle owned 288 slaves including two men called Farewell and three named January. They were increasingly left to their own devices possibly because of Denys Rolle's undertaking in 1783 to make them semi-independent. It may also have been due to the economic unviability of the estate: the main cash crop, cotton, failed across the Bahamas in the 1780s and Rolle admitted in parliament that since his father's death the estate had cost him between £400 and £500 annually. In one ten-year period he received £130 in revenue but spent £5,000 (£339,006.50). This was greater than his later emancipation award of £4,333 6s 9d (£293,805.92).[546] Rolle was also obliged to pay poll taxes on the enslaved: three shillings (£10.17) were annually due for each man and woman. In 1834 Rolle owed payments of £28 2s 3d (£1,906.06) and asserted that his island was exempt. Rolle was the largest landowner who refused to pay the tax.[547]

It was because of his reputation as a wealthy man that he was lambasted in a Devon newspaper for taking emancipation money in 1836.

> 'Poor Lord Rolle! he could not even abate the nine pennyworth of slavery but took the odd coppers to the utmost farthing. We suppose the nine pennyworth of freedom belonged to some happy piccaninny whose birth was to take place and so its liberty, Lord Rolle's munificence, was awaiting its arrival on earth.'[548]

For more than a decade before emancipation Rolle attempted to extricate himself from his financial losses by freeing his workers but was thwarted by the establishment. He was encumbered by Bahamian law in making his workforce completely free. In 1784, when his settlement began on Great Exuma, a tax of £90 (£7,749.41) was imposed on each manumission. This continued until 1827. Partial freedom may have been a means of circumventing this fee.[549]

The Rolle policy of partial freedom coincided with other Bahamian landowners' inability to deploy their enslaved in profitable work. Instead their workforces were expected to be self-sufficient; their working days were spent engaged in food production. In 1824 one commentator noted that the owners faced economic ruin whereas for the slaves:

> 'the effects have been ease, plenty, health and the preservation and increase of their numbers by native means, all in a degree quite beyond example in any other part of the West Indies'.[550]

Some Bahamian landowners responded to the agricultural crisis by transferring some 2,000 enslaved people to other West Indian islands. Between 1825 and 1828 Rolle also considered moving his workers to Trinidad, Cuba, Jamaica or Demerara. In 1825 he argued that he had spent £4,777 15s 4d for their maintenance in the previous seven years, that there was no viable means of making a profit in the Bahamas and that the slaves' removal to another colony would:

> 'promote the comfort and happiness of the slaves as well as render justice to your memorialist who seeks only to be relieved from an unreasonable burden accidentally devolved upon him under circumstances not within his control'.[551]

He also proposed to free his slaves once they earned in Trinidad their purchase price but in 1829 they refused to relocate. Their views were immaterial given the Colonial Office would not sanction the plan. Rolle instead moved sixty-one Bahamians to other islands in the Bahamas.[552] At that time they were 'in a state of great excitement' because it had been intimated to them that Rolle would punish any slave 'in a moderate and very limited degree' whose negligence or indolence had contributed to the financial losses of his Bahamian estate.[553]

The islands' governor wrote to the colonial secretary in 1828 that 'the prevailing opinion' among the enslaved was that Denys Rolle had provided safeguards for them in his will of 1797. Governor Grant wrote the enslaved believed:

> 'that they should never be sold or separated or otherwise severely dealt with. They themselves have this impression, and for many years it has been much confirmed in many quarters by the extraordinary indulgent treatment they have received in having their labour chiefly applied to their private benefit while the expense of their maintenance, etc. was supplied by Lord Rolle.'

Rolle's workforce went on strike and the agent reported

> 'they say they want the land to maintain themselves and they won't be flogged by any white man, neither will they remove from this place'.[554]

A subsequent plan involved relocating seventy-seven slaves from Great Exuma to Cat Island. The pretence was that the enslaved were being deployed to another of Rolle's plantations but in fact they were to be loaned to a different estate owner. This embroiled Rolle in scandal. In 1830 newspapers across England reprinted an Antiguan report alleging brutality. In the summer of 1830 forty-four men and women sailed for Nassau to testify to the governor but were intercepted, charged as runaways and severely punished. Five men were publicly given 50 lashes each while a boy and

▶ 38. A statue erected to Pompey at Great Exuma in about 2011. The statue is unusual not only in that it is golden but that another to Pompey was subsequently placed near it.

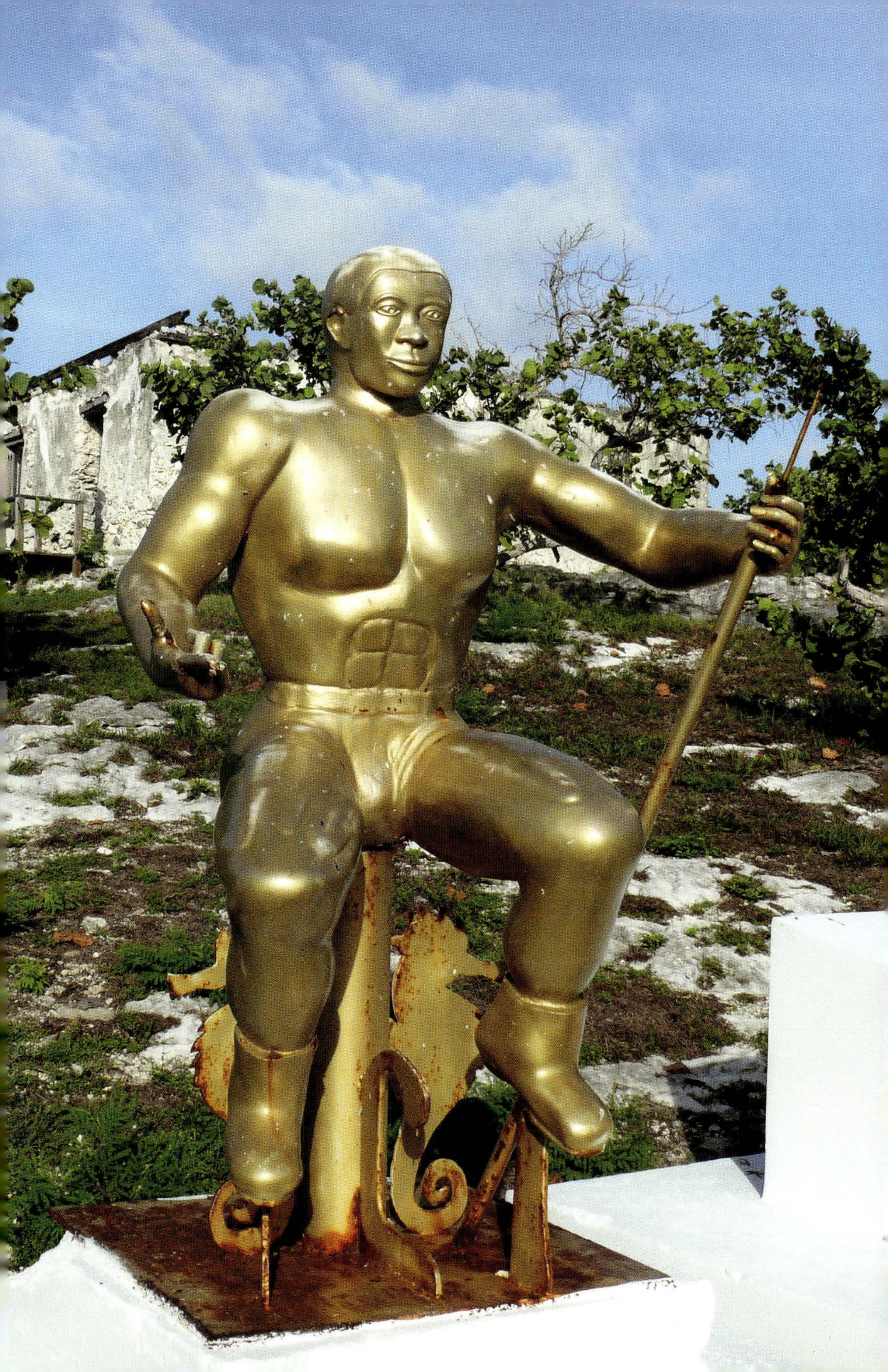

8 women had 39 lashes in the workhouse. Two of the women were nursing babies and a third was pregnant.

The due process of law regarding removals to other islands had not been followed and the agent, who was also a legislator, and three justices were deprived of their offices.[555]

When the slaves returned to Exuma they went on strike. Troops were deployed and thirty-nine lashes were given to the leader, Pompey. Two statues have recently been erected in his honour and a Nassau museum is named after him.[556] He was probably the man of that name listed as belonging to Rolle in 1831; he was a Creole born in about 1798.[557]

A Devon journalist reported the incident in order that:

> 'Lord Rolle may see to what treatment his poor slaves are subjected from his agents. We know his Lordship is not a reformer, but judging from his known humanity, we hope for once he will venture across the Atlantic and set the captives free'.[558]

The governor determined that the treatment was inhuman, unmanly, disgraceful and a 'brutal outrage upon humanity'.[559] Three years later the incident was cited in parliament.[560]

There was a war of attrition between owner and enslaved in 1833 and 1834. In 1833 another strike was prompted by insufficient provisions and in 1834 the governor sent troops three times to restore order.[561] In 1834, when Rolle intervened in the parliamentary debate over emancipation, he 'called the attention of ministers to the state of the Bahama Island where the slaves had refused to work'. Moreover, he complained he was financially responsible for their full maintenance despite they only worked for him part-time.[562]

A Devon journalist commented:

> 'It seems that Lord Rolle was himself a slave-owner, a matter not very generally known before, and we feel we may almost suspect not very well known to his Lordship himself, for when asked more than once in what island the property was situated, Lord Rolle said he obtained the plantation from his father in 1797, and that appeared to be all he knew about it. For his lordship's information we may state that it is in one of the Bahamas. But to the point, his Lordship stated that he had just received a demand for £1,000, which we understood was for the purposes of providing food and clothing for the poor slaves from whose labour his Lordship under the blessings of the cart whip, has perhaps annually received considerable remittances, or consignments of produce. We would ask Lord Rolle whether this £1,000 was not remitted in the common course of dealing. If the produce be sent to England for sale, is it not necessary out of its proceeds to make remittances to the agents to maintain the slaves and we would further ask whether his Lordship's plantations are under the best management, and whether this ought not to have been remitted some time before? And whether it not probable that the want of sustenance, which the delay of remittances occasioned, was not the cause of the insurrection among the slaves of which his Lordship complains; and that it was

in no respect attributed to the abolition act. It might not be worth his Lordship's while to make these enquiries. But Lord Rolle should not adduce charges against the policy of this great measure, without first ascertaining these facts. If Lord Rolle's slaves were brought to Bicton, their situation we know would be quite different. But it is one of the curses of the slave system, that a benevolent proprietor in England, might through his agent, become the indirect cause of as great cruelty as can disgrace human nature. Acts might be committed on the plantation at which Lord Rolle would shudder.'[563]

Rolle had said 'If I did not pay this bill the Negroes must starve – work they will not'.[564]

The incident inspired an Exeter poet:

My good Lord Rolle, I needs much say,
Sans profit from the 'Cane',
A thousand pounds for *Corn* to pay,
Is much – *against the Grain*![565]

The legal status of slaves in the Bahamas had been set out in the 1820s. Rolle was obliged to provide every enslaved person over the age of ten a peck of unground corn each week and with two suits of 'proper and sufficient clothing' every year. They were also entitled to land for a dwelling and garden. Aged and infirm slaves could be given their freedom but their former owners remained responsible for their maintenance.[566]

In 1838 Rolle presented a Devon petition to parliament calling for the immediate cessation of slave apprenticeship.[567] That year, on 1 August, he released his workers from their last year of apprenticeship. He said in parliament that he was unable to reconcile slavery with his conscience and now had the satisfaction of 'seeing them industrious, happy, contented and able to support themselves'.[568]

In addition to the moral consideration, this ended for Rolle a longstanding financial loss while for the enslaved it was a means of gaining full and early liberty. One historian has argued that 'by their uncooperative behaviour and actual resistance the slaves of Lord Rolle ostensibly won independence and land for themselves'.[569]

There is a tradition in the Bahamas that the enslaved were deeded Rolle's land in perpetual commonage. This was publicly acknowledged in 1838 when Rolle was praised for 'giving them in addition the free possession of all his lands, ships, implements of husbandry etc. without exacting or expecting any return but their gratitude'.[570] Five Lord John Rolle Commonage Estates continue on Exuma: Rolle Town, Rolleville, Steventon, Ramsey and Mount Thompson are protected by law and cannot be sold.

In 1838 an Exeter man received a letter from the Bahamas which stated that the former slaves:

'cannot thank their dear master sufficiently for his manifold kindnesses, and that they endeavour to bring up their children Christianly, virtuously, and industriously, so that they may be a credit to society and further to instil into their minds that they owe a part of their existence to their benevolent patron as they cannot hope ever to meet him in this transitory world, they sincerely pray that the great Redeemer, who only knows their hearts, will permit them to meet him, their affectionate master, in a happier world above'.[571]

The land transference had been made four years earlier. In the autumn of 1834 Rolle's agent spent a fortnight on Exuma finalising the details. Mr Lees had emancipated the workers, divided up the land amongst them and instituted a rental of two shillings per acre. The fee covered the annual quit-rent, a nominal fee paid by those living on land granted by the Crown, and it covered the maintenance costs of eight elderly former slaves. In that deal the land remained in Rolle's ownership. A number of senior men were appointed to act as a self-governing council. Cattle and other property was sold for the financial benefit of Rolle. Lees concluded:

'You have made upward of 300 people happy and contented, and you have saved yourself from immense expenditure and infinite vexation and the government here from continual trouble and annoyance.'

Earlier that year Rolle had written:

'I am induced to send out instructions to discharge my Negroes from their apprenticeship but first to request through you the cooperation of government. My instructions would be in my power of attorney… to convey the lands for the use of the Negroes during their apprenticeship'.

This was apparently rejected by the governor but instituted by Rolle a few months later.[572]

The decision to give the land had been anticipated a generation earlier. In 1792 a cleric wrote:

'A gentleman who has brought a good many Indians from the Mosquito shore to Cat Island wants to have them baptised, but I have hitherto deferred it because they have had very little religious instruction. This gentleman (who is 70 years of age) having no relations by blood, intends to give all his Indians freedom by his last will, and likewise to divide his property among them. At present he lets them live in too easy and indolent a way, which they feel the bad effects of, if they should ever have their freedom without property'.[573]

▶ 39. Photograph of Alexander Rolle of Old Blight, Cat Island, the Bahamas, taken 1935. His father or grandfather may have been one of the enslaved people on the Rolle estate.

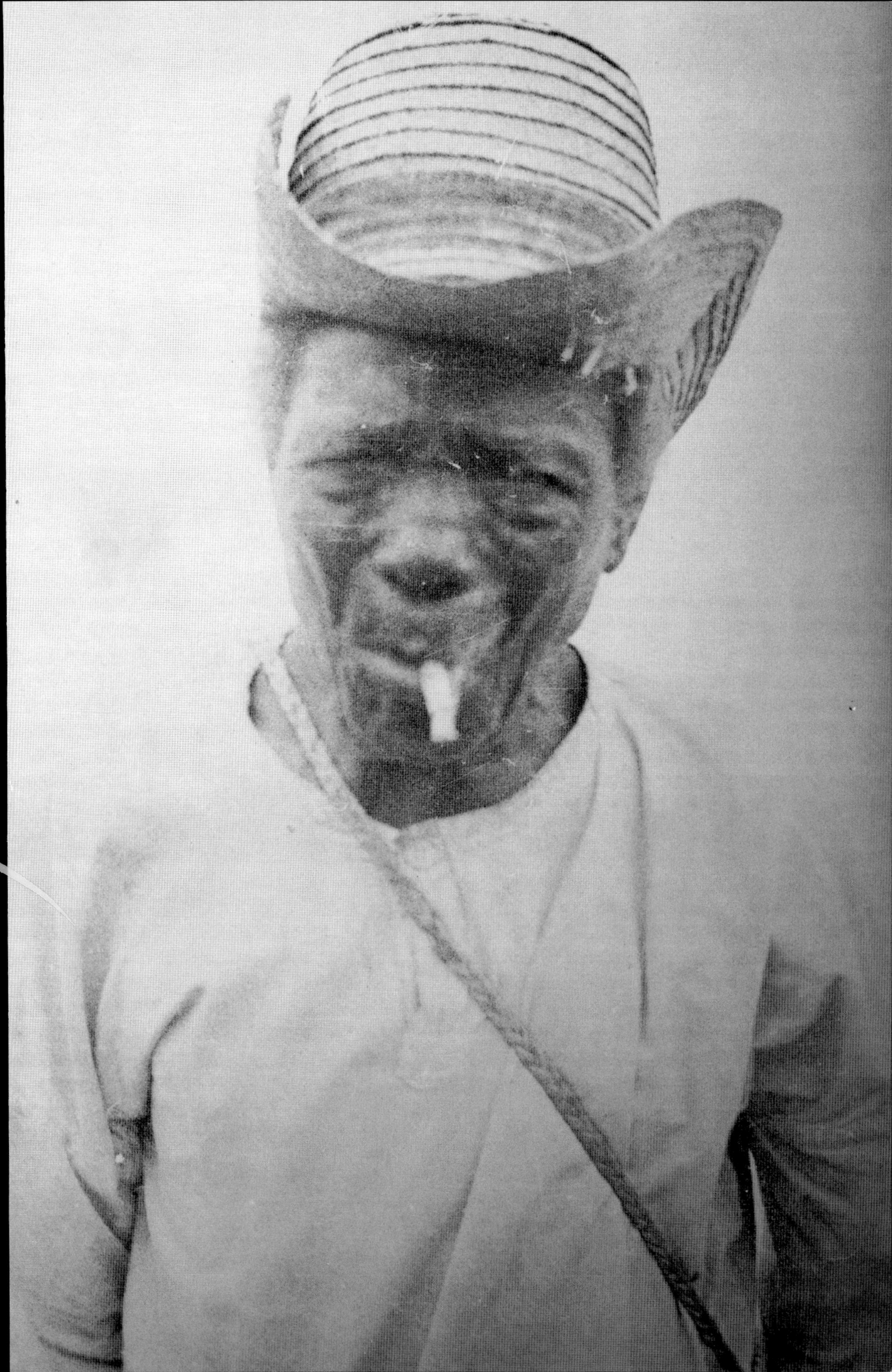

In 1887 a visitor remarked upon the prevalence of the Rolle surname:

> 'All the beneficiaries of course adopted the name of Rolle as a surname and the consequence is Rolles swarm all over the colony and it is impossible to get a dozen coloured people together without finding a Rolle or two among them'.[574] Some had taken the surname as early as 1825.[575]

Following emancipation it was believed that those men and women with the surname Rolle could claim land.[576]

Lord Rolle was childless when he died in 1842 and his surname was adopted by his heir, Mark Trefusis, his second wife's nephew but he had no sons and his line died out in 1907. One curious legacy of slavery is the prevalence of many thousands of Rolles on one side of the Atlantic.

One historian has concluded that 'conditions better than elsewhere in every respect seem to have been enjoyed by the population of slaves' owned by Rolle.[577] A demographic study of his Bahamian workers shows a population increase from 254 in 1822 to 376 in 1834. This has been attributed to 'a fortunate combination of demographic, familial, occupational and locational circumstances', in effect, conditions under Rolle were more benign than in other estates. He had not purchased additional human beings since at least 1784 and it was unusual for numbers to grow without new arrivals. The work conditions, partial freedom and the gift of the Great Exuma land have contributed to Rolle having, it was noted in 1978, 'an almost legendary reputation' for being 'a liberal master'.[578]

The Rolle history demonstrates, among many things, that enslavement was not economically viable in every colony. It illustrates how one wealthy and powerful individual attempted over many years to extricate himself from the institution of slavery but that the establishment only eventually and grudgingly allowed change. The financial difficulties estate owners had in the Bahamas were unusual and Rolle was an atypical Devonian. Even so, few others have left as rich a paper trail which allows not only an examination of the man himself but opens up comparisons with all of Devon's other slaveholders.

5

Devon's veiled slave-owners

'We cannot escape history',
Abraham Lincoln, message to Congress, 1 December 1862

While forty-three individuals have been identified who were resident in Devon in the late 1830s, received compensation and were agents or beneficiaries, this chapter examines others who were involved through other financial or legal associations with plantations and in some instances had priority over owners. The number in both groups is comparable. Some of course had multiple claims of differing kinds. Twenty-three individuals were agents acting on behalf of others; they comprised 10 executors, 1 executrix, 12 trustees and 1 sequestrator. Another eighteen individuals were beneficiaries in that they either had lent credit to slaveholders or were gifted financial sums by slave-owners. This group included 1 legatee, 1 mortgagee-in-possession, 8 mortgagees, 4 annuitants, 2 assignees and 5 judgement creditors. Biographical histories of each appear in one of the categories in which they were classed.

AGENTS: EXECUTORS, EXECUTRIX, TRUSTEES AND SEQUESTRATORS

Twenty-three men and women received twenty-four awards while legally acting on the behalf of others.

Executors and executrix

The following six individuals, along with William Bovell, Robert Houstoun, William Brooks King, Emanuel Lousada and Thomas Teschemaker who had multiple claims in different capacities, were compensated while acting in probate as executors of estates; the writer of a will had appointed them to carry out his or her wishes.

John Dennis Burdon, Kenton

Burdon received £1,946 9s 10d (£131,974.67) for the loss of 109 Jamaicans on the Vauxhall Estate. They were owned by Elizabeth Smyth who died aged 89 in Lympstone in 1833 before the compensation scheme.[579] The beneficiaries were Smyth's family members. She came from Devon and in her will of 1831 described herself as being 'of Exeter'. Despite living much of her life in the West Indies, she and her deceased husband, Jamaican-born Francis George Smyth, also had ties with Barnstaple and Northam where some of his children from a first marriage were born. The couple appear to have crossed the Atlantic on a number of occasions but it was in Exeter that Mrs Smyth died. The main beneficiary of her will was her daughter Federata, the wife of James Rodd who by 1841 lived at 'the Town House' in Doddiscombsleigh. Elizabeth Smyth was related to the Burdon families through a marriage with a member of the Rodd family.[580]

Frances Dent née Sanders, Stoke Damerel

Dent, born in St Kitts, inherited from her sister. She had married Digby Dent, the son of Rear Admiral Sir Digby Dent, on the island in 1786 and the couple subsequently lived in Plymouth near the dockyard in Stoke Damerel. Their six children were born there. Mrs Dent remained in Plymouth after her husband's death at the age of 34 in 1798. Her son Douglas lived at 88 Navy Row in 1830 and in 1841 she was the head of the household at Officer's Row, Dockyards. Ten years later she was living at 17 James Terrace, also in Stoke, with her son. Mrs Dent died at Wyndham Place in 1856. She had inherited a share in the Grove Estate as the heir of Mary Butler and received £711 8s (£48,233.84) in compensation in 1836.[581]

John Campbell Fisher, Merton and Harpford

Reverend Fisher was born in Somerset and served as the rector of Merton and Harpford by 1835 through to the early 1850s. He then moved to Exmouth but died in Somerset in 1855.

In 1836, while at Merton, Fisher received £6,571 9s 10d (£445,555.68) owed to him, as executor of a judgement creditor, from his maternal grandfather's estate which included two Jamaican plantations. One of these was Luana Pen and in 1822 Fisher's manager purchased Letitia from the workhouse: she was described as 'a Coromantee, 4 feet 10 inches, marked [branded] LH diamond between, has a scar round the small of her right leg'.[582] Fisher's father, John Fisher, also received two compensation awards.

Joseph Graham, Stonehouse

Graham, a naval captain, was possibly born in Trinidad where he married his wife Jane in 1826. By 1837 he was living at 24 East Emma Place in Stonehouse but left 'the neighbourhood' the following year. In 1840 he claimed compensation of £54 3s 10d (£3,674.27) for a single slave owned by Richard Jameson.[583]

Henry Phillpotts, Exeter

In 1835 Henry Phillpotts, Bishop of Exeter, received over £12,000 (£813,615.60) as executor of John William Ward, Earl of Dudley. An incautious use of the printed accounts, before the online Legacies of British Slave-Ownership project, led to his being named as a slave-owner. In 2006 the issue was raised in Parliament and the then current bishop was asked to apologise on his behalf. It was even widely claimed that the Church of England had enslaved people. Phillpotts had a second slavery connection in that his brother Thomas received part of the compensation of more than £12,000 for ten estates. Until 1838 Bishop Phillpotts did not feel that the enslaved should be freed: he admitted in Parliament that his opinion was that they would not be able to accommodate themselves to freedom.[584]

James King Went, Teignmouth

Reverend Went was born in Barbados and after graduating from Cambridge spent his clerical career on the island and married Elizabeth Ann Clinton. By 1861 they emigrated to England and took up residence in Paddington. Within four years he moved to St Mary's Lodge at Reed Vale in West Teignmouth. He lived there until his death in 1886.[585] Went inherited interests in four plantations in Barbados for which, as an executor, he received £1,438 18s 4d (£97,560.42) in compensation, including for Thurban and Chimborazo Estates, as well as £1,790 9s 8d (£121,397.10) for a further 80 individuals on Thorpe Cottage Estate. In 1829 and 1832 Mrs Went owned three enslaved people in her own right. In 1871 Went's son, James King Junior, married into the Alleyne family, Barbadian slaveholders who had moved to Devon.[586]

Trustees

Seven individuals, as well as James Cunningham, Thomas Hall, Henry Adolphus Hawkins, William Brooks King and Henry George Windsor who also received compensation in other capacities, received awards while acting as trustees.

Eliza Jane Addison née Prentice, Exmouth

Addison acted as a trustee or guardian for her daughters in claiming compensation of £34 19s (£2,369.66) for three enslaved Barbadians. She lived a transient life in accompanying her husband, General Joseph Addison, across the country in his military career. She had moved from Switzerland to 14 The Beacon in Exmouth shortly before her death on Christmas Day, 1900.[587]

John Dicker Inglett Fortescue, Buckland Filleigh and Dawlish

Fortescue acquired his surname through his grandfather Richard Inglett, the collector of customs at Dawlish, who in 1776 changed his name in the right of his mother, Rebecca Fortescue. He was heir to a considerable estate through his maternal grandmother. In 1837 Fortescue was successful as a trustee in obtaining £2,468 8s 8d (£167,362.99) for 124 Jamaicans on the Morgan's Valley Estate but unsuccessful in a second claim for 88 individuals on the Hope Estate in St Vincent. He was born in Dawlish in 1807 and moved to Cornwall after he sold his father's mansion at Buckland Filleigh in 1843.[588]

Francis Glanville, Egg Buckland

Glanville was probably one of the four trustees for Jasper Taylor Hall, a Jamaican and absentee slaveholder. In 1835 Glanville, a Cornishman, claimed £5,842 13s 2d (£396,139.83) possibly as part of a marriage settlement. Glanville lived in Egg Buckland in 1851.[589]

Samuel Trehawke Kekewich, Alphington

Kekewich was a trustee for Mary D'Urban of Topsham when in 1836 he handled her claim for £3,013 12s 7d (£204,327.98) for the loss of 113 individuals in Grenada. As an Exeter MP from 1826 to 1830 he had voted against the emancipation of Jews, favoured Catholic suffrage but in respect to slavery he was 'not opposed in principle to the extinction of slavery'.[590]

Samuel Parr, Clyst St George

Parr worked alongside Kekewich for Mary D'Urban and lived in Clyst St George at Knowle, now the headquarters of the Devon & Somerset Fire and Rescue Service. He was born in Exeter but died in 1858 shortly after moving to Lowestoft.[591]

John James Scott, Lynton

Reverend Scott, discussed more fully later, had a Jamaican award of £212 15s 2d (£14,425.29) as a trustee for Henry Cussens Scott but was unsuccessful in two further claims for £6,501 16s 11d (£440,833.60) because of an existing annuity granted to his mother by his father.

Constantine Estwick Trent, Stonehouse

Trent, born in Dorset, resided in Stonehouse by 6 June 1841 when the census enumerator recorded him as 'of independent means' and living in a boarding house in Durnford Street. He had served in the 14th Light Dragoons but in 1827 received a substantial bequest from Harrison Walke Sober, a Southampton owner of three estates in Barbados. Trent was one of his three trustees and executors, who received compensation on Sober's behalf in 1836, and died four years later in Stonehouse.[592]

Sequestrators

Devon's single sequestrator, the individual responsible to the court for the protection of an estate's assets, was John Lane who died in Paignton in 1860. His death notice recorded he was 'late of Demerara' but no other personal information was given other than that he was aged 62, lived at Gerston Terrace and was 'much respected'. He was probably the attorney of that name who was active in British Guiana from the 1830s through into the 1850s. Lane was the sequestrator for the Henrietta estate and in 1836 claimed compensation for a second estate of £325 16s 4d (£22,090.79) for five individuals.

Lane appears to have arrived in Paignton shortly before he died but had earlier local ties. In the 1820s he was the attorney in Demerara for Exeter-born Hugh Mill Bunbury, owner of the Devonshire and Devonshire Castle Estates.[593]

BENEFICIARIES: LEGATEES, MORTGAGEES, ANNUITANTS, ASSIGNEES AND JUDGEMENT CREDITORS

Eighteen Devon-associated enslavers benefitted in that their compensation claims came from having lent credit to slave-owners or had been left financial legacies.

Legatees

Devon had one legatee. Reverend John James Scott had an award for more than £800 but was unsuccessful in two further claims for £6,501 16s 11d (£440,833.60) because of an existing annuity granted to his mother by his father. Hinds Howell, failed to receive a compensation award through a legacy to his wife from her father. He had claimed for £242 14s 10d (£16,458.20) for 13 individuals in Barbados.

Mortgagees

Eight individuals had underwritten an estate by lending funds at interest in exchange for taking title of the debtor's property. They had prior claims for compensation awards. One of them was Miss Martha Euphemia Wilson who in August 1839 noted in her will that she was 'at present residing in Teignmouth'. She subsequently returned to London where she had been raised after leaving Tobago as a child. In 1798 she inherited from her Scottish father a plantation for which she received, as a mortgagee, £819 10s 2d (£55,563.74) in compensation for the loss of 40 individuals. She was then, in 1836, living in London. Her connection with Teignmouth appears to have been brief.[594]

John Anderson, John Nelson Bond, James Lee Brodbelt and Thomas Daniel were mortgagees but also had other types of compensation claims. John Bent, George Cole and George Pearse are discussed separately.

Annuitants

Four annuitants, three of them women, lived in Devon at various times in their lives. They received an annual income which had been secured from an estate via a marriage settlement or will.

Elizabeth Vidal née Allwood of Bishop's Tawton was one. She was born in Jamaica in 1774 and came to North Devon by 1840; the following year the census recorded her living at Newport Row in Bishop's Tawton. Ten years later she was a lodger in a neighbour's home and died there in 1858. By 1821 she had emigrated to England with her husband John James Vidal, an attorney, and they initially settled at Clifton outside Bristol where he died in 1823.[595] He was given an unusually long obituary:

> 'to the inexpressible grief of his disconsolate widow, his family and friends, John James Vidal, Esquire, who, by his irreproachable conduct and character, his suavity and mildness of manners, had acquired the esteem of all who had the pleasure of his acquaintance. Until the last few years this gentleman resided in the island of Jamaica and was formerly representative in the honourable House of Assembly for the parish of St Thomas in the Vale, and a judge of the Supreme Court of Judicature in that island, universally beloved, esteemed and respected'.[596]

Three years later Mrs Vidal moved out of their Bristol home. Her wealth is indicated by the luxurious household contents that were sold. These included:

> 'lofty and richly carved mahogany four post and tent bedsteads, with moreen and chintz furniture, and window curtains to correspond, sets of superior mahogany Trafalgar drawing room and dining parlour chairs, with Grecian sofa and couches to match'.[597]

Mrs Vidal's future husband saved her life in 1780 when a hurricane struck Jamaica. A journalist wrote that:

> 'No pen can describe the horrors of the scene which the morning presented to the sight of the few who survived to lament the fate of their wretched neighbours; the earth strewed with the mangled bodies of the dead and dying, some with broken limbs, who, in that situation, had been tossed about during the storm, and afterwards left on the wet, naked earth, to languish out the night in agonies, with no hand to help, or eye to pity them. Humanity recoils at the contemplation of such unheard of calamities; and every feeling heart must melt at the bare recital!'[598]

According to family tradition the seventeen-year-old Vidal rescued his six-year-old cousin. In one account he helped her 'cling to a spar when the tidal wave engulfed their house' and in another she and her two brothers 'were saved by their faithful Black nurse who, with the help of another slave, rushed them up to higher ground as the waters rose'. Vidal married her eleven years later.

In 1817 her enslaved people on one estate were listed as comprising four individuals, each was described as either a 'Creole' or 'Negro'; they were Peter, aged 21, Luna, 25, Rosina, 25 and Frances, 3 months old.[599] Mrs Vidal did not collect compensation for the 143 Jamaicans on her husband's Berkshire Hall estate because she had an agreed annuity. In 1836, when she made her initial claim, Mrs Vidal was living at Ideford near Newton Abbot with her son, Reverend Francis Vidal, who had been appointed curate two years earlier. In 1835 he had married Mary Theresa Johnson of Great Torrington and the couple sailed to Australia in 1839 for missionary work. It was at this time that Elizabeth Vidal moved to North Devon. She spent nearly twenty years of her life in the county. She may have been the Mrs Vidal who in 1838 was a member of the Exeter Branch of the Ladies' Society for promoting the early education and improvement of the children of Negroes and of People of Colour in the British West Indies.[600]

The remaining annuitants, Rebecca Ann Weekes of Sidmouth, John Campbell of Budleigh Salterton and Hannah Barnes of Dawlish, are discussed elsewhere.

Assignees

Two men who lived in Devon claimed compensation because, as assignees, they had a financial claim on a slave-owner and the debt had been legally made over to them. One was successful.

In 1836 Richard Collins was granted £4,821 7s 7d (£326,895.78) for 247 Jamaicans on the Mount Moses estate. The coffee plantation had been owned by Reverend Edward Marshall who had been born in Exeter and became rector of Kingston on the island. He died in about 1822 and presumably owed a debt to Collins who was noted as being 'of Exeter'. This may have been the merchant of that name who lived in Southernhay and was aged 86 in 1836. His obituary noted eleven years later that:

> 'He was one of the oldest inhabitants of this city and his kindness of disposition and straight-forward uprightness of character had earned him the respect and esteem of an extended circle of friends'.[601]

In 1836 Nicholas Russell Garner was unsuccessful in two claims for 49 people in Barbados part of which he had argued was due to him through a mortgage in 1825 but received through another claim £1,119 10s 6d (£75,905.25) for 56 enslaved people on the Vineyard estate in Barbados. Less than a year later Garner died in London of influenza. He had lived in Budleigh Salterton from at least 1830.[602]

Judgement creditors

Five individuals (James Lee Brodbelt, James Cunningham, Thomas Daniel, Emanuel Lousada and Robert Semple) who lived in Devon secured debts on slave estates through court judgements. They had priority in compensation claims. One who was unsuccessful was the widow of John Upham, a merchant and insurance broker in

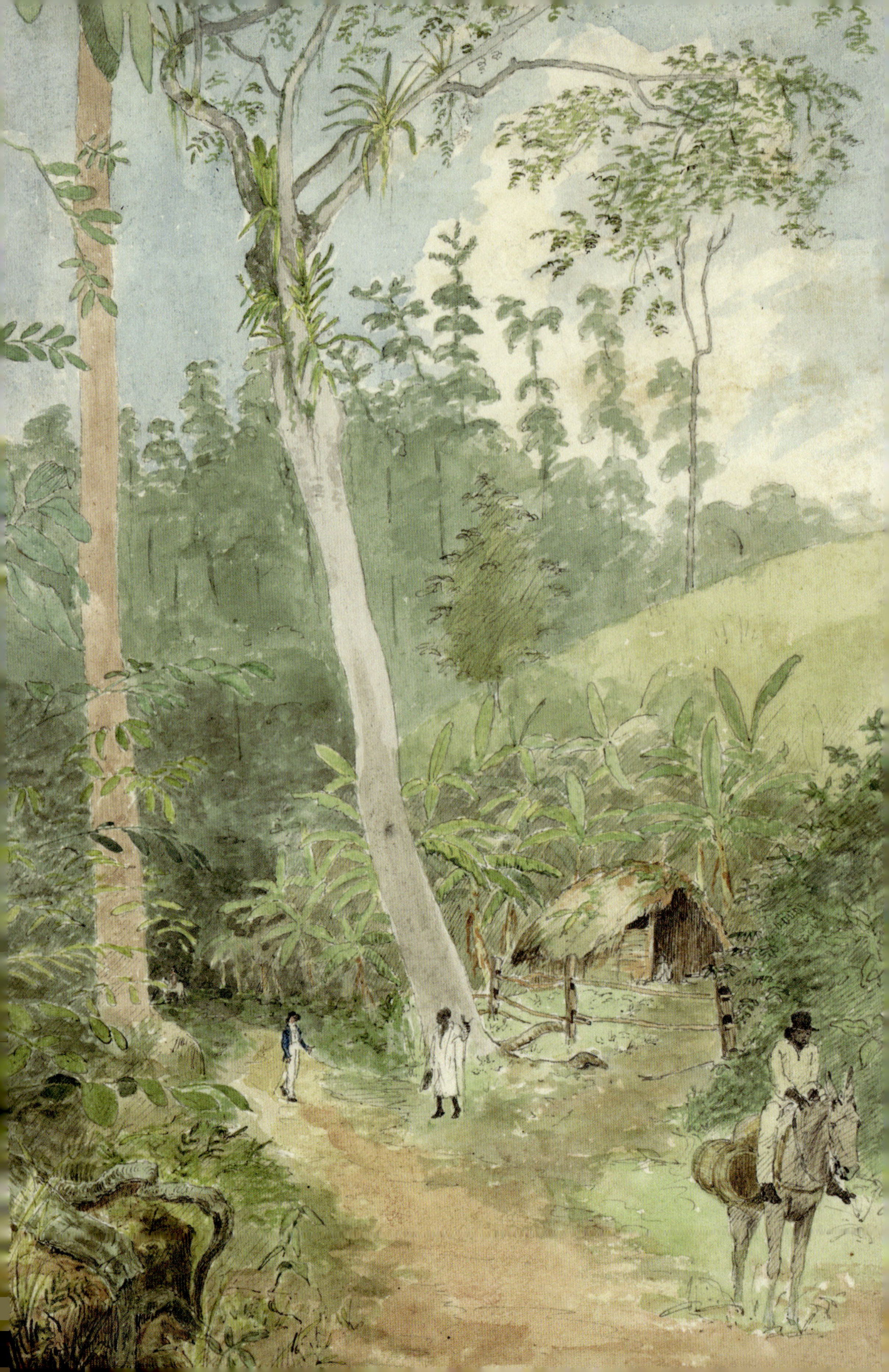

London and Jamaica in the 1790s and early 1800s. He died in 1813 having been married to Anne Rogers for only seven years. By 1828 she had moved to Exeter where she lived immediately outside Rougemont Castle at Bradninch House. Her house was described as:

> 'that large and convenient family house and premises with a small walled garden behind the same, situate in Bradninch Place … long the residence of Samuel Pierce, solicitor. It is well calculated for the residence of a large and respectable family and also contains a spacious music or drawing room at the back thereof, which was erected at considerable expense by the late proprietor'.[603]

She had moved from Upper Phillimore Place in Kensington which she and her husband may have become familiar with through two other residents. Exonian Thomas Finnimore Sanders was one neighbour and William Jackson, a former Chief Justice of Jamaica, was another.

In 1836 Mrs Upham unsuccessfully claimed, as a judgement creditor to the owner, for compensation of 88 enslaved Jamaicans. She continued to live in Exeter for another ten years: Upham died at Bradninch Place in 1846.[604]

UNSUCCESSFUL CLAIMANTS

A number of other individuals with Devon connections were also unsuccessful in claiming compensation. These individuals were thwarted by pre-existing financial obligations on their estates. One example is Joseph Sleigh, a 'working cutler' from St Thomas outside Exeter, who had hoped to have compensation through Francis Guscott's Jamaican estate but he was too late in his application.[605]

Mary Bucknor Clark née Mowatt, Sidmouth and Bideford

Jamaican-born Clark arrived in Devon following the death of her husband in 1845. By 1851, when she was aged seventy-one, Mrs Clark had moved from London to 2 Denby Place in Sidmouth and then to Springfield Terrace at Bideford where she died aged 88 in 1868. Her husband was the mortgage holder of Berkshire Hall, a Jamaica estate, but was unsuccessful in his claim for compensation which was given as part of an annuity to Elizabeth Vidal of Ideford and Bishop's Tawton.[606]

The Baijer family, Exeter

Baijer Otto Baijer was of Dutch ancestry and was left an Antiguan estate by his father John Otto Baijer of Exeter: he held Otto's Plantation from 1817 to 1834 but withdrew his claim to ownership in 1835. The Baijer family lived at Franklyn House in St

◀ 40. A Jamaican plantain walk by William Berryman, early 1800s.

Thomas through the eighteenth century and into the mid nineteenth. Compensation was paid elsewhere on 208 individuals. In the late eighteenth century, when the Baijer family held estates, there were 133 enslaved people on Lady Cooke's plantation and another 122 on Five Islands plantation.[607]

Clifton Wintringham Loscombe, Exmouth

Bristolian Loscombe and his St Kitts-born wife Maria Frances lived in Exmouth after their marriage there in 1807. They mortgaged their estates in St Kitts and were unsuccessful later in their claims to compensation in 1837. Shortly afterwards the couple moved to Bristol. Their marriage settlement noted two plantations (Endraught and Mon Repos) in Demerara as well as others on St Kitts.[608]

John Nugent Fraser, Exeter

Fraser was born in Exeter in 1807 and he may not have returned to Devon after he entered military service as a teenager. Fraser married in Ireland in 1832, retired in 1839 and emigrated to Jamaica where he was unsuccessful in claiming compensation of £630 17s 1d (£42,772.73) on a claim that his Liverpool-born mother had owned plantations including Chatsworth.[609]

Ann Napier née Stirling, Sidmouth and Exeter

This Scottish widow unsuccessfully claimed compensation for two estates in Tobago through her husband Archibald. She was staying at the Bedford Hotel in in Sidmouth in 1841 but had moved to St Sidwell outside Exeter ten years later. Curiously she was then noted in the census as a lace-maker. Soon afterwards she relocated to Brighton but died in Bristol in 1866.[610]

John Reece, Exeter and Devonport

In 1837 Reece, an annuitant, unsuccessfully applied for compensation for the Thurban estate in Barbados where he had been born in 1795. Reece lived in Somerset in 1837, was in Exeter between 1844 and 1847 and then at 4 Upper Somerset Place in Devonport by 1849 until 1852. In 1851 his household included two female servants. His wife Emma died in 1852 and he subsequently moved to London where he himself died in 1869. The claim for 67 individuals was eventually paid to Reverend James King West of Teignmouth.[611]

William and Eleanor Tringham, Tiverton

In 1851 Commander Tringham brought his family to Tiverton following thirty years' service in the Royal Navy. He had been tried in court for the loss of HM Steam Packet *Spitfire* in 1842 in the West Indies but was honourably discharged. Tringham ended his career serving on the royal yacht. He was on half-pay from 1844 and four years later was in London's Debtor Prison. The court heard how during his naval career Tringham's family had lived in Sheerness and Portsmouth while he also had lodgings in Middlesex.

There are no apparent Devon connections to explain the subsequent move to Tiverton in 1851: Tringham had been born in Jamaica, his wife Eleanor was Welsh and they married in Warwickshire. From at least 1852 the couple rented Franca Villa, the former home of Martin Dunsford, the town's first historian. Two sons were educated at Blundell's and it appears that their daughter composed 'The Tiverton Galope' in 1855. In 1859 Tringham died at the age of fifty-seven and his wife stayed for at least two more years: in 1861 she was noted in the census as a lodger with one daughter at Brunswick House. By 1871 she had moved to London and died that year. The couple had unsuccessfully claimed for an estate in Grenada which had 256 enslaved people. It had been the property of the family of Mrs Tringham's first husband, Henry Tarleton, whose family were Liverpool slave traders and slave-owners.[612]

William Vassall Junior, Berry Pomeroy

When Vassall died aged about 90 at Berry Pomeroy in 1843 it was said he 'was a gentleman beloved and respected by all who knew him'.[613] Seven years before he had unsuccessfully claimed compensation for 198 individuals in Jamaica. He, like his father, William Vassall Senior, was born in Boston in the United States. Vassall Senior was an American Loyalist who emigrated to Surrey at the time of the Revolution. He had owned the Green River estate since 1740 but later it was heavily in debt; in 1805 it was mortgaged for £8,400 (£569,530.92). Vassall Junior lived at Weston House near Totnes from at least 1812.[614] His wife was Anne Bent whose family were Totnesians. They had married into the Farwell family, local people who likewise owned plantations. One of the Bent sisters, Mary, had married George Farwell, a Totnes solicitor, and they also resided at Weston House. Vassall was a witness to their marriage in 1810.[615] Among his enslaved people at the Green River Plantation were two men called Glasgow, another named Green River and there were nearly two hundred other men besides women and children.[616]

Alice Anne Welch née Preston, Lynton and Exmouth

Mrs Welch, born in Ireland, was not entitled to claim on her husband's estate in Jamaica because it had been heavily mortgaged. She had six children with her Jamaican husband Richard and some time after he died in 1809 Mrs Welch moved from Middlesex to Devon. In 1841 she was recorded in the census as living in Lynton with two daughters. Within three years they had moved to 13 Claremont Terrace in Exmouth where Mrs Welch died in 1847 'at an advanced age'. She was 76. It is uncertain why she moved to Devon and lived on both the north and south coasts. Her motivation does not appear to have been connected with her family: her two sons were in the navy and one, Arthur, had died in 1838 after falling off his horse.[617]

Other individuals utilised slave labour but did not own estates. The Jamaican firm of merchant Robert Robertson, for example, was contracted from 1817 to 1829 to provide enslaved people for work in military camps. In 1815 Robertson sailed from Jamaica and less than ten months later he married his former business partner's seventeen-year-old daughter in London. He was aged thirty-nine. She had a dowry of a sixth share in her father's estate worth £400,000 (£27,120,520). Six years later the couple purchased the Auchleeks estate in Perthshire and built a country mansion. They later owned homes in Bath, London, and from 1827, their most prestigious property was Membland in the South Hams. This appears to have been their chief residence and their summers were spent in Scotland. The Devon property, which included nearly two thousand acres, cost £53,400 (£3,620,589.42) and was advertised nationally. The London auction room was said to have been crowded on the day of the sale.[618]

In 1843 the house was offered for rent and had:

> 'on the first floor a drawing room about 35 feet by 17, a dining room and breakfast room and water closets, below which are servants' hall, butler's pantry and housekeeper's room and other necessary offices. On the second floor four principal bedrooms, two dressing rooms and water closet. On the upper floor are three secondary bed chambers, dressing room and nursery and two rooms for servants with water closet'.

In the West Wing were a dairy, cheese room, dairy maid's scullery, lumber room, apple and fruit room, dairy maid's room, and three bedrooms whereas the East Wing had a kitchen, scullery, brew house, laundry, maid's bedroom and two additional bedrooms. The stables accommodated fourteen horses and the coach house held six carriages. The garden was three acres in extent, had brick walls, a pinery, melon beds and hot and green houses.[619]

No reason has been found for Robertson choosing Devon for his fourth home. He was a magistrate in Perthshire as he later became in Devon. He served as High Sheriff of Devon in 1837. Robertson died at his Bath home in 1859 but his widow continued to live in Devon. Membland was sold and she relocated to Torquay where she lived at Parkwood, a villa in Park Hill Road. In 1881, shortly before she died, her household included six servants. By coincidence, the Robertson family's earlier coat of arms features a man shackled in chains.[620]

Dorothy Burke, a widow from Antigua, may have been another slaveholder who no longer owned a plantation. She died in Exeter in 1837 and two years previously received £26 5d (£1,764.25) for two Antiguans. Her husband had been the island's Attorney General and famously lost his composure when addressing the Duke of Clarence in 1787. Mrs Burke appears to have sold his estate in about 1824 before she migrated to England.[621] She was in Exeter from at least June 1836 but possibly not much earlier and was probably residing with her heir, fellow Antiguan Leonora Hankinson Lindsey, the wife of a naval officer who led a peripatetic lifestyle and who had a daughter born in Exeter six months after Mrs Burke died. Capt. Lindsey's family were also slave-owners. Neither Burke or Lindsey were listed in the Exeter directory of 1835.[622]

Part Two: Devon and slave-ownership, 1834

The compensation awards establish that there were many ways of financially benefiting from slave ownership and that this considerably extends the number of individuals personally involved. In this Devon was like other counties but further examination of those owners deemed eligible to receive emancipation compensation reveals patterns which outline a previously unknown character to that history.

6

Devon's slave-owners

'My envied wealth be said to have taken wings and fled away, yet the wreck remains and when renovated by time, will like the giant refreshed by his slumbers, again be great but in the mean time, sorrows deep and bitter have been and still are mine', Louisa Carolina Colleton Graves, 1821

Slaveholders had a multitude of types of connections and associations with Devon. Some were casual such as that of Mary Dalzell, a Cheltenham woman whose link was a visit in 1851 to her daughter at Ilfracombe. Likewise, Wilhemina Petgrave, a Jamaican who had a compensation award, rented a room in a East Budleigh lodging house in 1861.[623] It is not known if she had a longer-lasting connection with Devon. Similar to her circumstances are others who came for their health and died shortly afterwards. The popularity of Devon's resorts brought many thousands of tourists each year and amongst them would have been many other as yet unidentified former enslavers.

Other connections were more solid but defining what makes a slave-owner a Devonian is also problematic. Is the criterion birth in the county or is it securing a place of residence of any duration? Even if this is a second or third home? Can those who had parents from Devon be considered local men and women?

In order to understand these individuals it is necessary to untangle each life. For instance, in 1836 Elizabeth Charity Drake was awarded £1,202 8s 9d (£81,526.83) for her losses in Stoney Gut, a Jamaican estate. Nine years earlier it had belonged in part to another Elizabeth Charity Drake who was possibly her mother: a Bristol woman who married in Somerset and whose children were subsequently born in Jamaica, Dorset or Devon (Colyton). Her husband William, who was born in Axminster, had died in Jamaica in 1809.[624]

Amelia Mais' association with Devon was organised for her: in 1876 she was committed to the Plympton Lunatic Asylum. For the previous twenty seven years she had lived in a Somerset institution. Mais died in Plympton St Mary thirteen years later. She had inherited her uncle's Silver Hill plantation in Jamaica and in 1835 she received £2,547 19s 3d (£172,755.17) for her loss of 121 Jamaicans. By coincidence her Devon home was Plympton House, formerly owned by Captain Paul Henry Ourry whose portrait now at Saltram includes Jersey, his African servant, in about 1748.[625]

George Lowman Tuckett appears to have fitted Devon into a life complicated by multiple crossings of the Atlantic. He was Somerset-born and had two long stints in the West Indies where he practised law. He was known for two cases: in 1818 Tuckett prosecuted ten Taunton neighbours for attempting to abduct his teenage niece and fourteen years later he saved the life of a Baptist missionary following the Christmas Rebellion in Jamaica.[626]

Tuckett was in Grenada by 1799 and stayed there until 1808. He served as Solicitor General and married Martha Lowman, a seventeen-year-old first cousin, on the island. Tuckett was aged thirty. In 1809 she gave birth to a daughter in Budleigh Salterton, presumably a place recommended because of its relatively warm climate. From this time until at least 1822 he practised law in Taunton but returned to the West Indies by 1826. He was appointed a judge of the Vice-Admiralty court in Jamaica and in 1831 became Chief Justice. Shortly afterwards he returned to England, moved to London, in 1837 his wife died in Tiverton and in 1851 he was living in Ilfracombe with three of his daughters and one son. That year he died aged 80 in Cardiff.[627]

Tuckett's father had previously been in the West Indies and it may have been through him that he inherited five enslaved people on a Jamaican plantation. This brought a compensation settlement of £128 7s 1d (£8,702.58).

Mary Ann Barnett had what might have been a two-year connection with Devon. In 1846 this seventy-eight-year-old London widow was buried in the churchyard at Bishop's Tawton outside Barnstaple. She had married her Bristol-born husband William Barnett in 1787 in Jamaica and lived there for some twenty years. They owned three estates, Biddeford, Trelawny and Sportsman's Hall, until 1808. The couple returned to live in England, notably Bristol, but the reasons for Mrs Barnett's subsequent residence at Newport Terrace in Barnstaple for a few years are unknown.[628]

The most plausible reason for some individuals being in Devon was for proximity to family members. For instance, Elizabeth Bryan née Rodon, a forty-six-year-old Jamaican-born widow, lived with her daughter in Ilfracombe from about 1839. By 1851 they moved to Cornwall and she died in Penzance in 1859. The compensation in 1836 for six enslaved people on her estate, Hall's Delight in Jamaica, had amounted to £128 3d (£8,679.41).[629] In 1826 Bryan owned seven Jamaicans. They included Maria Ives and her two daughters and three sons as well as another woman who was named Elizabeth Bryan. The latter was thirty years old, Ives was thirty-one and her children's ages ranged from two to thirteen.[630]

At the time of Emancipation Admiral Sir Edward Codrington was Devon's only MP who owned human beings. He represented Devonport, lived in London and in 1832 was questioned during the hustings over his plantation. He was forced to withdraw his denials of ownership and to admit to being a joint owner with his brother. Codrington stated that he 'had the misfortune' of having inherited enslaved people and claimed he would support a bill for abolition. The issue developed into a

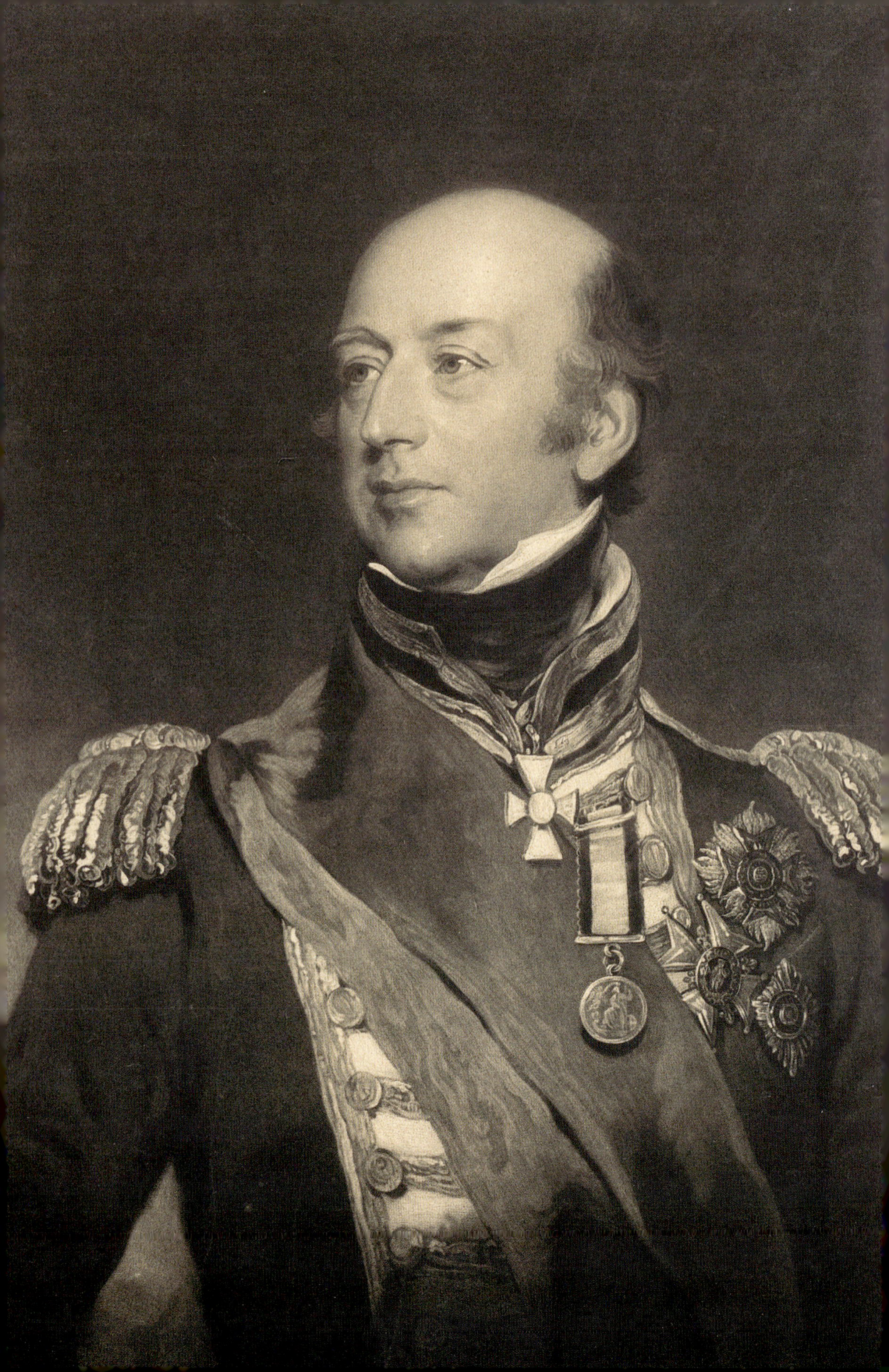

political row which was heard in the King's Bench.[631] Three years later Codrington received £2,588 6s 6d (£175,491.80). His nephew, Bethell Walrond of Broadhembury, also had a share in the family's Antiguan plantations.

No comments from Devonians' emancipated slaves have been found although it was claimed that Lord Rolle's former enslaved people were grateful for their liberty and his land.'[632] Rolle received one of the highest compensation awards to a resident Devonian; he was given £4,333 6s 9d (£293,805.92). Others include Caroline Robley, a Londoner who died in Tiverton, who received £9,543 4s 3d (£647,042.21) and Hugh Mill Bunbury, a former Exonian who lived in Berkshire, who had £24,169 1s 3d (£1,638,693.86). The Porter brothers moved from Demerara to Devon where they lived in great luxury partly through sharing £55,256 2s 8d (£3,746,437.67). Finally, Thomas Daniel, a Bristol merchant who purchased a Devon country mansion, received £68,512 8s 7d (£4,645,231.76).[633]

There are four categories in which slaveholders connected with Devon have been identified; fourteen were born in the county and nearly all the rest migrated from elsewhere to Devon. Some were employed by the navy at Plymouth but the majority enjoyed a life of leisure in Devon. A minority of them were born in Britain and the remainder were colonials. Nearly all slave-owners connected with Devon came after they made compensation claims.

DEVON-BORN

Fourteen enslavers who had compensation awards were born in Devon. Anna Binney née Marshall was not one of them. She was a slave owner who does not appear to have owned an estate nor did she receive compensation. She was born in Ashprington in 1801 and baptised in Totnes. Her father Edward was an Exeter clergyman who served as the rector of Kingston in Jamaica and in 1794 had married the daughter of James Horn, a slaveholder who had died in 1788. Anna was partly raised in Jamaica but married in Putney in 1822. Her husband Lieut. John Binney subsequently captained packet ships sailing between Falmouth and the West Indies.[634] Between 1831 and 1836 she lived in Cornwall and moved to Tiverton following her husband drowning at sea in a hurricane in 1835: he was described as 'a smart, active and meritorious officer respected and beloved by his crew as well as by all who had the pleasure of his acquaintance'. She was there at least by 1841 but subsequently moved to Tunbridge in Kent by 1851 and she died in Hungerford in 1871. She led a peripatetic life.[635]

From the age of sixteen Binney had owned Jamaicans on the Mount Moses estate. The highest recorded number of workers was 238 individuals in 1831.[636] Amongst them in 1817 were two men named Tiverton and Topsham.[637] The remaining fourteen Devonian slave-owners received compensation.

◀ 41. Portrait of Edward Codrington, later an MP for Devonport, 1830.

Table 9

Devon-born slave-owners who had compensation, 1834.

Name	Place of birth	Place of death	Comp.
G. Beare	Topsham	Grenada	£313
J. Beare	Topsham	Grenada	£106
H. M. Bunbury	Exeter	London	£24,169
G. Cole	Dawlish	Somerset	£4,610
T. Davy	Exeter	Ottery St Mary	£1,101
M. D'Urban	Topsham	Exmouth	£3,013
A. C. Grant	West Alvington	London	£10,914
H. A. Hawkins	Exeter	London	£384
H. S. Highatt	Brampford Speke	Australia	£1,502
G. Pearse	Tiverton	Bradninch	£4,390
W. Pole	Shute	Shute	£2,648
J. Rolle	Chittlehampton	Bicton	£4,333
T. Rossiter	Tiverton	Tiverton	£1,062
J. J. Rowe	East Down	Morchard Bishop	£306

Colonials

Seven Devonians received compensation awards and had first-hand experience of slave plantations in the colonies.

George and James Beare, Topsham

These brothers were born in Topsham in 1782 and 1792 and were the youngest sons of eight siblings. Men of that name, with connections to Topsham, were subsequently in the West Indies and are likely to have been the same individuals. By 1815 George Beare had become Comptroller of Customs for Grenada, Tortola and Antigua[638] and in 1832 he married Sophia Willis in Barnstaple. He died in Antigua five years later. In the 1820s Beare wrote a series of letters regarding the cruelty towards enslaved people.[639]

Two compensation awards were made in 1835 for estates in Grenada and Antigua for seventeen individuals; he had an award of £313 7d (£21,223.78). Edward Connett, formerly of Starcross, then acted as his attorney in Grenada.[640] In 1834 Beare's Grenadian enslaved people comprised fifteen individuals.[641]

Table 10
George Beare's enslaved people, 1834.

Name	Age		Colour	Country
Harry	47		black	Africa
Simon	66	(blind in one eye)	black	Africa
Robert	9½		black	Creole
George	2¾		black	Africa
James	2½		black	Africa
Betty	43		black	Africa
Janet	37		black	Creole
Lucy	51		black	Africa
Agnes	25		black	Creole
Margaret	15		black	Creole
Elizabeth	11½		black	Creole
Anne	9		black	Creole
Eleanor	8½		black	Creole
Eliza	1 month		black	Creole
Caroline	2 months & 12 days		black	Creole

Brother James was a merchant in Grenada by 1815; that year he imported goods from London.[642] He owned one Grenadian estate and received £106 12s 11d (£7,230,73) for his five enslaved people. Beare died in 1842 when he was noted as being from Topsham.[643]

Hugh Mill Bunbury, Exeter

Bunbury was born in Exeter in 1766 and seventy years later received £24,169 1s 3d (£1,638,693.86) for 478 enslaved people on the Devonshire and Devonshire Castle estates in Demerara. In about 1788 he had emigrated to St Vincent where he married three years later. Among his children was Edward, thought to have been of mixed-race. By 1799 Bunbury had purchased 'bush land' in Demerara which he developed into his two slave estates.

Bunbury's father was Irish but his mother, Mary Mill, came from Exeter. His brother later lived in Devon: Benjamin, who was also born in Exeter, lived in Teignmouth for many years but died in a riding-accident in Berkshire where he served as Deputy Lieutenant.[644]

Hugh Mill Bunbury returned to Ireland in 1816 and subsequently lived in Wandsworth and Regent's Park in London. He died in 1838, shortly after he received his compensation awards. In his will Bunbury referred to himself as being 'of Devonshire Castle in the United Colony of Demerara and Essequibo'. He should not be confused with his better-known rake of a son with whom he shared his name; he, in 1825 at the age of 23, was imprisoned at Cambridge for having incurred extravagant

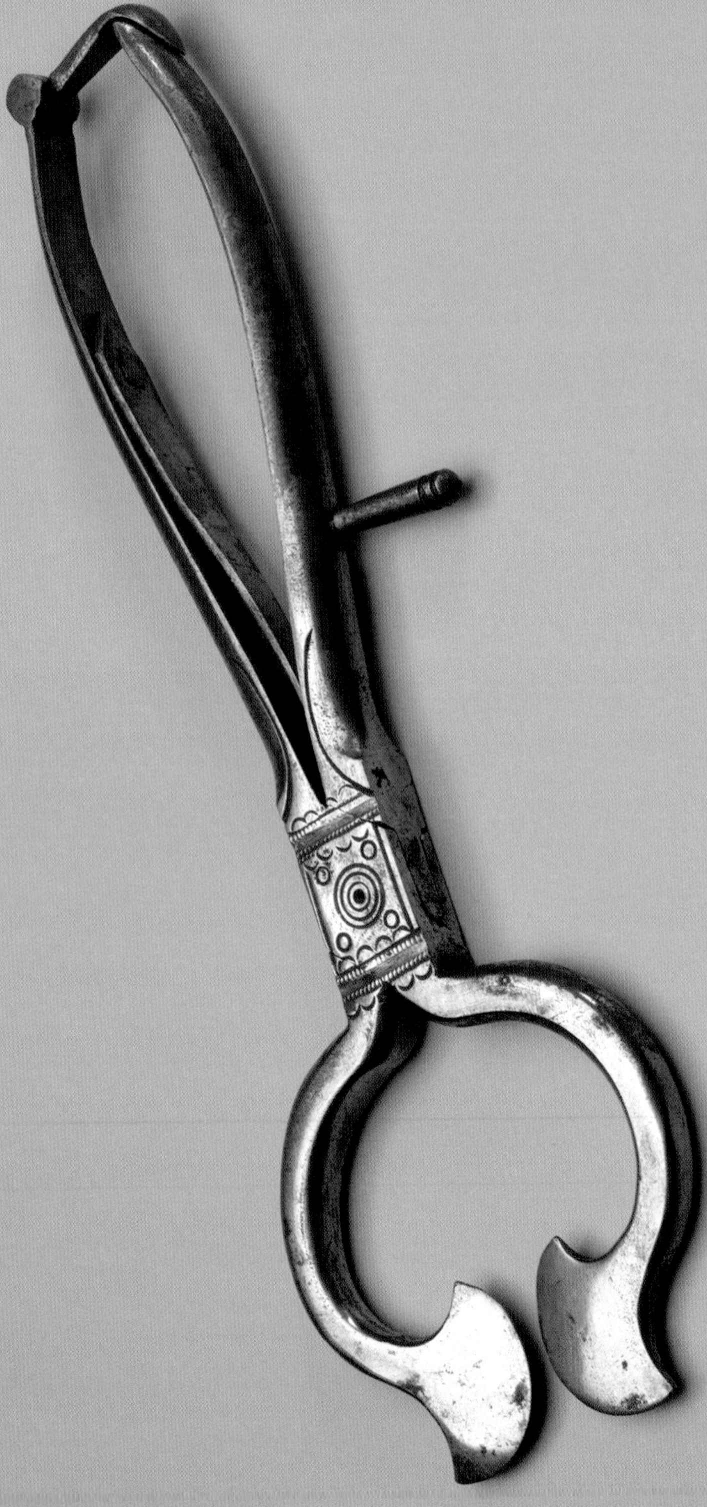

debts by false pretences. In court he was described as 'a person of very dashing appearance' which, along with his father's estates in Demerara, may in part explain his appeal to his four wives. In court he spoke of his father's immense wealth.[645]

George Cole, Dawlish

Cole was born in Dawlish in about 1785 and the family lived at Holcombe, just outside the resort. He moved to Glasgow by 1805 and was engaged in shipping between Trinidad and Glasgow up to about 1840. He appears to have been a frequent traveller to the West Indies. Cole married in Scotland and returned to Devon possibly as late as 1841 when, as a widower, he was living in May Cottage in Sidmouth. In 1842 he remarried and moved to Fortfield Terrace. Seven years later Cole returned to Dawlish: he was living at Laurel Cottage or 'The Cottage' at 133 Weech Street. He died only two years later, at the age of 68, at Wellisford Manor near Wellington in Somerset.[646]

Cole's had compensation money for three estates. In 1837 he received £4,610 6s (£312,584.33) for 86 enslaved Trinidadians; nearly half was as a mortgagee for the Mount Stuart Estate. In 1816 he had recorded purchasing one enslaved woman in Trinidad: she was Louisa Buckley, 'colour Mulatto', who was employed as a Dominican-born servant, aged 23 and five feet high in stature.[647]

Sir Alexander Cray Grant

Grant, later nicknamed 'Chin' because of his 'gross physiognomy', was born at Bowringsleigh near Kingsbridge in January 1782 and in that sense can claim to be a Devonian. However, this inheritor of about 609 Jamaicans did not appear to have had any subsequent association with Devon. He was raised in Hampshire, visited Jamaica from 1810 to 1811 and later lived in Whitehall Gardens, London. From 1812 to 1843 Grant served as an MP for constituencies outside Devon. During at least two of the hustings he was shamed for ill-treating his enslaved people. His compensation amounted to £10,914 6s 7d (£740,005.71) on Spring Vale Pen, Albion Estate, Rio Magno Pen and Berwick Estate. In parliament he spoke in favour of the West Indian slaveholders.[648]

In 1836 a Jamaican Special Magistrate designated August 1 as a holiday and he was criticised for his comments about Rio Magno Pen. Three island justices wrote it had:

> 'tended to weaken their confidence in their managers. Special Justice Palmer's observations to the apprentices, as deposed to by Mr Worger of Rio Magno in telling them *that they had a right to take that day or any other day*, making them judges of the law, injudicious and improper. Also, that the injudicious advice given to the apprentices relative to locking their doors, turning out to work at the shell blow, and making them judges of the time to draw off from rain by saying *could the managers tie your feet*, could not fail to destroy all authority and control of the overseers'.

◀ 42. Sugar cutters, c1820.

Two years later, in 1838, the national press reported that Grant had liberated 'an extensive class of his Negroes in Jamaica'. He died in London in 1854.[649]

Henry Adolphus Hawkins, Exeter

Hawkins was born in Exeter but spent his working life as a surgeon mostly in Berkshire or London. In his twenties, from 1814 to 1824, he was in Jamaica employed as a surgeon in the Middlesex Regiment of Horse. It was probably then that Hawkins acquired shares in three plantations and in 1835, while at Victoria Terrace in Exeter, requested compensation for 102 Jamaicans. He was successful in two personal claims and received £384 5s 2d (£26,053.21) for 18 individuals. A third claim involved the trusteeship of a minor. In 1832 Hawkins was listed as owning seventeen enslaved people who comprised eight males and nine females. Three men had been born in Africa. No females had second names recorded but were listed as Dorothy (Negro, aged 15), Mary (Mulatto, 48), Elizabeth (Quadroon, 19), Sabrina (Negro, 30), Ellen (Sambo, 25) and Malvina (Negro, 2). After his stint in Jamaica Hawkins may have returned to Devon for two years before moving to the South East.[650]

Thomas Rossiter, Tiverton

Rossiter was born in Tiverton in 1772, made his riches in Jamaica and returned home by 1810 when he married his second wife, became a leading member of the civic community and died in 1839 at the age of 67. He lived in Westexe.[651]

In 1835 Rossiter received an award of £1,064 9s 4d (£72,172.22) for 55 Jamaicans on Pear Tree Grove, the estate he acquired through his first wife. His daughter Mary Ann later inherited the property.[652] In 1829 there were sixty-eight enslaved people, of whom twenty-nine were female and thirty-nine male. Their number had increased from 1817 when he owned thirty-three individuals.[653] Pear Tree Grove plantation had more slaves in 1822; Rossiter then owned 182 men, women and children. Some men had topographical names (Bristol, London, Oxford and York as well as Devon and Tiverton). In 1826 he recorded female slaves by name, colour, age, whether African or Creole and made some remarks on parentage:

> Eleanor, Negro, 2 years & 8 months, Creole, daughter of Letitia
> Pussy, Negro, 45, Creole
> Franky alias Sarah Hamilton, Negro, 34, African
> Harriet alias Catherine Graham, Negro, 36, African
> Barbary Graham, Negro, 8, Creole, daughter of Harriet
> Charlotte Ferguson, Negro, 5, Creole, daughter of Harriet
> Fanny, Negro, 1 year & 9 months, Creole, daughter of Harriet
> Patty alias Celia Williams, Negro, 41, African
> Elizabeth, Negro, 40, African
> Isabella alias Jennet Hare, Negro, 23, Creole
> Fanny, Negro, 18, Creole

Clara, Negro, Creole, daughter of Celinda
Margaret Adams, Negro, Creole, daughter of Ann Chambers[654]

Rossiter married Elizabeth Sophia Jones, a Jamaican woman in 1795, probably not long after he arrived, and they had six daughters. Rossiter was a widower in 1809, shortly after he returned to Tiverton where he married a second time, had additional children, became a trustee of various local charities and was elected mayor in 1838. Rossiter crossed the Atlantic in 1812, 1818 and 1827 but Tiverton appears to have remained his main home.[655]

Absentee owners

The remaining seven Devon-born slave-owners were absentee owners, that is, they hired men as agents, managers or overseers to run their affairs and estates.[656] In Barbados one magistrate commented overseers were 'a low order of men… without education… trained up to use the whip… knowing nothing else save the art of flogging'.[657] Lord Rolle and Reverend James Rowe have been discussed earlier.

Mary Elizabeth Stewart D'Urban née Mitchell, Topsham

D'Urban spent her entire life living along the Exe Estuary. Her father Samuel Mitchell had served as president of the Grenada Assembly while her father-in-law was not only governor of Antigua but also of British Guiana, Demerara-Essequibo and the Cape of Good Hope.

She was born in Topsham at Newport House, her mother's family home, and she married William James D'Urban in the parish church in 1833. Five years later her home was rebuilt.[658] Mrs D'Urban lived at Newport, with five servants, until about 1879 when she moved to Exmouth, first at Beacon Hill and then Moorlands where her son lived. She died there in 1892 at the age of 89.

In 1803 Samuel Mitchell bequeathed to his daughter the Hope Vale (formerly *Chemin*) estate in Grenada. In 1836 compensation of £3,013 12s 7d (£204,327.98) was paid, as part of her marriage settlement, for 113 Grenadians. Three years earlier it was recorded that she owned sixty-one male servants and fifty-seven women including children. One man had lost an eye and two of the others had either an arm or leg amputated.[659]

Thomas Davy, Ottery St Mary

Dr Davy, a house surgeon at Guy's Hospital, was born in Exeter in 1773 and married an Exeter woman twenty-six years later. His brothers James and Edward emigrated to Jamaica and in 1803 the latter bequeathed an estate to him. Davy's estate, held jointly with his sister Rebecca, was run first by his brother James and afterwards by John Davy, probably his nephew, who were both attorneys. A second estate, Topsham, may have been sold in 1824. Dr Davy died in about 1852.

Davy lived in one of Ottery St Mary's most prominent buildings, Raleigh House in Mill Street. It was rebuilt in 1805 following a fire. This was two years after he inherited his plantations and thirty years before Davy received £1,101 3s 8d (£74,661.66) in compensation for the loss of 59 Jamaicans on the Knowsley Park estate. In 1829 he had fifty-five enslaved Jamaicans and three years later there were fifty-seven. In 1817 40 individuals were listed by name, colour, age and birth place. The mothers of those born in the West Indies were also noted.[660]

Table 11

Thomas Davy's enslaved people, 1817.

Name	Race	Age	Place of birth	Mother
Males				
Luke	Negro	40	African	
Joe	Negro	25	African	
Tom	Negro	19	African	
Quaco	Negro	25	African	
John	Negro	29	African	
George	Negro	25	African	
Bob	Negro	28	African	
Quamina	Negro	30	African	
Peter	Negro	45	African	
Robert	Negro	14	Creole	Joyce
Sammy	Negro	9	Creole	Jessy
William	Negro	7	Creole	Bessy
Edward	Negro	5	Creole	Amba
Kenny	Negro	4	Creole	Bessy
James	Negro	4	Creole	Cuba
Dick	Negro	4	Creole	Amba
Adam	Negro	3	Creole	Fanny
Ben	Negro	3	Creole	Bessy
Peter	Negro	2	Creole	Amba
Remas	Negro	1	Creole	Bessy

Females

Jessy	Negro	30	African	
Joyce	Negro	28	African	
Abby	Negro	23	African	
Quasheba	Negro	22	African	
Sally	Negro	27	African	
Amba	Negro	25	African	
Cuba	Negro	23	African	
Bessy	Negro	25	African	
Fanny	Negro	23	African	
Amy	Negro	24	African	
Margaret	Negro	22	African	
Celia	Negro	28	African	
Sukey	Negro	20	African	
Mary	Negro	21	African	
Diana	Negro	12	Creole	Jessy
Billy	Negro	13	Creole	Sally
Sarah	Negro	12	Creole	Joyce
Cynthia	Negro	6	Creole	Jessy
Eliza	Negro	3	Creole	Jessy
Catherine	Negro	1	Creole	Amba

John Fisher, East Budleigh

Fisher was a Somerset barrister who later worked in Devon. By 1813 he lived at Tidwell House in East Budleigh. This substantial eighteenth-century brick home had been the home of John Rolle in the mid 1780s and early 1790s. By 1815 Fisher had refinanced the Archibald, Union and Luana Pen estates in Jamaica. His property was held in trust when in 1826 it was reported he owned 268 enslaved men and women in one parish. The compensation was later paid to his son John Campbell Fisher. In 1835 and 1836 Fisher received £289 17s 9d (£19,654.75) for thirteen other Jamaicans who probably included Margaret, Sibly, Nancy, Bryan, Dan, James, William, Toby, John and John Wright. Fisher died aged 81 in 1839 in Budleigh Salterton.[661]

Henry Stogdon Highatt, Brampford Speke

Highatt was born in Brampford Speke and at the age of nine was awarded his first of two compensation payments which were placed in trust: in total he had £1,502 18s (£101,898.57) for 71 enslaved Jamaicans on the Orange Grove estate. He and his parents lived at Lower Cleeve but in 1831 his father, aged twenty-six, died suddenly off Lundy while sailing to Jamaica. Months later Highatt's mother remarried and presumably moved from Devon. By 1835 they were living in Yorkshire. Highatt subsequently emigrated to Australia where he died in 1885.[662]

Sir William Templer Pole, Shute

Pole's was born and died at Shute near Colyton and the 7th Baronet spent his entire life on his ancestral estate. He served as Deputy Lieutenant and High Sheriff of Devon and upon his death in 1847 was given uncommon praise. One journalist commented:

> 'He was one of the few existing relics of the Old English Country Gentleman of the first class, devoting his entire life to acts of kindness and benevolence, and enjoying in return the respect, esteem and veneration of an entire population'.[663]

Another journalist was even more effusive. He wrote:

> 'His uniform attention to the duties of hospitality, and the kindness and urbanity of his manners, endeared him to all who enjoyed the pleasure of his immediate intercourse; whilst his perpetual interest in the welfare of the poor, and his liberal charities, proved the goodness of his heart, and will cause him to be long remembered as their benefactor by the objects of his care. As a magistrate, he was vigilant and judicious; and as a landlord, kind and generous. In the exemplary discharge of his duties as a country gentleman, he won for himself the golden opinions of all, and the news of his death elicited a general expression of regret from all classes, far and near.'[664]

Years before, in 1835, a poet dedicated his book, *Seaton Beach*, to Pole as 'a gentleman whose elegant taste in polite literature is only exceeded by the splendour of his moral virtues'.[665]

Pole's direct interests appear to have been focused on Devon rather than the West Indies. His life was centred on Shute House built in the 1780s by the sixth baronet. It was described in 1830 as having:

> 'a delightful view in front with a very handsome lawn and is about four miles from the sea. The plan of the house is a square of about sixty-eight feet, with two handsome wings, connected with the body by corridors. The principal rooms are a dining parlour forty feet by twenty-three, fifteen in height, a drawing room thirty-six feet by twenty-three of the same height, a large breakfast parlour and a handsome library. The entrance has a portico of the Doric order with columns and the vestibule fifteen feet wide leads to a very grand geometrical Portland stone staircase.'[666]

43. Slave shackle, made of iron, of an uncertain date, found in Surinam. ▶

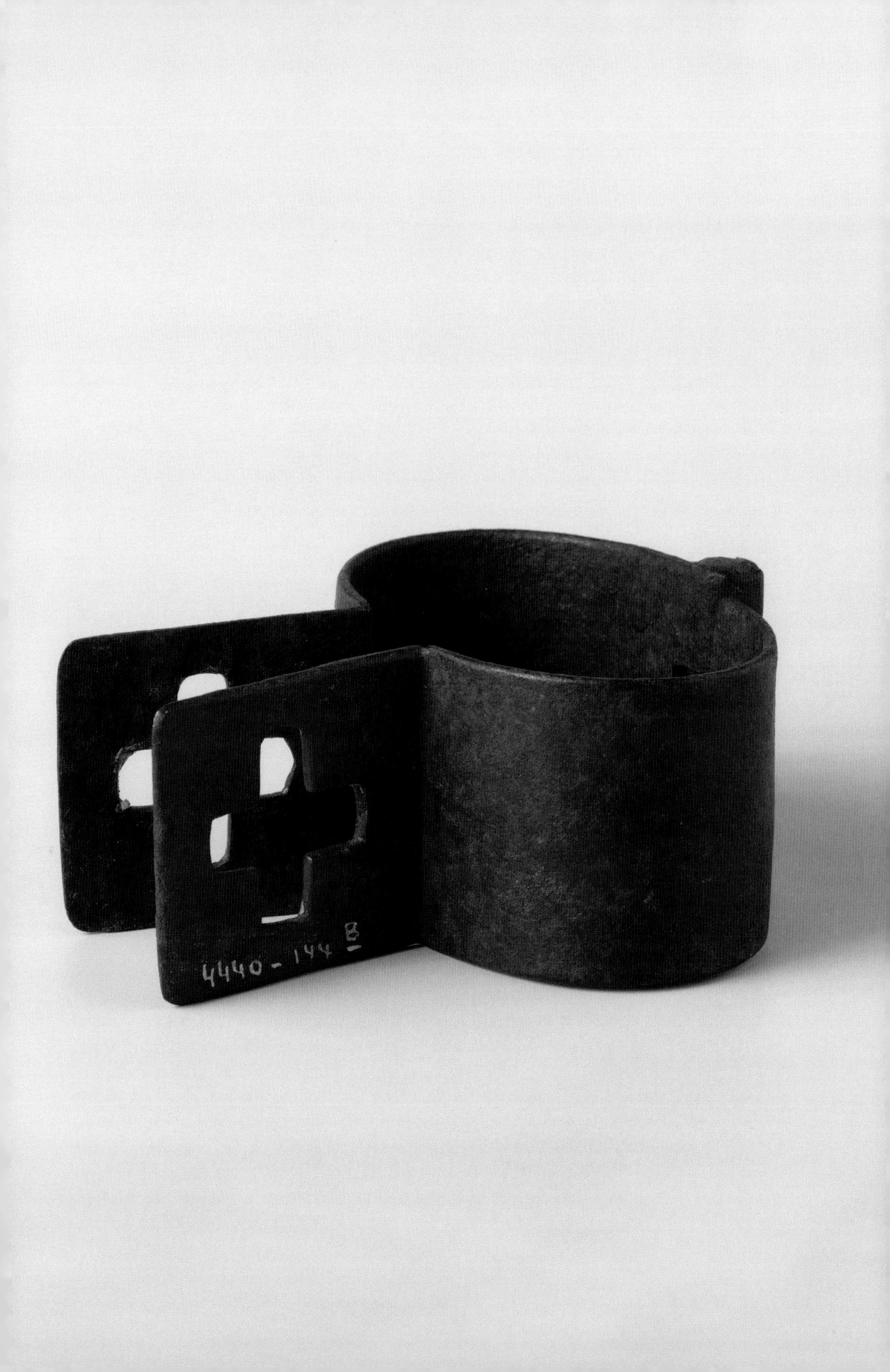
4440-144 B

It was later claimed that the family were cursed with the line of succession being interrupted.

'In a field of standing corn he built,
In a field of straight green corn,
His eldest son shall never be heir,
Nay, never his eldest born.'

Shute Hill had been known for its horse racing: in the 1780s events lasted three to four days.[667] In 1829 Pole had a grand celebration for 20,000 people, in what was described as 'almost a revival of medieval festivity', for his son's coming of age.[668] He had previously been commended by the Royal Society for the Encouragement of Arts, Manufactures and Commerce for growing oak trees at Shute: in 1821 he won the Ceres Medal for having raised nearly 900,000 trees. It was claimed he had more oak trees on his estate than any other gentleman or nurseryman in the West Country.[669]

His maternal grandfather, John Mills of Woodford in Essex, bequeathed him half of two plantations in St Kitts. He was awarded £2,648 8s 2d (£179,565.53) for 170 individuals on the Golden Rock and Mills Estates. Pole retained his plantations through his life. Two hundred years earlier the family had a Black servant. Sir William's great, great, great, great grandfather had one of the earliest servants of African descent in Devon: the parish register for Colyton recorded the burial in 1619 of Katherine, 'a blackamoor servant' of Sir William Pole.[670]

ARMED SERVICES

Six slaveholders came to Plymouth while pursuing their careers in the armed services. In 1806 one commentator noted that the White population of the West Indies had been augmented by men formerly in the navy and army[671] but these six plantation owners had active military careers.

Manley Dixon, Plymouth

Admiral Dixon led a peripatetic life. He was born in Nova Scotia in 1757 and lived in various parts of the Atlantic world. In the 1760s his siblings were born either in Plymouth or Hampshire, his marriage took place in Jamaica and his first set of children were born in Devon in the 1780s. He married a second time at Fremington in North Devon and had more children born in Brazil and Wales. Dixon served in the navy from the age of thirteen and it was later recollected that there was nothing in his record 'of a censurable nature, nothing but what is cheering and animating'. In 1830 he returned to Plymouth as Commander in Chief for three years before retiring to Exmouth where he died in 1837. That year he received £271 14s 2d (£18,422.18) for the Hall's Prospect Estate in Jamaica inherited by his three daughters from his first wife.[672]

Edward Rodon Huggins, Plymouth

Huggins was a Hampshire-born naval officer who moved to Plymouth shortly after his marriage in 1830. He had inherited enslaved people through Miss Jane Ellis. In 1823 Huggins owned thirteen Jamaicans and six years later their number had increased to twenty-one.[673] In 1835 he was on HMS *Andromache* in China when his wife Emily wrote 'the task of bringing to a settlement his affairs in Jamaica devolves to me'. She handled two compensation claims for the St Catherine estate; for 23 individuals they received £385 2d (£26,104.07). Huggins had owned the plantation since 1817 and noted in his will that it was 'a mountain settlement'. The couple lived at 5 Laira Green Cottages. He died in 1842 and she three years later.[674]

John Martell, Devonport

Martell, a shipwright, was another slaveholder who came to Plymouth because of the dockyard. The census of 1841, which placed him at Ker Street in Devonport, noted he was a shipwright born 'in foreign parts'. This was probably Jamaica where his children were born in 1823 and 1832. By 1835 he had emigrated to England from where Martell submitted his claim for an award of £63 16s 1d (£4,326.01) for three Jamaicans.[675]

George Frederick Rich, Devonport

Admiral Rich was one of the six illegitimate children of Sir Thomas Rich, 4th Baronet of Sonning, Berkshire and his mistress, Elizabeth Burt, the daughter of a general. London-born Rich served in the navy from 1795 through to the 1840s. He was posted to the Royal Naval Victualling Yard at Devonport in 1842 and upon his retirement returned to London where he died in 1863. In 1836 Rich received a compensation award of £2,145 15s 9d (£145,487.18) on behalf of his first wife, Jane Agnes Wilhelmina Fraser who died at Stoke Damerel in 1842. Her part ownership of a plantation at British Guiana was inherited from her mother, the wife of C. H. Fraser, a diplomat. Admiral Rich remarried in 1854.[676]

Houston Shaw Stewart, Plymouth

Admiral Stewart not only had a distinguished naval career but also served as a Liberal MP in 1852. He came to Devon in 1856, at the age of sixty-four, on his appointment as Admiral Superintendent of Devonport Dockyard and was promoted four years later as Commander-in-Chief at Plymouth. He left Devon in 1863. Stewart had inherited an estate in Tobago through his father and in 1836 received £2,998 8s 8d (£203,297.68) for 143 individuals. He retired to his native Scotland where he died in 1875.[677]

Isaac Toby, Kenton and Plymouth

Colonel Toby received £690 3s (£46,793.07) for 36 enslaved people on the Sherwood Park plantation in Tobago. His wife Anne and her three sisters had inherited interests. She had been born in Dunkirk, the daughter of a Tobago merchant from Glasgow. Toby was born in Kenton and by 1829 was in Plymouth where he served in the Royal Marines. He appears to have lived for some time in Saltash but by 1851 lived with his wife and two indoor servants at 55 Durnford Street in Stonehouse. Toby ended his career as the barrack master and died in 1869.[678]

THE BRITISH AT LEISURE

A number of British slaveholders who had compensation moved to Devon where they had a life of leisure. John Hyde Doyle, a Londoner, was one. He married at the age of twenty-five in 1830 and two or so years afterwards moved to Devon with his wife. They had two children in Exeter. By 1839 they were living in Exmouth, had three more children and continued there until about 1870 when they moved to Bath. Doyle subsequently returned to London. Their reason for choosing Devon is not known. Doyle inherited the Body Ponds estate in Antigua from his maternal grandfather and in 1836, shortly before he moved to Withycombe Raleigh, received £1,704 11d (£115,536.52) compensation for 102 individuals. In 1850 he was one of a handful of gentlemen resident in the parish and was listed in the census the following year as a land owner or owner of houses. Doyle died in London in 1894.[679]

Some former enslavers had short or casual Devon associations. This includes Alexander Scott Broomfield, an Irishman with a plantation in Trinidad, who came to Torquay in 1846, possibly for his health, and died a few months later.[680] Likewise, Mary Elizabeth Dalzell owned slaves in Barbados but her connection with Devon appears to be a family visit to Ilfracombe in 1851.[681] In contrast, others lived substantial periods of their lives in Devon. More than a dozen have been identified but it is probable that many others are yet to be found. Some had their compensation while living in Devon and others came to the county afterwards.

Hannah Barnes née Nicoll, Dawlish

Barnes was born in Bristol in 1766 and subsequently lived in Jamaica with her husband Joseph, a native of Cumbria who was a senior judge. Following his death in 1829 Barnes returned to England. It is uncertain why she chose Dawlish but she was resident there by 1835 when her compensation claim was made. Barnes had interests in two plantations and wrote to the government on 21 November:

> 'I am the widow of the late Joseph Barnes of Kingston, Jamaica, and that myself, my daughter and her children are entirely dependent for support on what we receive from his estate; that in consequence of the non-receipt of our remittances for many months past, I am much in want of money.'[682]

At this time she was sharing Barton Cottage with her daughter, five grandchildren and her son-in-law's mother. Barnes' shortage of cash was exacerbated by her son-in-law William Trutch. He had been incarcerated as a debtor in the parish of St Thomas outside Exeter but obtained a rope and escaped. Described as a man 'of dashing exterior', he deserted his family and left them in the financial care of his mother-in-law. Trutch was described in newspapers as being:

> 'about 38 years of age, about 5 feet 9 inches high, blue eyes, fresh and fair complexion, round features, and a fine and handsome man, having the Somersetshire dialect. He has the initials of his name imprinted on his left arm, between the wrist and elbow, with blue ink. He was born at Ashcott, in Somerset; is of prepossessing and insinuating manners, and was formerly Clerk of the Peace in the Island of Jamaica. He married the daughter of the Honourable Joseph Barnes, late a judge of the Supreme Court of Judicature in Jamaica, and his wife and family are now living with her mother at Dawlish, and *his* mother… it is supposed that he is cohabiting with a young woman, of about 23 years of age, a native of Exeter, and they have been passing by the name of Mr and Mrs Pearce in Bath. They were also seen together at Weymouth, on Thursday, 13th inst., passing by the name of Mr and Mrs Smith.'

Trutch was recaptured but does not appear to have reconciled with his wife. Instead he fathered several additional children with a servant. Five years later Barnes died in her native Bristol.[683]

From 1836 to 1837 Barnes was paid £157 8s 9d (£10,674,47) for nine Jamaicans and acted as an executor and trustee for a second award of £626 11s 5d (£42,482.32) for 132 enslaved people. In 1838 she owned three men and five women whereas six years earlier a return made by her agent listed seven individuals by name, 'colour', age and whether African or Creole:[684]

Philip Dennis, Negro, 26, Creole
James Waters, Sambo, 25, Creole
Richard Christopher, Negro, 14½, Creole
Thomas Wiltshire, Negro, 9 years 8 months, Creole
John Beacher, Negro, 7 years 10 months, Creole
Sarah Denniss, Negro, 30, Creole
Mary Williams, Sambo, 27, Creole

John Nelson Bond, Torquay

Bond was born, married and lived in London. In his thirties he moved to Folkestone, Hastings and Brighton but his last three years were spent at Cliff View in Tor Hill Road, Torquay, where he died at the age of eighty in 1878.[685] Bond had been a partner in a firm of London attorneys and in 1835 was successful, partly as a mortgagee, in receiving compensation money for part of three Jamaican estates but unsuccessful in a fourth: his share came to £2,701 6d (£183,133.01).

John Campbell, Budleigh Salterton

On his death Campbell was termed 'the father' of Budleigh Salterton. He had settled in the resort in his early thirties, possibly after his marriage in 1804 but certainly by 1813.[686] In 1841 his obituarist wrote Campbell was:

> 'a staunch, zealous, and consistent Reformer throughout the whole of his long life; a steady, faithful, and attached friend to all who had the privilege of his intimate acquaintance and a kind, generous, and benevolent friend to all beneath him. He was literally the father of Salterton, having settled there 40 years ago. His advice was eagerly sought, and readily obtained. His example was worthy of all imitation, and as he had lived respected and beloved, so is his memory cherished by the people of Budleigh Salterton with an affectionate veneration'.

He died at the age of 71. Campbell was probably born in London as were his siblings, married in Dublin and he and his wife Mary rented Umbrella Cottage in Fore Street Hill, near what is now the Fairlynch Museum. His claim of £2,004 11s 2d (£135,911.66) for 102 Jamaicans on the Saltspring estate came through on 13 August 1841, nine days after the probate of his will was completed. The plantation was part of the estate of his father, Duncan Campbell of The Adelphi in St Martin in the Fields, a merchant who later leased his ships as prison hulks. John Campbell had already inherited, in 1803, other Jamaican plantations.[687]

Charles Devon, Rackenford

Devon, a Middlesex-born magistrate who owned Jamaicans but spent his life in the South East of England, had a Devon connection when, in 1821, he purchased Cruwyshayes, now known as Rackenford Manor, possibly as a shooting estate. He owned it until his death in 1869. In 1851 the census enumerator recorded he spent the night of 30th of March in the gamekeeper's cottage. Otherwise his family residence was in Middlesex. Devon appears to have been particularly interested in the game in his Rackenford property and prosecuted poachers. In 1836 he claimed compensation of £2,000 (£135,602.60) regarding the Lucky Valley estate in Jamaica to fulfil the requirements of his wife's marriage settlement.[688] A drawing made in 1808 shows a large number of buildings including two overseers' houses, a trash house, corn store, cattle pen, cooper's building, hospital, mill house, boiling and still houses, rum store, piggery and poultry house with sheep pen.[689]

Thomas Drane, St Marychurch

More is known about the character and personal life of Drane than of many other Devon slave-owners. He was born in Limehouse in 1794 and became an East Indian merchant. His youngest child of four, Augusta, is best known as Mother Francis Raphael, a Dominican nun, who described her family life in great detail in her memoirs.

She wrote that her parents had married young, that her father was the managing partner in the firm and that he possessed estates in New Zealand, Australia, India, Ceylon and Mauritius. In 1837 his three plantations in the latter colony provided him with compensation of £6,868 7s 1d (£465,682.34) for 206 enslaved people.

His daughter wrote that before his marriage Drane:

> 'had already begun to be a book collector and something of an artist and musician. These tastes he continued to cultivate all through his life. His library grew to a considerable size and its contents determined the direction of my education. His musical instruments were of all kinds: organ, piano, harp, flute and French horn, but his knowledge of music was not scientific.'

His greatest interest, she wrote, was in landscape painting. During the early part of the marriage Drane had considerable wealth and the captains of his East Indian ships brought curiosities for Mrs Drane who was 'an almost constant invalid'. The family's relocation may have been caused by a series of family deaths but Drane also had severe business losses. He retired from work and brought his family to Devon in 1837, the year he received his compensation. It was by chance that he had seen Devon and fixed upon Torquay for the family home. His daughter later wrote:

> 'Anyone who only knows Babbacombe as it is now can form no idea of its perfect beauty forty years ago. It contained seven houses and no more. The downs above were wide, unenclosed, and lonely in their expanse. Torquay was just emerging from the fishing-town, and had not yet become the watering-place. There was no railway nearer than Salisbury. The Torquay shops were so few and so barbarous, that, when we wanted to shop, we drove to Exeter, over the beautiful Haldon Hills. Between Torquay and Babbacombe the country was perfectly unbroken by houses; and in the fields now occupied by Bishopstowe I have seen the pheasants feeding in the quiet evenings.'[690]

Eight years later, in 1844, further losses brought the family into reduced circumstances. In 1846 the family home, Middle Westhill, was offered at auction. It had three parlours on the ground floor, seven bedrooms and the garden extended to two acres. Drane was living at Melville Lodge in Tor Mohun when he died in 1864.[691]

Catherine Campbell Griffith née Shakespear, Barnstaple

Griffith was born in London in 1774 but it was in Jamaica where her parents married, her siblings were born and she married John William Spencer Griffith, an attorney. In addition, until 1811 each of her children were born on the island. Their daughter Frances, however, was born in Bideford in 1812 and after living in Jersey in around 1841, she and her two daughters Frances and Mary moved to Newport in Barnstaple by 1850. They were at 1 Newport Terrace when Mrs Griffith died five years later. Their reasons for choosing Devon are not apparent.

In 1817 Griffith registered thirty-three enslaved Jamaicans including women named Tamar, Gift, Harriet, Myra, Rachel, Grace, Bessie, Myrtilla, Louisa, Eliza, Clarissa, Lucky, Sally, Kitty, Eve, Minerva, Violet, Annie, Elizabeth, Molly, Ruthie and Mary. Six years earlier Mr Griffith had a daughter, Fatima Campbell Shakespear, with Eleanor Smith, a 'sambo', but neither were listed as being enslaved. In 1836 Mrs Griffith received £685 8s 11d (£46,447) for 37 Jamaicans.[692]

James Hackett, Newton Abbot

Hackett's working life from the 1820s through to the 1850s was as a local official in Demerara. In 1871 his widow referred to him as having been in the Colonial Civil Service. The Irishman had died two years earlier in Newton Abbot and was noted then as being formerly of Demerara and Boulogne-sur-Mer. Hackett appears to have moved to Devon shortly before his death. His widow lived at Courtenay Terrace in Newton Abbot and their son remained in the town through his adult life. Hackett received compensation of £2,247 15s 11d (£152,403.48) for 42 individuals. In 1832 he had registered 57 enslaved people on the Onderneeming estate in Demerara.[693]

Sir Alexander Hamilton Hamilton of Topsham

Alexander Hamilton Kelso, a Scot, changed his name to Alexander Hamilton Hamilton in order to inherit the estate of his uncle, Alexander Hamilton, in 1809. The latter was remembered in 1810 by Joseph Farington who passed by Hamilton's Topsham home, The Retreat. The diarist recalled that Hamilton had been the captain of an East Indies ship:

> 'and afterwards with his wife got possession of large property and altogether by his sagacity and perseverance made up a fortune said to be £100,000. But a few years have removed them both from this affluent situation and the Retreat is occupied only by servants, the heir of Sir Alexander being abroad and not to come into possession till [he becomes] 25 years old'.[694]

One of Sir Alexander Hamilton's executors in 1809 was his 'good friend' fellow slaveholder Thomas Porter of Rockbeare.[695]

Hamilton Hamilton was born in 1783 and as a young man entered the service of the East India Company in India. In 1809 he married Maria Rosalie Colbiornsen, the daughter of a former Danish official, in Madras and they returned to England the following year.[696]

In August, just before the couple left India eighty-three of 'the principals of all classes of the native inhabitants of Tranquebar' wished them a quick and prosperous voyage as well as perfect health, long life and every happiness. Their address was printed in the *Madras Courier*.

> 'It has been our misfortune to learn that you are about to leave this country. When we reflect that your honour has governed us with wisdom, impartiality and benevolence

and that our present comfortable state is to be attributed to your attention to our wants, we are at a loss to express our sorrow and disappointment at your early departure.

From the period of your arrival here we have always considered your honour as the friend and benefactor of our country but since your departure is with your own, and your most respectable family's, good will, we much content ourselves with presenting our grateful thanks for the justice and comfort we have enjoyed during your honour's administration'.[697]

Hamilton had been appointed assistant to the collector of the Western Polygar Peishcush and of Arcot, north of the river Palar, in 1802, the subordinate collector of Coimbatore in 1807, judge and magistrate of the Zillah of Mangalore in 1807 and finally as British Commissioner at Tranquebar in 1810.[698]

In 1810 he took residence in his uncle's home, The Retreat, which was a converted sugar factory of the early eighteenth century. Hamilton's uncle had purchased the building shortly before he added a storey in 1786. It may have been the work of a 'Mr Gray' who was also then working at Arlington Court.[699]

Hamilton Hamilton raised a family of nine children. In 1851, two years before he died, the household staff comprised four male servants and five females. His estate was worth over £250,000 on his death. This included £3,184 15s 3d (£215,931.04) which he received in 1835 as compensation for the loss of 140 Grenadians on two estates. Amongst his uncle's properties was the Samaritan estate. A few pages of accounts for 1809 to 1810 survive which detail the export on various ships of sugar and rum from the island. That estate had 38 enslaved people in 1834.[700]

Mrs Hamilton took some interest in the conditions of the West Indies' enslaved people: in 1838 she was a member of the Exeter Branch of the Ladies' Society for promoting the early education and improvement of the children of Negroes and of People of Colour in the British West Indies.[701]

Hamilton may have been the 'Grenada proprietor' who wrote in 1826 from Exeter to the editor of the *Grenada Free Press*. That writer corrected the newspaper for suggesting slaves did not own property. He wrote:

'As a Grenada proprietor, I can assure you that many of my people are in possession of ample funds …'[702]

In 1833 a former enslaved man, John Lewis, returned to Hamilton's Samaritan estate after an absence of twenty-three years. He was arrested, placed in prison and pleaded for his freedom. Lewis explained that he had been born in slavery on the estate but 'absented himself' on 17 April 1810 and sailed to England the following year. He explained to the judge that he had married a White woman in England and had two children with her. After serving eight years in the navy Lewis returned to the West Indies in February 1833 in order to see his parents but was arrested by the estate manager. In May the judge determined that Lewis was still enslaved but expressed the hope that the estate owner would pardon him 'which would be a termination of his case very consistent with humanity and the liberality of the times in which we live'.[703]

There were difficulties at the Samaritan Estate following emancipation. In 1839 a strike was organised across a number of estates and solders were sent to re-establish order: a report noted that the former apprentices had described the manager as 'a severe, bad man and they would not work with him'.[704]

Philip Haughton James and his family, Sidmouth

Five members of this London family claimed compensation money and lived together in one of Sidmouth's better-known houses. James and his wife Mary Anne, sister Caroline, aunt Mary and mother-in-law Rebecca shared Helens, described in 1838 as 'an excellent family dwelling'.[705] In 1837 he was successful in claiming £3,401 10s 8d (£230,628.38) for 187 Jamaicans on one estate and £3,018 6s 9d (£204,674.21) for another 155 on the Haughton Hall estate. James had resided in Sidmouth by 1836 but sailed to Jamaica late in 1837 partly for his health but there were also family concerns over the non-payment of compensation. He returned the following year and resumed living in Sidmouth.[706]

Rebecca Ann Palmer then Weekes née James resided in Sidmouth from at least 1832.[707] In 1841 the census recorded that the sixty-eight-year-old widow headed a household which included six servants. Her first husband was John Palmer of Jamaica and she later married Nathaniel Weekes of Barbados. She had financial interests in two Jamaican plantations (Palmyra and Rose Hall) through her first husband's second wife Rosa who in turn acquired them from her first husband.

Weekes had moved from Jamaica in about 1808; in her husband's will he noted that they were about to sail for England. She was an annuitant in two Jamaican claims.[708] Herbert Jarrett James, a slave-owner who lived for a short time in Dawlish, acted for her in Jamaica from 1826 in securing payments and in claims on the Rose Hall and Palmyra Estates.[709] His correspondent was Philip Haughton James and the level of detail suggests some exiles were highly informed of developments in the West Indies. Eighteen days after emancipation Herbert Jarrett James wrote to him:

> 'The first of August has passed off as quietly as could reasonably be expected. In St Ann's the negroes positively refused to work without they were [sic] paid. Some special magistrates were sent there with a body of troops. Some of the most refractory were tried and severely punished with the cat upon their backs and shoulders. When they consented to work as the law directs them in some other parts some examples have been made not however until persuasion and remonstrance were found unavailing. It is, however, a very bad law for all parties and causes much dissatisfaction. We must submit and try and make the best of it. We are also annoyed at the proceedings of the Commissioners of compensation who really appear to be causing as much unnecessary trouble and expense. The negroes are all to be valued and the Valuers are to be paid so much per hundred. Certificates are to be taken from the Secretary's office of the last return under the registry act without which the valuation cannot take place. Now there

is only one set of books containing these returns and probably one of them may contain returns of 2 or 3 parishes. Thus how are they to be obtained or how long will it be before the Certificates and valuation of 300,000 Negroes can be completed. What is the use if the Certificates does not contain the names of the Negroes but only of such as were born or who died between 1829 and 1832 when it was made? Why are they to be valued? We are not to be paid the value and then nothing will be allowed for invalids or old helpless negroes whereas they must be maintained at the expense of their master for the next six years. It is a complete fraud and robbery.'[710]

In 1841 Mrs Weekes shared Helens with her daughter and son-in-law. The couple remained in the cottage following Weekes' death five years later and continued until 1873. By the time Philip Haughton James died in 1880 his wife had predeceased him and he was living near Hyde Park in London. In 1851 the household at Helens also included Mary Partridge James, a seventy-five-year-old maiden aunt, who in 1829 had been a part owner of two other Jamaican plantations. She died in 1856 in Sidmouth. The family continued to own Burnt Ground Pen in Jamaica through to at least 1872.[711]

James' sister Caroline Haughton Clarke was also noted in one unsuccessful compensation claim as being of Sidmouth. She appears to have been a resident in the late 1830s but had left Sidmouth for London by 1840.[712]

Caroline Robley née Blake, Bickleigh

John Robley, a thirty-one-year-old London merchant, sailed from London soon after 27 November 1807 and within three months had reached Barbados. He left his London-born wife and children behind and apparently never saw them again. Some eighteen months after his departure his wife gave birth to a son, Henry. She named the father as John Robley. In his will he named three children with his wife (Fanny Ann, John Horatio and Adelaide) but not Henry.[713]

The Robley family had been active in the West Indies since the mid eighteenth century. In 1820 one writer referred to Robley's uncle's innovations in cultivating spices and cotton on Tobago, suggested Robley was a 'true friend to humanity' and questioned why there was not a statue erected to his memory.[714] He was president of the Council of Tobago and together with his father, John Senior, had bought land from about 1760 from the crown and Sir William Young. By 1801 John Robley Junior was promoting the cultivation of cotton over that of sugar.[715] His mercantile firm, John Robley & Company, was a partnership with his brother-in-law, Charles Brook of Bristol and London. It held over 3,000 acres of land in Lowlayton Plantation in Jamaica, Old Road Plantation in Antigua and Calliaqua Plantation, Pembroke Plantation and The Villa in St Vincent. There were also other plantations.

In 1802 he had been in business at Dunkirk selling West Indian products and supplying estate-owners with stores.[716] By his death in 1821 Robley's firm had invested in Jamaica, Tobago and St Vincent and from 1835 to 1836 his widow received compensation awards for the latter two islands which totalled £9,543 4s 3d

(£647,042.21). These were Pembroke and Villa Estates in St Vincent and Friendship, Betsey's Hope, Golden Grove, Richmond, Goldsborough and Cove Estates in Tobago. A watercolour painted in 1782 represented the Pembroke Estate within a dramatic landscape.[717]

In 1821 Mrs Robley shared her husband's wealth with several Caribbean women with whom her husband had children. He had died at Golden Grove in Tobago in 1821 and in his will left legacies to some enslaved people including granting freedom to 'my Mulatto woman named Betty and my Negro woman named Peggy'. Two daughters were given £5,000 (£339,006.50) each. It was reported in the *Morning Advertiser* that three codicils in his will 'establishes the right of his numerous West India wives and children to very large annuities and of his slaves to a present of 100 hogsheads of tobacco'. The will was contested in 1839 and the judge noted that:

> 'At his departure, he left his wife with three children in England, and shortly afterwards another child was born, and his will was in favour of his family. When he arrived at Tobago he became acquainted with a free mulatto woman, named Eliza M'Kenzie, by whom he had several children, many of whom died, but three survived him, Phyllis Aida, Sybil, and Clara, the last of whom died an infant unmarried.'[718]

In 1808 Robley had purchased the freedom of Eliza Mackenzie, described as a Mulatto, in St Vincent, for £120 (£8,136.16). The fee was twenty pounds higher than that he paid for a male slave named Finch and a girl called Friendship and the price of two others, Olivia and Margaret, who he sold at this time.[719]

In 1820 Golden Grove Plantation had 187 males in slavery and 189 females. Their numbers were supplemented by five male babies, each noted as being Black (Christmas, Martinique, Duncan, Arthur and Lincolnshire), and five female babies (Abigail, Lucy, Dolly, Lizette and Phoeba). Robley had recently purchased Ben, Dublin, Henry, Robert and Jacobus as well as Betty, Belinda, Eve, Grace, Jessie, Eleanora, Big Nancy, Little Nancy, Peggy and Venus.[720]

Mrs Robley's purpose in moving from Russell Square in Bloomsbury to Tiverton is unknown. There was no apparent family connection. She had recently been in Cheltenham with her son John Horatio with whom she may have been close. Her daughter-in-law wrote the following year that he 'has never recovered the shock of his mother's death, but I hope the beautiful climate [of Madeira] will restore him'. Five years later he was admitted to Moorcroft House, a private asylum in Middlesex.

Mrs Robley may have arrived in Tiverton not long before her death on 5 November 1843, perhaps she had moved for her health. In her will, written on 20 August, she referred to herself as 'at present residing in Tiverton'. Her burial took place a few miles away in Bickleigh. It is a coincidence that this was also the churchyard in which Colonel John Stedman, a Dutch slave-owner from Surinam, was buried. Like Robley's

▶ 44. Possibly a self-portrait by John Gabriel Stedman in Surinam, later of Tiverton, 1794, with the caption *'From different parents, different climes we came, at different periods*, Fate still rules the same. Unhappy youth while bleeding on the ground, twas YOURS to fall but MINE to feel the wound'.

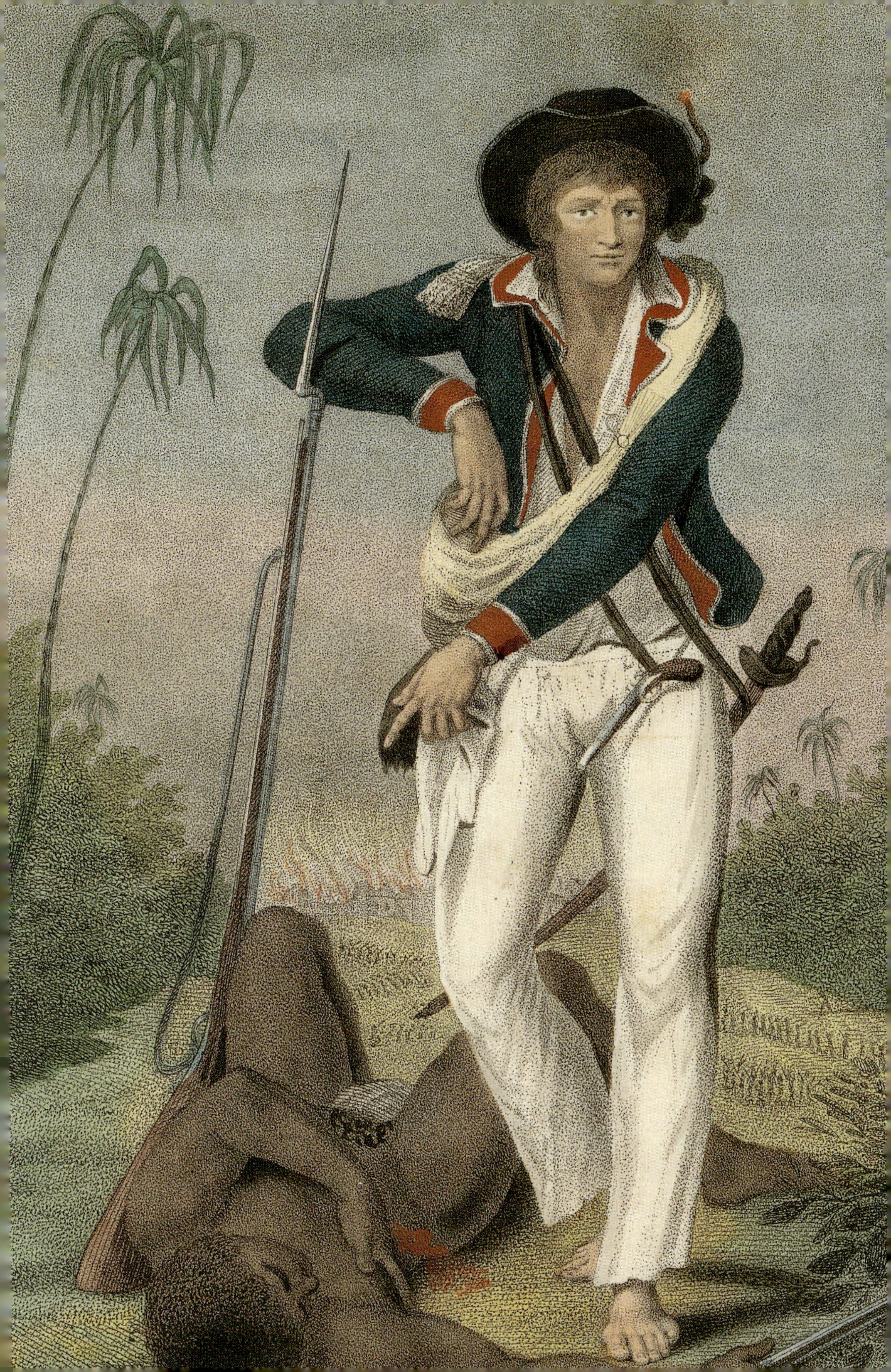

husband, he had a mixed-race child but raised him partly in Tiverton. Father and son died many years before Robley arrived in Devon.[721]

Henry Stuart, Sidmouth

Stuart, a former captain in the 16th Light Dragoons, arrived in Sidmouth by 1820 with his wife Catherine Julia, niece of Thomas, 1st Viscount Anson. There were no obvious connections with Devon. The couple may have already moved to Devon in 1815 when one of their slaves on the New Hampshire estate, a man named Pelagie, died suddenly from drinking an excessive amount of rum.[722]

They leased Old Cotmaton House and Stuart lived there until his death in 1837.[723] Cotmaton, one of the best known dwellings in Sidmouth, was described as:

> 'commanding a picturesque sea and land view, and calculated for the accommodation of a large family, with a coach house, stable, green house, extensive kitchen and flower garden, a lawn and shrubbery, and from 10 to 20 acres of excellent pasture land'.[724]

Stuart had part-owned two plantations in Dominica and Grenada and they provided awards in 1835 totalling £1,935 9s 10d (£131,228.85) in compensation for the loss of 71 slaves. In 1833 he had owned thirty-eight males and thirty-one females on the New Hampshire estate in Grenada. Each of whom was described as Black and born in either Africa or Grenada. Some men were named after place names such as Aberdeen, Calais and Cambridge.[725]

In 1829 Lindsay Ross, an enslaved man on the New Hampshire Estate, complained that Samuel Heron, the estate manager, had violently assaulted him and placed him in the stocks. The complaint was dismissed. Less than a year later an inquest was held on the body of Scipio, another slave, who was found in the garden of the estate.[726]

COUNTRY HOUSE BUILDERS AT EMANCIPATION

In general little or no evidence has yet been found to associate the majority of Devon's country houses with slavery. Prominent buildings such as Arlington Court, Castle Hill, Compton Castle, Endsleigh, Hartland Abbey, Killerton, Knightshayes, Mount Edgcumbe, Powderham Castle, Saltram, Tawstock and Ugbrooke were not built with slavery profits. However, a more minor house, Oxton in Kenn, had clear associations with slavery in the late eighteenth century.

Two of the nine Devon mansions owned by the National Trust were recently noted as having slavery links (Buckland Abbey and Old Shute) but it is significant that this commissioned report overlooked the former having been purchased and renovated with wealth generated by slave goods. Sir Francis Drake's privateering career comprised the seizure of Iberian bullion, jewels and trading commodities which had either been stolen from Indigenous Americans or produced through slave labour. It is puzzling why it also ignored Killerton as the home of a key abolitionist: Sir Thomas Dyke Acland was a deputy secretary of the Society for the Extinction of the Slave Trade and for the Civilization of Africa and prominent at local abolition meetings.[727]

The Landmark Trust has four buildings (The China Tower at Bicton, Millcombe Villa on Lundy, Shute Gatehouse and Stevenstone) whose connections to slavery are examined in this book. No historic properties in Devon that are owned by English Heritage have identifiable associations with slavery nor those by the district or city councils of East Devon, Mid Devon, North Devon, Teignbridge (Forde House), Torridge or West Devon. The exceptions are South Hams (Follaton House) and Exeter. The latter's ancient guildhall held prominent abolition meetings and the Custom House recorded ships trading forced-labour goods and four ships were noted in 1699, 1757, 1760 and 1762 as slavers. In respect to unitary authorities, no connection has been found with a historic building for Torbay (Oldway) or Devon (Bellair). Plymouth City Council owns 3 Elliot Terrace, gifted by Nancy Astor whose American family were slaveholders and whose father fought for the Confederacy.

Four houses in North Devon and on Lundy were likely to have been built in part or entirely from compensation money or from the profits of slave labour. Other buildings may have been erected by slaveholders of 1834 with earlier slave income.

Emancipation and country houses

The Rolle houses of Heanton Satchville and Stevenstone were built before they acquired slave estates and Bicton was remodelled in about 1800 when it is unclear if the family's plantations were profitable and if they could have contributed to the costs. New Shute was built by the Pole family before the emancipation award was given and it is not known how much money the family had previously received from the plantations which were owned by relations in Essex.

Three Devon mansions were erected by slave-owning families before they had emancipation compensation. Follaton House is one. It was inherited by George Stanley Cary in 1822 and rebuilt in 1826, nine years before he claimed for Shadwell Park, Westhope Estate and Grange in St Kitts. In 1835 Cary received £3,547 19s 2d (£240,556.33) for 219 Kittians. When rebuilding he would have had plantation income but the extent to which it contributed to the family's overall wealth will be known once, or if, estate records are found. Follaton comprises two storeys with a nine window façade. A four column Ionic portico is the dominant feature of this classical style building. The family lived in splendour; in 1851 they had eight indoor servants (lady's maid, cook, laundry maid, housemaid, footman, kitchen maid, butler and washerwoman). The family was resident for nearly a century but since 1967 Follaton has been owned by South Hams District Council.[728]

The estates were inherited from Cary's maternal great grandfather, Gilbert Fane Fleming, a former Lieutenant General of both St Kitts and the Leeward Islands. His inheritance was shared with a cousin, Sir Wastel Brisco of Bohemia Mansion, East Sussex. Cary himself, although born in London, was part of the Cary family at Torre Abbey. Follaton was designed by George Stanley Repton, architect. Cary's father Edward also owned an estate in St Croix in 1822.[729]

A prominent Sidmouth mansion may be another. Its owner, Emanuel Lousada, was born, lived and died in London but also had a second home in Sidmouth: he owned Peak House, a prominent house to the west of the town. The walk up Peak Hill, a place name since the thirteenth century, had been popular amongst genteel visitors for at least twenty years before his uncle Emanuel Baruh Lousada built the house by 1794. Although Sidmouth was described in 1779 as 'a trifling place', it was then developing as a watering place and Lousada was an early, but not founding, resident of Sidmouth as a seaside resort.[730] The house was briefly described in 1820:

> 'The mansion itself, which has been built by that gentleman, with its grounds and gardens, in which still further improvements are projected, is a delightful abode.'

In the grounds stood a small 'fanciful building' with battlements to give it the appearance of a fort.[731] In 1831 Emanuel Lousada inherited the house and two plantations in Barbados and Jamaica which in 1836 and 1838 provided him with compensation of £1,268 9s (£86,002.56) for 63 Jamaicans and Barbadians. He also claimed for another estate for which he acted as a trustee and had interests in two other properties.[732]

In 1834 G. H. Julian, a London architect who had recently moved to Exeter, oversaw 'extensive alterations' which were said to have transformed Peak House from being an 'unsightly building' to 'one of the most chaste and beautiful mansions in the neighbourhood'.[733] Thirteen years later it again had 'great improvements'.[734] In 1838 the house was praised in print for having been:

> 'considerably enlarged and beautified by its present owner and occupant, E. Lousada, Esquire, who has manifested much true taste in a new arrangement and disposition of the adjoining pleasure grounds, which will be more apparent, as every succeeding year, by adding growth to the young plantations, will add increasing beauty to the scene. The alteration of the house was designed by Mr Julian of Exeter and does credit to his architectural abilities'.[735]

John Claudius Loudon visited in 1842 and concluded the house had 'some good pictures, statues and books'. Although the house was complimented for being 'replete with arrangements requisite for comfortable and elegant enjoyment', it was suggested that it would take a few years longer for Lousada to acquire good taste.[736]

In 1851 the household servants comprised a butler, footman, coachman, lady's maid, cook, house maid, dairy maid and under house maid. Lousada was prominent in Devon: in 1842 he served as High Sheriff, the first Jewish man to do so outside of London. Peak House was a plain classical building of two storeys and had a four-column portico. Lousada died in 1854 and fifty years later his mansion was demolished and replaced with the current building.[737]

45. The *kingdom of Lundy*, painted by Charles Thomas Burt, 1857. ▶

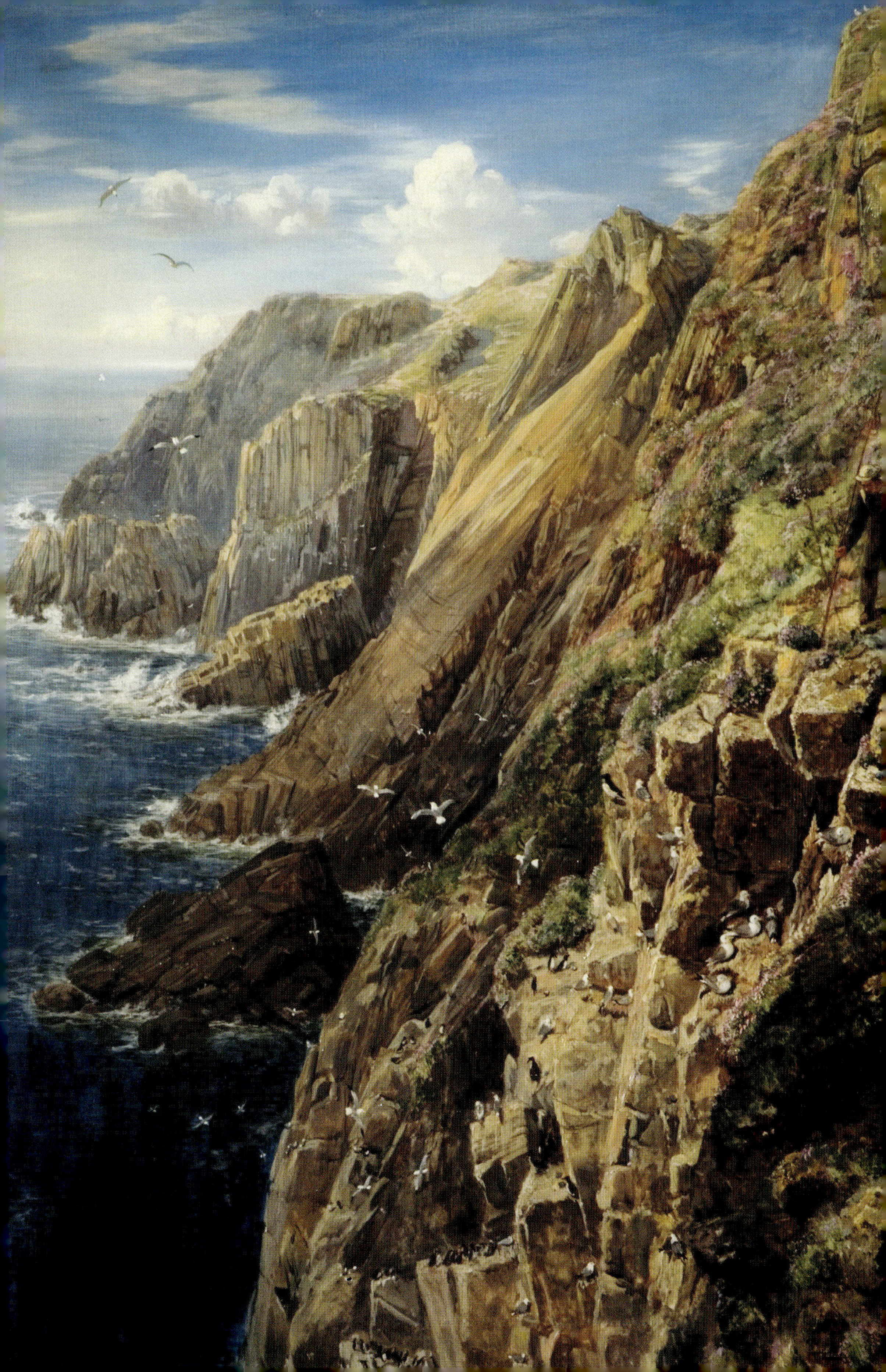

Dulford House in Broadhembury, near Cullompton, may be another example. It was probably in the 1790s that the 7th Earl of Mountrath built Strawberry Hill in the parish and after his death in 1802 it was purchased by Lyons Walrond, 6th Marques de Vallado, who had returned from Antigua. He renamed it Montrath House and after his death in 1819 it remained the home of his widow and of his mother through to their deaths. It was subsequently the home of Lady Janet Walrond who was famously estranged from her husband Bethell.[738] The couple were abroad from 1837 until 1852 but had separated in 1850. The family were said to be 'of Montrath' (1828–) and 'of Dulford House' (1831–). This also appears to have been the same property.[739]

Dulford House was demolished in 1930. Bethell Walrond did not receive £3,626 12s 1d (£245,888.48) which was paid for the loss of 233 Antiguans on the Lower and Upper Walrond Estates. The money was paid to his father-in-law James St Clair Erskine as part of the marriage settlement for Caroline, Bethell Walrond's wife. It is possible that Dulford House was reconstructed with income from Walrond's plantations in Antigua. He had a second claim for which in 1835 he received £862 15s 2d (£38,496.14) for 63 Antiguans. Admiral Sir Edward Codrington also had portion of the claim. In 1830 Walrond had been elected in London to the standing committee of the West Indies proprietors.[740]

Four of the compensated slaveholders, all born outside Devon, built substantial domestic properties with extensive grounds in the county. Three relocated to Devon.

William Hudson Heaven and Millcombe House, Lundy

Heaven, a Gloucestershire tea importer educated at Harrow and Oxford and who was described as 'a quiet, amiable country gentlemen', died on Lundy Island in the house he had built in the late 1830s. He had purchased the island in 1836 although he attempted to sell it four years later.[741]

In 1807 Heaven was eight years old when his godfather William Hudson died in Jamaica. Thirteen years later he inherited six Jamaican estates. Heaven had married three years earlier and the couple would have ten children. It had been intended that the family would keep Bristol as their main home and use Lundy as a summer retreat but it became a permanent home in 1851. The staff comprised a cook, house maid, laundry maid and a sick nurse in 1881 and Heaven remained there until his death two years later.[742]

Heaven received £11,742 13s 2d (£796,167.50) compensation for 538 Jamaicans on 19 October 1835 and 15 February 1836. He owned Ramble Pen, Silver Grove, Golden Grove and Bean's Estates. It was presumably after Heaven received his awards that he paid £9,870 for Lundy. His annual income has been estimated at between £5,000 and £6,000 but a drop prompted Heaven to attempt to sell the island in 1840.

▶ 46. Oil painting entitled 'At Linton, North Devon', 1842, by John Upham. The wild nature of the landscape of Lynton appealed to the late Georgian English traveller.

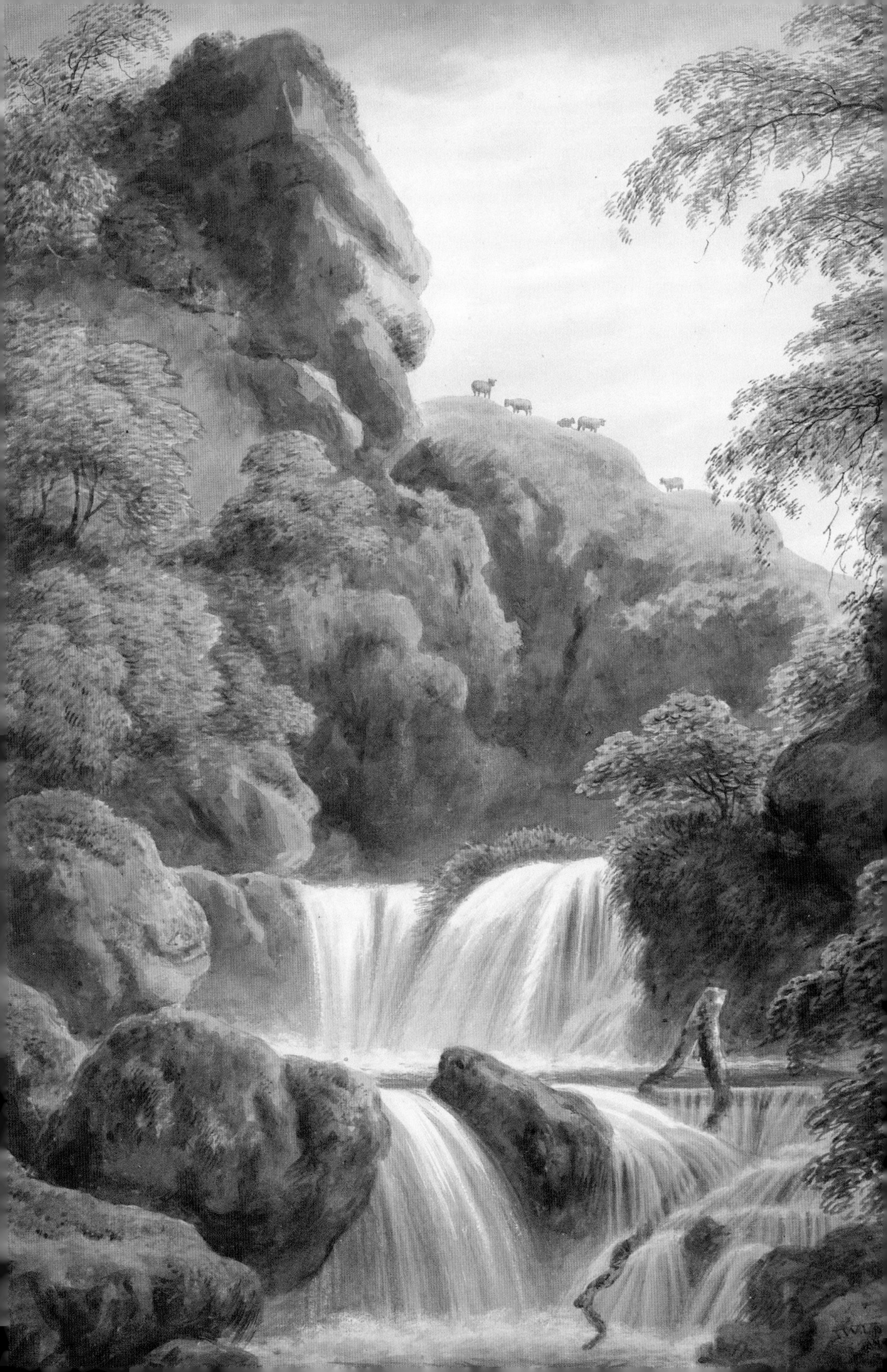

Ramble Pen had been purchased in 1822. In 1824 a conspiracy between the workers and some of the surrounding estates was discovered.[743] Nine men (John Clarke, Alick Heaven, William Harding, Edward Hughes, Henry McKenzie, George Waite, Sam Goldsworthy, Sam James and William Downer) were subsequently charged with attempting to obtain their freedom by force. Seven were found guilty and were hung at the gallows.[744]

Heaven employed a Bristol architect, Edwin Honeychurch, and Millcombe House, initially known as Millcombe Villa or just as The Villa, was erected within two years.[745] The two storey building lies in a sheltered valley and was built in a plain classical style. This Grade II listed building is held by the Landmark Trust.

John James Scott and Combe Park, Lynton

In 1787 an intrepid traveller visited Lynton only to find it 'an indifferent village of poor thatched houses'. Only a few years later another visitor saw the landscape's potential when he wrote it was 'a most astonishing romantic place … the place for wildness and grandeur of scenery [which] beggars all description'.[746] Lynton began enticing wealthy people not only to visit but to build elegant homes in what was largely an unknown part of England. It became known as the Switzerland of England.[747]

One such individual was Reverend Scott, born in London in 1807, who in his mid twenties created Combe Park, his country mansion. It was described as a beautiful mansion in 1840:

> 'The house, which has been recently erected of stone, regardless of expense, and now in a perfect state of repair, is in the Gothic Style with a tower entrance containing a valuable clock and bell. On the ground floor are entrance hall and vestibule, drawing room, dining room, breakfast room and library, all of good dimensions, and a water closet. On the second floor are four best bedrooms and two dressing rooms, two nurseries, two servants' bedrooms and a water closet. The offices include large and commodious kitchen, scullery and larder and brew house, and male servants' dormitories over … in the centre of the buildings is a quadrangular court, 60 feet by 37, tastefully laid out as a flower garden. On one side of the quadrangle is a large hall, 44 feet by 19 feet 6 inches and 16 feet high which might be easily converted into a music room or picture gallery.'[748]

In 1835 Scott, as a trustee for a family member, received £212 15s 2d (£14,425.29) for twelve Jamaicans. His parents were both born there and their families had long ties with the island. Scott's father, 'a silly, vain, chattering blockhead', had served as president of Jamaica's council. He returned to England, died in 1813 in Norfolk and left small legacies to eight of his illegitimate mixed-race children living on the island. In contrast, his son John was in England and appears to have become a wealthy man. By 1833 Scott had moved to North Devon where two years later he began his clerical career as curate of Countisbury and Lynton.[749]

Combe Park was built between 1833 and 1839. During this time, according to his obituarist, he also built a road from Lynton to Watersmeet and restored Countisbury church. Later Scott substantially contributed to the building of a second Anglican church in Barnstaple and it was said at his death that this gift had 'crippled his means'. The corner stone for Holy Trinity Church was laid in 1843 and although there had been some uncertainties with Scott over his promised gift the church had been built and he served as vicar for ten years. However, in 1853 the building was deemed unsafe, closed to the public and was rebuilt with the exception of the tower.[750] Scott's sudden departure from Devon may have been caused by his murky financial dealings with the church's building. His contribution was dependent upon the sale of his Jamaican estate The Retreat but it was suggested that Scott had acted dishonourably.[751]

Scott already had personal experience of building demolition. In June 1840 he had a farewell meal at Combe Park for 400 to 500 local people and moved twenty miles to Barnstaple. That year Scott attempted to sell his mansion with its eighty acre estate, which included the Swiss cottage known as Watersmeet, but failed to find a buyer. The consequence was that his newly-built mansion was demolished a year later and the materials were auctioned that autumn. The surveyor for the parish tithe map noted that his map of 1840 was accurate despite 'several alterations took place about this house during the time of survey'.[752]

Walter Stevenson Halliday and Glenthorne, Countisbury

Reverend Halliday had a greater impact on Lynton than Reverend Scott; he arrived earlier and stayed longer, until his death in 1872. Halliday may have been born in India and started visiting Lynton by at least 1827 when he was in his thirties. An obituarist claimed that it was while he was with relatives:

> 'he was so much charmed by the beauties of the locality that he made purchase of several considerable estates and built the delightful abode in which he has since resided – inferior, it may be said, in its situation and surrounding beauties to few seaside mansions in England.'

Halliday's mansion lies in Countisbury, the parish which borders Somerset, and he named it Glenthorne, now a Grade II listed building. In 1882 it was named as 'the show of the neighbourhood'.[753]

In 1826 Halliday was a member of the United Company of Merchants Trading to the East Indies.[754] His middle name was derived from his maternal grandmother from whom he inherited the Castle Wemyss estate in Jamaica. Neither he nor his parents appear to have visited the island but relations had been born there. Halliday purchased land in Devon in the late 1820s but it was after his father's death in 1829 that he inherited £30,000 and his West Indian estate. Halliday married the following year and built Glenthorne. In 1836 he was compensated for 165 Jamaicans with £3,168 12s 8d (£214,837.46).[755] The estate had become less profitable by the time Halliday had inherited and after Emancipation he considered leasing, selling or abandoning the estate.[756]

A visitor later commented Halliday's 'pretty Tudoresque mansion' was beautifully situated 'though I frankly own it looked somewhat lonely'.[757] The 'Decision Stone' marks the spot on which he is supposed to have decided to erect his mansion. In 1841 the estate itself was relatively small, at 94 acres, but the house had at least five household servants as well as a gardener. Eventually he purchased the entire parish which comprised 3,227 acres 2 roods and 30 perches.

Besides some additions, Glenthorne remains largely the Neo Tudor house which was built nearly two hundred years ago. Halliday is also credited with building Clooneavin, another picturesque house in Lynton, as well as Watersmeet, a Swiss villa, which Halliday subsequently sold to Scott.[758]

Thomas Daniel Junior and Stoodleigh Court, Stoodleigh

In 1841 'the king of Bristol' purchased Stoodleigh Court, now a Grade II* listed building. His firm, Messrs Thomas Daniel & Company of London, had recently received some £137,024 17s 2d (£9,290,463.53) for enslaved people in estates across the West Indies. Thomas and John Daniel presumably were equal partners and received £68,512 8s 7d each. Stoodleigh was Daniel's base in Devon but he appears to have left it unoccupied.

Daniel was born in Barbados in 1762 and came to England with his family two years later. He inherited his father's mercantile businesses before his father's death in 1802. Daniel opposed not only abolition but Catholic emancipation. Daniel and his brother John owned more than three dozen plantations and made 52 compensation claims. Twenty-seven were successful and their awards covered the loss of more than 4,000 enslaved people. Daniel personally owned an additional 200 individuals.[759]

Stoodleigh Court had been owned from 1773 by Mathew Brickdale, MP for Bristol from 1768 to 1774 and 1789 to 1790. He had plantations in the West Indies but his bank went bankrupt in 1817 and Stoodleigh was sold to another MP, John Nicholas Fazakerley, who used it during the summer season.[760]

By 1840 Daniel had purchased Stoodleigh but it may have been a whim: he preferred his Bristol home at 20 Berkeley Square or his country residence outside the city at Henbury in Gloucestershire. It was later claimed that the 'delicate health' of Daniel's wife prevented their living there.[761] Daniel is the most striking example of the geographical reach in Devon of the Bristol slave-owners.

Stoodleigh Court was described in 1846 as 'a large property' and 'a substantial edifice'. It is unclear if Daniel rebuilt the mansion but the next family member to hold the name (Thomas Daniel III) was more involved with the locality. When he died at Stoodleigh in 1872 a Tiverton journalist noted he had transformed the estate. It had been:

> 'originally consisting of ill-constructed farms and of cottages of the meanest class (the typical condition unhappily of most Devonshire villages), it now stands a model village surrounded by model farms. Labourers' cottages, rebuilt with tasteful architectural effect and substantial comforts, have replaced the squalid cabins swept away – farms restored or rebuilt with the addition of every modern improvement in machinery and

useful appliance – unfertile lands drained and rendered profitable by the unstinted employment of capital, all testify to the beneficence of him who has just passed from among us.'[762]

In 1876 the estate comprised 5,751 acres.[763]

His son, Thomas Carew Daniel, subsequently preferred to live three miles distant at Stuckeridge House, a Grade II listed building, in Oakford but rebuilt Stoodleigh from 1883 to 1885. Some internal features, including the dining and billiard rooms, were retained. The architects, Sir Ernest George and Harold Peto, built the house in the form of the letter L from stone quarried on the estate. The new designs were initiated by 1877 and the first plan was rejected. The finished building comprised four reception rooms, twenty-six principal and secondary bed and dressing rooms and five bathrooms in addition to the domestic offices.[764]

A year later, in 1886, Stoodleigh Court was offered for rent. The grounds had two features, the largest orchard house in Devon, standing at 280 feet in length and 8½ feet in width, and a rose house which was some 500 feet long. The mansion was sold, with nearly 5,000 acres, in 1895 to E. H. Dunning, a Devonian who made his fortune in gold and diamond mines in South Africa.[765]

COLONIALS

As seen in the preceding pages, the Devon-born owners were augmented by a far larger number who came from elsewhere. In addition to those already noted, fourteen men and women who had compensation have been identified who were born in the colonies and migrated to Devon. Some had existing ties with the county but it is difficult to identify the remainders' personal reasons for choosing Devon.

Lady Nelson was probably the most famous West Indian to have lived in Devon. She had been born in Nevis nearly fifty years before she retired to Exmouth in 1807, two years after Lord Nelson's death. She initially lived at 6, The Beacon before moving to Louisa Place. Frances Nelson became part of local society such as, for example, when in 1821 she hosted a ball and supper for 'most of the persons of distinction of the town and vicinity'.[766] She died in 1830 and was buried in Exmouth. Lady Nelson had a Black companion who was named after either Cato the Elder or Younger.[767]

Other West Indians include Ellen and William Adlam O'Halloran who also did not receive compensation for losses. They had interests in the Essex Valley and Upper and Lower Warminster estates in Jamaica and were likely to have been the plantations' owners. They were both probably born in Jamaica and were cousins. The couple left Jamaica in 1843 and purchased a house at St Marychurch in Torquay they named Adlamville. They lived there for two years. He died in 1846, she remarried and died in London in 1867.[768]

Fourteen other colonials were living in Devon when they claimed compensation.

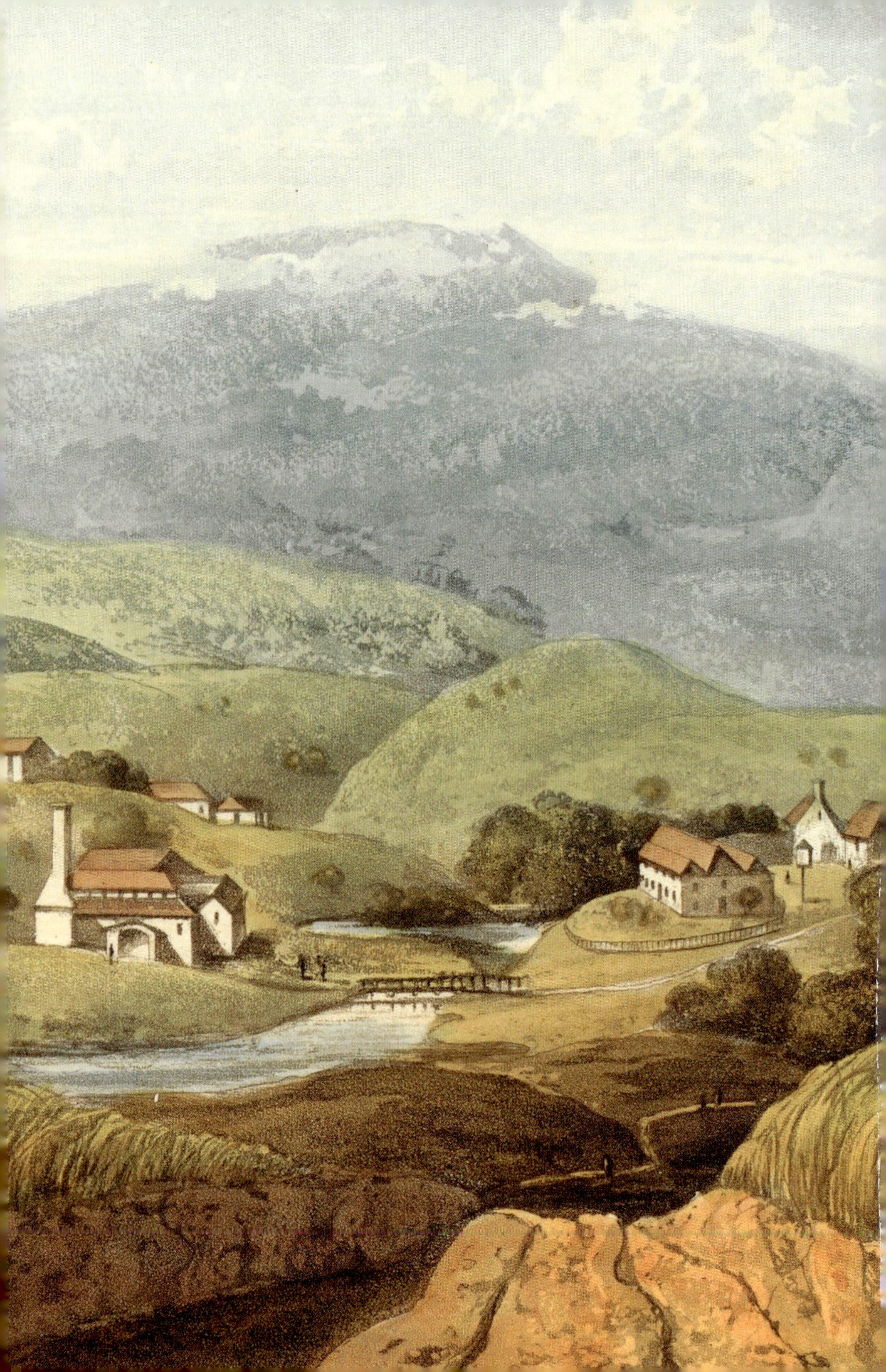

Eliza Abell, Alphington

Eliza Abell was only fourteen when her compensation was paid in 1836. She was living outside Exeter in Alphington where her paternal grandmother had died the previous year. Her parents had owned the Devon plantation in Jamaica with Samuel Glanville formerly of Ottery St Mary. Her father William had purchased it in 1817 and three years later married Margaretta Parsons Neyle of Ambrook House in Ipplepen where her family had been resident for several centuries. In 1813 he was listed as a planter in the parish of St Elizabeth and was resident through to at least 1819.[769]

Presumably the newly-married couple sailed for Jamaica shortly after their marriage when Eliza Abell was born in Jamaica in 1822. Four years later the couple, along with Eliza and an unidentified son (termed 'Master Abell') returned to England. A year later, in 1827, another passenger list recorded that William and Margaretta had returned to Jamaica but no mention was made of their children. The couple had a second daughter three years afterwards: Catherine was born in Jamaica in 1830.

A third voyage proved disastrous: William died in 1833 while sailing on the *Briseis* to England. Mrs Abell may have been with him because she had returned to England by June 1834: that month she remarried in Torquay. Her second husband was Dr James Lewis Davy, a resident of Jamaica who was appointed Custos Rotulorum but more importantly had been a friend of her deceased husband and acted as an executor of his estate. Their marriage was short-lived: six years later Davy died of yellow fever, aged 42.[770]

Eliza was living with her grandmother in 1834, the year of her mother's remarriage. Neither woman has been found in the census of 1841 and it may have been that they had returned to Jamaica. In 1851 she and her daughter Catherine were living in Exeter where they continued to reside with each other after Catherine's marriage in 1860. No further mention of Eliza has been found.[771]

William Abell left in his will a legacy and lump sum to Eliza whom he referred to as his 'reputed daughter'. She may have been illegitimate. She also had £287 16s 4d (£19,514.34) in compensation for seventeen slaves. In 1829 she had owned nine individuals.[772] Her family's connection with Alphington may have originated with her grandfather Francis who died in the village in 1826 at the age of 87.[773]

Thomas Hall, Exmouth

Jamaican-born Hall moved to England as a toddler and spent his adult years in the family home at Englefield Green in Egham, Surrey or at Portman Square in London. He was entitled to a portion of the Williamsfield estate in Jamaica which had 270 individuals. He had several law suits including a claim for £6,000 (£406,807.80) specified in his marriage settlement in 1787 out of the compensation of £9,495 4d (£643,773.63) for three plantations.

◀ 47. Williamsfield Estate, Jamaica, owned in part by Thomas Hall of Exmouth, 1825.

Amongst the enslaved people who died on the Williamsfield estate in 1826 was Trim, described as a male Negro who was born in Africa aged forty six. Another man with the same name was murdered in the garden of the estate six years later.[774] Hall had moved to Exmouth by 1831 and died there eight years later. It is not known if Hall knew of the circumstances of Trim's death although they were reported in *The Jamaica Watchman* and there was a on-going rebellion on the plantation. In court the overseer described Trim as being aged about sixty years old and as a 'weakly, sickly man'. A solider, Patrick Murphy, was accused of murder and claimed that Trim 'was saucy to him' and would not give him directions. Despite the testimonies of several witnesses Murphy was found innocent.[775]

The Hewitt family, Exeter

Jamaica was the location for William Kellett Hewitt's birth in 1757, his marriage in 1782 and the births of his twelve children. Nevertheless when he died in 1812 he was living in Exeter and his memorial was placed in the cathedral. It was then Hewitt was from Cashoo, one of his plantations. Two decades later his slavery compensation was paid to his children, most of whom appear to have lived and died in Jamaica. Several daughters however came to Exeter.[776]

Two, Eliza and Raby, had compensation awards in 1833. Eliza married Captain William Gardner Burn who inherited the Burn family home at Colleton Crescent. They subsequently moved to Byrleigh House in Bradninch and were there in 1833 and possibly three years later when the compensation was paid. They probably moved to Bradninch to be near Raby Williams Hewitt who in 1827 married George Pearse, a solicitor and son of a Rear Admiral. The couple lived in Bradninch House. He was elected the town's mayor in 1833 and in 1843 the Prince of Wales appointed him his gamekeeper for the manor of Bradninch.

Pearse had compensation totalling £4,390 4s 3d (£297,662.11) for 228 enslaved people. His brother-in-law Burn received compensation for 19 Jamaicans of £414 4s 3d (£28,084.15) on Content Hall Estate as did a third sibling, Mary Kellitt Hewitt. She was born in 1795 but no details have been found of her life.[777]

Ellen Lytcott Hinds, Plympton St Mary

Hinds was born in Barbados and inherited two slaves for whom she had £46 12s 1d (£3,159.82) in compensation. They were Molly Frances aged six and Beckey (or Rebecca) who was twenty-six. The latter she had owned since at least 1823 and had been a gift of her father. Hinds made her compensation claim in 1836, presumably when she had arrived in Devon, but died at the age of 37 the following year in Plympton St Mary. It was then noted that she 'had come to England for the recovery of her health'. She was a patient in the asylum and had been admitted in 1835.[778]

Hinds Howell, Washfield, Shobrooke and Bridestowe

Reverend Howell was born in Barbados as were his parents, grandparents, sisters, wife and mother in law. He was educated at the Codrington College Grammar School, an institution which was run with the profits of slave plantations. Aged twenty he came to England in 1828 and later recalled:

> 'My father died before I was sixteen and from that time I have been my own master. I came to England with the determination to be a missionary and studied, not only theology, but medicine.'[779]

Howell later served in the churches at Washfield (1833–7), Shobrooke (1840–46) and Bridestowe (1847–55). A premature death announcement was printed in January 1899. He died seven months later at the age of 91 and it was then remembered:

> 'He had married while yet an undergraduate, and his domesticities hindering his remaining at Oxford to try for honours, he rushed off to Budleigh Salterton. When his wife and little daughter were getting over a dangerous illness, he sent to the rector of the parish, and offered himself for any work that he liked to give, pending his ordination. Soon after, one of the good old hunting squires of Devonshire called on him, and said, *Do you want a curacy, Mr Hinds Howell, because a curate is wanted in my parish, and I have heard of you.* This led to the young man's speedy ordination and the beginning of his clerical career at Washfield, near Tiverton.'

Howell's daughter wrote a memoir of her father in which she penned:

> 'Within a week of his arrival he sought an interview with the squire and quietly asked what was to be done about a school. The squire answered, "Nothing." "Will you give me some land to build one?" pursued the curate. "Certainly not," was the encouraging answer. Then and there my father determined that a school of some sort there must and should be, and, assisted by his wife, actually held one four days a week in his dining room. At the end of six months the squire galloped up to the house and gave a view halloo [a show given by a hunter]. "Still mad about this school?" he asked abruptly as the curate came to the door. "Still resolved to have one," he answered laughing. "Well, I must say," went on the squire "that the children have improved manners, so if you can come with me now I'll show you a bit of land you may have." Having obtained the land my father asked for building materials, and was told that he might draw stone from a quarry belonging to the squire. Washfield School cost about £400, of which £100 was contributed by the rector, my father and mother finding the rest.'[780]

In 1855 Howell moved to Norfolk because of his poor health.

In 1836 he had through inheritance compensation of £3,194 9s 7d (£216,589.84) for 161 individuals on two Barbadian estates. His mother-in-law Mary Ann Goodridge lived with him in Bridestowe and also received compensation for 12 Barbadians of £310 13s 5d (£21,063.89).[781]

Herbert Jarrett James

James, a forty-five-year-old Jamaican who had been a senior court official on the island, lived in Dawlish for seventeen months after receiving slavery compensation. He received £581 7s 11d (£39,419.39) for four claims and died shortly afterwards, in 1840, in Bristol.[782]

The survival of a letter book establishes there was a frenetic exchange of correspondence between him in Jamaica and absentee planters. Financial matters dominate the letter book including of compensation claims. In April 1836 he received compensation for his three minor claims which involved eight Jamaicans but pointed out that he was short £4 6s 8d in the case of two 'head domestics'. James wrote:

> 'The man was not brought up for valuation as he is a cripple and unable to walk as far as the court house but had I understood that his presence was absolutely necessary he should have been carried there. The trifle awarded for him is not of so much consequence but I have to pay 3s 4d per week for allowance to clothe him and pay doctors' bills for four years. What will then become of him and of a multitude of others in a similar situation I am at a loss to imagine.'[783]

While in Jamaica James imparted local news and enquired about the island while living in Dawlish. He was anxious to read Jamaican newspapers. Of Emancipation Day he noted some called it 'the Day of Confusion' and noted 'God grant it may pass over quietly'.[784]

Perhaps more interestingly, the letter book provides insights into the otherwise hidden lives of some West Indian exiles. In one letter written in Jamaica in 1829 his views on death are revealed when he informed Mrs Millward of the death of her son:

> 'In this Country you are well aware how suddenly our friends and acquaintances are taken from us, in the course of a few days and frequently in a few hours. The strongest and most healthy are picked out from amongst us and we see them no more, so short a step is it here from this world to the next. It is now my painful duty to convey to you the afflicting intelligence of such an instance which occurred only the day before yesterday, Monday, before any of your friends were aware of your son being unwell or even complaining and before the doctor could be called to his assistance he breathed his last and his remains were yesterday followed to the grave by the young men residing within town and deposited in the family vault, which Duncan and myself saw closed up afterwards. I have from time to time called your attention to the idle life he has long been living which is sure to pave the way to other bad habits and I would willingly keep from your knowledge the cause of his sudden death were I not fearful that it reach you from other quarters in an aggravated form, and you might blame me for not informing you in the first instance and preventing your mind from being harassed a second time

at a distant period… I have been informed his custom when he had any money [was for] drinking spirits to excess and [he] continued doing so until Monday morning when he complained of a heat in his stomach like fire. He then drank 7 or 8 jars of water and about 3 o'clock in the evening the people about him became alarmed and sent for Dr Turner who found him laying at length on the sofa unable to speak but with a catching or movement of his mouth on one side. He thought him in an apoplectic fit and was about to bleed him but it was too late, his respiration became difficult, his pulse ceased, his eye gradually sank and your unfortunate son was alas a corpse.'[785]

James wanted to leave Jamaica partly because of his own health (he had Erysipelas) but he also doubted the viability of the Jamaican economy after emancipation and discussed migrating to the United States or Canada. He left Jamaica in July 1837 and four months later arrived in Dawlish where his wife had been living since 1830. He explained to an associate:

'I came down here last week for the purpose of seeing my children and finding the air mild and agreeable and wishing to avail myself of Mr Goss's medical experience I have taken a house for a month on trial and if it suits me and my health improves I shall remain here for the winter months.'

Within weeks he wrote that he felt 'the cold already very much, and expect this winter will be a severe trial to my broken constitution'.[786]

James acutely missed his family. In 1828 he explained from Jamaica:

'the separation of children from their parents is one of the greatest miseries to which we who reside in the colonies are subject and most deeply do I regret the impossibility of joining mine and superintending their education.'[787]

He finally saw his children and wife after an interval of at least fifteen years. In that time he sent his daughter lockets of his hair for a broach. James himself had one with his deceased son's hair.[788] In 1839 he purchased land in Australia for his sons and admitted to a contact there that he did not know them. James wrote:

'as far as I am able to form an opinion they appear to be well disposed and free from vice and will I trust acquit themselves to your satisfaction'.[789]

The James family established themselves in Dawlish. They lived at Park House, later a summer residence of Lord and Lady Courtenay, which had three sitting rooms and five bedrooms.[790] In 1839, during a time of food shortages, James imported rice for the local poor. Other ties were more long-lasting: his eighteen-year-old daughter Elizabeth announced her engagement to a local man and James was anxious.

'My daughter fancies herself old enough to undertake the cares and management of a family and has engaged herself to her medical attendant Dr Goss at Dawlish. I fancy she is rather in haste but suppose it is useless my repeating such a disagreeable notion to a young lady in such a matter and shall therefore give my consent to her marriage at once'.

The couple married and lived at 3, Barton Terrace.[791] Some family members remained in Devon. His eldest son married in Ilfracombe, the second son lived in Whitestone, Honiton and Pinhoe while the youngest moved to Bideford.[792] Mrs James had been a widow for forty years when she relocated to Barnstaple where she died in 1880.[793] She may have become acquainted with the town through her own mother; Elizabeth Vidal had lived there for some twenty years before she died in 1858.

In about 1850 youngest son Richard Boucher returned from Australia and became known as 'Squire James' in Bideford. He acquired a reputation as a skilled breeder of sheep and horses and exhibited at the West of England Show. He lived at North Down Hall and then Glenburnie in Bideford before moving to Hallsannery. Upon his death in 1908 one death notice referred to him as 'an empire builder'.[794]

James' letters illustrate close personal connections with other former slave-owners in Devon and indicate there was a community of slave-owning exiles. In addition to his friendship with William Brook King at Teignmouth, his brother-in-law and his mother-in-law lived seven miles away in Ideford, he was related to the James family at Sidmouth and was a business associate of both Thomas Rossiter at Tiverton and Dr Brodbelt in Plymouth.

James, like several other colonials, brought two Black servants with him. One made an unusual decision: he returned to the Caribbean. In 1838 James wrote:

> 'the black servant who came with me from Jamaica is desirous of returning before the cold weather commences. Should you hear of any person requiring his services I can recommend him most faithfully in every respect, both for his conduct on board ship as well as since he has been with me here. I shall be sorry to part with him but he cannot stand the cold in winter.'

Joseph Brown had left Jamaica with James in 1836. His son recorded that they departed Spanish Town with two servants: in addition to Brown there was 'William, long known as cook and groom of my father's establishment'. He was probably the second servant who corresponded with Brown as he embarked from London on the *Elizabeth & Jane*.[795] Both of these men appear not to have been apprentices as was also the case of Julian, a servant he had anticipated freeing some years before.[796]

James' two Black servants may have met Margaret Taylor, the mixed-race slave-owner who was living in Dawlish at the time they arrived from Jamaica. Taylor may even have been serving in the James' household.

▶ 48. Copper buttons with the initials of Thomas Porter, used to identify an enslaved person as his property with second pewter button, early 1800s.

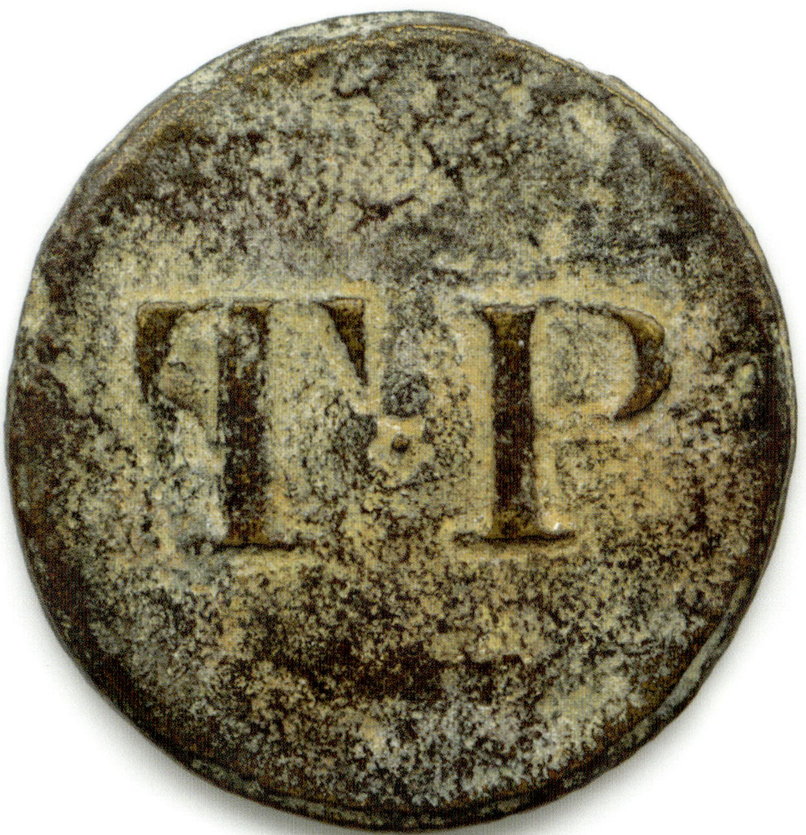
TP

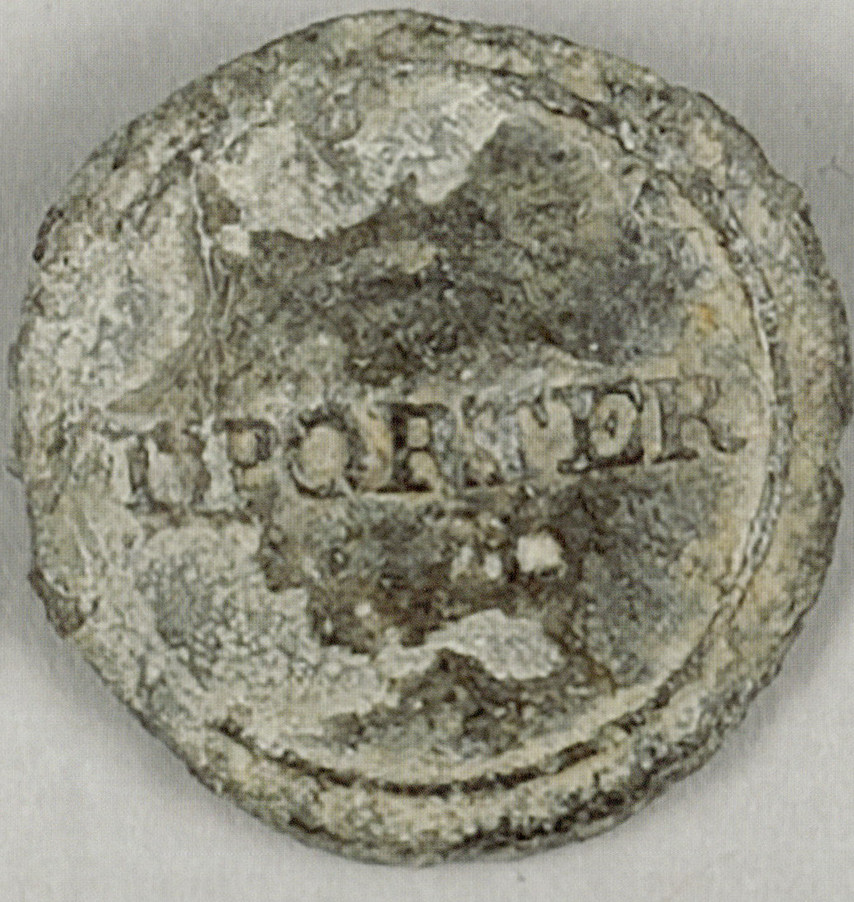
PORTER

John Panton Passley, Teignmouth

Captain Passley served in the 60th Royal Rifles[797] and came from Jamaica where he had twice married. From his first wife, Clementia Grant Anderson, he had inherited a financial interest in the Rothiemurchas estate. In 1828 he offered this estate for letting and it may have been at this time that Passley moved to England. By 1833 he was in Teignmouth with his second wife and their four children. In 1835 he claimed for 80 Jamaicans on three plantations for £1,503 8s 4d (£101,933.60). Passley died in London in 1840 and a few months later his widow died in Teignmouth.[798]

The Porter family

The Porters were among the most conspicuous of the West Indian estate-owners to relocate to Devon. Their wealth helped them firmly establish themselves in the upper ranks of society.

Thomas Porter Senior, Rockbeare

Thomas Porter was born in Somerset in 1748, the son of Jasper Porter who had unusual grievances towards his family: he marked 'the cruel and unnatural will of my father' and 'the villainy and artifice of my sister' by setting aside a sum of money in his own will for the annual burning of his sister and father in effigy.[799]

Thomas Porter arrived in Demerara in 1782 and according to Francis Mackenzie, 1st Baron Seaforth, who was Governor of Barbados, Porter introduced cotton growing. Porter 'first got it afloat and discovered the superior fitness of the salt lands for the growth of cotton'. Mackenzie explained that:

> 'About 1782 Mr Porter of Tobago, a ruined man owing £10,000 more than he was worth, left Tobago to recover a debt for 20 Negroes sold to Mr Elliott of Demerary. He succeeded by his address and during his negotiations with the French Governor to prevail on him to compel Elliot to restore the Negroes, he wished to employ his time and the little money he had to advantage and having been accustomed to cotton planting, he exerted himself in that line and acquired Lot 27 on the east side of the Demerary; this lot he acquired, not because he particularly approved of it, but because it was then cheap (he gave 6,000 florins for it). His Dutch friends gave him up as lost and thought him mad for enterprising in such a lot. To his surprise he found it more productive of cotton (and that cotton of better quality) than those lands commonly reckoned cotton lands. He suspected the real cause, extended his cultivation and his purchases, grew rich, and is now possessed of an immense fortune. Other people observed his progress and followed his example and in the course of 10 years this new discovery has entirely changed the face of the country and the views of its inhabitants.'[800]

▶ 10.52. Four painted figures made of paper and glue formerly part of a diorama depicting men and women in Surinam, early 1800s.

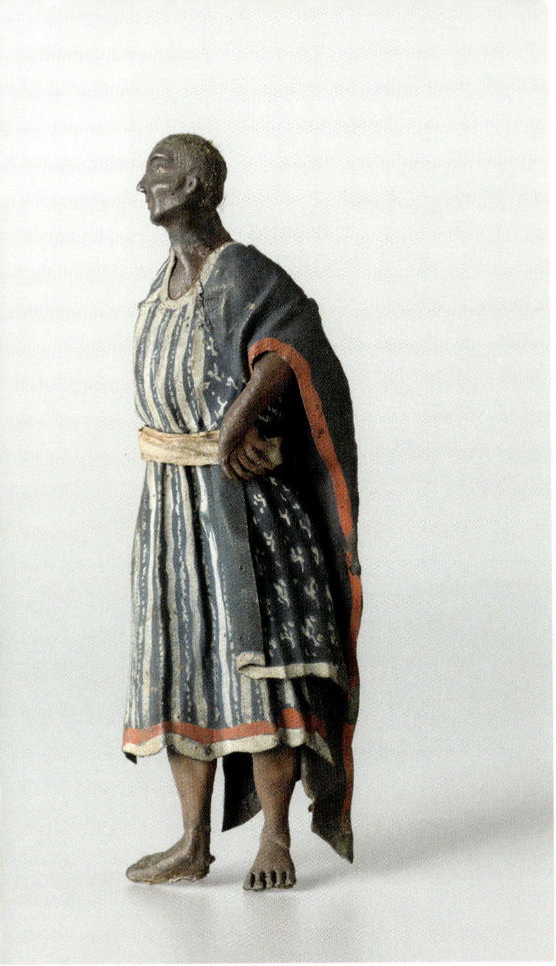
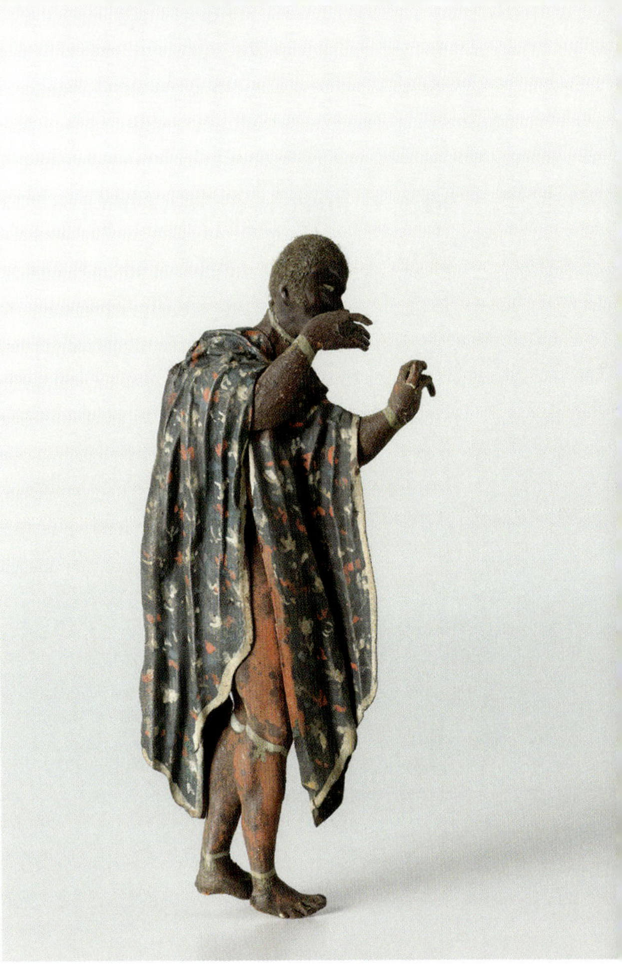
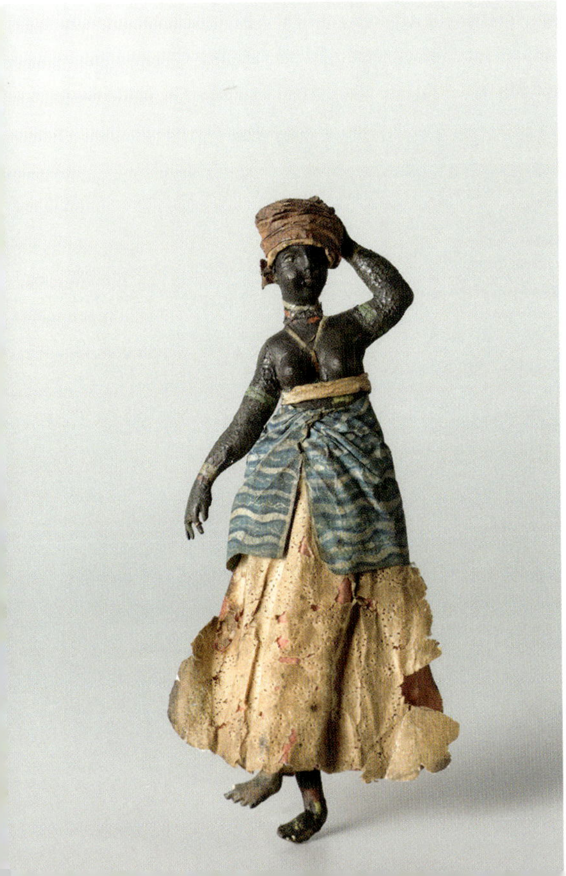
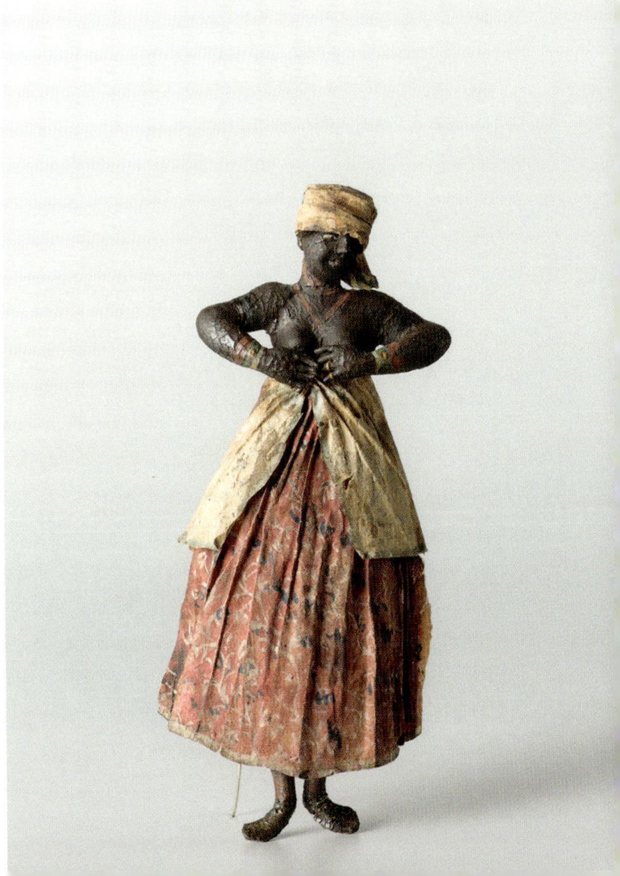

Porter returned to England in May 1796. He was observed by a surgeon on a naval vessel:

> 'the *Grenada* proceeds to take in a cargo of cotton or sugar in order to return with all speed to England. Her cabin is already engaged by a Mr Porter who is about to quit the fatigues of a tropical world, and to retire to Europe with his family. This gentleman was one of the earliest planters who ventured to direct his labours to the cultivation of the sea coast, instead of the banks of the river, and who has turned his industry to a profitable account; his well-merited success enabling him to return to England possessed of a very large fortune'.[801]

Porter purchased Rockbeare House shortly afterwards. It had been the home of Sir John Duntze, one of Devon's most powerful cloth merchants. The estate was nearly four hundred acres in size. In August that year, a few months after Porter arrived in England, the house was described in its sale notice as being:

> 'modern and highly finished with some superior rooms in it and the whole was planned by the late possessor who had a refined taste in architecture and modern gardening'.[802]

Nevertheless, shortly afterwards, he rebuilt and had 'on its site a handsome mansion for his own residence'.[803]

Porter then entered polite society. In 1800 he was publicly singled out for his benevolence in feeding the poor of Exeter and shortly afterwards was on the ruling body of the Exeter Lunatic Asylum, the West of England Infirmary and the Society for Promoting the Education of the Poor. He was also President of the Exeter Humane Society and in 1804 served as High Sheriff of Devon. Porter died in 1815 at the age of 67 and was reported to be:

> 'a gentleman of high respectability, whose death is sincerely regretted by all who had the pleasure of his acquaintance'.[804]

Porter's wealth was estimated as being £120,000 (£8,136,156) at his death. This included plantations in Demerara (Paradise, Good Faith, Adventure, Hope and Enmore) and Tobago (Perry Wood). One of his executors was Alexander Hamilton Hamilton, a Devon owner of a Grenada estate.

Thomas Porter II, Rockbeare and Lympstone

In 1815 Porter, as the elder son, inherited his father's estate at Rockbeare which had grown to some nine hundred acres. It was said at the time that 'his equipage of four horses was one of the most dashing and when he came forth *en grande tenue* [in full dress] the country folk rubbed their eyes.' In 1833 he had £19,295 8s (£1,308,253.20) for 385 enslaved people who mainly produced sugar, cotton and coffee on Paradise estate in Demerara.[805] However, Thomas Porter's fortunes would come to fail him.

Porter was born in Demerara in 1790 and came to Devon as a six-year-old. Like his father he became part of high society although not with the same degree of success. Porter gave generously to local charities, regularly entered the local Floricultural Shows, was appointed a magistrate and was one of three candidates for High Sheriff in 1822 although his name was not pricked.[806]

Six metal buttons, now in Washington, indicate that Porter was trafficking slaves in the American South at this time. They have been stamped T*P or TPORTER and were cast in London. It is thought that they were used on the clothing of slaves and were found in Georgia and South Carolina.[807] The buttons were in the tradition of the livery clothing worn by servants in Devon and elsewhere.

In about 1840 Porter rented his second home, Upper Nutwell, which he had acquired through his wife's dowry. The census in 1841 does not indicate financial difficulties at Rockbeare House: there was a large household staff looking after the family. However, ten years later the enumerator found him with his brother in Clyst St Mary while his wife was living at 8 Beacon Hill in Exmouth. One servant, a gardener, was in residence at Rockbeare House. The following year a journalist commented 'Mr Porter, the generous squire, became an impoverished man. He had to put down his equipage, abandon his large house, for his West Indian property has melted away like a tropical mist.'[808]

In 1845 a family friend, Lord Canterbury who was then the Speaker of the House of Commons, died while living 'in a very retired manner' at Rockbeare House. At his death he was being visited by his illustrious sister-in-law, the Countess of Blessington. Shortly afterwards Rockbeare House was offered for letting and Porter moved into Upper Nutwell. It was also at this time, in 1852, that Porter entered into a public dispute with the rector of Lympstone. He accused the rector of having illicitly sold leases. On 1 May Porter died at the age of 67. His wife had passed away the preceding day.[809]

Henry Porter, Clyst St Mary

In 1796 Porter, a younger son, was only five years old when he voyaged from Demerara with his family to England. In 1820 he married the India-born daughter of Sir Henry Russell, 1st Baron Swallowfield. Within two years of his marriage Porter purchased Winslade House, a mansion which would act as a very public backdrop to his position in society. He also inherited land in Somerset.[810]

Winslade is located in the parish of Clyst St Mary, five miles from Rockbeare House and only four from Exeter. It was offered for sale in the summer of 1821 upon the death of its owner, Josias Du Pre Porcher, an East Indies merchant who was the son of a South Carolina planter. Before him it was owned by Edward Cotsford, another East Indies figure. The mansion was 'suited to a family of the highest respectability'.[811] Porter moved in by December.[812]

The house became the family's showpiece. In 1836 it was noted as 'a princely mansion, the grounds and gardens are delightful, the furniture superb and everything in the most elegant style'.[813] When John Claudius Loudon visited seven years later he was impressed by the grounds: he praised the terrace, noted the rosary had been laid out and planted by Pince of St Thomas and observed that Mrs Porter had designed various rustic structures. The house, he wrote, had valuable articles of V*irtu*, sculpture, paintings and books. He also observed a collection of stuffed foreign birds including 'the bellbird of Mr Watson'.[814]

Porter soon became a prominent figure through generous donations to the Devon & Exeter Infant School, Institution for the Blind, Society for the Promotion of Christian Knowledge and the Devon & Exeter Horticultural Society. He also served as a trustee of Bedford Chapel, vice-president of the Devon & Exeter Female Penitentiary and president of the Devon & Exeter Hospital. He was a magistrate from 1831.[815]

The couple raised fifteen children at Winslade and their mansion featured in public family events regularly reported in local newspapers. During the Christmas season of 1840 a journalist noted that the family hosted 'a large party of fashionables', this included Lord and Lady Aylmer and Miss Rose Paynter. The latter was featured the previous year in *The Book of Beauty* edited by the Countess of Blessington, sister to Porter's sister-in-law.[816] In 1843 it was reported Winslade had a Grand Ball for 400 members of the nobility and gentry. The reporter added:

> 'Everything went off just as it must where Henry Porter, Esq and his amiable lady are host and hostess. If Porter had been reporter, we could have given further particulars.'[817]

An eye-brow could be raised regarding the unusually high number of news stories in which Porter was lauded and often the recipient of public adoration. For instance, in 1826 when a son, Whitworth, was born and baptised it was reported:

> 'Winslade House, the seat of Henry Porter, Esquire has been, and it is intended shall continue during the week, a scene of old English hospitality and festivity, to do honour to the birth of a son and heir. On Monday the infant was baptised at St Mary Clyst church by the Rev. Whitworth Russell by the name of Henry Elmore. On that day a family party partook of the good cheer provided for the occasion, on Tuesday there was a dinner party in the invitations for which were included the officers of the 17th Lancers stationed here. This evening (Wednesday) the tenantry, tradesmen, and servants, with their families, are to be entertained with an excellent supper, to be followed by the merry dance; and on Friday, the whole of the working people, and persons in the neighbourhood, are to be regaled on the lawn in front of the house.'[818]

Porter presented himself as an English gentleman and there was only one mention in the news stories of his associations with British Guiana.

In 1857 the village celebrated the wedding of Porter's third son, Henry.

> 'The early morning was ushered in by the firing of cannons at different points on the Winslade estate here and there the stalwart labourers were busily at work transferring huge clumps of fir trees to the central points of the village, and ere the sluggards of town life had scarcely made their morning toilet, the village was gaily decorated with fir

trees, triumphal arches, flags, and other emblems of festivity. The nuptial party reached the church of St Mary Clyst which was gaily decorated with evergreens and flowers about eleven o'clock, the bride being attired in white brocade, with a magnificent lace fall, and wreath of orange blossoms. She was accompanied by eight bridesmaids, attired in white muslin, edged with pink… At the conclusion of the ceremony the marriage party returned to the parsonage, where a sumptuous cold collation was served up, the bride cake, which was a gem in point of design, and supplied by Mr Cuthbertson of this city, being a conspicuous object. The happy pair having been duly pledged in a bumper, they proceeded in the nuptial carriage to Exeter, amid the rejoicings of the villagers, and were soon en route for Bath. In the afternoon the villagers of St Mary's Clyst were regaled in the school house by the father of the bride with substantial cold collation, consisting of beef, vegetables, and beer. At a subsequent period the females and children of the parish were also assembled in the School House, and liberally supped with tea, cake, and other customary refreshments, the principal members of the Winslade family, and of the household the Rev. Mr Strong, being present, and administering, with their usual condescension, to the wants of their poorer neighbours. In the evening there was a brilliant display of fireworks in the village, and some hundreds of persons from the adjacent country flocked into Clyst to join in the nuptial revels, which were kept with much spirit until midnight, while at Winslade House Henry Porter, Esquire, entertained some of the principal members of the two families and their immediate friends at a sumptuous banquet, embracing every delicacy of the season. Thus closed the nuptial rejoicings of St Mary Clyst, an event which will long live in the remembrance of the villagers, old and young.'[819]

A year later the village again turned out to celebrate a family wedding. A journalist reported:

'The kind-hearted Squire of Winslade House is so well-known for his liberality, and the house has become so proverbial in the county for the good old system of English hospitality which it maintains, that it is hardly necessary for us to say that the festival in honour of the bride and bridegroom was a very delightful and magnificent one. The weather, although somewhat hot and oppressive, was not inappropriate to the *interesting occasion*. The avenues to the church were prettily decorated with flowers, evergreens, and flags; the villagers of Clyst St Mary displayed their customary holiday spirit by adorning the street with juvenile fir trees, evergreen arches, quaint floral devices and banners, bearing affectionate mottoes, and the heart's best wishes for the happiness and prosperity of the *happy couple*. The Clysters have rejoiced on so many *interesting occasions* lately, that the visitor to that valley of historical renown is not surprised to witness the respectable position which they have attained in the decorative art. The *deafening roar of cannon* smote the ear of the slumbering Clyster at the early hour of *cock-crow*, and the violent ringing of the church bell (not *bells*, we believe) excited afresh those holiday feelings which had been awakened in his loyal bosom on the previous night.'[820]

An earlier event had also asserted public enthusiasm for Porter and his family. In July 1855 Major Whitworth Porter arrived home from the Crimea and over the following months he wrote *Life in the Trenches before Sebastopol* at Winslade. Porter was seriously injured and five months passed before a public celebration was held to mark his return. A journalist felt compelled to mark the villagers' sentiments:

> 'The Porter family are deservedly popular in the village of Clyst St Mary and the neighbouring places. The venerable Squire does not, we are informed, take advantage of his high social position to intermeddle unduly in parochial affairs, but always consults the interests and feelings of the parishioners in any measure which he may introduce. He is therefore much esteemed by the agricultural Clysters, who are very jealous of parochial interference, either by Squire or Clergyman. Mr Porter is also most liberal in dispensing his wealth among his poor neighbours, and the kindness and charitable conduct of the worthy Squire, of Mrs Porter, of Major Porter and his lady, and of the Misses Porter, are the theme of universal praise in the district, where they are much beloved.'

A long procession wound its way through the village, with music and banners, and they were greeted at Winslade by the family at the front door. Cannon boomed and church bells rung. Roast beef, boiled mutton, vegetables, plum pudding, rum punch and beer was provided to 140 villagers and afterwards the vicar toasted Henry Porter ('Mr Porter, the worthy Squire of Winslade, was not only respected by all among whom he lived for the Christian conduct which he exemplified and for the estimable manner in which he discharged all the duties of social life; but what was most important he was beloved by all for the kind interest he had always shown to those in distress, and the readiness with which his heart and hand were always open to relieve the wants of those about him').

Interestingly, the clergyman noted that Porter had plantations in British Guiana and had recently received a medal for his sugar and rum at the Paris Exhibition. The villagers presented Major Porter with a silver claret jug. Fireworks and dancing rounded off the day.[821] Another reporter noted that the event 'was one of those pleasant and gratifying revivals of the ancient English feeling, which read to people at a distance like bits cut out of mediaeval history'.[822]

The family socialised at Teignmouth and the Starcross Regatta but there were also long periods of travel. In 1832 it was reported:

> 'On Saturday, 18th, Henry Porter Esq and family returned to their seat at Winslade when the high estimation in which they are held was clearly evinced by the manner in which they were received. About eight o'clock in the evening nearly 200 persons assembled on Clyst Bridge. On their arrival the horses were taken off and the inhabitants (particularly the poor who are much indebted to their bounty) eager to show their gratitude, drew them up to their mansion, into which they were ushered amid the ringing of bells and the most joyful acclamations'.[823]

Part Two: Devon and slave-ownership, 1834

In the summer of 1837 the family returned from the continent after several years.

'The village of Mary Clyst was all on the *qui vive* [on the lookout] on Wednesday the 16th *ultimo.*, expecting the arrival to his mansion at Winslade of Henry Porter, Esq., who has been absent on the continent for some years back, with the greater portion of his family. From the earliest part of the day a general spirit of joy was spread through the whole population of the place, and there was not a cot[tage], however humble, which did not display a flag or festive bough expressive of the pleasure felt by the occupier. Soon after five o'clock in the afternoon, the carriages containing the family and domestics were seen advancing on the road from Honiton, upon which the villagers proceeded to receive them, at the bridge leading into Mary Clyst, when they quickly unhorsed the carriage and four in which Mr and Mrs Porter were riding, and drew it to the entrance of the house at Winslade. To add to the general expression of joy, Mr Porter sent £5 to Mr Taylor, the worthy landlord of the Maltster's Arms, to be spent upon the population at his discretion.

Mine Host wisely judging that if so great a sum were all spent upon the male population, it would be too much for those whose hearts were already overflowing with joy, resolved to retain a portion of the money for the enjoyment of the female part of the inhabitants, a class too often overlooked on such occasions. Accordingly the mothers, old and young, of the villagers, accompanied by their children, assembled on Thursday, cup and saucer in hand, to enjoy an excellent tea, provided for them at a long table neatly laid out by Mr Taylor, before the inn door. The number of females could not be less than 50 and twice or thrice as many children sat down after their elders had finished. The good old ladies were loud in their praises of the excellent tea provided for them, and it may well be believed that the younger portion of the guests were not less warm in their commendations of the share that fell to their lot.

Soon after six o'clock, Mr and Mrs Porter walked into the village, and upon shaking hands with the poor people, whose wants have never been neglected even during their absence abroad, we are not exaggerating when we state that not a dry eye was seen. It is by such acts as this, that the gentry of England, can endear themselves to the classes inferior to them, and callous must be that breast which would prefer such a welcome home to the splendour of the metropolis, or the ceaseless turmoil of foreign travelling'.[824]

Other notable demonstrations of devotion to their tenants include a Christmas meal in 1842.[825]

Porter died at Winslade seventeen months after his brother. His obituarist wrote in 1858 he was:

'distinguished for his warm and generous hospitalities, and for his human and truly benevolent disposition. In him the poor of St Mary Clyst and the neighbouring parishes have lost a generous benefactor; the tradesmen of the neighbourhood and of Exeter a liberal patron; and his numerous domestics a kind and considerate employer, cast a gloom over neighbourhood, one expression of feeling, that of deep regret and sorrow at the death of so estimable a gentleman and neighbour'.[826]

In 1835 Henry Porter received £35,960 14s 8d (£2,438,184.47) for the loss of 709 individuals in Demerara. He continued to own plantations after emancipation and employed his nephew, Thomas Porter III, to look after them. In 1841 the workforce at Enmore Plantation was increased with twenty liberated Africans. Despite his lavish lifestyle, Porter claimed in 1846 that his plantations in British Guiana were marginally profitable. He wrote that in those years their revenue of £10,000 barely covered their costs.[827]

Thomas Porter III

Thomas Porter III sold his father's home at Rockbeare and became the agent in Demerara for his uncle Henry and later for his cousin Henry, the absentee owners of plantations including Enmore which had been named after the family's home parish in Somerset.

He was born in about 1813, educated at Eton and Oxford, migrated to Demerara but in 1839 he returned to Rockbeare and a journalist commented 'he looked in remarkably good health and was welcomed back to his home with every demonstration of affection and joy. The bells of the parish church rung merrily through the day'.[828] A year later, in 1840, he returned to the colony and married Charlotte Wolseley whose family had arrived in Exeter in 1832 and lived in Heavitree. Lady Patterson noted in her diary that they had come from the West Indies and were acquainted with Lady D' Urban of Topsham (who owned a Grenada estate). Charlotte's father, William Bertie Wolseley, lived at 1 Stafford Terrace and owned enslaved people in Antigua.[829] One of his neighbours in this short row of buildings was Rebecca Potter.

Thomas Porter III managed the family's estates in the colony following his father's death in 1857 and he was joined by his cousin Ludovico. Both men eventually returned to England. The census enumerator found him at home in Berkshire in 1861, 1871 and 1881. Thomas Porter III died at Whiteknights in Reading in 1897 and was then described as 'a man with considerable means and generous sympathies'.[830]

Rebecca Cresse Potter née Evans, Heavitree

Reduced income probably contributed to Mrs Potter, a Jamaican, eventually having to leave her home, 5 Stafford Terrace in Heavitree. It was a family house, with a stable and coach house, which was advertised for sale in 1829:

> 'has been erected only a few years and consists of a very good breakfast room, dining room, large drawing room, divided by sliding doors, a kitchen, back kitchen, with a larder and cellars on the ground floor, and on the second floor there are six good bedrooms and a store house.'[831]

Mrs Potter's second husband, James, had died the year before at the family home in Heavitree.[832]

In 1817 her husband owned 33 females (Jennett, Yellow Nancy, Black Nancy, Christmas, Fastina, Princess, Rachel, Sophia, Lydia, Betty, Pru, Charlotte, Christian, Ellie, Ruthie, Alfie, Helen, Easter, Dolly, Mary, Charity, Fanny, Rose, Old Ruthie, Jenny, Peggy, Olive, Hager, Charlotte, Sarah, Malvina, Betty and Susan) and 36 males (Tom, Primus, Dick, James, Robert, Ben, William, Adam, Storer Tom, Isaac, Jacky, Peter, Johnny, Billy, Sam, Lucky, Romulus, Henry, Old John, Papa John, Quaco, Congo Tom, Marcus, Sancho, Harry, Andrew, Pleasant, Billy, Prince, Scipio, Sandy, John, Goodluck, James, Sandy, Edmund) on his plantation in Jamaica.[833]

In 1838 the finances of the forty-nine-year-old would be supplemented by an award of £135 19s 9d (£9,220.13) for 8 individuals on her Jamaican plantation but a few years later she was humiliated by her financial situation being reported in a local newspaper. Her household then included three daughters and a son. In 1843 she was cited by two drapers for a debt of £84 10s (£5,729.21). It was explained in court that items were purchased for her daughters' dowries. By then she was living at South Wonford House, also in Heavitree, but moved to Yorkshire shortly afterwards to live with her son.[834]

John and Thomas Teschemaker, Ilfracombe, Tiverton and Exmouth

Two brothers of Dutch ancestry moved to Devon as young men in the 1820s and 1830s and spent the rest of their lives in the county. They had criss-crossed the Atlantic and lived in England, Holland, the West Indies and the United States. Their reasons for relocating to Devon are unknown. In 1837 Dr John Teschemaker received an award of £5,293 6s 1d (£358,892.90) for 106 individuals on an estate in British Guiana while Thomas had awards totalling £15,668 3s (£1,062,320.94) for his part in nine estates, including Amersfoort and Nieuw Oosterbeck. In one he may have been an executor and the brothers may have shared the Amersfoort estate. Some 335 people had been enslaved on his properties.

Family tradition relates that an ancestor first arrived in Demerara in about 1700. The family moved to Boston in New England in 1796 and emigrated to England in 1801.

John was born in Demerara in 1792 while his younger brother was born in London in 1801. That same year the family relocated to Holland. Their father John Senior returned, with his son Thomas, to Demerara when the French invaded in 1810. John Junior was educated at Oxford where he graduated in 1813 and the following year studied law at Leyden. He served at the battle of Waterloo in 1815 and more than fifty years later, in 1867, he resurrected his military uniform at a fancy dress ball in Exmouth. It was reported that 'the costume of Dr Teschemaker was most interesting, it being the same uniform which that gentleman wore at the battle of Waterloo'.[835]

The brothers continued to cross the Atlantic. They returned to Demerara in 1819 and two years later John Junior returned to England. His brother Thomas remained in the colony and married there in 1828 and, again, in 1831. He was still there in 1834 when a son was born.

John Junior's first child was born in Amsterdam in 1822 and it may have been at this time that a Dutch clock by Jan Hendrik Kuhn, made for a Teschemaker ancestor in the eighteenth century, was brought back from Amsterdam. This musical clock was given by a descendant to the Royal Albert Memorial Museum in Exeter.

Teschemaker had more children born at Bath and Exeter. The family's main residence however appears to have been outside Bath at Bathford Cottage[836] which was acquired in 1826 on a seven year lease. It was advertised as being:

> 'pleasantly situated at the bottom of Bathford Hill, 3 miles from Bath, containing 2 parlours, 6 bedrooms and numerous convenient offices with coach house, capital three stall stable and excellent garden'.[837]

In 1833 they moved to Ilfracombe where two more children were born.

Five years later, in 1838, they were living in Tiverton. That summer Gotham House, a prestigious building in the centre of the town, was offered for letting. It had:

> 'a vestibule, dining room 20 feet by 15, drawing room 16 feet 8 inches by 16 feet, room opposite 17 feet 6 inches by 15 feet, library 16 feet 6 inches by 9 feet, four very comfortable and spacious bedrooms, and dressing room, six other bedrooms, a good kitchen, wine cellar, and all requisite offices, stabling and coach house'.

The walled garden comprised an acre and there was an acre of meadow land.[838] It was leased by John Teschemaker.

It was also at this time that younger brother Thomas moved from Demerara to Tiverton and lived in nearby St Peter Street. His household in 1841 included four live-in servants. Both men sent their sons to Blundell's School. The fact that the two men had only recently arrived in Tiverton was commented upon in 1840 in a local political squabble: Thomas was referred to as having a 'fleeting countenance' while his brother John was noted as having a 'transitory influence'.[839]

Just over a decade later, in 1849, both men once again relocated, with their families, to Exmouth. The older brother lived at 9 Claremont Terrace and the younger one at 22 Beacon Hill. The latter entertained on a lavish scale not long after his arrival. Both men died in the resort. The elder brother was noted at his death in 1867 as being 'a highly respected resident of this town'.[840] Two years later John Teschemaker's family donated to the Royal Albert Memorial Museum in Exeter 'a large collection of specimens of natural history from all parts of the world'.[841] Some objects may have been derived from the widow and two sons of Thomas Teschemaker. The three emigrated to New Zealand following Thomas' death in 1850.

Henry George Windsor, Budleigh Salterton

Windsor submitted a compensation claim on 29 November 1835 while in Budleigh Salterton but his association with the resort is uncertain. It is thought that he was Canadian-born, served as a naval purser and was a merchant in Barbados. Windsor may have been one of the naval men who were noted as giving up their naval careers in order to become 'peaceful citizens and industrious planters'.[842]

Windsor is credited with starting the Barbados Chamber of Commerce. He married on the island in 1821 and had four children, including one born on a voyage to England in 1833. Windsor died in Barbados in 1841 but his business address had been London in 1834. He may have been a visitor.[843] Windsor was successful in three claims which brought compensation of £319 7s 6d (£21,654.04), was unsuccessful in a fourth and acted as a trustee for a fifth estate all of which were in Barbados. In 1834 he had owned five males and three females who were all listed as having been born in the island and whose skin colour was noted as being black. The women were domestics, three of the men were labourers and there were two children aged three and six year-old.[844]

Other colonials

Some two dozen men and women have been identified as moving to Devon before or after their awards were claimed.

Ann St John Maxwell Adams née Trefusis, Exeter

The lives of Thomas Maxwell Adams and his wife Ann demonstrate the difficulties of attributing topographical identities. He was a West Indian whose family had a long history in Barbados by the time he died in 1807 in Exeter.

In 1792 Adams married Ann St John Trefusis, the sister of the 17th Baron Clinton. She had been born in Westminster. As his widow she inherited the Adams Castle estate and in 1836 claimed compensation of £4,400 8s 7d (£298,354.82) for 216 Barbadians.

Mrs Adams was in Barbados by 1802, when and where her son Francis was born, and moved to England not long after. She was once again in Barbados in 1834 but subsequently returned to England where she died in Bath in 1845.

Mr Adams' character had been impugned in 1795 when his wife's aunt, the Dowager Lady St John, wrote 'there was not any falsehood or any fraud that Mr Adams might not be capable of to gain a point'.[845] The local connection may have been through the Trefusis family who lived partly in Devon.

The couple lived at Duryard Lodge in Exeter which preceded Reed Hall, the main building on the principal campus of the University of Exeter. Before Adam's death the lodge was offered for sale. It was advertised as a 'commodious dwelling house' with an estate of 27 acres.[846]

Elizabeth Mary Alleyne née Lowe, Exeter

Miss Lowe was born in Barbados and lived there until sailing to England by 1842 when her second husband James Holder Alleyne died in Cheltenham.[847] In 1865 she moved from Hove to Exeter where on 2 April 1871 the census enumerator found her, aged 79, with three indoor servants at 32 East Southernhay. She lived there until her death six years later. It is probable Alleyne chose Exeter because her son Arthur was the rector of St Edmund's Church from 1863.[848]

In 1836 she claimed £3,064 7s 7d (£207,768.89) as compensation for 135 Barbadians whom she inherited on the Greggs Estate from her father Joseph Lowe. Her enslaved people in 1817 included Andrew (driver), Ben (house servant), Benny (mason), Will (cattle keeper), Dick (boiler), Billy (cook), John (carpenter), Prince (groom) and Teddy (picks grass). Many of those listed as 'Coloured' rather than as Black worked as domestic servants.[849]

John Anderson, Starcross

Anderson settled at Warren House in Starcross by 1850 via the Isle of Wight and Southampton where he had lived at Anspatch House, the former home of the celebrated Margravine of Anspatch. The census enumerator recorded in 1851 that he had no profession. Anderson was awarded £2,686 9s 4d (£181,145.93) for nearly two hundred Jamaicans on the Flower Hill Estate where he had been born in 1793. He was unsuccessful in a second claim as an assignee. His wife Anne died in 1836 and he moved to Devon with an older sister, a son and daughter. Anderson appears to have left Jamaica by 1821. The reasons for his move to Devon are unclear.[850]

William Bovell, Plymouth

Bovell was born in Jamaica in the late 1790s and became a partner in a Liverpool merchant firm up to his emigrating to England in about 1838. He chose to live in Plymouth and occupied a substantial property at Saltram Place. He later lived at North Hill Place where he died in 1851. In 1836 Bovell had claimed for four estates in Barbados, including The Hope, Chance Hall and Oxford Estates, and another in Trinidad. His compensation money amounted to £7,299 3s 3d (£494,892.71) and he acted as the executor of another estate which brought in the sum of £567 10d (£38,446.16). In 1831 Bovell had two male servants on Trinidad; they were James Poyer, a domestic, and William Sandiford, a cook.[851] His list of 1834 for Chance Hall Estate on Barbados recorded the details of a further 127 individuals, nearly all of whom had been born on the island.[852]

Sarah Oxley Cadogan née McIntosh, Topsham

In 1801 Sarah McIntosh married fellow Jamaican Ward Cadogan on the island and later moved to England where they purchased Brinkburn Abbey in Northumberland.

Their house, now known as the Manor House, remained in family ownership despite their moving to Exeter probably in 1828 when they rented Northbrook Lodge (otherwise called Northbrook House) from Henry Seymour who had moved to Wells. This mansion had a six acre lawn, two gardens and a twelve-stall stable. It was 'elegantly furnished' and 'very pleasantly situated' so as to take advantage of views of the river Exe.[853]

Five years later, on 7 August 1833, a grandchild was born in the house but eleven days later Ward Cadogan 'suddenly' died. His memorial stone noted he lived at Brinckburn but died at Northbrook.[854] It was probably because of his death that shortly afterwards Mrs Cadogan left Devon for London where she lived for the remainder of her life. Northbrook was then let to the Marchioness of Headford, was demolished a century later and is now the site of the city's crematorium.[855]

In his will Ward Cadogan noted that he felt 'alarmed' by the Emancipation Bill 'fearing it will render the estates of no value to the proprietors'. Despite this, Mrs Cadogan and her daughter inherited Harrow, Crab Hill and Pickerings Estates in Barbados which brought them compensation of £11,249 12s 9d (£762,740.05) for 515 Barbadians. She claimed in 1836 and 1837, shortly after leaving Devon. Pickering Plantation had 167 individuals listed in 1834 of whom nearly all were labourers and not domestics.[856]

In 1833 Cadogan left £50 to his 'Black servant John Day' who died four years later at St Sidwells in Exeter. He was noted in 1837 as 'a man of colour and known in the neighbourhood as a waiter at dinner and evening parties'.[857] In Barbados Cadogan had owned a number of enslaved people with the first name John and some had second names such as John Adam, John Backey, John Barrow, John Cambridge, John Campbell, John Escott, John James, John Johnson, John Nitre, John Richard, John Sambo, John Thomas, John Thorne, John Top and John Wonda. There was also Little John. John Bailey was listed as Coloured rather than black and this would have made him more suitable as a domestic worker.[858]

John Tharp Clarke, Lympstone and Exmouth

Clarke was born in Jamaica in 1794, entered military service by the age of seventeen and retired in 1856. In 1836, when it is uncertain where he was living, possibly Budleigh Salterton, he received compensation of £163 14s 9d (£11,101.62) for eight Jamaicans. In 1841 the census noted him as a visitor to the household of Philippa Cocks in Lympstone and ten years later he was once again visiting her at 9 Clarence Road in Exmouth. The household was extensive: it comprised John Clarke (born in East Budleigh, c1830), Frances Clarke (East Budleigh, c1834), Myra Clarke (Lympstone, c1836), Alexander Campbell Clarke (Lympstone, 1838), Thursa Clarke (Devon, 1840), Louisa Clarke (Lympstone, c1843), Eliza Claudia Clarke (East Budleigh, c1844), Clarissa Clarke (East Budleigh, c1845), Charles Clarke (East Budleigh, 1848) and Edward James Clarke (Exmouth, c1850).[859]

They wed on 13 April 1857 but the marriage does not seem to have been a happy one. Two months later he placed an advertisement in a Devon newspaper:

> 'I hereby give notice that I will not be responsible for any debt or debts that my wife Philippa, now or late residing in New Town, Exmouth, in the County of Devon, may contract, dated this 22nd day of June, 1857, John Tharp Clarke'.

He died two years later.[860]

John George Cox, South Molton

Captain Cox of the 11th Regiment moved from Porlock in Somerset to South Molton shortly before he died in 1852. His intention was probably to be near his daughter who had recently married William Gould Smyth of Fort House. In 1851 the census recorded that Cox lived in East Street with one female servant.

He was born in St Vincent, he married his first wife in Somerset in 1795 and then his second wife in Ireland in 1816. His children were born in St Vincent (1798–1801), Kenton (1819–21) and Somerset (1825–7). In 1836, when he was living in Porlock, he claimed for two enslaved people in St Vincent for which he received £44 17s 10d (£3,043.71). He had written the previous year 'Having two apprentices in the island of St Vincent named Louise and John – for whom I claim compensation – may I be permitted to know how and how much?'. Cox was worth less than £100 at his death. His son Harry Alexander was given only five pounds because of 'his disobedience and folly'.[861]

James Cunningham, Sidmouth

Cunningham was a Jamaican whose Scottish father owned a number of plantations. The family was one of the wealthiest in Jamaica.[862]

Cunningham was born in 1780, married a Londoner in the 1820s, emigrated to England and settled in Bristol. Their children were born in either Jamaica or Bristol. By 1839, and possibly earlier, Cunningham held property in Sidmouth where he died aged 72 in 1852. The couple lived at Witheby which may have been paid for through five compensation awards from 1836 to 1837 of £14,448 13s 5d (£979,638.67) for 703 Jamaicans on six estates including Biddeford, Bellfield and Hopewell Estates and Ramble and Retrieve Pens. Cunningham was also a trustee for two other plantations.

In 1838 Witheby was described as 'a large and elegant cottage orné'. It comprised:

> 'on the ground floor an entrance hall leading to a breakfast room, 41 feet 6 inches by 17 feet 8 inches, opening with French windows to a veranda 100 feet long, a morning room, 17 feet by 12 feet, a conservatory fitted up in the Gothic style with stained glass windows, leading to a dining room, 20 feet 6 inches by 14 feet 6 inches.'

On the upper floor was a drawing room, eight best bedrooms and another four for servants.'[863] In 1851 Cunningham had five servants whereas his plantation in the parish of Trelawny in Jamaica had 234 slaves.[864]

Edmund Haynes, Exeter

Haynes, a Barbadian, moved to Exeter by 1838 and lived at 11 Higher Summerlands Place until his death five years later in Cheltenham. His home, which was destroyed in the Second World War, comprised breakfast, dining and drawing rooms as well as five bedrooms.[865] At his death the local honorary secretary of the Church Missionary Society noted that Haynes had 'done a great deal of good in the West Indies'.[866] He may have been referring to his petition to the House of Assembly of Barbados in 1822 to allow the Moravian Mission to become 'instructors of the Negroes in Christianity'.[867] Haynes' enslaved adults and children attended Moravian-taught classes three times a week. In 1838 Mrs Hayne was secretary of the Exeter Branch of the Ladies' Society for promoting the early education and improvement of the children of Negroes and of People of Colour in the British West Indies.[868] His memorial in St John's Church in Barbados commemorated 'his Christian exertions and munificent contributions in the re-erection of this sanctuary after the destruction of the former one in the hurricane of 1831'. In 1834 Hayne built Villa Nova, a domestic building which was later purchased by Sir Anthony Eden, in Barbados.

In 1832 Haynes corresponded with the London agent of the Barbadian assembly about the implication of emancipation in the colony. In 1836, probably before he moved to Exeter, Haynes received £5,649 1s 10d (£383,015.76) for 272 Barbadians on Haynesfield. Two weeks after emancipation an unfavourable report appeared in the *Mercury* about the former apprentices on the Haynes Field estate. It was claimed that they:

> 'have idled their time away since the 1st of August and have refused to come under any contract … they have expressed themselves dissatisfied with their freedom.'

Haynes sold the estate before his death in 1843.[869]

His widow Lucretia died nearly forty years later, in 1874. She had moved to Colyford Villa in Longbrook Street and it was there that another former Barbadian, Philip Lovell Phillips, died while on a visit. Haynes was related to the Reed family, who also settled in Exeter, via his second wife Lucretia Reed.[870]

Mary Gerald Kearton née Colcroft

In 1851 the census enumerator recorded Kearton as living in Barnstaple but the reasons for her choosing the town and the length of time she was there remains uncertain. She was born in St Vincent in 1791 and at the age of nineteen married George Kearton of Kearton, a sugar plantation which comprised 250 acres. They had seven domestics (Cathy, Maria, Augusta, Bolton, Mary, Georgiana Eboe and Jem) to look after them.

KEARTONS ESTATE in the ISLAND OF ST VINCENT

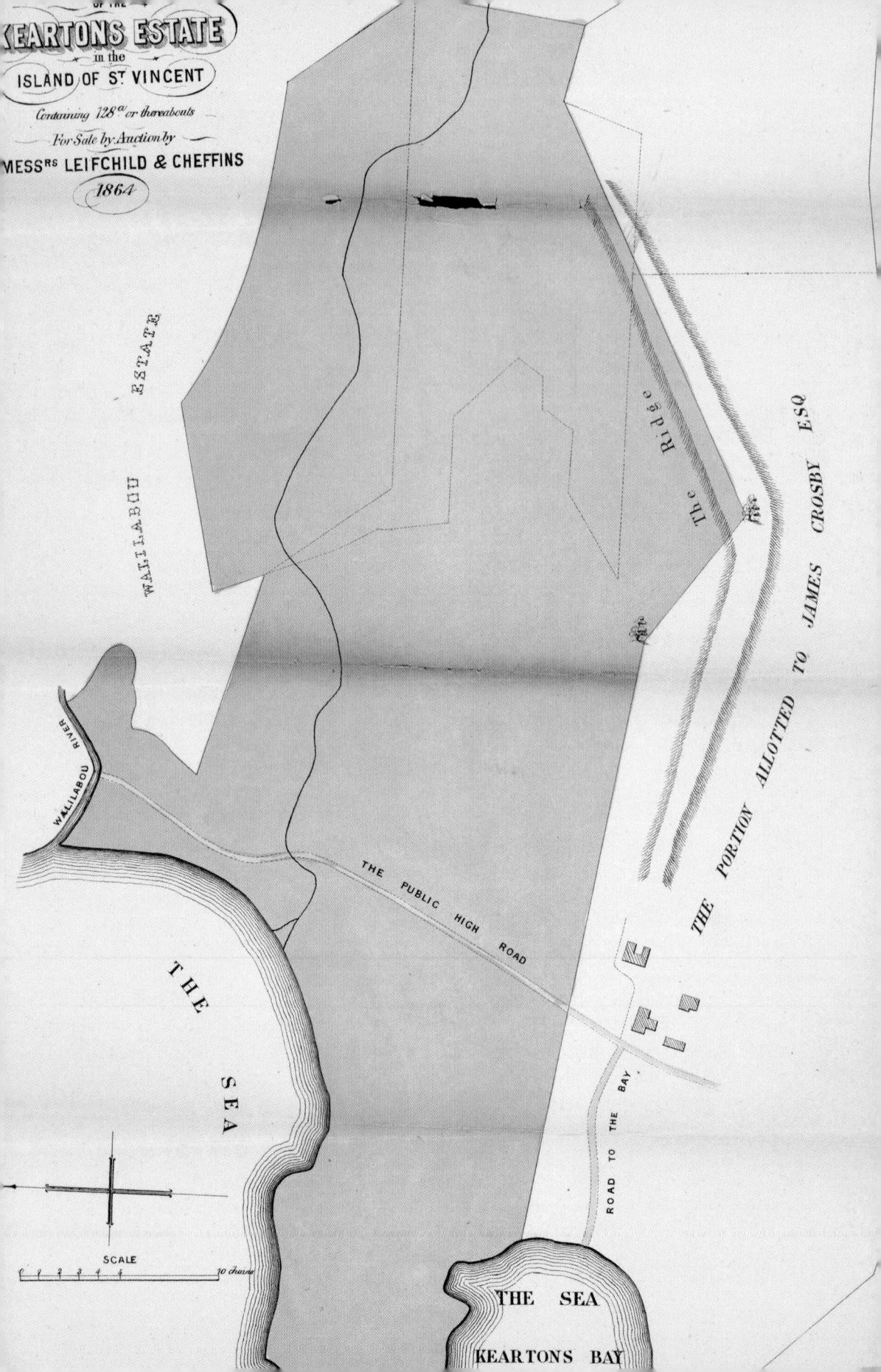

Containing 128ᵃ or thereabouts
For Sale by Auction by
MESSʀˢ LEIFCHILD & CHEFFINS
1864

WALLIABOU ESTATE

The Ridge

THE PORTION ALLOTTED TO JAMES CROSBY ESQ

WALLIABOU RIVER

THE PUBLIC HIGH ROAD

THE SEA

ROAD TO THE BAY

SCALE 10 chains

THE SEA
KEARTONS BAY

In 1823 the couple sailed for England and may not have returned to the West Indies. They had re-financed the estate for an annual payment of £500 (£33,900.65). George died four year later in London and his memorial was placed in a Somerset church.[871]

In 1836 Mrs Kearton successfully claimed compensation for the loss of 10 enslaved people and received £301 5s 10d (£20,427.97). Among those she had owned in 1827 were Baptiste, Billy, Cato, Dorset, Dick, Egypt, Fortune, George, Jingo, Jacky, Liverpool, Little Liverpool, Peter, Sampson, Little Sampson, Catherine, Hannah, Juba, Little Juba, Molly, Margaret, Penny, Posey, Phoebe, Little Phoebe, Susannah and Susy.[872] It was reported shortly after emancipation in 1838 that there had been 'good disposition' shown by the freed apprentices on the Kearton estate into entering into work contracts.[873]

In 1851 Mrs Kearton lived alone in Barnstaple with a servant, Mary Staple, who had been born in Ilminster in Somerset. She died in Bedford in 1869 at the age of 78.[874]

Ann Clarke McClery, Seaton

McClery was another late comer to Devon. She was born in Jamaica in 1810. She came to England by 1841 when she began a peripatetic lifestyle living in Hertfordshire, Somerset, Wiltshire and by 1881 she shared 4 Violet Terrace in Seaton with her sister Judith. Their mother had left them equal shares in Galloway Estate and in 1836 she received £179 13s 5d (£12,181.92) for the loss of 12 Jamaicans. William Jones, David Clarke, James Williams, Charles Douglass and John Peat were some of the enslaved men who were listed in 1832 and would have gained their freedom two years later.[875] In 1891 she was living with her niece at The Elms in Beer Road also in Seaton.

Elizabeth Mary Mayne née Hewitt, Sidmouth

On first glance Mayne's connection to Devon would appear to be with Sidmouth where she died in 1875 but another through her mother may have been more important. She was born in Jamaica in 1809 and came to England sometime before 1840. That year she married Captain Dawson Mayne, who had been stationed in the West Indies from 1821 to 1832, in Shropshire. They may have originally met in Jamaica. Shortly before his marriage Mayne had been appointed the county's Chief Constable. This may have been arranged through his cousin Rowland Hill, a Member of Parliament for Shropshire. Hill's and Mrs Mayne's mothers were sisters and both had been born in Exeter. Mayne retired in 1859 and in 1871 the couple lived in Leamington Spa with his unmarried sister. Brother and sister visited their brother in Ireland in 1872 and died within a month of each other. Mrs Mayne appears to have then moved to Sidmouth where three years later she died at 2 Clifton Terrace

◀ 53. Map of the northern part of Kearton Estate, noted as a valuable sugar and arrowroot estate, 1864, in St Vincent.

at the age of 65. In 1838, shortly before her marriage, she had an award of £190 9d (£12,884.79) for her loss of 24 Jamaicans.[876]

Martha Moody née Clement, Exeter

A few individuals owned only one slave. They included Martha Moody who spent 1851 to 1853 in Devon; in her late sixties she lived with three of her children at 7 Bystock Terrace in Exeter in 1851, and possibly at 6 Baring Crescent two years later, before moving to Hampshire. She had been born in Barbados and lived in British Guiana before emigrating to England where she mostly lived in London and Essex. Her compensation award in 1835 of £35 9s 10d (£2,406.38) for one enslaved person on a British Guiana estate is not representative of the wider and longstanding investment by her family; her Dutch father had plantations in Barbados. Nor does it convey the considerable role that Moody's husband, Thomas, had in abolition and in informing slave policies in the West Indies.[877] Among his government work was commenting upon Lord Rolle's proposal to relocate his enslaved people from the Bahamas to Trinidad.[878] One of Moody's near neighbours at Bystock Terrace was Anne Cranstoun, Baroness Scotland, who had been born in the West Indies.

Phillip Lovell Phillips, Torquay

In 1869 Phillips went to Exeter for 'a change of air'. His doctor had recommended leaving Torquay for his health but he died not long afterwards. He stayed at Colyford Villa with Lucretia Haynes, the widow of Edmund Haynes, another West Indian planter. Phillips had been born in Barbados but relocated to Torquay by 1838. His elderly father, John Randall Phillips, moved that year from Edinburgh to spend his last seven years with him at Torville.

Durants Estate in Barbados had passed to Phillips through his mother. In 1836, just before Phillips moved to Devon, an award of £1,576 16s 11d (£106,912.20) was made for the loss of 86 individuals. In 1832 there had been 206 people enslaved. Many were recorded without second names including Dogood, Christmas, Apollo, London, Cambridge, Windsor, Princess, Present, Duchess and Polidore.[879]

It was noted at Phillips' death in 1869 that he was a large landowner in Barbados. Despite being an absentee owner he wrote, in 1845, *An essay on Tropical Agriculture*. A reviewer suggested:

> 'This important and opportune pamphlet has been written with the view of stimulating the West Indian Planter to overcome the difficulties arising from a deficient supply of labour, the adoption of the aids which science holds out to them, no less than to our home agriculturist. The author is a West India Planter, and is, therefore, competent to appreciate and point out the incalculable benefits which would accrue, not only to the Planters, but to the consumers of their produce, from the employment of the much improved agricultural implements, and the recent discoveries in agricultural chemistry, in so far as they are applicable to the peculiar character of tropical cultivation. The

work contains much useful information respecting draining and the management and scientific application of various manures. It is in a small compass, and is, moreover, cheap (2s 6d). We strongly recommend it the perusal, and attentive consideration, of all in any way concerned in West Indian cultivation or prosperity.'[880]

Amongst his enslaved people in Barbados was a man called Exeter.[881] Phillips does not appear to have practised medicine while living in Torquay.

John Prettejohn, Exmouth

Prettejohn inherited the Constant Plantation in Barbados and in 1837 three trustees were paid his compensation of £1,873 16s 9d (£127,048.62). Part of the original claim was awarded elsewhere because of financial obligations made in 1777 and another, regarding a marriage settlement, was in dispute from the 1830s through to at least 1852. Amongst the men that Prettejohn owned in 1834 were Sambo, Philas, Benny, Bob, John Edward, Nat, Frederick, Quaman, Billy, Richard, Bouman, Pollydore, Thomas, Ben Horn, Monday, King and Tom Boy. They were all described as Black and Barbadian. Prettejohn also owned several hundred other men, women and children.

Prettejohn had been born in Barbados in about 1778, married in Bath, spent many years in Berkshire and then moved to Exmouth in about 1850. His family lived at 3 Claremont Terrace until his death three years later. This short period of residency appears inconsequential but Prettejohn was not merely another retiree who relocated to Devon's coastal resorts to die. His father had been born in Exmouth in 1731 and emigrated to Barbados where he died in 1803. In moving to Exmouth Prettejohn was returning to his family's roots.[882]

Charles Schaw, Torquay

Major Schaw, a Jamaican, spent his adult years serving in the army or as a government official before retiring to Torquay in 1858. His military service included time in the West Indies but in 1833 he moved his family to Tasmania where he was appointed a police magistrate. In 1838 he was awarded £196 11s 11d (£13,329.45) for 8 Jamaicans. Schaw had owned 16 enslaved people in 1823 and 10 in 1826.[883] While in Tasmania he built Schawfield, a thirty-room mansion. Concerns were expressed about Schaw when he was appointed and Tasmanians summarised him as having an autocratic temperament, a short temper, being haughty, of harbouring strong prejudices and living on the edge of bankruptcy.[884]

Schaw's last sixteen years of his life were spent at Torquay and devoted to the Church of England. His obituarist in Torquay noted:

'When others, like him, find they have lived too active and orderly a life of duty, to be content and happy without something to give a point and character to the daily life of old age, may they find, as he did, that the church offers a work as well as a refuge for the old and the lonely, and in learning to die, leave the light of a Christian life behind them.'[885]

Schaw's character in retirement contrasted with that in Tasmania which had earned him the resentment of local people and 'a universal feeling of indignation' of his peers.[886] Cheltenham Villa was his first Torquay home which he shared with his wife and two of his eight children. He later moved to 4, Modena Terrace. He died in 1874 aged 88.[887]

Catherine Seaman née Blake, Teignmouth

Blake was born in Jamaica in 1798, the daughter of a clergyman. She married Dr William Boog Seaman, an army surgeon, who died in 1819 not long after the birth of their third child. Mrs Seaman and her children subsequently moved to England and by 1838 they were in Devon: that year her daughter Christian Anne was married in Heavitree church. Shortly afterwards Mrs Blake was living in Teignmouth where she died in 1864. They had a number of addresses (Bitton Street, Carlton Place and Landscore Villa) but her reason for choosing this resort is unknown. Her award was for six Jamaicans on the Devon Pen estate for whom she received £185 18s 6d (£12,605.96) in 1835. In 1817 she owned Judith Brave and her two young children, each described as a 'Mulatto'. In 1823 and 1829 Blake had thirteen individuals on her plantation. In the latter list a number of name changes were recorded. Mary Smith had formerly been known as Jane, Sarah Smith had been Sally Smart, and Caroline Smith had been called Phyllis.[888]

Robert Semple, Torquay

Semple may have come to Torquay in 1845 for his health given he was admitted to Stafford county asylum four years later and died the following year at the age of about fifty two. Semple was born in Demerara, married in Glasgow and raised his family in Demerara in the 1820s before sailing to Liverpool in 1830.[889] In 1834 he received £581 8s 1d (£39,419.96) for ten individuals. They did not include Princess, who in 1823 had complained about the treatment Semple had given her. She testified in court:

> 'That this morning she saw a woman of the name of Cuba sitting down asleep; she said to her *What was you doing last night that you did not sleep*? At the same time Mr Semple came out of his bedroom and asked me what I said. I told him. He said *You always have something to say. Better shut your mouth.* I answered him again, *Master I don't speak with you. I speak with Cuba* and then I came downstairs and went into the kitchen. Master followed me into the kitchen and told me I had better go to my work than meddle

54. Stewart Castle Plantation in Jamaica, 1840, owned by Robert Shedden of Torquay. ▶

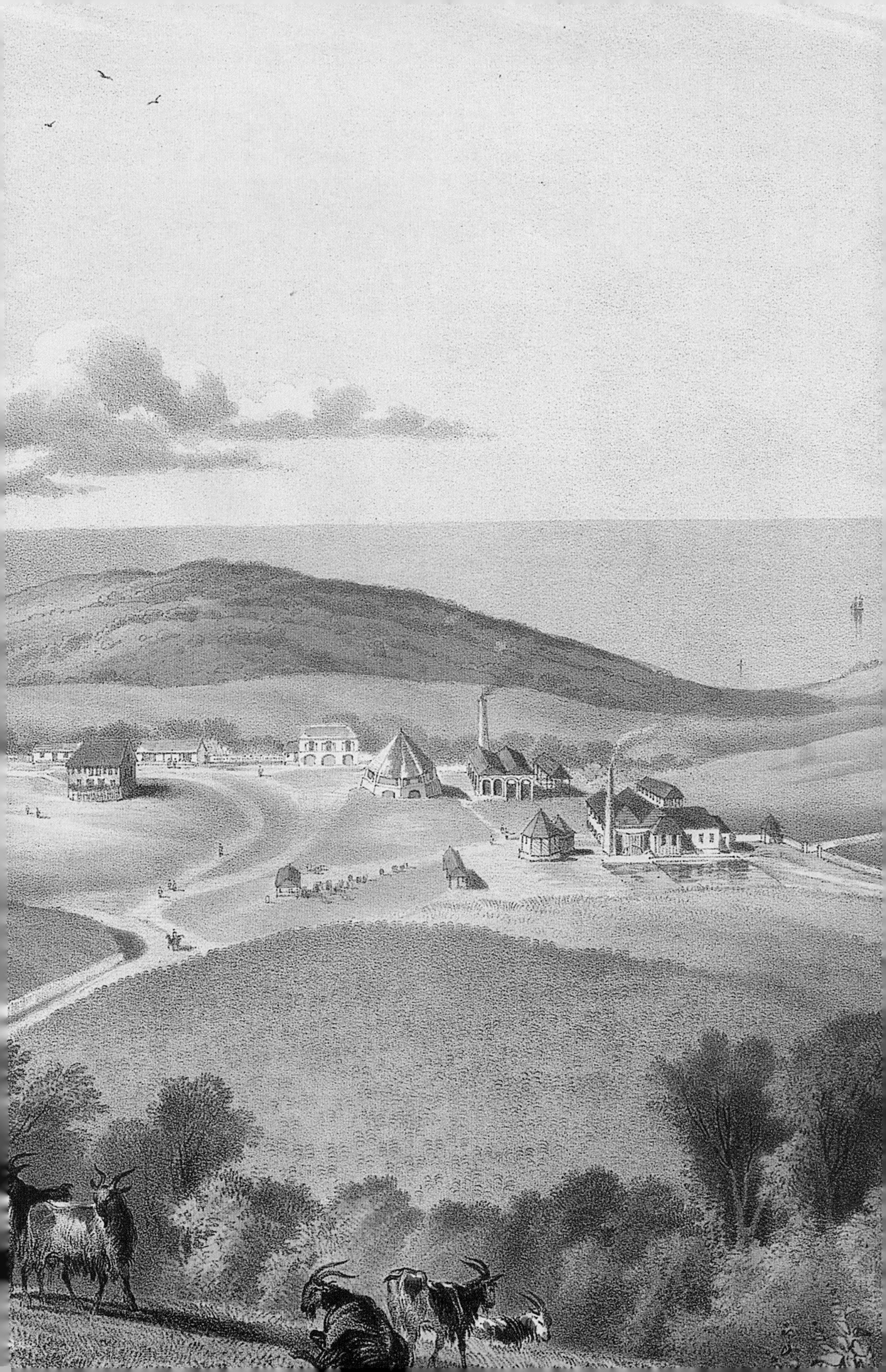

my tongue. I answered him *I am doing my work, and you come to trouble me; I was not speaking to you*. Then he went to the store and took a horsewhip and began to flog me. I asked him for what he flogged me; he said for badness. I told him *So long as you flog me for nothing, I shall go to the Fiscal* and I came away.'[890]

By 1846 Semple and his family lived at Brotherton House in Torquay. One daughter married in Tormohun Church. Her husband was from Demerara. Semple's Torquay home was large; it had five bedrooms with separate accommodation for servants, a large drawing room, a dining room, a stable for four horses and a coach house.[891]

Robert Shedden, Torquay

In 1840 Robert Shedden Sulyarde Cary was twelve years old when he inherited the Torre Abbey estate in Torquay. His maternal grandfather, Robert Shedden, managed it on his behalf as a trustee until he turned twenty-one in 1849. In 1854 it was discovered that the estate had poor financial management; Cary moved to Wales, the contents of the abbey were auctioned and land was sold. He returned to Torquay two decades later.[892]

His grandfather Shedden had been born in Virginia in about 1777, married his wife in London twenty-five years later and became a partner in a merchant firm based in London, Robert Shedden & Sons. In 1835 he received £934 14s 10d (£63,376.70) for his share in a Jamaican plantation. In 1823 he had owned 280 Jamaicans at the Stewart Castle plantation. Some of them, such as Mercury Crosby, Charlotte Dallas, Queen Duncan, Tom Dalrymple, Venus Pusey and Amy Faith, appear in lists from 1817 onwards and may have lived until emancipation in 1834. Cary died in 1856, aged 82, while at the abbey.[893]

Maria Manuella Strickland née Sorzano, Exmouth and Dawlish

Sorzano, of Spanish descent, was born in Trinidad in 1795, married her Lancashire-born husband Martin on the island in 1814, moved with him to Liverpool and sometime after his death settled on the south coast of Devon. She was still in Lancashire in 1841 but by 1851 had moved to 1 Prospect Place in Exmouth and then Marine Parade in Dawlish where she died in 1857. Compensation was not administered until 1857 when it was paid to her descendants; this amounted to £2,876 10s 1d (£195,030.72) for an estate in Trinidad which had 58 enslaved people. In 1822 Mrs Strickland had owned in her own right three individuals and the family's estate of Torrecilla then had forty-four slaves.[894]

▶ 55. View of Kingston from Windsor Farm, Jamaica, the property of Thomas Reid Tharp of Topsham, 1820–1, drawn by James Hakewill.

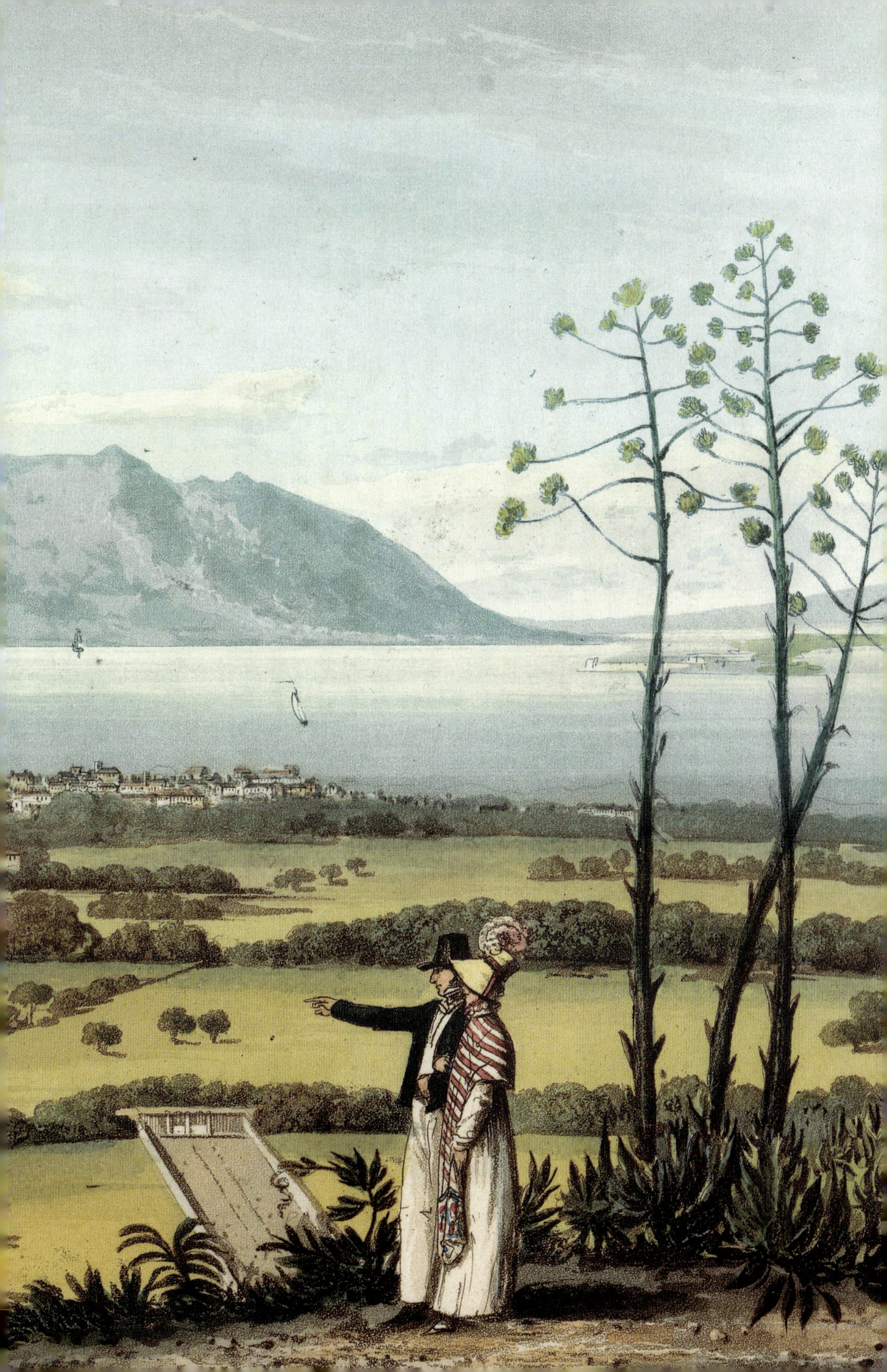

Edward Butler Taylor, Teignmouth

Taylor, an attorney, was in his native Barbados in 1836 when he had his award of £1,079 14s 5d (£73,206.48) for 43 enslaved people on Arthur Seat Estate. In 1817 his eight household slaves were Isaac (black, 42, born in Africa), Simon (black, 22, Barbadian), Diana (black, 28, a Creole from Grenada), Adel (black, 28, a Creole from Martinique), Juliet (black, five months old, a Creole from Martinique), Fanny (Coloured, 42, Barbadian), Kitty Ann (Coloured, 7, Barbadian) and Charlotte (Coloured, 4, Barbadian). Twelve years later, in 1829, he owned 39 human beings.

Taylor relocated to Bristol in the late 1830s before settling down at West Teignmouth. By 1851 he was at Tuckers Garden with his married daughter and two servants. Taylor died two years later in Teignmouth and was buried in Bristol.[895]

Thomas Reid Tharp, Topsham

Jamaican Tharp relocated with his parents to Devon possibly as a young man in the 1820s. He inherited a share in the Windsor plantation for which Tharp received £745 7s 11d (£50,538.81) as emancipation compensation. His father William, who was noted as being 'formerly of St Servians, France and late of Bradninch', had died seven years earlier in Heavitree, presumably where the family was then living.

Tharp was probably 'T. Tharp Esquire' who sold his genteel household furniture from Seldon Cottage in Moor Lane in 1824. He was 'going abroad'. If so, he returned by 1851 for he was living at Seabrook in Topsham with his mother Mary, also a beneficiary of the plantation. She died at Seabrook in 1854 aged one hundred. Ten years later Tharp moved to Barton Cottage, also in Topsham, and died in 1878.[896]

Elizabeth Wallen née Ford, Exeter

Wallen, possibly a visitor, died at Mount Radford in Exeter in 1835. She had been born in Canada in about 1791 and fifteen years later married Major Edward Pinnock Wallen, later a customs officer, in Jamaica. They had three children born on the island and emigrated to England by 1821 when a third daughter was born in Reading. Major Wallen died there the following year. He owned thirteen individuals that year whereas in 1817 the total number had been twenty-three. The colour of their skin was noted as either Quadroon (3), Mulatto (5) or Negro (15). Only three men had been born in Africa, the others were listed as Creoles. Mrs Wallen's claim of £477 10s 10d (£32,377.95) for the loss of her 18 Jamaicans was paid on 2 November 1835, a few days after her death at Radnor Place.[897]

There are various ways in which to try to understand these individuals and to discover their role in Devon. It is harder to define their legacies. William Hudson Heaven endures in his villa on Lundy while others, like the Colleton family, are remembered by having lent their names to streets or buildings. Most had families and their descendants today may or may not be aware of their history. Outside the county, in the former slave colonies, Devon names remain attached to former estates and the descendants of the enslaved bear former owners' surnames.

At the time this disparate group of a hundred or so men and women were outnumbered by the many others whose livelihoods were associated in other ways with the British Empire. It is difficult to see how former slaveholders could easily be distinguished from other colonials unless they had Creole accents. It is not known how freely they admitted to owning other human beings.

The wealthier of them, in this rigid class-ordered society, mixed with like people and were attended by men and women who were less likely to know how their employers' incomes originated or at least understand what portion was contributed by forced-labour profits. Jane Hunt, a house servant from Sandford, most likely knew of the Barbadian origins of her Exmouth employer John Prettejohn but did she, by 1850, associate him then with slavery? Elizabeth Tucker, a kitchen maid born in Harberton but employed at Follaton House outside Totnes, may not have been aware how much George Stanley Cary's award of £3,547 19s 2d (£240,556.33) contributed to her salary. In contrast, John Delve, a butler from Barnstaple, would have realised that his employer, Henry Porter of Winslade, was a sugar plantation owner. The extent and origins of his wealth were well-known in Devon let alone to Delve along with Edmund Patch, a footman from Otterton, Mary Ann Davis, a cook from Broadclyst, and another nine other live-in servants.[898] How many of the staff did not whisper of his grant of £35,960 14s 8d (£2,438,184.47)?

In addition to how slaveholders were seen by others, there remains the question of how they saw themselves. No personal insights were recorded except those of Lord Rolle who cited his conscience in 1838. The journalist noted he said:

> 'He had been left a large number of slaves by his father. He could not reconcile it to his conscience to be the possessor of slaves and upon his accession to the property he had given them full liberty, and he had the pleasing satisfaction of saying that they were now very industrious, they supported themselves and were contented and happy'.[899]

Rolle may have been misquoted or he was already writing his own history. Although slavery was only one of many divisive issues, it had been unpopular with the British public for many years. When he made this speech in the last days of emancipation, Rolle may have been considering how he, as with other former slave-holders, would be remembered by subsequent generations.

Conclusion

'All the singers are said to have been slaves. Slavery does not seem to have injured them in the least, for they are good specimens of the Negro race, merry and vigorous, and supremely satisfied with themselves and their surroundings.' Exeter, 1877

The most useful means of understanding Devon's Regency slave-holders is through their biographies. It is only in unravelling their life stories do we begin to understand these men and women. It slowly becomes apparent how some were connected and that others were drawn to one another while living in Devon.

Their mobility is astounding. Some led truly peripatetic lives and only a handful remained rooted to one place. Most individuals were not just well travelled but lived in a number of counties if not countries.

Devon's mid nineteenth-century slaveholders were not a homogenous group. Some were Devon born and bred but they were outnumbered by retirees from the West Indies and other parts of Great Britain: most were former owners who largely favoured the new seaside resorts over Exeter and Plymouth or the countryside. These men and women were typical of the thousands of other cosmopolitan 'incomers' who sought a lifestyle comparable to other fashionable coastal parts of Great Britain. Some stayed for less than a year, others for several decades. Some most likely chose Devon because money went further than it did in more developed parts of the country.

Most led quiet and anonymous lives but a few immigrants rose to considerable local prominence such as the Lousadas at Sidmouth and the Porter brothers at Rockbeare and Winslade. The latter house was described as being synonymous with old English hospitality but was more akin to plantation life which Plymouth's Lady Astor later longed to return to.[900] A few individuals, such as Lord Rolle and William Templer Pole, were from their births leading figures in Devon. Some served as High Sheriffs, town mayors or on the committees of local charities.

▶ 66. A medal, by Joseph Davis, commemorating the abolition of the apprenticeship system in the West Indies, 1838.

LIBERTY PEACE. AND INDUSTRY

DAVIS BIRM.
MDCCCXXXVIII.

They held estates in colonies across the Caribbean and one owned plantations in Mauritius. The most straight-forward category of a Devonian slave-holder is of those resident in the county on Emancipation Day: these thirty-four men and women owned 4,957 enslaved people which is 0.8 per cent of those who were emancipated. They received awards of £138,634 18s 11d (£9,399,629.55) which was 0.8 per cent of the £16,356,668 given to all slaveholders. These thirty-four individuals were 0.09 per cent of all 37,407 slaveholders who received compensation claims.

However, these are just some of the individuals who were directly associated with slavery. Many other former slave-owners subsequently came to Devon: nine more were resident at the time of their awards in the late 1830s and at least another 45 came afterwards. Nearly all were White but a small number were mixed-race descendants of West Indian slave-owners.

The distinctiveness of Devon's history will be better understood when comparative in-depth studies of other counties are written. Questions immediately arise from this volume. Given Cornwall had a lower population and was more remote from London than Devon, did it have a lower level of slave-ownership? Were seaside resorts in other counties as attractive to retired colonials as they were in Devon? Did economically vibrant urban centres of the country have a higher level of investment in slave colonies?

It is clear, even without other county studies, that Devon had notable but not unsurprising associations with two parts of England; a considerable number of both male and female enslavers came from London and Bristol. It is also apparent that neighbouring counties had dissimilar connections with Devon: the numbers of migrating slave-holders from Cornwall and Dorset were negligible while those from Somerset were high. This may in part reflect population levels but also those counties' histories of slave-owning.

Devon's great county families were not Regency enslavers with the exception of a junior branch of the Cary family at Totnes, the Poles of Shute and the Rolles of Bicton. The latter family found their forced labour estate had become a financial burden and freed their slaves before they were legally required. Few country houses were built by these slaveholders and this may have been because plantations were less financially lucrative in the generation preceding emancipation.

The Rolle family, the most prominent of all of Devon's slave-holders, devoted some of their great wealth to colonisation and attempted to create what has been hailed as Utopia but was, in reality, a society divided by race: the White settlers were financially underpinned by Black enslavement. The next generation of the Rolles found slavery was a financial drain and the head of the family, one of Devon's most powerful and well-connected men, was unable for years to end enslavement despite his energetic efforts. His proposals for his estate in the Bahamas anticipated emancipation across the slave colonies.

Devon's slaveholders included a surprisingly high number of Church of England clergymen although their views on the morality of slave-ownership were unrecorded. There was also a universal reticence by obituarists in mentioning the enslaved or the wealth generated by them.

Some enslaved people were brought to Devon where they were then free. They would have encountered lower numbers of others of African descent than in major urban centres in the country but Devon had a resident Black man as early as the late fifteenth century. Until the twentieth century the numbers were too small to term a community: subsequent children appear to have been born from unions with White Devonians and generations later their descendants were indistinguishable from the rest of society.

Slavery became more visible in Devon after 1834: just as emancipation came into effect 'slave entertainment' swept through England. One early performer was Thomas Dartmouth Rice, a White New Yorker who appeared in blackface in 1840.[901] But as a reviewer later noted, audiences wanted 'genuine' Black men and in 1867 sixteen former enslaved men performed across Devon. The Great American Slave Troupe sang and danced 'in that peculiar and mirth provoking manner characteristic of the Negro Race'. It was reported:

> 'This troupe possessed the advantage of being real unmistakable darkies and though some of them had evidently deepened their line (a mistake in the way of taste we think) still they were genuine Negroes and not imposters in the shape of coloured White men.'[902]

The generation that achieved emancipation legislation abroad enjoyed entertainments featuring slave caricatures and racial stereotypes at home.

Blackface became an established part of local culture and continued for more than a century. They also had whiteface. At Dartmoor Prison in 1814 American prisoners were segregated; White actors performed as The Dartmoor Thespian Company and Black performers had their own theatre. In one instance the latter enacted *Romeo & Juliet*. A fellow prisoner later recollected watching 'a tall strapping Negro, over six feet high, painted white, murdering the part of Juliet to the Romeo of another tall darkskin'. The tradition included mimicry of White people.[903]

Devon has struggled to understand the many forms of its African slavery legacy. The name of the county itself was first appropriated as a name for enslaved men and hundreds of years later it is held by many hundreds, if not thousands, of individuals who are unaware that they have a 'slave name'.[904] Owner's surnames, such as Rolle, likewise continue generations after slavery was abolished as do the names of former forced-labour estates.

The question of reparations is rarely discussed in Devon today but it was raised fifty years after emancipation when the Dean of Exeter preached at Plymouth. He urged:

> 'England owed to the black man a debt which was certainly not extinguished by the gift of twenty million [pounds] to the West Indian planters. To that oppressed and downtrodden race they owed a debt which they ought to recognise and exert themselves to pay'.[905]

A generation later a contributor to *The Journal of Negro History* questioned how society should best address the topic of slavery. He commented on Devon-born John Hawkins that 'to apply our twentieth-century moral code to the man would be to invoke an eternal curse upon him'.[906] Nearly a century later, in 2019, John Hawkins Square in Plymouth was renamed because of his slaving voyages but only a few months earlier a statue was erected to Lady Nancy Astor, Plymouth's MP from 1919 to 1945, on the grounds she was the first woman to take her seat in the House of Commons. Her direct associations with American slavery were disregarded.[907] Public disarray on how to accept and acknowledge Devon's associations in enslavement history will in all likelihood continue for many years to come.

The issue is complicated in that this remains only part of a much wider history. Devon's enslavers in 1834 were not, of course, the county's last. John Bent, for example, retained enslaved people outside the empire in Surinam. He had been living in Sussex for some fifteen years when he died in 1848[908] but previously resided at Weston House in Berry Pomeroy. He was described as 'a Devonian of humble origin' who rose to become a Surinam commissioner from 1813 to 1814 and member of Parliament for Totnes in 1820. Bent and his brother-in-law, Christopher Farwell, a former mayor of Totnes who also had family in Ashburton, owned enslaved people in British Guiana and Surinam.[909]

Our interest in and understanding of transatlantic enslavement is increasingly influenced by the continuation of slavery in modern society. Some 10,000 instances in the country were reported to the authorities in 2019.[910] Nearly two hundred years have followed emancipation and yet we still live with slavery albeit it is hidden in disguised forms. We often ask ourselves how previous generations were able to live with enslavement and yet we conveniently overlook the purchase of foreign goods made with forced labour. Sadly, the generation of 1834 were not Devon's last slave-owners. It may be that we are doomed to repeat this history but we must first learn it. The history of emancipation in 1834 is not just Black history but also, among others, that of White colonists, of their mixed-race children and of those Asians brought to the West Indies as paid labour. Their history matters. Our history matters, all history matters.

57. 'A lady holding a Negro mask', c1800, by John Raphael Smith. ▶

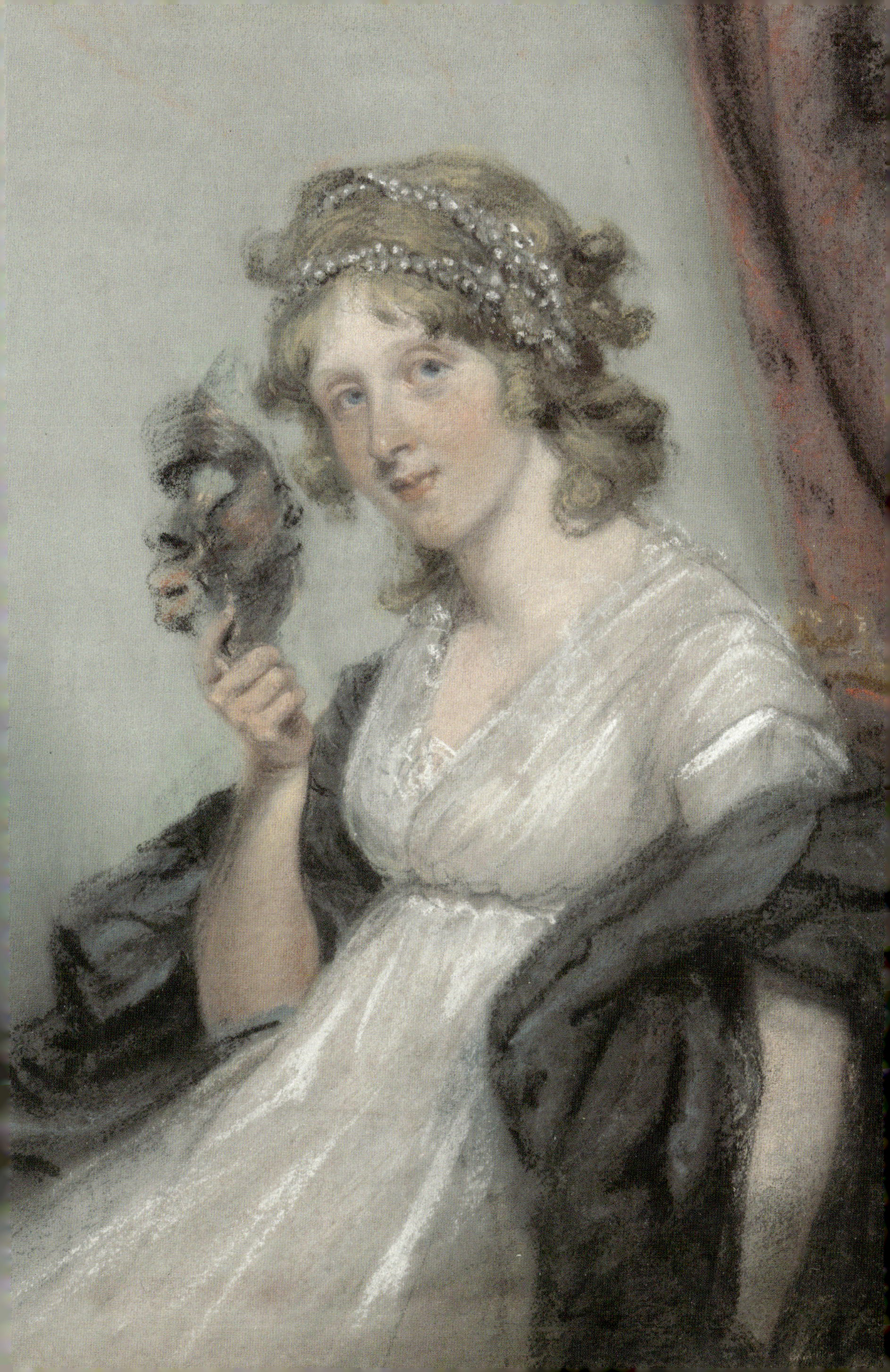

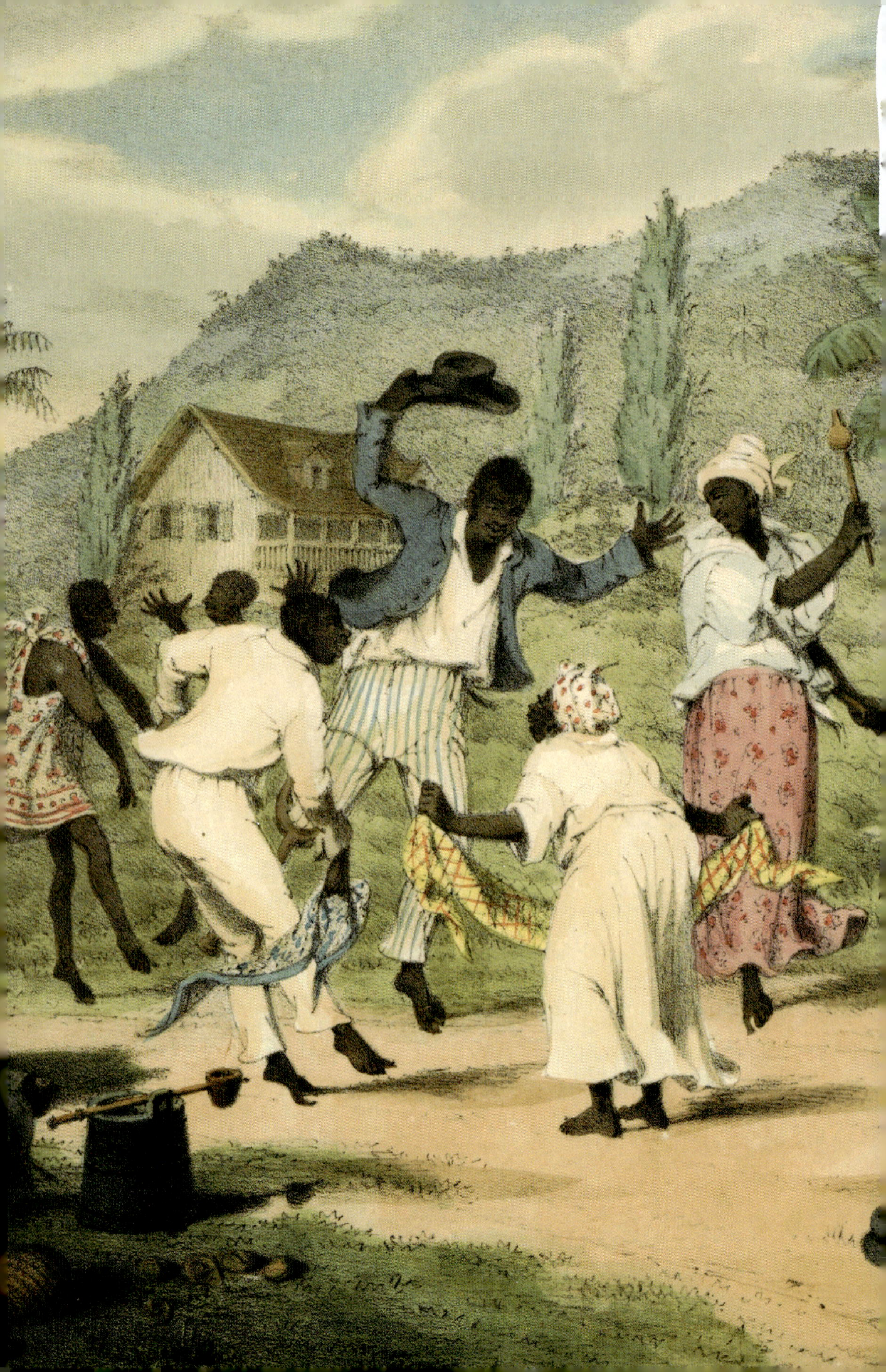

Appendix

Letter of A. J. Lees to Lord Rolle, 22 January 1835

Source: TNA, CO23/95, Folios 208-210

'Nassau, 22 January, 1835

My dear Lord,

I had the pleasure two days ago of receiving your Lordship's letter of the 16th of October, and sometime previous to the sailing of the last packet I received your power of attorney. I would then have written to you but being much occupied at the time, I requested Mr Dyer to mention to you that I had received it and to say I was immediately going to Exuma and would write to you on my return.

I returned about three weeks ago and this is the first packet which has since sailed. You will see therefore that I did not receive your power of attorney till long after Governor Balfour had written to you, and that I have lost no time in acting upon it. I was about a fortnight at your plantations. I have given the Negroes their emancipation with the exception of eight very old ones who are incapable of maintaining themselves and to whom the magistrates very properly objected that emancipation should be given.

The Negroes were of course extremely delighted at obtaining their freedom and are now perfectly happy. They will, I have no kind of doubt, maintain themselves with the greatest ease and will be able to acquire not only the necessaries but many of them the comforts and (to them) luxuries of life. I have taken great pains to share out the land among them so as to prevent any quarrels or disputes respecting it. I have also appointed a few of the oldest and best characters among them to be a sort of council to settle disputes and regulate their affairs and offered them freely and at all times my own advice and assistance, should they require it.

I have given them a building, which was formerly a cotton house, for a church and have appointed one of them who can read and write to preach to them every Sunday – a regulation with which I am happy to say they seem much pleased.

◀ 58. Detail from a lithograph entitled 'Negro dance', c1838, by Richard Bridgens.

I have not given them the land absolutely rent free but have reserved rent of about 2s sterling per acre for that which they cultivate, in order to raise a fund to maintain the 8 old people before alluded to and to enable me to pay the annual quit rents for the land. This small sum they can most easily afford to pay and it will besides have the good effect of keeping them in mind that the land is still your lordship's and that they are your tenants. Otherwise they might fancy that the land is absolutely their own.

Mr Hall has been discharged from your service, there being now no longer any occasion to pay an overseer. I have allowed a man and his wife, named Clarke, to remain in the dwelling house upon condition that he will take care of the premises and property generally, look after the old people and give them their clothes and allowances and do anything else that I may require of the sort without expense.

You will not I think be ever called upon to pay another farthing, as the only expense now will be the quit rents of the land and the maintenance of the 8 old persons and the rent of the land, if paid, will more than cover such trifling expenses as these.

I am now making arrangements for the sale of the cattle and other property on the estate and as soon as I have completed them, I will send you regular accounts of all my proceedings and of all monies received on your account, and will either retain them to assist in paying the quit rents and maintenance of the 8 old people above mentioned, or will forthwith remit them to you as you may think proper to direct.

The Negroes were all officially registered and you will therefore have no difficulty in obtaining the compensation money. I shall take every care of your interest in this respect. I have got a copy of the registration of your slaves, which I intend to send to you, but must wait till I can get some private conveyance, as the expense of sending so large a document by the packet would be too great.

I cannot conclude without congratulating your Lordship on the step you have taken. You have made upward of 300 people happy and contented, and you have saved yourself from immense expenditure and infinite vexation and the government here from continual trouble and annoyance.

The Lieutenant Governor, Mr Balfour, has been most kind in offering me every advice and assistance in his power and has taken great interest in the welfare of your Negroes. You will probably see him in London. Most sorry am I that he is about to leave us. Begging my compliments to Lady Rolle and to Captain Trefusis when you see him,

I am, A. J. Lees'

Illustration Sources

Frontispiece and cover illustrations: Ira Aldridge as 'The Captive Slave', 1827, by John Philip Simpson (Art Institute Chicago, 2008.188); 'Cotton plantation', 1840. (Yale University Art Gallery, 1946.9.614) and portrait of Lady Frances Rowe in Jamaica, 1835. She was the wife of Chief Justice Joshua Rowe and the daughter of James Bate, a Londoner who lived in Woodford, Essex and later resided at 1, Claremont Grove, Exeter. When Lady Frances married in 1823 her husband's family lived at Torpoint House in Cornwall. The following year he was called to the Bar and in 1832 they emigrated to Jamaica where he had been appointed Chief Justice. The portrait was painted by Isaac Mendes Belisario. (Yale Center for British Art, B2007.3)

I would like to thank three private individuals (**1, 38**: Heather and Brett Anderson); Devon Heritage Centre (**2**: P&D 086930); North Devon Athenaeum (**3**: B2M/ZI); the churchwardens of the Church of St James, Christow (**4**); J. Paul Getty Museum (**5**: 84.XB.932.4.10); Yale Center for British Art (**6** & **47**: T683, folio A; **7**: B1986.29.7; **8**: Folio A 2011-24; **9**: B1981.25.79; **12**: B1981.25.83; **17**: B1977.14.346, **19**: Rare Books, Folio A 2010 10; **23**: B1981.25.2639; **24** & **35**: B1981.25.2403; **25**: B1981.25.2399; **26-8**: Folio A 2010 22; **30**: B1975.4.1370; **33**: B1975.4.1808; **34**: B1976.7.100; **41**: B1990.22.17; **44**: Rare Books, F2410 S81 179; **54**: T686, folio C; **55**: T383, folio A; **56**, Rare books and Mss, Cabinet O; **57**: B1977.14.6285); Metropolitan Museum of Art (**10**: 10.64.3); Rijksmuseum (**11**: RP-P-OB-11.590; **14**: NG-2007-50; **21**: SK-A-4087; **43**: NG-C-2012-7; **49-52**, NG-2007-63-A-M); National Museum of African American History & Culture (**13**: 2008.10.4, **16**: 2010.21.1.2; **48**: 2009.32.4 & 2); Library of Congress (**15**: 2017889496; **22**: DRWG 1, Berryman, no. 127; **40**: DRWG 1, Berryman, no. 13; **39**: 2007660249; **53**: 2016586053; **58**: PGA - Bridgens); Yale University Art Gallery (**18**: 2001.87.3463; **32**: 1962.45.180; **42**: 1954.27.2); New York Public Library (**20**: b11486940); National Gallery of Art (Washington) (**29**: 1987.37.1; **31**: 1987.27.1); National Archives (**36**: MPD 1/6); Lupton House (**37**); Birmingham Museums Trust (**45**: 1933P75); Museum of New Zealand (**46**: 1957-0009-251). **Map**: J. Pinkerton, *A Modern Atlas* (1818). The cameos and illustration 59 are courtesy of the Library of Congress (DRWG1 – Berryman, nos 130, 133, 137 & 290).

References

The National Archives holds the records of the Slave Compensation Commission (T71, AO14 and NDO4) and the details of individuals' compensation were printed by the House of Parliament in *Accounts of slave compensation claims: for the colonies of Jamaica, Antigua, Honduras, St. Christopher's, Grenada, Dominica, Nevis, Virgin Islands, St. Lucia, British Guiana, Montserrat, Bermuda, Bahamas, Tobago, St. Vincent's, Trinidad, Barbadoes, Mauritius, Cape of Good Hope* (1838) and *Parliamentary Papers, 1837-8*, Vol. XLVII (215). These have been extracted by the Centre for the Study of the Legacies of British Slavery and published on its website along with expanded biographical details. Compensation details cited in this volume have been derived from these printed and electronic sources unless National Archive documentary references have been provided.

Ethnicity details for each former colony have been derived from the World Directory of Minorities and Indigenous People (Minority Rights Groups International, 2015).

The quotations introducing each chapter have been derived for chapter one from *Exeter Flying Post*, 12 October 1815; chapter two (William Cobbett, *The Parliamentary History of England from the Norman Conquest in 1066 to the year 1803* (1806-1820), XXVIII, columns 41-2); chapter three (Richard Robert Madden, *A twelvemonth's residence in the West Indies*, 1835, I, 196; chapter four (Frederic G. Kenyon, (ed.), *The letters of Elizabeth Barrett Browning*, 1897, I, 14-15); chapter five (Roy P. Basier (ed.), *The Collected Works of Abraham Lincoln*, 1953, V, 537; chapter six (Louisa Carolina Colleton Graves, *Desultory Thoughts on Various Subjects,* Brussels, 1821, 25-6; conclusion (*Exeter & Plymouth Gazette*, 31 March 1877)

Abbreviations

Ancestry	Ancestry.com
BL	British Library
DAT	*Devonshire Association Transactions*
DHC	Devon Heritage Centre
DNB	*Oxford Dictionary of National Biography*
E&E	*Express & Echo*
EFP	*Exeter Flying Post*
EPG	*Exeter & Plymouth Gazette*
GM	*Gentleman's Magazine*
LES	*London Evening Standard*
RGJ	*Royal Gazette of Jamaica*
NDJ	*North Devon Journal*
NDRO	North Devon Record Office
TNA	The National Archives
WT	*Western Times*

Notes

1. *Aberdeen Press*, 19 Feb. 1940.
2. Peter J. Parish, *Slavery; History and Historians* (New York, 1989), ix-xi.
3. https://www.youtube.com/watch?v=grAylhm2qbA&t=326s
4. Charles Kingsley, *Westward Ho!* (1856), 1, 89.
5. *EFP*, 29 March 1821.
6. *EPG*, 21 Dec. 1830.
7. *Port of Spain Gazette*, 30 July 1833.
8. Edward Cheshire, 'The results of the census of Great Britain in 1851', *Journal of the Statistical Society of London* (May, 1854), vol. 17, no. 1, 46.
9. *EPG*, 25 Jan. 1878; George Oliver and Pitman Jones (eds), *A view of Devonshire in 1630* (Exeter, 1845), 31.
10. John Prince, *The Worthies of Devon* (1810), 69, 315, 403, 472, 586, 621, 666; W. Pengelly, 'Notes on slips connected with Devonshire, part II', *DAT* (1878), XII, 261.
11. Henry Ellis, 'On certain passages in the life of Sir John Hawkins', *Archaeologia* (1850), vol. 33, issue 2, 205-6; Harry Kelsey, *Sir John Hawkins* (New Haven, 2003), 31-3; NDRO, B2M/Z1.
12. There is no mention in the single history of the eighteenth century: Richard Polwhele, *Historical Views of Devonshire* (Exeter, 1793-1806), three volumes.
13. Daniel & Samuel Lysons, *Magna Britannia: Devon* (1822), vol. 6, xc.
14. Robert C. Davis, *Christian Slaves, Muslim Masters* (Basingstoke, 2003), 23; Todd Gray, 'Turkish Piracy and Early Stuart Devon', *DAT* (1989), CXXI, 159-71.
15. Benjamin Waterhouse, 'A journal of a young man of Massachusetts', *The Magazine of History with Notes and Queries* (1911), Extra no. 10, 174.
16. W. G. Hoskins, *Devon* (1954); Robin Stanes, *A History of Devon* (Chichester, 1986); Oliver and Jones, *A View of Devonshire in 1630*; Tristram Risdon, *The Chorographical Description or Survey of the County of Devon* (1811).
17. Thomas Moore, *The history and topography of the county of Devon* (1831), II, 94.
18. Moore, *History and topography*, II, 94-5.
19. R. N. Worth, 'Sir John Hawkins: Sailor, Statesmen, Hero', *DAT* (1883), XV, 255-7; J. Henry Harris, *My Devonshire Book* (Plymouth, 1907), 13; W. G. Hoskins, *Devon and its people* (Exeter, 1959), 105. Plymouth's histories are largely silent until 1993: Henry Francis Whitfield, *Plymouth and Devonport* (Plymouth, 1900), 37-9; Crispin Gill, *Plymouth, A New History* (Tiverton, 1993), 378, 176; R. A. J. Walling, *The Story of Plymouth* (1950), 36.

20 DRO, D1508M-1/T/1/6/12; http://landedestates.ie>LandedEstates>jsp>estate-show accessed 26 May 2021.
21 F. C. P. Naish, 'Extracts from a Slaver's Log', *Mariner's Mirror* (1920), VI, 3-10; Nigel Tattersfield, *The Forgotten Trade* (1991); James. A. Rawley, *The Trans-Atlantic Slave Trade* (1981), 243.
22 Todd Gray, *Devon and the Slave Trade* (Exeter, 2020 edn).
23 Len Pole and Zoe Shearman, *Cargo* (Plymouth, 2007).
24 J. A. Froude, 'The conditions of historical study', *DAT* (1870), IV, 19, 39; Andrew Fish, 'The reputation of James Anthony Froude', *Pacific Historical Review* (June, 1932), I, no. 2, 179-93; Ian Hesketh, 'Diagnosing Froude's Disease: boundary work and the discipline of history in late-Victorian Britain', *History and Theory* (Oct. 2008), XLVII, no. 3, 373-95.
25 James Anthony Froude, *The English in the West Indies* (1888), 43-4.
26 The author was J. J. Thomas. See also Charles Spencer Salmon, *The Caribbean Confederation* (1888).
27 H. Walrond, *Historical Records of the 1st Devon Militia* (London, 1897), 21.
28 *House of Commons Parliamentary Papers, 1837-8* (215), vol. 48; https://www.ucl.ac.uk>lbs.
29 *LES*, 9 April 1862; *Southern Times*, 12 April 1862; *WT*, 12 April 1862; *Edinburgh Evening Courant*, 2 May 1857; Ancestry, Census, 1851 (Haddington), Census, 1861 (Tormohun) & Cruickshank/Houstoun family tree.
30 *St George's Chronicle*, 31 Jan. 1835. He was resident at Clerkington: National Records of Scotland, SC40/20/223/9.
31 *Morning Post*, 26 May 1834; *The Navy List* (1838), 132.
32 R. R. Madden, *A Twelvemonth's Residence in the West Indies* (1835), I, 200.
33 *RGJ*, 5 Nov. 1825, 10 March 1827, 12 May 1827; *Documents relating to foreign relations*, vol. 30, 13; *RGJ*, 24 March 1827; *Morning Post*, 26 May 1834.
34 Sarah Harrison (ed.), *A Jamaican Master in Chancery; The Letter-Books of Herbert Jarrett James, 1821-1840* (no date or place of publication), 148 & 156.
35 *The Laws of Jamaica passed in the sixth year of the reign of King William the fourth* (Kingston, 1836), 9-10; *WT*, 25 Aug. 1838; DHC, 313M-O/F/2; *EPG*, 23 June 1838.
36 Harrison, *Letter-Books*, 261, 265.
37 *EFP*, 17 Dec. 1884; *Morning Post*, 16 Feb. 1866; *Bridport News*, 30 May 1884.
38 *EPG*, 19 May 1884.
39 http://www.jamaicanfamilysearch.com/Members/JamesHughetc.htm, accessed 24 May 2021.
40 DHC, 1959M/12/1; TNA, PROB 11/1898/248; *Bath Chronicle*, 18 April 1822; *EFP*, 20 Dec. 1838; Ancestry, Census, 1841, 1851, 1861 (St Sidwell); *WT*, 4 Oct. 1845; *EPG*, 9 May 1846; *EPG*, 27 May 1874.
41 Ancestry, Census, 1851 (Tormohun); TNA, C101/6291.
42 Ancestry, Census, 1851 (Charles).
43 Gray, *Devon and the Slave Trade*, 207-209.
44 Thomas L. Johnson, *Twenty-eight years a slave* (Bournemouth, 1909), 220-2.
45 Kingsley, *Westward Ho!*, I, 224.
46 David M. Whitford, *The Curse of Ham in the Early Modern Era* (Abingdon, 2009).
47 Laura Lomas, 'Mystifying mystery: the inscriptions of the oral in the legend of Rose Hall', *Journal of West Indian Literature* (May 1994), vol. 6, no. 2, 70.
48 *The Daily Gleaner*, 21 Nov. & 5 Dec. 1965.
49 Leonard Wibberley, *The King's Beard* (New York, 1952; In 1812 a story set in Exeter about

a West Indian planter appeared in issue 43 of *The Lady's Magazine*. *The Sealed Message*, published in 1907 and written by Fergus Hume, featured Adonis Geary, a one-eyed Black publican in the fictional Devon village of Denleigh, who married a tall Barnstaple woman with whom he had six children.

50 *The Wit's Museum* (c1789), 32; G. K., *The Festival of Wit* (1789), 181-2; *The Bouquet* (1796), vol. II, no. VII, 33.
51 Edward B. Rugemer, *Slave Law and the Politics of Resistance in the Early Atlantic World* (Cambridge, Mass., 2018), 33.
52 Bryan Edwards, *The History, Civil and Commercial of the British Colonies in the West Indies* (Philadelphia, 1806), II, 200-201.
53 *EPG*, 12 Dec. 1835.
54 DHC, CC6B/116; CC17/12; CC20/101; Chanter 857, 208-210; Chanter 861, 136-8; Chanter 867, 500-501; Chanter 856, 449-50.
55 Gray, *Devon and the Slave Trade*, 8; *EPG*, 27 June 1840. It was also used as a name for cattle: *Davy's Devon Herd Book* (1892), 120.
56 *EPG*, 29 Aug. 1840.
57 Fred. W. P. Jago, 'English Changes of Celtic Cornish Names', *The Western Antiquary* (March, 1885), vol. 4, no. 10, 202; *EPG*, 9 March 1833.
58 Todd Gray, *Not One of Us; Individuals set apart by choice, circumstances, crowds or the mob in Exeter, 1451-1952* (Exeter, 2018), 161-3; *WT*, 5 July 1876.
59 Edwards, *History*, II, 205.
60 Alison Carmichael, *Domestic Manners and Social Conditions* (1833), I, 18.
61 W. Noel Sainsbury (ed.), *The Calendar of Stage* Papers *Colonial: North America and the West Indies, 1574-1739* (1880), vol. 5, 15 April 1664.
62 Carmichael, *Domestic*, I, 59.
63 *EPG*, 17 April 1830.
64 Jack D. Forbes, 'The use of the terms *Negro* and *black* to include persons of Native American Ancestry in *Anglo* North America', *Explorations in Ethnic Studies* (July 1984), vol. 7, no. 2, 11-12.
65 These citations from parish registers were first listed by a volunteer research project of the Friends of Devon's Archives in 1999: https://www.foda.org.uk and widely used including in Imtiaz Habib, *Black Lives in English Archives, 1500-1677* (2007).
66 The parish registers are at the Devon Heritage Centre or North Devon Record Office. In the 1990s I brought together some of these details for a volunteer project organised by the Friends of Devon's Archives and these are listed on its website; Nabil Matar, *Turks, Moors and Englishmen in the age of discovery* (New York, 1999), 6-7.
67 J. F. Chanter, 'On Certain Documents Relating to the History of Lynton and Countisbury', *DAT* (1906) XXXVIII, 240; TNA, PROB 11/52/367; Gray, *Devon and the Slave Trade*, 26-7.
68 P. E. H. Hair, 'Attitudes towards Africans in English Primary Sources on Guinea up to 1650', *History in Africa* (1999), vol. 26, 55.
69 For instance see C. Raymond Beazley, *Voyages and Travels* (1903), I, 29-130; Kaufmann, *Black Tudors*, 70.
70 Parish registers are located in the archives at Barnstaple, Exeter and Plymouth; Charles Herbert Levermore, *Forerunners and Competitors of the Pilgrims and the Puritans* (Brooklyn, 1912), I, 310; John Hemming, *Red Gold* (1987 edn), 11; Rugemer, *Slave Law*, 13.
71 Todd Gray, *Strumpets & Ninnycocks* (Exeter, 2016), 6.

72 F. T. Elworthy, 'Fourteenth report of the committee on Devonshire verbal provincialisms', *DAT* (1895), XXVII, 53; R. Pearse Chope, 'The dialect of Hartland', *DAT* (1891), XXIII, 428.
73 Edward Parfitt, 'The fauna of Devon', *DAT* (1888), XX, 333. For a wider use see Joseph Anderson, 'Galls of Gymnetron Villosulum', *The Entomologist* (Nov. 1882), XV, no. 234, 263; *WT*, 19 Dec. 1835.
74 George Clement Boase & William Prideaux Courtney, *Bibliotheca Cornubiensis* (1878), II, 435; Charles William Peach, 'On the Nigger or Cotton Spinner of the Cornish Fisherman', *The annals and magazine of natural history* (1845), XV, 171-4.
75 John Mayo of Southampton married Isabella Bell on 23 December 1797 at Withycombe Raleigh; Gloucestershire Record Office, D2091/F14; https://www.readingtheforest.com.
76 DHC, Chanter 862/143 & 170; Gray, *Devon and the Slave Trade*, 8-9.
77 https://www.englandsimmigrants.com/person/59749 version 1.0, 13 December 2020; W. Mark Ormrod, Bart Lambert and Jonathan Mackman, *Immigrant England, 1300-1550* (Manchester, 2019), 190.
78 DHC, CC23/237; Chanter 866/22-8; CC25/141; CC6/156; Chanter 867/957; CC6/180; CC7/88.
79 Hakluyt, *Principal Navigations*, vol. 25, pt 4, 132-3.
80 Douglas Hall, 'Jamaica', 195, in David W. Cohen and Jack, P. Greene (eds), *Neither slave nor free* (Baltimore, 1972).
81 Hugh Thomas, *The Slave Trade* (2006 edn), 63.
82 Thomas Atwood, *The History of the Island of Dominica* (1791), 210.
83 James A. Thome and J. Horace Kimball, *Emancipation in the West Indies, a six month's tour in Antigua, Barbados and Jamaica in the year 1837* (New York, 1838), 26.
84 F. W. N. Bayley, *Four years' residence in the West Indies* (1830), 331-2.
85 Thome & Kimball, *Emancipation*, 79.
86 W. G. Sewell, *The Ordeal of Free Labour in the British West Indies* (New York, 1861), 44.
87 Monk Lewis, *Journal of a West India Proprietor Kept during a residence in the island of Jamaica* (1834), 74.
88 Sewell, *Ordeal*, 67-8.
89 Hall, 'Jamaica', 211.
90 Thome & Kimball, *Emancipation*, 31-2.
91 Edwards, *History*, II, 214; Bayley, *Four years*, 492: Lewis, *Journal*, 106; James Stephen, *The Slavery of the British West India Colonies Delineated* (1824-30), I, 27.
92 Edwards, *History*, II, 214.
93 *EPG*, 23 April 1842.
94 *EPG*, 16 Sept. 1864.
95 *WT*, 27 July 1844.
96 Gray, *Devon and the Slave Trade*, 112-34.
97 Gray, *Not One of Us*, 23-4, 251-5.
98 *EPG*, 12 Dec. 1835.
99 DHC, 3104B/MF/1-6; *EPG*, 3 Nov. 1827; *NDJ*, 12 Jan. 1832, 20 June 1833, 24 April 1834.
100 DHC, 2104B/MF/1-3; TNA, T71/497-8. Seven years earlier he was listed as a tailor: TNA, T71/493; BL, St Vincent Deed Book, 1824-31, EAP668/1/1/75, 304.
101 *Sun*, 17 March 1947; *EFP*, 26 May 1803, 11 Jan. 1827, 29 Oct. 1835; *NDJ*, 28 Jan. 1830; *EPG*, 21 July 1832, 10 Jan. 1835, 23 Sept. 1837; *WT*, 11 May 1833, 2 Aug. 1834, 10 Oct.

1835; DHC, 1926B/B/L/4/81; Ancestry, Census, 1841 (Topsham), Census, 1851 (St Sidwell).
102 TNA, PROB 11/1904/418.
103 Joseph Sturge & Thomas Harvey, *The West Indies in 1837* (1838), 170.
104 *Grenada Free Press*, 11 Sept. 1839; NDRO, 2309B/O/FS/27/1; TNA, PROB 11/1916/239 & 11/1944/43.
105 *Grenada Free Press*, 29 Aug. 1838; Edward L. Cox, *Free coloreds in the slave societies of St Kitts and Grenada, 1763-1833* (Knoxville, 1984), 61.
106 TNA, T71/462.
107 *The Edinburgh Medical and Surgical Journal* (1824), vol. 22, 444; *The Scotsman*, 4 Aug. 1824.
108 *Columbus Messenger*, 9 May 2008.
109 *Norfolk Chronicle*, 11 Aug. 1821; *Law Times Reports* (6 Nov. 1858), vol. 32, 65-6.
110 TNA, PROB 11/1295/243; *DNB*, Natalie Zacek, 'Anne Brodbelt née Penoyre' (2004).
111 *Hereford Journal*, 21 April 1824; TNA, PROB 11/1726/250.
112 TNA, T71/1 & 3.
113 *Jamaica Courant*, 22 April 1822; J. M. Bulloch, *The Making of the West Indies* (privately printed, 1915), 23-4.
114 TNA, PROB 11/1918/326.
115 Haverfield may have been related to T. W. Haverfield who was a churchwarden at Great Torrington in 1716: J. J. Alexander & W. R. Hooper, *History of Great Torrington*, (2010 edn, Norwich), 38; *RGJ*, 30 Aug. 1817.
116 https://adb.anu.edu.au/biography/haverfield-robert-ross-3733, acc. 26 May 2021; *Baldwin's London Weekly Journal*, 11 April 1818; *RGJ*, 13 January 1816.
117 Todd Gray (ed.), *Travels in Georgian Devon* (Tiverton, 1995), I, 28.
118 https://adb.anu.edu.au/biography/haverfield-robert-ross-3733, accessed 26 May 2021.
119 *London Courier*, 28 Sept. 1813.
120 TNA, PROB 11/2168/391.
121 *RGJ*, 15 Dec. 1827.
122 *RGJ*, 1 Oct. & 3 Dec. 1814.
123 TNA, T71/1607; Draper, *The Price*, 162.
124 TNA, T71/111 & T71/79 & 87.
125 *NDJ*, 7 Feb. 1833.
126 Herbert G. de Lisser, *The White Witch of Rose Hall* (1929); Johnny Cash, 'The Ballad of Annie Palmer' (1973).
127 Lewis, *Journal*, 60.
128 *WT*, 20 Oct. 1827.
129 Nicholas Draper, *The Price of Emancipation* (Cambridge, 2010), 69-70; *Evening Mail*, 26 Nov. 1841.
130 *WT*, 16 June 1848.
131 *WT*, 26 June 1841.
132 *EFP*, 25 Jan. 1810.
133 I am grateful to Diane Walker for supplying a photograph of this monument.
134 TNA, PROB 11/1512/480.
135 *The addresses, speeches, squibs, songs &c which were circulated during the recent general election* (Exeter, 1818), 120; TNA, T71/178.
136 *Morning Post*, 31 Oct. 1821; *EFP*, 26 July 1821.

137 *EFP*, 28 Nov. 1822.
138 *WT*, 16 Sept. 1837; *EPG*, 16 Sept. 1837; *WT*, 28 March 1840.
139 *EFP*, 21 Sept. 1837.
140 *WT*, 16 Sept. 1837.
141 Draper, *The Price*, 160; *The Annual Register or a view of the history, politicks and literature for the year 1765* (1766), 72; Gray, *Not One of Us*, 130-1.
142 *Sun*, 6 March 1830; TNA, PROB 11/1768/180.
143 *NDJ*, 8 Nov. 1866; *The Pall Mall Budget* (1871), vol. 5, 36.
144 Mable Nembhard, *Nembhard of Jamaica* (c1909), 11.
145 *Bristol Times*, 5 June 1869; *The Post Office Directory of Devon* (1866), 769; *WT*, 16 May 1871; *Taunton Courier*, 10 May 1871; Ancestry, Census, 1841 (Milverton), 1851 & 1861 (Oxfordshire), 1871 (Colyton).
146 Ancestry, Census, 1851 (Tiverton).
147 TNA, PROB 11/1975/193; *E&E*, 23 April 1888.
148 Edwards, *History*, I, 190.
149 *WT*, 18 Aug. 1832.
150 Thomas, *Slave Trade*, 89, 21-129.
151 L. P. Jackson, 'Elizabethan seamen and the African slave trade', *Journal of Negro History* (Jan. 1924), vol. 9, no. 1, 2.
152 Gray, *Devon and the Slave Trade*, 15-82; Rawley, *Trans-Atlantic Slave Trade*, 243.
153 Michael MacCarthy-Morrogh, *The Munster Plantation* (Oxford, 1986), 121-2; http://landedestates.ie>LandedEstates>jsp>estate-show, accessed 26 May 2021.
154 Hair, 'Attitudes', 66-7.
155 Henry A. M. Smith, 'The Colleton family in South Carolina', *The South Carolina Historical and Genealogical Magazine* (Oct. 1900), vol. 1, no. 4, 338-40,'The Baronies of South Carolina', (July, 1912), vol. 12, no. 3, 124-5 and 'The Baronies of South Carolina', vol. 11, no. 4, 198-9; DHC, Withycombe Raleigh, PR1; Charity Scott-Stokes & Alan Lumb (eds), *Sir Francis Henry Drake* (Devon & Cornwall Record Society, 2019), NS 62, 40-1.
156 Smith, 'The Baronies', vol. 11, 201-202.
157 Louisa Carolina Colleton Graves, *Desultory Thoughts on Various Subjects* (Brussels, 1821); William Gillmore Simms, *The History of South Carolina* (1840), 277; John B. Irving, *A Day on Cooper River* (1842), 28; Smith, 'The Baronies', vol. 11, 201.
158 Smith, 'The Baronies', vol. 11, 201-202.
159 *St James Chronicle*, 19 Nov. 1814.
160 Graves, *Desultory Thoughts*, 14-15, 42-7, 51-2.
161 *The Lady's Magazine*, XVIII (1787), 559.
162 Graves, *Desultory Thoughts*, 93-4.
163 Graves, *Desultory Thoughts*, 104-5.
164 *EFP*, 25 March 1802.
165 *Cornwall Gazette*, 11 Sept. 1813; *Jamaica Journal*, 11 & 18 Sept. 1824; TNA, PROB 11/1699/80.
166 TNA, PROB 11/1765/21 & DHC, 3779B/MF/1.
167 TNA, PROB 11/1485/48, PROB 11/1667/301, PROB 11/1822/67; *EFP*, 6 Sept. 1804; *RGJ*, 29 March 1817, 18 April 1818 & 29 Oct. 1825; *EFP*, 16 July 1818
168 Henry Maddock, *Reports of cases argued and determined in the court of the vice chancellor* (1817), vol. 1, 467-88.
169 Frank Cundall, *Historic Jamaica* (1915), xxiii; Craig Bailey, *Irish London; Middle class*

170 *Morning Post*, 19 March 1805.

171 T. C. Hansard, *The Parliamentary Debates from the year 1803 to the present time* (1812), vol. 8, 833.

172 DHC, DEX/7/b/1/1802/33; *EFP*, 23 March 1809 & 4 Oct. 1837.

173 *EPG*, 5 Feb. 1831; *Dorset County Chronicle*, 17 Feb. 1831; *WT*, 20 Feb. 1830; DHC, 58/9/ box 67-9.

174 *EFP*, 22 Nov. 1810.

175 John Maurice Turner, *Washfield, the Story of a Devonshire village* (Tiverton, 1947), 39; *Bath Chronicle*, 3 Dec. 1789; Frank Gibbon, 'The Antiguan Connection: Some New Light on Mansfield Park', *The Cambridge Quarterly* (1982), vol. 11, no. 2, 298-305; Robert Clark (ed.), *Jane Austen's Geographies* (e-book).

176 *The Trial of Richard Vining Perry, Esq.* (Bristol, 1794), 23-5; DHC, DEX/7/b/1/1816/97; TNA, PROB 11/1598/59; *Bath Chronicle*, 7 Jan. 1813.

177 *EFP*, 19 Jan. & 12 Oct. 1815; *Pigot and Company's National Commercial Directory* (1993 edn), 129; Simon D. Smith, *An introduction to the plantation journals of the Prospect sugar estate* (2004); *EPG*, 15 Nov. 1828; *Bath Chronicle, 30 Aug. 1832; WT*, 6 May 1837; *Norfolk Chronicle*, 4 Aug. 1838.

178 *EPG*, 26 July 1828; *Sun*, 21 July 1828; TNA, PROB 11/1744/95; *WT*, 14 Feb. 1829.

179 *EFP*, 23 Feb. 1809; *London Courier*, 5 June 1810; *Oxford Journal*, 22 Sept. 1810; *Bury & Norwich Post*, 29 Feb. 1832; DHC, 5139B.

180 DHC, 1160M/title deeds/Jamaica/1.

181 *Sherborne Mercury*, 2 Oct. 1797; DHC, 1160M/C/J1-30; His daughter Eliza 'of Barnstaple' married Richard Cross on 22 May 1801. This was a few years after John Reeder's death and she may have been living with her aunt: *EFP*, 28 May 1801; Ancestry, Land Tax Redemption Records, Fremington, 1798.

182 TNA, HO42/24/229.

183 NDRO, 3704M/FC7.

184 NDRO, 3704M/FC11.

185 Gray, *Devon and the Slave Trade*, 57-73.

186 DHC, 1160M/C/J3 & J30.

187 DHC, 1160M/T/Jamaica/1.

188 Goucher, 'John Reeder's Foundry', 40-41; DHC, 1160M/C/J1-30; *Hereford Journal*, 15 July 1789; *Caledonian Mercury*, 11 July 1789; Danby Pickering, *The Statutes at Large* (1794), XXXVIII, 160. The governor made the grant in 1782. In 1790 the Jamaican Assembly passed a private act awarding Reeder the rights to his discovery of a varnish for copper and 'of joining the seams of copper and making the same water-tight without soldor': *Acts of Assembly passed in the island of Jamaica in the years 1789 and 1790* (1790), iv.

189 DHC, 1160M/T/Jamaica/1.

190 *Daily Advertiser*, 26-8 May & 1 June 1791.

191 Candice L. Goucher, 'African metallurgy in the Atlantic World', *African Archaeological Review* (1993), vol. 11, 206, 212, 'Iron sails the seas; a maritime history of African diaspora iron technology', *Canadian Journal of Latin American and Caribbean Studies* (Nov. 2013), vol. 38, no. 2, 183 and 'Rituals of Iron in the Black Atlantic World', 112-113 in Akinwumi Ogundiran and Paula Sanders (eds), *Materialities of Ritual in the Black Atlantic* (Bloomington, 2014).

192 Candice L. Goucher, 'John Reeder's Foundry: A Study of Eighteenth-Century African-Caribbean Technology', *Jamaica Journal* (1990), 23 (1), 39-40.
193 Candice Goucher and Kofi Agorsah, 'Excavating the Roots of Resistance', 151, in James A. Delle, Mark W. Hauser and Douglas V. Armstrong (eds), *Out of Many, One People* (Tuscaloosa, 2011).
194 Frederick C. Knight, *Working the Diaspora: The Impact of African Labor on the Anglo American World, 1650–1850* (New York, 2010), 117; Theresa Singleton, 'Islands of Slavery', in Noel Lenski and Catherine M. Cameron (eds), *What is a Slave Society?* (Cambridge, 2018), 302. For similar comments see Terry Weik, 'The Archaeology of Maroon Societies in the Americas', *Historical Archaeology* (1997), vol. 31, no. 2, 85 and Teresita Majewski, 'Current Research', *American Antiquity* (Jan. 1992), vol. 57, no. 1, 147.
195 DHC, 1160M/C/J1-30.
196 DHC, 1160M/T/Jamaica/1.
197 Goucher, 'John Reeder's Foundry', 41. James Nalby, Edward Thomas, Alexander Mortimer, George Gillepsie and John Clinton were buried between August 1779 and September 1783.
198 *The Jamaica Mercury and Kingston Weekly Advertiser*, 6, 13, 20 & 27 Nov. 1779.
199 Goucher, 'John Reeder's Foundry', 42, note 4; DHC, 1160M/C/J1.
200 Goucher, 'Iron sails', 183.
201 *EFP*, 18 Oct. 1808; DHC, 4056M/E/8 & 971A/PO4; Ancestry, Clark-Waymouth family tree.
202 TNA, T71/253; *Sherborne Mercury*, 14 Feb. 1831.
203 *DNB*, J. A. Hamilton & Hallie Rubenhold, 'Lopes, Sir Manasseh Masseh, first baronet, landowner and politician' (2004); Catherine Hall et al, *Legacies of British Slave-ownership* (2014, Cambridge), 273; *Belfast Newsletter*, 8 April 1831.
204 TNA, PROB 11/1527/68.
205 *Bristol Mirror,* 15 Aug. 1829; *NDJ*, 23 April 1840; Ancestry, Creativegraces family tree.
206 Gray, *Devon and the Slave Trade*, 149-89.
207 *Plymouth & Devonport Weekly Journal*, 13 Dec. 1832.
208 *WT*, 12 Jan. 1850; *EFP*, 27 Dec. 1865.
209 'Biographical sketch of the late John Prideaux', *Annual Reports and Transactions of the Plymouth Institution* (1865), I, 25-7.
210 *WT*, 5 July 1834.
211 For example, for Exeter see *WT*, 6 April 1833 & 16 Dec. 1837.
212 *NDJ*, 2 & 16 Sept. 1830; *EPG*, 11 Sept. 1830.
213 *NDJ*, 12 Jan. 1832.
214 *EPG*, 6 April 1833.
215 *Dudley Guardian*, 12 Dec. 1874; *EPG*, 7 April 1878.
216 *WT*, 19 & 26 March 1853; *Western Courier*, 22 Dec. 1852; John Brown, *Slave Life in Georgia* (1855), 245.
217 *WT*, 13 Jan. 1871 & 20 April 1866.
218 James Bickford, *James Bickford* (1890), 10.
219 *WT*, 9 August 1834.
220 Bickford, *Bickford*, 118.
221 Richard B. Sheridan, *Sugar and Slavery* (Baltimore, 1973).
222 *Sketches and Recollections of the West Indies by a resident* (1828), 26.
223 Samuel M. Wilson, 'The cultural mosaic of the Indigenous Caribbean', *Proceedings of the*

British Academy (1993), vol. 81, 37-66; Frederick A. Ober, 'Aborigines of the West Indies', *American Antiquarian Society* (April, 1894), vol. 9, 280.

224 Edwards, *History*, II, 205-6.
225 TNA, T71.
226 R. Montgomery Martin, *History of the West Indies* (1837), I, 93-7.
227 Henry Bolingbroke, *A voyage to the Demerary* (1807), 43-4.
228 Martin, *History*, II, 129-30.
229 Jerome S. Handler and JoAnn Jacoby, 'Slave Names and Naming in Barbados, 1650–1830', *The William and Mary Quarterly* (Oct. 1996), 3rd Series, vol. 53, no. 4, 685-95.
230 A. Meredith John, *The plantation slaves of Trinidad, 1783–1816* (Cambridge, 1988), 74; These are found in T71 at the National Archives which is now available through Ancestry.
231 Susan Benson, 'Injurious names', Gabrielle vom Bruck & Barbara Bodenhorn (eds), *An Anthropology of Names and Naming* (Cambridge, 2006), 189-91.
232 TNA, T71/164, T71/258, T71/233, T71/228.
233 TNA, T71/65.
234 DHC, Churston Ferrers, PR1, burial, 20 June 1750. A memorial stone for Philip Scipio, who died on 1784, is at St Martin's Church in the former Devon parish of Werrington.
235 DHC, Chanter 866/248-59; Todd Gray (ed.), *Devon Parish Taxpayers, 1500–1650*, DCRS (2016), vol. 2, NS59, 265; Jannine Crocker (ed.), *Elizabethan Inventories and Wills of the Exeter Orphans' Court*, DCRS (2014), vol. 1, NS57, 292.
236 Ancestry, Census, 1841 (for all these parishes).
237 A Jamaican Chudleigh may be connected to Devon.
238 Stanley L. Engerman & B. W. Higham, 'The demographic structure of the Caribbean slave societies in the eighteenth and nineteenth centuries', in F. W. Knight (ed.), *General History of the Caribbean* (2003), III, 50-1; The population of Mauritius was poorly recorded. This figure has been derived from Sadasivam Jaganada Reddi & Shetal Sheena Sookrajowa, 'Slavery, health and epidemics in Mauritius, 1721-1860', *The Palgrave Handbook of Ethnicity* (2019), 8.
239 Madden, *A Twelvemonth's Residence*, I, 56.
240 R. Bickell, *The West Indies as they are or a real picture of slavery* (1825), 57.
241 H. N. Coleridge, *Six Months in the West Indies in 1825* (1826), 230.
242 Jo Anne Ferreira, 'Madeiran Portuguese Migration to Guyana, St Vincent, Antigua and Trinidad: A Comparative Overview', *Portuguese Studies Review* (Jan. 2006), 73; Carl. E. James, 'Antigua and Barbuda', Patrick Taylor, Frederick I. Case and Sean Meighoo (eds), *The Encyclopedia of Caribbean Religions* (Chicago, 2013), 60.
243 Draper, *The Price*, 139; Martin, *History*, II, 311; *Slave Population {Slave Registries}* (1833), 2.
244 *GM* (1796), vol. 66, pt 1, 444; Gray, *Devon and the Slave Trade*, 95-105; Gray, *Travels in Georgian Devon*, II, xi; Oliver, *History of Antigua*, I, 23 & III, 106.
245 TNA, C 13/710/20.
246 DHC, 72/1/2/12; Peter Maunder, *Tiverton Cloth* (Tiverton, 2018), 331.
247 *WT*, 6 Sept. 1834.
248 Frances Lanaghan Flannigan, *Antigua and the Antiguans* (1844), I, 149.
249 Sewell, *Ordeal*, 141-2.
250 Joseph John Gurney, *A Winter in The West Indies* (1840), 69; Thome & Kimball, *Emancipation*, 5.
251 Thome & Kimball, *Emancipation*, vi, 52.
252 Minority Rights Group International, *World Directory of Minorities and Indigenous Peoples*

253 Martin, *History*, I, 283.
254 Martin, *History*, II, Appendix B; *Slave Population {Slave Registries}* (1833), 2.
255 Howard Johnson, 'The share system in the Bahamas in the nineteenth and early twentieth centuries', *Slavery & Abolition* (1984), vol. 5, issue 2, 141.
256 *A sermon preached before the incorporated Society for the Propagation of the Gospel in Foreign Parts* (1797), 45-7. See also F. A. Cox, *History of the Baptist Missionary Society* (1842), II, 266-7.
257 Lambeth Palace Library, FP/XV, 87-93.
258 Rawson W. Rawson, *Report on the Bahamas for the year 1864* (1866), 7.
259 Charles C. Wakefield, 'Mission Work in the Bahamas', in J. J. Halcombe (ed.), *Mission Life* (1876), VII, part 1, 87.
260 Howard Johnson, *The Bahamas from slavery to servitude, 1783–1933* (Gainesville, 1996).
261 *EPG*, 9 Aug. 1834.
262 Thome & Kimball, *Emancipation*, 53.
263 Martin, *History*, II, 204-205.
264 Coleridge, *Six Months*, 125-6.
265 Rugemer, *Slave Law*, 11-34; Simon P. Newman, *A New World of Labor; the Development of Plantation Slavery in the British Atlantic* (Philadelphia, 2013), 54; Linford D. Fisher, 'Dangerous Designs, the 1676 Barbados Act to Prohibit New England Indian Slave Importation', *The William & Mary Quarterly*, vol. 71, no. 1 (Jan. 2014), 99-124.
266 Martin, *History*, II, 203-204.
267 Thome & Kimball, *Emancipation*, 57.
268 Thome & Kimball, *Emancipation*, 57.
269 *Slave Population {Slave Registries}* (1833), 2; Martin, *History*, II, Appendix B; Draper, *The Price*, 139.
270 Ancestry, Census, 1851 (Cadbury).
271 Thome & Kimball, *Emancipation*, 55; Sturge & Harvey, *The West Indies in 1837*, 150-2.
272 William A. Green, 'The Apprenticeship in British Guiana, 1834–1838', *Caribbean Studies*, vol. 9, no. 2 (July 1969), 58-60; Dave Ramsaran & Linden F. Lewis, *Caribbean Masala* (University Press Online, 2008), 21.
273 Edward Bancroft, *An Essay on the natural history of Guiana in South America* (1769), 365-6.
274 *WT*, 27 June 1835; *Sun*, 11 Sept. 1834; http://www.simeons.org.uk>hyndmans-trust-history.
275 Green, 'The Apprenticeship', 44-5.
276 *Slave Population {Slave Registries}* (1833), 2; Martin, *History*, II, Appendix B.
277 Martin, *History*, II, Appendix B; Draper, *The Price*, 139.
278 *Slave Population {Slave Registries}* (1833), 2.
279 Martin, *History*, II, 180-3.
280 Martin, *History*, II, 129-30.
281 DHC, 3939M/Z/1.
282 *WT*, 4 Feb. 1843; TNA, PROB 11/1818/497; *Morning Post*, 18 June 1855; Edmund F. Moore, *Reports of cases heard and determined by the judicial committee and the lords by her majesty's most honourable privy council* (1854-5), vol. 9, 439-51.
283 *Oxford University and City Herald*, 21 June 1828.
284 *Tavistock Gazette*, 16 Oct. 1868; *The Times*, 15 Aug. 1868; *Pall Mall Gazette*, 17 Aug. 1868;

Sir George William Des Voeux, *Experiences of a Demerara magistrate* (Georgetown, 1870), 90; *Post Office Directory of Devon* (1866), 784.

285 Atwood, *History*, 208.
286 Draper, *The Price*, 139; Martin, *History*, II, 284-6.
287 *Sketches and Recollections*, 71.
288 Joseph A. Borome, 'How crown colony government came to Dominica by 1898', *Caribbean Studies* (Oct. 1969), vol. 9, no. 3, 26.
289 Coleridge, *Six Months*, 148-9.
290 Gurney, *A Winter*, 72.
291 Beverley A. Steele, 'Grenada, an island state, its history and its people', *Caribbean Quarterly* (March, 1974), vol. 20, no. 1, 11.
292 Steele, 'Grenada, an Island state', 13-14.
293 Martin, *History*, II, Appendix B and I, 266; Draper, *The Price*, 139.
294 Coleridge, *Six Months*, 97-8.
295 DHC, 2147B/add/M/T/67-8; 2147addB/M/FW/17; 2147B/1/M/EB/3-4; 2147B/1/M/EC/2; 2147B/1/M/ET/5-8; 2147B/1/M/FW/23.
296 *EFP*, 22 Nov. 1804; *Hampshire Chronicle*, 6 April 1807; TNA, PROB11/1576/242.
297 George Richardson Porter, *The Nature and Properties of the Sugar Cane* (1830), 329; Chris Evans and Louise Miskell, *Swansea Copper* (Baltimore, 2020), 191, n24.
298 Madden, *A Twelvemonth's Residence*, I, 60; *EPG*, 22 Sept. 1838.
299 Sewell, *Ordeal*, 89; Steele, 'Grenada', 14.
300 Sewell, *Ordeal*, 84-5.
301 Martin, *History*, I, 88.
302 Madden, *A Twelvemonth's Residence*, I, 67-113, 140-1 & II, 5.
303 TNA, T71/1593. Hawkins was in Bideford on 16 Feb. 1837; Martin, *History*, II, Appendix B; Draper, *The Price*, 139.
304 Martin, *History*, I, 120-3.
305 Lewis, *Journal*, 110.
306 Martin, *History*, I, 94-6.
307 Sewell, *Ordeal*, 169-70.
308 Sewell, *Ordeal*, 170-304.
309 E. Ethelred Brown, 'Labour Conditions in Jamaica prior to 1917', *The Journal of Negro History* (October, 1919), vol. 4, no. 4, 351.
310 Coleridge, *Six Months*, 179.
311 Draper, *The Price*, 139.
312 *DNB*, David Small, 'George Tobin' (2004); *WT*, 18 Dec 1830; *EFP*, 19 April 1838; *EFP*, 9 March 1815; TNA, PROB 11/1572/45.
313 *WT*, 5 Dec. 1829.
314 'On the 11th of October last died at Nevis in the West Indies, Mr Robert Paul, a native of this city': *EFP*, 10 Jan. 1805.
315 Gray, *Devon and the Slave Trade*, 135-8; Ancestry, Census, 1851 (Colyton). The plantation may be the one offered for sale in 1807 by a Colyton solicitor: *EFP*, 22 Jan. 1807.
316 Draper, *The Price*, 139; Sewell, *Ordeal*, 163.
317 *EPG*, 11 Oct. 1834.
318 *EFP*, 29 Jan. 1835.
319 Coleridge, *Six Months*, 203.
320 Vincent K. Hubbard, *A History of St Kitts* (Oxford, 2002), 115-119.

321 Gurney, *A Winter*, 46.
322 Bickford, *Bickford*, 27.
323 Bickford, *Bickford*, 31; Ferreira, 'Madeiran Portuguese Migration', 73.
324 Carmichael, *Domestic*, I, 3-4.
325 Carmichael, *Domestic*, I, 242, 295-6.
326 Draper, *The Price*, 139.
327 Coleridge, *Six Months*, 105-106; Carmichael, *Domestic*, II, 299; Bayley, *Four Years*, 196.
328 William Young, *A tour through the several islands of Barbadoes, St Vincent, Antigua, Tobago and Grenada in the years 1791 and 1792* (1801), II, 272.
329 Bickford, *Bickford*, 27-8.
330 Sewell, *Ordeal*, 78-81.
331 J. H. Wylie & James Wylie, *Report on the Records of the City of Exeter* (1916), 41, 203, 205.
332 Eric Williams, *History of the People of Trinidad and Tobago* (New York, 1962), 76-7, 99, 97, 123-4, 129.
333 Young, *A tour*, II, 272.
334 Martin, *History*, II, Appendix B & I, 243-5; Sewell, *Ordeal*, 90-1.
335 Draper, *The Price*, 139.
336 Draper, *The Price*, 128; *EFP*, 10 Dec. 1818; BL, St Vincent Deed Book 1808, EAP688/1/1/19.
337 *EFP*, 5 Feb. 1801; DHC, 3939M/Z/1.
338 DHC, 5257B; TNA, PROB 11/2005/119 & T71/501; *St James Chronicle*, 14 Oct. 1843 & 31 Jan. 1835. Charles Lamb listed slaves on two plantations named Montrose and La Recconisance: TNA, T71/513.
339 W. J. Adam, *Journal of Voyages to Marguaritta, Trinidad & Maturin* (1824), 16.
340 Jo Anne Ferreira, 'Madeiran Portuguese Migration to Guyana, St Vincent, Antigua and Trinidad: A Comparative Overview', *Portuguese Studies Review* (Jan. 2006), 73; Williams, *History*, 96-7; Rhoda Reddock, 'Freedom Denied; Indian Women and Indentureship in Trinidad and Tobago, 1845–1917', *Economic and Political Weekly* (26 Oct. 1985), vol. 20, no. 43; K. O. Laurence, 'The Settlement of Free Negroes in Trinidad Before Emancipation', *Caribbean Quarterly* (March/June 1963), vol. 9, no. 1/2.
341 Ramsaran & Lewis, *Caribbean Masala*, 21.
342 Williams, *History*, 65, 70, 72.
343 Gray, *Devon and the Slave Trade*, 201-56.
344 Carmichael, *Domestic*, I, 116.
345 TNA CO23/81 & CO23/74.
346 Martin, *History*, II, Appendix B & I, 228; Williams, *History*, 78-9, 87-9.
347 Williams, *History*, 76-7, 97, 99.
348 Williams, *History*, 91.
349 Sewell, *Ordeal*, 95-105.
350 Sewell, *Ordeal*, 107.
351 A. F. Fokeer, 'The Negroes in Mauritius', *The Journal of Negro History* (1922), vol. 7, 197, 202-203; Charles Pridham, *An Historical, Political and Statistical Account of Ceylon and Its Dependencies* (1849), 173; John Parish (ed.), *A voyage to the Isle of Mauritius* (1775), 100.
352 A Bengal Civilian, *Journal of Five Months' Residence in the Mauritius* (Calcutta, 1838), 55.
353 *Journal of Five Months*, 58.
354 *Slave Population {Slave Registries}* (1833), 2; De Burgh-Edwardes, *History of Mauritius*, 70-2.
355 Martin, *History*, II, Appendix B.

356 James Holman, *Travels in Madras, Ceylon, Mauritius, Cormoro Islands, Zanzibar, Calcutta* (1840), 163.
357 *Devonport Telegraph & Plymouth Chronicle*, 6 Oct. 1832.
358 Parish, *Voyage*, 98-102; William Henry Gregory, *A Transport Voyage to the Mauritius and Back* (1851), 136-9; Patrick Beaton, *Creoles and Coolies* (1859), 170-4; Williams, *History*, 99; J. J. Freeman, *A Tour in South Africa* (1851), 372-3.
359 Gray, *Not One of Us*, 256.
360 John Robley, *A permanent and effectual remedy suggested for the evils under which the British West Indies now labour* (1808), 39-41.
361 J. R. Ward, *British West Indian Slavery, 1750-1834* (Oxford, 1988), 105-108, 222-3; Peter Pope, *Fish into Wine* (Chapel Hill, 2004), 27, 96, 380-1.
362 Cheshire, 'The results of the census of Great Britain in 1851', 46, 58.
363 Todd Gray (ed.), *The Exeter Cloth Dispatch Book*, DCRS (2020), NS63, 24-42.
364 W. G. Hoskins, *Industry, Trade and People in Exeter, 1688–1800* (Exeter, 1968 edn), 89-91, 160-2.
365 National Records of Scotland, GD214/681/8. Porcher purchased the house from the estate of Edward Cotsford, another East India Company official: *EFP*, 7 June 1810.
366 Mrs Mary Burgoyne Brunton née Jackson died at Dawlish on 17 Dec. 1809 in Dawlish: *The Scots Magazine* (1810), LXXII, 79.
367 *EFP*, 10 Jan. 1811.
368 National Records of Scotland, GD1/1153/11, letters 2, 5, 13; TNA, PROB 11/1518/25; Brunton's death notice referred to him as '3rd Regiment Native Infantry on the Madras Establishment and late Military Auditor General at the Presidency of Fort St George': *Oxford Journal*, 24 Nov. 1810. Mrs Brunton died at Dawlish by July 1810: *Madras Courier*, 3 July 1810.
369 *Bombay Gazette*, 16 Aug. 1837.
370 Frederic G. Kenyon, (ed.), *The letters of Elizabeth Barrett Browning* (1897), I, 51, 10-31; *DNB*, Marjorie Stone, 'Browning, Elizabeth Barrett, poet and writer', (2008); Hall et al, *Legacies*, 192-6; Jeanette Augustus Marks, *The Family of the Barrett* (New York, 1938), 418-23.
371 'Description of Budleigh', *The Weekly Entertainer* (1 July 1805), vol. 45, 511.
372 *Pigot*, 78.
373 *Grenada Free Press*, 29 March 1828; Craton & Saunders, *Islanders in the Stream*, 202.
374 Ancestry, Census, Minehead (1861), East Budleigh (1871), St Sidwell Exeter (1881, 1891) *Whites Directory for Devon* (1878), 202; *E&E*, 15 March 1892.
375 Wilbur H. Siebert, *The Legacy of the American Revolution to the British West Indies* (Columbus, 1913), 32; Michael Craton and Gail Saunders, *Islanders in the Stream* (Athens, 1992), 222-4; TNA, T71/129.
376 Christiana C. Hankin, *Life of Mary Ann Schimmelpennick* (1858), 93.
377 Martin Dunsford, *Miscellaneous observations in the course of two tours, through several parts of the West of England* (1807), 87.
378 Richard Warner, *A walk through some of the Western counties of England* (Bath, 1800), 222.
379 Daniel Carless Webb, *Observations and remarks during four excursions made to various parts of Great Britain* (1812).
380 Somerset Heritage Centre, DD/ES/14/2.
381 W. Spreat, *A new guide to the city of Exeter* (1825), 118-119.
382 *Pigot*, 63-4.

383 *Pigot*, 64.
384 Edmund Gibson, *Britannia* (1753), I, 43.
385 Andrew Brice, *The Grand Gazetteer* (Exeter, 1759), 551.
386 Andrew Oliver (ed.), *The Journal of Samuel Curwen, Loyalist* (Salem, 1972), I, 455.
387 Bath Record Office, diary of Thomas Moy.
388 *Pigot*, 78.
389 *Pigot*, 79.
390 TNA, T71/202.
391 TNA, T71/304.
392 TNA, T71/328.
393 Plymouth Archives, 308/50.
394 Gray, *Travels in Georgian Devon*, I, 36-7.
395 William George Maton, *Observations relative chiefly to the Natural History, Picturesque Scenery and antiquities of the Western Counties of England* (1797), II, 71-2; Warner, *A walk*, 117.
396 W. G. Hoskins, *Devon* (Newton Abbot, 1954), 414.
397 J. Banfield, *A guide to Ilfracombe* (Ilfracombe, 1840), 11-12.
398 Lady Jackson, *The Bath Archives* (1873), I, 134.
399 Somerset Heritage Centre, DD/ES/14/2.
400 *EPG*, 12 Jan. 1850; *Pigot*, 84-5.
401 *Barbados Agricultural Reporter*, 11 Sept. 1868; *Port of Spain Gazette*, 30 July 1833; Ancestry, Census, 1841 & 1851 (Ilfracombe).
402 John Lloyd Warden Page, *The Coasts of Devon & Lundy Island* (1895), 87; Amy Slade King, 'Notes on the Older Times of Ilfracombe', *DAT* (1879), XI, 167; *Ipswich Journal*, 20 Oct. 1796.
403 Gray, *Travels in Georgian Devon*, I, 44.
404 Maton, *Observations*, II, 91.
405 Bath Record Office, diary of Thomas Moy.
406 John Walker, *The Universal Gazetteer* (1798), no page number.
407 Somerset Heritage Centre, DD/ES/14/2.
408 Pedestres, 'A Pedestrian Tour', *The Metropolitan Magazine* (April, 1836), vol. 15, no. 60, 319.
409 Spreat, *A New Guide to the City of Exeter*, 114.
410 *The Sidmouth Guide* (Sidmouth, 1818), 30.
411 *EPG*, 2 April 1831; TNA, PROB 11/1789/72.
412 Ancestry, Census, 1861-71 (Sidmouth); *Morning Post*, 29 & 30 Oct. 1879.
413 Malcolm Brown, 'Anglo-Jewish Country Houses from the Resettlement to 1800', *Transactions & Miscellanies* (Jewish Historical Society of England, 1981-2), vol. 28, 34.
414 ***, 14.
415 *Pigot*, 124.
416 TNA, T71/295.
417 W. Hyett, *Guide in a tour to the watering places and their environs on the south-east coast of Devon* (Exeter, c1800), 15-16.
418 Spreat, *A New Guide to the City of Exeter*, 117.
419 University of Manchester Library, GB 133 MAM/FL/6/11/17; *Pigot*, 129.
420 Oliver, *Curwen*, I, 461.
421 Dunsford, *Miscellaneous*, 106.

Notes

422 University of Manchester Library, GB 133 MAM/FL/6/11/18.
423 *Pigot*, 129; *EFP*, 20 March 1823.
424 *The Complete Gazetteer of England and Wales* (1775), II, no page number.
425 *Pigot*, 135.
426 M. A. P., 'On Torquay and its environs', *South Devon Monthly Museum* (Jan. to June, 1835), vol. 5, 226.
427 Ancestry, Census, 1851 (Tormohun); TNA, PROB 11/2243/35.
428 Brice, *The Grand Gazetteer*, 181-2.
429 Plymouth Archives, 308/50.
430 Brice, *The Grand Gazetteer*, 138; *Universal British Directory*, II, 313.
431 *Royal Gazette*, 15 March 1823.
432 *Pigot*, 47. Some comments were taken directly from Richard Warner's account of 1800: Warner, *A Walk*, 122.
433 *Pigot*, 48; The letter was written by Capt. Thomas N. Stewart: William Renwick Riddell, *The Slave in Canada* (Washington, 1920), 75.
434 *NDJ*, 9 Aug. 1838, 22 Feb. 1838, 31 Jan. 1850, 5 Nov. 1840.
435 The Lysons brothers noted in 1822 that flannel was formerly made in Uffculme for the West Indies: Lysons, *Devon*, 538.
436 Brice, *The Grand Gazetteer*, 182.
437 Plymouth Archives, 308/50.
438 *Universal British Directory*, II, 436.
439 Warner, *A walk*, 124.
440 *Pigot*, 50.
441 *Pigot*, 52; DHC, 7785M/1/1/a-b.
442 Hawkins was in Bideford on 16 Feb. 1837 and Exeter the following month: TNA, T71/1593-4.
443 Warner, *A walk*, 57.
444 *Pigot*, 113-115.
445 Somerset Heritage Centre, DD/ES/14/2.
446 TNA, T71/553.
447 *Plymouth and Devonport Weekly Journal*, 28 June 1832.
448 Brice, *The Grand Gazetteer*, 545.
449 *Pigot*, 47.
450 Daniel Carless Webb, *Observations and remarks during four excursions made to various parts of Great Britain* (1812).
451 *Pigot*, 66-8.
452 *The Complete Gazetteer of England and Wales* (1775), II, no page number.
453 *Lady's Magazine* (1783), Vol. 14; Plymouth Archives, 308/50.
454 Gray, *Travels in Georgian Devon*, I, 29.
455 Maton, *Observations*, II, 53-4.
456 *Pigot*, 137.
457 *Pigot*, 137; DHC, 189M/1/F/2/16a-b, 189M/3/F/5/13, 189M/1/F/6/3 and 189M/1/E/6/8.
458 *Pigot*, 95; Ancestry, Census (1851), Ottery St Mary.
459 *The Complete Gazetteer of England and Wales* (1775), II, no page number.
460 *Lady's Magazine* (17830, Vol. 14.
461 Somerset Heritage Centre, DD/ES/14/2.
462 *Pigot*, 96.

463 Gibson, *Britannia*, I, 38.
464 *Universal British Directory* (1790), IV, 617-618.
465 Shirley Woolmer, A *Concise Account of the City of Exeter* (Exeter, 1821), 77.
466 *Pigot*, 131.
467 *Pigot*, 132.
468 TNA, T71/125.
469 TNA, T71/125.
470 TNA, T71/440.
471 TNA, T71/438.
472 *EPG*, 29 Aug. 9 Sept. & 30 Nov. 1885.
473 Oliver, *Curwen*, I, 199.
474 *Pigot*, 134.
475 Charles Knight, *Knight's Tourist Companion Through the Land We Live* (1853), 14-15.
476 *Pigot*, 134; TNA, T71/77 & 224.
477 *The Complete Gazetteer of England and Wales* (1775), II, no page number.
478 Warner, *Walk*, 186-7.
479 *Pigot*, 138.
480 Devon Heritage Centre, Totnes parish register.
481 *Bath Chronicle*, 16 May 1844; *Bristol Mercury*, 18 May 1844.
482 *WT*, 13 Sept. 1834.
483 Numbers of Black prisoners vary from between 950 and 1,174: Robin F. A. Fabel, 'Self-help in Dartmoor: Black and White Prisoners in the War of 1812', *Journal of the Early Republic* (Summer, 1989), vol. 9, no. 2, 165-90; Alan Thomas Lipke, *The strange life and stranger afterlife of King Dick* (2013), 4-11; W. Jeffrey Bolster, *Black Jacks* (Cambridge, 1997), 102-3.
484 Todd Gray, *Exeter Remembers The War* (Exeter, 2005), 164.
485 The census listed 369 Irish in Exeter and 1,652 in Plymouth. More than 5,000 Irish immigrants lived across Devon.
486 Ancestry, Census, 1841 & 1851.
487 They were Edgar Johnson of Honiton, Charles Lewis of Exeter St Stephen and Mary Williams of Exeter St Sidwell: Ancestry, Census, 1841.
488 Most of these references are derived from a volunteers' project conducted by the Friends of Devon's Archives in the late 1990s. Each entry has been verified with the original document but the notes regarding Charles Phoenix and Thomas Bathurst have not been found. The latter did have his marriage recorded in 1798 but with different personal details.
489 Ancestry, Broadbent family tree; *EPG*, 30 Aug. & 6 & 20 Sept. 1828.
490 *NDJ*, 13 July 1827.
491 *WT*, 3 Nov. 1827.
492 *EPG*, 29 Nov. 1834; *Western Morning News*, 10 July 1860; *Western Daily Mercury*, 15 June 1863.
493 *EPG*, 4 & 19 June 1830.
494 Gray, *Not One of Us*, 258-9; *EPG*, 22 Feb. 1840.
495 *EFP*, 23 Feb. 1815.
496 *EPG*, 21 Nov. 1829; *Royal Cornwall Gazette*, 21 Nov. 1829.
497 *EFP*, 4 July 1822.
498 *EPG*, 22 Feb. 1834; *WT*, 1 March 1834; DHC, DEX7/b/1/1834/72.
499 *EFP*, 19 June 1834; *EPG* & *WT*, 21 June 1834; *Bristol Mercury*, 28 June 1834.

500 *EFP*, 22 Jan. 1807 & 5 Feb. 1818; *Exeter Directory*, 217; *EPG*, 18 May 1833; *WT*, 12 May 1838; *EPG*, 7 July 1838; TNA, PROB 11/1896/93.
501 *EFP*, 2 Jan. 1817.
502 WT, 15 Dec. 1875.
503 NDJ, 11 Jan. 1917, 22 May 1941; Ancestry, Pete Gurney family tree.
504 *NDJ*, 21 Nov. 1901.
505 *NDJ*, 18 April 1907
506 *WT*, 18 May 1916.
507 There were none in the remaining eight colonies of Anguilla, Bermuda, Cape of Good Hope, the Caymans, Honduras, Mauritius, Montserrat, St Lucia or the Virgin Islands.
508 Figures from the census taken a few years earlier supplement those given by Dr Draper: Draper, *The Price*, 139.
509 Bermuda's census of 1831 recorded 3,920 slaves and that of the Caymans reported 950. Draper, *The Price*, 138, note 3, 139, 154; Cheshire, 'The Results', 46, 58. The figure for all slave-holders who received compensation awards was calculated by Professor Richard Lobdell in 2000 as 82 per cent of the 43,678 gross claims. I am grateful to him for sharing his research: 'The Price of Freedom: Financial Aspects of British Slave Emancipation, 1833-1838, notes on research in progress', unpublished paper presented at the annual meeting of the Social Sciences History Association, October, 2000, 10. The £535 figure has been calculated from the £16,356,668 estimated to have been given by Draper.
510 Of these thirty-three, Alphington, Clyst St Mary, Countisbury, Exeter, Heavitree, Ilfracombe, Ottery St Mary, Rockbeare, Shute, Stevenstone, Totnes and Washfield had one each whereas Bradninch, Dawlish, Exmouth, Sidmouth, Teignmouth, Tiverton and Topsham had two each. Plymouth had three while Budleigh Salterton was the only place with four.
511 Figures from the census for Mauritius taken a few years earlier supplement those given by Dr Draper: Draper, *The Price*, 139.
512 Draper, *The Price*, 154.
513 In 1830 they were classified as being either noble, gentry or members of the clergy: *Pigot*.
514 Draper, *The Price*, 7-8.
515 R. Polwhele, *Traditions and Recollections* (1826), II, 435.
516 *Kentish Gazette*, 5 Sept. 1797; Charles L. Mowat, 'The Tribulations of Denys Rolle', *The Florida Historical Quarterly* (July, 1944), vol. 23, no. 1, 1; *GM* (1797), LXXXII, 885; Charles Loch Mowat, *East Florida as a British Province, 1763–1784* (Berkeley, 1943), 71; Robert Legg, *A pioneer in Xanadu, Denys Rolle: 1725–97* (Whitchurch, Hants, 1997); Somerset Heritage Centre, DD/DN/4/1/27/31.
517 *Ipswich Journal*, 19 May 1764; *Manchester Mercury*, 19 Nov. 1765; *Caledonian Mercury*, 23 July 1766; *Salisbury & Winchester Journal*, 29 Dec. 1766. In April 1767 another 93 men, women and children sailed from Falmouth to Rolle's settlement and in May 1767 it was reported Rolle was recruiting labourers and mechanics in Ireland: *Caledonian Mercury*, 4 April 1767 & *Stamford Mercury*, 21 May 1767.
518 *The Scots Magazine*, 1 Aug. 1767; *GM* (1767), XXXVII, 429.
519 James Grant Forbes, *Sketches, historical and topographical of the Floridas* (New York, 1821), 81; Ralph H. Brown, *Mirror for Americans* (New York, 1943), 150.
520 Mowat, 'The Tribulations', 1-2; Carita Doggett Corse & James Grant, 'Denys Rolle and Rollestown, a Pioneer for Utopia', *The Florida Historical Society Quarterly* (Oct. 1928), vol. 7, no. 2, 126; Legg, *A pioneer in Xanadu*.

521 *Narrative of a voyage to the Spanish Main in the ship Two Friends* (1819), 154.
522 John Lee Williams, *The Territory of Florida* (New York, 1837), 188. See also Charles Vignoles, *Observations upon the Floridas* (New York, 1823), 73 who referred to the women as 'a certain class of unhappy females… from the purlieus of Drury Lane'.
523 *Florida Standard Guide* (unknown, 1922), 25. In 1925 they were referred to as 'a motley collection of persons assembled from the gutters of London' and in 1943 they were termed 'wretched people': Carol Bohnenberger, 'The Settlement of Charlotia (Rolles Town), 1765', *The Florida Historical Quarterly* (July 1925), vol. 4, no. 1, 46 & Brown, *Mirror*, 152.
524 Archibald Clavering Gunter, *The Power of Woman* (New York, 1897), I, 272.
525 Legg, *A Pioneer*, 119, 124-7.
526 Denys Rolle, *To the Right Honourable the Lords of his Majesty's Most Honourable Council* (1790), 81; Legg, *A Pioneer*, 80.
527 TNA, T77/15, 194.
528 TNA, T77/15, 213, the general state of the settlement or plantation of Denys Rolle in East Florida, 1783.
529 TNA, T77/15, 198.
530 *Sun*, 25 Dec. 1818; *Jamaica Journal*, 6 Nov. 1824.
531 *Salisbury & Winchester Journal*, 17 April 1769; James Munro (ed.), *Acts of the Privy Council, Colonial Series* (1912), VI, 612-613.
532 Legg, *A Pioneer*, 129; Thelma Peters, 'The American Loyalists in the Bahama Islands: Who They Were', *The Florida Historical Quarterly* (Jan. 1962), vol. 40, no. 3, 238; *Saunders' Newsletter*, 5 Nov. 1787. Rolle claimed ten to twelve died on the voyage: TNA, CO23/15.
533 TNA, T77/14.
534 Wiltshire & Swindon History Centre, 9/35/232. Rolle was with the king in Devon in 1789: Bedfordshire Archives & Records Service, L30/15/33/4 & 8.
535 *RGJ*, 5 Aug. 1826.
536 *Derby Mercury*, 28 Aug. 1767.
537 Robert Dosie, *Memoirs of Agriculture* (1768-71), I, 4.
538 *Kentish Gazette*, 5 Sept. 1797; *Devonshire* (Exeter, c1867), 113.
539 J. B. Andrews, 'Chittlehampton', *DAT* (1962), XCIV, 275; *GM* (1797), 1125; *The Weekly Entertainer* (11 Dec. 1797), XXX, 461-2.
540 'Of the late Dennis Rolle', *The Monthly Magazine* (1797), IV, 316.
541 *Criticisms on the Rolliad, a poem* (1785); *The Rolliad* (1795), xxvii, 187. There were a number of editions. In 1784 he had been mocked: Bedfordshire Archives & Records Service, L30/14/333/282. One observer noted 'The verses in *The Public Advertiser* on Mr Rolle are not altogether bad, especially the last seventeen lines which are I think really good, I suspect Sheridan or Fitzpatrick'.
542 *DNB*, J. M. Rigg & Roland Thorne, 'Rolle, John, Baron Rolle' (2009); Mary M. Drummond, 'Rolle, John (1756-1842) of Stevenstone, Devon', in L. Namier & J. Brooke (eds), *The History of Parliament: the House of Commons, 1754–1790* (1964).
543 NDRO, 3704M/FC/Corr. 1790.
544 Wiltshire & Swindon History Centre, 9/35/232; Plymouth Record Office, 1259/1/51. The election was estimated to have cost £40,000: *Hampshire Chronicle*, 5 July 1790.
545 Alexander Jenkins, *History of Exeter* (1806), 220.
546 TNA, T71/457; *The Debates in Parliament – Session 1833 – on the resolutions and bill for the abolition of slavery in the British colonies* (1834), 24; *The Literary Magazine and British Review* (June 1790), IV, 153-4; Gail Saunders, *Bahamian Loyalists* (1983), 25.

547 TNA, TS25/2046, folios 295-8.
548 *WT*, 7 April 1838.
549 Stark, *History of the Bahama Islands*, 450-1.
550 Craton, 'Hobbesian', 354.
551 TNA, CO23/74, folio 275.
552 Craton & Saunders, *Islanders*, 225-6; Michael Craton, 'Hobbesian or Panglossian? The Two Extremes of Slave Conditions in the British Empire, 1783 to 1834', *William & Mary Quarterly* (April, 1978), vol. 35, no. 2, 352-3; TNA, CO23/81, folios 107 & 109.
553 TNA, CO23/81, folio 109.
554 Craton & Saunders, *Islanders*, 382. Rolle's will of 1792 does not have any such stipulations: TNA, PROB 11/1298/41.
555 Craton & Saunders, *Islanders*, 383-6; *Sun*, 12 July 1830; *Devizes and Wiltshire Gazette*, 23 Sept. 1830; *Nottingham Review*, 23 July 1830; James Martin Wright, *History of the Bahama Islands* (1905), 476-7.
556 Michael Craton, 'We shall not be moved; Pompey's slave revolt in Exuma Island, Bahamas, 1830', *New West Indian Guide* (1983), vol. 57, no. 1, 27-9; Wright, *History of the Bahama Islands*, 506.
557 TNA, T71/459.
558 *WT*, 9 Oct. 1830.
559 *Star*, 9 Oct. 1830; *Hull Packet*, 2 Nov. 1830.
560 *The Debates in Parliament, Session 1833* (1834), 908.
561 Craton & Saunders, *Islanders*, 389-91.
562 *Cambridge Chronicle*, 15 Aug. 1834; *Morning Advertiser*, 12 Aug. 1834.
563 *WT*, 6 Sept. 1834.
564 *Port of Spain Gazette*, 28 Oct. 1834.
565 *EPG*, 30 Aug. 1834.
566 Stark, *History of the Bahama Islands*, 446.
567 *Morning Chronicle*, 4 May 1839; *EPG*, 26 May 1838.
568 *Sun*, 23 May 1838; *Morning Chronicle*, 23 May 1838; Gail Saunders, *Race and Class in the Colonial Bahamas, 1880-1960* (Gainesville, 2016), 16.
569 Craton, 'We shall not', 29-30; *The Debates in Parliament,* 24.
570 *EPG*, 15 Dec. 1838.
571 *EPG*, 15 Dec. 1838.
572 TNA, CO23/92, folio 496; Craton & Saunders, *Islanders*, 390.
573 Lambeth Palace Library, FP/XV, 87-93.
574 L. D. Powles, *The Land of the Pink Pearl* (1888), 298; A. R. Hope Moncrieff, *The World of Today* (1911), V, 22.
575 *Slave Population* (1826), 115. Anne and Elizabeth Rolle were manumitted in consideration of their services on October 31.
576 Saunders, *Race and Class*, 16.
577 Craton, 'Hobbesian', 325.
578 Craton, 'Hobbseian', 327.
579 *EFP*, 5 Dec. 1833.
580 Ancestry, Census, 1841 (Doddiscombsleigh & Kenton); *EFP*, 2 Jan. 1840, 5 Dec. 1833; TNA, PROB 11/1855/308; TNA, PROB 11/1091/159.
581 *Pigot*, 11; *St James Chronicle*, 12 July 1856; Ancestry, Census, 1841 & 1851 (Stoke Damerel).

582 TNA, T71/1608; *Royal Gazette*, 27 April 1822; *EPG*, 10 Nov. 1855; *Weston Super Mare Gazette*, 10 Nov. 1855.
583 *Western Courier*, 26 July 1837 & 27 Jan. 1841; Ancestry, Census, 1841 (Stonehouse); *Dublin Weekly Register, 1 July 1843*.
584 Eric Williams, *Capitalism and Slavery* (1944), 43; Lucy MacKeith, *Local Black History: A Beginning in Devon* (2003), 21; Gray, *Devon and the Slave Trade* (2007 edn), 199-200; *Morning Advertiser*, 30 March 1838.
585 Ancestry, Census, 1861 (Paddington); 1871 & 1881 (West Teignmouth); *Home News*, 20 April 1867; *White's Directory of Devon*, 1878-9, 774; *Worcestershire Chronicle*, 8 March 1879; National Probate Calendar (Index of Wills and Administrations), 1898, West.
586 TNA, T71/541 & 548; *Morning Advertiser*, 25 Dec. 1871.
587 Ancestry, Census, 1851 (Chelsea), 1861 (Richmond), 1871 (Sandhurst), 1881 (Yateley); *Exmouth Journal*, 29 Dec. 1900; *Glasgow Evening Post*, 22 Nov. 1890.
588 TNA, PROB 11/1191/234; *LES*, 8 Oct. 1836; *WT*, 19 Dec. 1840; *NDJ*, 10 Dec. 1840; Ancestry, Census, 1851 (Poundstock); *Post Office Directory of Cornwall* (1856), 89; *WT*, 18 Aug. 1860.
589 Ancestry, Census, 1851 (Egg Buckland) & 1861 (Brampton); *Royal Cornwall Gazette*, 29 April 1881; *Naval & Military Gazette*, 11 May 1881.
590 Terry Jenkins, 'Kekewich, Samuel Trehawke, of Peamore House, nr Exeter, Devon' in D. R. Fisher, *The History of Parliament: the House of Commons, 1820-1832* (2009).
591 *EFP*, 23 Sept. 1858; *WT*, 1 Dec. 1855.
592 *Caledonian Mercury*, 2 Jan. 1815; TNA, PROB 11/1722/96.
593 *British Daily Mail*, 8 April 1850; *LES*, 12 Dec. 1860; *WT*, 22 Dec. 1860; *LES*, 15 May 1863.
594 TNA, PROB 11/1355/181 & 2133/304.
595 *Bristol Mirror*, 24 Nov. 1821 & 1 Nov. 1823; Ancestry, Census, 1841 (Bishop's Tawton).
596 *Bell's Weekly Messenger*, 2 Nov. 1823.
597 *Bristol Mirror*, 9 Dec. 1826.
598 *RGJ*, 14 Oct. 1780.
599 TNA, T71/1.
600 Draper, *The Price*, 146, 190; Ancestry, Census, 1851 (Bishop's Tawton); *EFP*, 4 Nov. 1858; *NDJ*, 16 July 1840; *The fourteenth annual report of the Ladies' Society for promoting the early education and improvement of the children of Negroes and of People of Colour in the British West Indies* (1839), 84-5.
601 *EFP*, 11 March 1813; *Pigot*, 67; *EPG*, 25 Sept. & 30 Oct. 1847; Ancestry, Census, 1841 (St David).
602 *WT*, 4 Feb. 1837; *Pigot*, 79.
603 *RGJ*, 12 July 1794; *Oxford University and City Herald*, 13 March 1813; *Exeter Itinerary and General Directory* (Exeter, 1828 & 1831), 218; *EFP*, 21 Sept. 1837.
604 *Pigot*, 68; *EPG*, 14 Feb. 1846; TNA, PROB 11/2038/151.
605 TNA, T71/1607. He was applying on behalf of the deceased's brother and five sisters. Sleigh had married Sarah Guscott in Exeter in 1813: Ancestry, Guscott family tree.
606 Ancestry, Census, 1851 (Sidmouth), Young/Fletcher/Tullis family tree.
607 Oliver, *History of Antigua*, III, 18, 26 & !, 23; *GM* (1796), vol. 66, pt 1, 444.
608 Somerset Heritage Centre, DD/SAS/C/432/43; *Bath Chronicle*, 12 March 1807; *EFP*, 14 Sept. 1815; *EPG*, 1 Dec. 1827; *EFP*, 13 Dec. 1838; *Salisbury and Winchester Journal*, 24 Jan. 1842; *Bath Chronicle*, 22 Dec. 1853.

609 *The Pilot*, 14 May 1832; Ancestry, Menes family tree.
610 Ancestry, Census, 1841 (Sidmouth), 1851 (St Sidwell), 1861 (Brighton); *Sussex Advertiser*, 20 Dec. 1866.
611 Ancestry, Biographical Research by William de Villiers; Census, 1851 (Stoke Damerel).
612 *Morning Post*, 5 May 1831; *LES*, 26 Jan. 1843 & 24 Sept. 1844; *EPG*, 11 Oct. 1845; *Hampshire Chronicle*, 6 May 1848; Ancestry, Census, 1851 & 1861 (Tiverton), 1871 (Kensington); *WT*, 20 Oct. 1849; *EPG*, 29 Dec. 1855; *Post Office Directory* (1856), 301; *EPG*, 17 Dec. 1859; & 10 March 1860.
613 *EFP*, 7 Dec. 1843; Charles Maclear Calder, *John Vassall and his Descendants* (Hertford, 1921), 28.
614 DHC, 3799M/O/L/92/6; *EFP*, 1 Feb. 1816.
615 *WT*, 7 Nov. 1846; DHC, DEX/7/b/1810/525.
616 TNA, T71/190.
617 *Morning Post*, 15 April 1802; *Dublin Evening Packet*, 24 March 1838; Ancestry, Census, 1841 (Lynton) & 1851 (Exmouth); *EPG*, 16 Oct. 1847; *Pigot*, 63; William White, *History, Gazetteer and Directory of Devonshire* (Sheffield, 1850), 235.
618 *RGJ*, 29 Jan. 1814 & 29 April 1815; *Durham Country Advertiser*, 24 Feb. 1816; *RGJ*, 5 April 1817; *Dundee Advertiser*, 26 Nov. 1897; *Chester Chronicle*, 7 Dec. 1827.
619 *EPG*, 26 Aug. 1843.
620 *EPG*, 1 Aug. 1846; Ancestry, 1851 (Bath), 1861 & 1871 (Tormohun); *Falkirk Herald*, 31 March 1859; *Morning Post*, 28 March 1859 & 8 Oct. 1884.
621 J. Luffman, *Antigua and the Antiguans* (1844), I, 119-20; *EPG* & *WT*, 4 Feb. 1837; TNA, ADM 354/221/364 & PROB 11/1879/298.
622 *Besley's Exeter Directory for 1835* (Exeter, 1835); Ancestry, Lindsey family tree.
623 Ancestry, Census, 1861 (Budleigh).
624 TNA, PROB 11/1743/31; A. J. P. Skinner, 'Kirkham of Feniton, Westofer of Yardbury, Colyton and Drake of Yardbury', *Devon & Cornwall Notes & Queries* (1913), vol. 7, 267.
625 Ancestry, Census, 1881 & 1891 (Plympton St Mary), jsisbeybritton family tree.
626 *Kirby's Wonderful and Eccentric Museum* (1820), vol. 6, 402; *Morning Post*, 28 July 1818; William Fitzer Burchell, *Memoir of Thomas Burchell* (1849), 217.
627 *St Georges Chronicle*, 20 Sept. & 24 Oct. 1799; *St James Chronicle*, 3 Oct. 1820; *RGJ*, 25 Nov. 1826 & 14 April 1827; *Jamaica Watchman*, 16 Nov. & 17 Dec. 1831, 11 April 1832; Ancestry, Census, 1851 (Ilfracombe); *Merthyr Guardian*, 15 Nov. 1851.
628 *Bath Chronicle*, 18 Feb. 1813; *Bristol Mirror*, 9 June 1827 & 10 May 1823; *Evening Mail*, 2 Nov. 1846.
629 Son-in-law John Michell was an attorney in Ilfracombe: White, *Directory*, 593; *EFP*, 27 Aug. 1835; *NDJ*, 3 Sept. 1835; Ancestry, Census, 1841 (Ilfracombe), 1851 (Madron).
630 TNA, T71/60.
631 *Royal Devonport Telegraph*, 18 Aug. 1832; *Plymouth and Devonport Weekly Journal*, 6 Dec. 1832; *EFP*, 21 Nov. 1833.
632 *EPG*, 15 Dec. 1838.
633 *Tablet*, 4 Aug. 1894; *NDJ*, 7 Sept. 1827; *EFP*, 6 Sept. 1827.
634 *RGJ*, 24 Dec. 1825.
635 *Globe* & *West Kent Guardian*, 16 Jan. 1836; Ancestry, Census, 1841 (Tiverton), 1851 (Tunbridge); *London Daily News*, 4 April 1871.
636 It may be that Richard Collins of Exeter was connected to the Marshall slave plantations: *EPG*, 25 Sept. 1847.

637 TNA, T71/125.
638 *St George's Chronicle*, 9 March 1815 & 17 Feb. 1819; *WT*, 26 Feb. 1842; Gillian Allen, 'Two Devon families in Jamaica', *Maritime South West* (2008), no. 21.
639 *Slave Trade; Further papers relating to Captured Negroes* (1825), 9, 26.
640 *EFP*, 14 Nov. 1839; *St George's Chronicle*, 31 Jan. 1835.
641 TNA, T71/334.
642 *St George's Chronicle*, 18 March 1815.
643 *St George's Chronicle*, 31 Jan. 1835; *WT*, 26 Feb. 1842; *GM*, 1842, 223.
644 *NDJ*, 7 Sept. 1827; *EFP*, 6 Sept. 1827; *British Daily Mail*, 8 April 1850; *LES*, 12 Dec. 1860; *WT*, 22 Dec. 1860; *LES*, 15 May 1863; *Tablet*, 4 Aug. 1894; *NDJ*, 7 Sept. 1827; *EFP*, 6 Sept. 1827; *The Times*, 27 April 1839; Ancestry, Urney Park & Beyond family tree.
645 TNA, PROB 11/1903/408; *Morning Advertiser*, 5 Jan. 1825; Neil Sammells, 'Rediscovering the Irish Wilde', in C. George Sandulescu (ed.), *Rediscovering Oscar Wilde* (1994), 362.
646 Ancestry, Census, 1841 (Sidmouth), 1851 (Dawlish), Cole Knapp Family Tree; White, *Directory*, 402; *LES*, 27 April 1853.
647 TNA, T71/507.
648 National Records of Scotland, GD18/2342. Grant was baptised on 28 January 1782; David R. Fisher, 'Alexander Cray Grant', in D. R. Fisher, *The History of Parliament: the House of Commons, 1820–1832* (2009); *RGJ*, 10 Aug. 1816; Draper, *The Price*, 69-70; Ancestry, Grant Thorold family tree.
649 *Falmouth Post*, 30 Nov. 1836; *EFP*, 31 May 1838; TNA, T71/41; *Morning Post*, 1 Dec. 1854.
650 *RGJ*, 10 Dec. 1814; *EPG*, 19 Jan. 1833; Ancestry, Census, 1841 (Berkshire), 1851 (Middlesex), Randall family tree; TNA, T71/11; *St James Chronicle*, 4 Oct. 1856; TNA, PROB 11/2241/393; *GM* (1856), vol. 201, 660.
651 *NDJ*, 1 Aug. 1839; *Somerset County Gazette*, 3 Aug. 1839; *Sherborne Mercury*, 16 Sept. 1839; Peter Maunder, 'Thomas Rossiter of the *Endeavour*', *Tiverton Civic Society Newsletter* (April, 2021), no. 95, 21-2; *Pigot*, 132.
652 DHC, 49/9/3/201a-b, 5214M/T/52-4 & 213M/T/192-200.
653 TNA, T71/31 & 25.
654 TNA, T71/28.
655 DHC, 213M/T/195; *RGJ*, 7 Nov. 1818 & 11 July 1812; *RGJ*, 10 April 1813; Draper, *The Price*, 188; *Dorset County Chronicle*, 7 Sept. 1826; *Morning Post*, 22 June 1827; *RGJ*, 20 Oct. 1827; *Bristol Mercury*, 10 Oct. 1835; *NDJ*, 1 Aug. 1839; *Somerset County Gazette*, 3 Aug. 1839; *Sherborne Mercury*, 16 Sept. 1839; DHC, 49/9/3/201a-b.
656 Thome & Kimball, *Emancipation*, vi.
657 Thome & Kimball, *Emancipation*, 77.
658 DHC, WSL, R. W. Mitchell (mss, 1991), 'The History of Newport House, Topsham, Devon 1798–1980'; Jan Betteridge, 'Samuel Mitchell: from plantation to Newport House', *Topsham Times* (2018), issue 21, 24-35; *The Asiatic Journal* (Sept. – Dec. 1833), NS12, 284.
659 TNA, T71/324.
660 TNA, T71/65; Gillian M. Allen, 'Slavery and two Ottery St Mary families', *Heritage, Journal of the Ottery St Mary Heritage Society* (Summer, 2009), no. 30, 3-5.
661 TNA, PROB 11/1916/137; DHC, 2741M/F/C/15/4a-b & 48/22/1/3; *EFP*, 22 March 1804; Black Cultural Archives, GALE/1/11-16; TNA, T71/169 & 137; *WT*, 17 August 1839.
662 *EFP*, 2 Feb. 1826; *EPG*, 5 May 1827; *EPG*, 26 March 1830; *EPG*, 26 March 1831; *Dorset County Chronicle*, 27 Oct. 1831; Ancestry, Census, 1841 (Yorkshire).

663   *Caledonian Mercury*, 12 April 1847.
664   *EPG*, 10 April 1847.
665   J. B. Smith, *Seaton Beach* (1835), iii-iv.
666   Edmund Butcher, *A new guide descriptive of the beauties of Sidmouth* (Exeter, 1830), no page numbers.
667   NDRO, 3704M/FC7.
668   M. F. Bridie, *The Story of Shute* (Axminster, 1955), 156, 170, 178; George P. R. Pulman, *The Book of the Axe* (1875), 766-7. It is unclear where Bridie obtained the story of the curse.
669   *Transactions of the Society for the Encouragement of Arts, Manufactures and Commerce* (1821), Vol. 29, 3-5.
670   DHC, Colyton Parish Register, PR1, 1 June 1619.
671   Edwards, *History*, II, 203.
672   J. Ralfe, *The Navy biography of Great Britain* (1828), III, 32; William R. O'Byrne, *A naval biographical dictionary* (1849), 292; Ancestry, Clarke family tree; *Sherborne Mercury*, 27 Feb. 1837; *Dublin Evening Packet*, 21 Feb. 1837
673   TNA, T71/8 & 21.
674   *Western Courier*, 26 Sept. 1838; Draper, *The Price*, 214; TNA, PROB 11/1969/262.
675   *RGJ*, 30 Dec. 1826; Ancestry, Census, 1841 (Devonport) & Menes family tree.
676   Draper, *The Price*, 181-2; *Bath Chronicle*, 31 July 1828; *Sun*, 9 Aug. 1839; *Western Courier*, 14 Feb. 1850; Ancestry, Census, 1841 (Middlesex), 1851 (Devonport) & Royals, Peerage & Famous People tree; *Examiner*, 13 May 1854; *Reading Mercury*, 2 Dec. 1854; O'Byrne, *A New Naval Biographical Dictionary*, I, 972.
677   Ancestry, Thomson family tree & Census, 1861 & 1871 (Stoke Damerel).
678   *EPG*, 9 Aug. 1834 & *Sherborne Mercury*, 28 Nov. 1831; *EPG*, 26 July 1834; *Royal Cornwall Gazette*, 2 April 1808; *St James Chronicle*, 10 Feb. 1829; *Western Courier*, 21 July 1847 & 24 May 1843; Ancestry, Census, 1851 (Stonehouse); *Cirencester Times*, 6 Sept. 1869.
679   *Besley's Exeter Directory for 1835* (Exeter, 1835), 77; *White's Devon* (1850), 254; Ancestry, Census, 1851 & 1861 (Withycombe Raleigh), 1871 (Bath), 1881 & 1891 (Wimbledon); *EPG*, 5 June 1891.
680   *Torquay Directory*, 16 June & 4 December 1846.
681   Ancestry, Census, 1851 (Ilfracombe). Dalzell stayed at 2 Down Place. She was born in the West Indies but had moved to Cheltenham by the 1850s.
682   *Carlisle Patriot*, 18 July 1829; TNA, T71/1608, T71/1592 & PROB 11/1791B/118; Draper, *The Price*, 227-9; *Bristol Mercury*, 7 Aug. 1841.
683   *WT*, 15 Feb. & 19 April 1834; *EPG*, 15 March 1834; *EFP*, 20 March, 24 April & 23 Oct. 1834; *Taunton Courier*, 12 Oct. 1836; *Morning Chronicle*, 17 Oct. 1849.
684   TNA, T71/118.
685   *Morning Chronicle*, 12 Feb. 1831; Ancestry, Census, 1851 (Cheriton), 1861 (Hastings); *Torquay Times*, 28 March 1874 & 30 Oct. 1875; William White, *History, Gazetteer and Directory of Devon* (1878-9), 803.
686   *EFP*, 9 Dec. 1813.
687   *Pigot*, 79; *WT*, 13 March 1841; DHC, East Budleigh tithe apportionment and map; *EFP*, 2 Nov. 1848.
688   Ancestry, Census, 1841 (Sussex), 1851 (Rackenford), 1861 (Addington); *EFP*, 2 Nov. 1848; *Morning Post*, 15 July 1822; *NDJ*, 8 Jan. 1835; *EFP*, 15 Dec. 1836; *EPG*, 16 Sept. 1837 & 28 Sept. 1844; *WT*, 12 Sept. 1846 & 1 Jan. 1848.

689   British Library, Add.43379, Item E. Four other drawings made by William Berryman have not survived.
690   'The late Mother Francis Raphael, O.S.D.', *The Irish Monthly,* vol. 22, no. 255 (Sept. 1894), 501; Bertram Wilberforce (ed.) *A memoir of Mother Francis Raphael O. S. D. (Augusta Theodosia Drane)* (1904), xv-xxxvi.
691   *EPG,* 13 Sept. 1845; *Torquay Directory,* 10 April 1846; *EPG,* 29 April 1848; Ancestry, Census, 1851 & 1861 (St Marychurch); *WDM,* 23 July 1864; *WT,* 29 July 1864.
692   NDRO, 942.3/BAR/NOR, Basil J. Northover, Newport Terrace, vol. 2, section 29; TNA, T71/164.
693   Menezes, Mary Noel. "The Dutch and British Policy of Indian Subsidy: A System of Annual and Triennial Presents." *Caribbean Studies* 13, no. 3 (1973): 64-88; *Slave Population {Slave Registries}* (1833), 7; *General Report of the Emigration Commissioners* (1837), I, 26, 40-43, 144; *WMN,* 3 Aug. 1869; Ancestry, Census, 1871 (Wolborough); White, *History, Gazetteer & Directory of Devon, 1878–9,* page 563.
694   James Greig (ed.), *The Farington Diary* (1926), VI, 153-4.
695   TNA, PROB 11/1502/73.
696   *Madras Courier,* 27 Feb. 1810; *London Courier,* 9 Sept. 1819.
697   *Madras Courier,* 28 Aug. 1810.
698   *Madras Courier,* 16 Dec. 1807 & 3 May 1809; *Record of Services of the Honourable East India Company's Civil servants* (1885), 83.
699   Gray, *Devon and the Slave Trade,* 145-7; NDRO, 3704M/FC8, letters of 18 January and 16 November 1786.
700   DHC, 4297Z/E/1; Ancestry, Census, 1851 (Topsham); TNA, T71/330. In 1835 it was reported that 139 enslaved people had been freed on these two estates: *St George's Chronicle,* 21 Feb. 1835.
701   *The fourteenth annual report of the Ladies' Society for promoting the early education and improvement of the children of Negroes and of People of Colour in the British West Indies* (1839), 84-5.
702   *Grenada Free Press,* 28 Sept. 1826.
703   *Port of Spain Gazette,* 14 May 1833.
704   *Grenada Free Press,* 4 Dec. 1839.
705   Theodore Hands Mogridge, *A descriptive sketch of Sidmouth* (Sidmouth, 1838), 43.
706   Harrison, *Letter-Books,* 192, 198, 230, 236, 239.
707   Harrison, *Letter-Books,* 119, 125, 139, 174, 203, 214, 223, 236.
708   Harrison, *Letter-Books,* 119.
709   Harrison, *Letter-Books,* 130.
710   Harrison, *Letter-Books,* 163.
711   DHC, 2793Z/L/1; TNA, C 101/1842; Ancestry, Census, 1841 (Sidmouth); *London Daily News,* 17 Dec. 1846; *EPG,* 19 Dec. 1846; TNA, PROB 11/2049/293.
712   Ancestry, Michelin-Townend family tree & Census, 1841 (Hampstead, Middlesex), 1851 (Paddington).
713   *Sun,* 10 Sept. 1805; *Carlisle Journal,* 28 Sept. 1805; *Sun,* 16 Sept. 1806 & 3 Jan. 1822; BL, St Vincent Deed Book 1808, EAP688/1/1/19, 13, 20, 26, 35.
714   Edward Blaquiere, *A statistical, commercial and political description of Venezuela, Trinidad, Margarita and Tobago* (1820), 348-9.
715   DHC, 152M/C1801/OC/54.
716   *The English Reports* (1901), vol. 5, 705-723.

717 The painting by Augustin Brunias was sold at Christies on 25 April 2012.
718 TNA, PROB 31/1192/206 & PROB 11/1671/56; *Morning Advertiser*, 19 April 1823; *LES*, 11 July 1839; *Reports of cases argued and determined in the several courts of law and equity, in England, during the year 1839* (New York, 1840), II, 132-7.
719 BL, St Vincent Deed Book 1809, EAP688/1/1/20, 279, 528, 529.
720 TNA, T71/466.
721 hhtps://www.robley.org.uk; *Bristol Mercury*, 18 Nov. 1843; Gray, *Devon and the Slave Trade*, 112-34.
722 *St George's Chronicle*, 22 April 1815.
723 DHC, 1855A/PW3. Cotmaton House was lived in by Miss Bethill in 1831; *EFP*, 22 July 1819, 10 Aug. 1820, 27 April 1837; *The Monthly Repository* (1815), vol. 10, 522-3.
724 *Taunton Courier*, 17 Oct. 1816.
725 TNA, T7/324. The number was reported as 70 in a Grenada newspaper: *St George's Chronicle*, 28 Feb. 1835.
726 *Grenada Free Press*, 29 April 1829 & 31 March 1830.
727 Sally-Anne Huxtable, Corrine Fowler, Christo Kefalas & Emma Slocombe (eds), *Interim Report on the Connections between Colonialism and Properties now in the Care of the National Trust, Including Links with Historic Slavery* (Swindon, 2020), 97-104; *EFP*, 23 Oct. 1861; *Report of the Committee of the African Civilization Society* (1842); *EFP*, 11 Aug. 1814.
728 Ancestry, Census, 1851 (Totnes); *Torbay Express*, 13 March 1967.
729 *DNB*, Richard Riddell, 'Repton, George Stanley, architect' (2004).
730 DHC, QS/113A/176/1 & 3; Charles Burlington, *The modern universal British traveller* (1779), 469; J. E. B. Gover, A. Mawer & F. M. Stenton, *The Place-Names of Devon* (Cambridge, 1932), II, 598; Oliver, *Curwen*, I, 252-5; DHC, QS/113A/176/1; Edward Jamilly, 'Patrons, clients, designers and developers: the Jewish contribution to secular building in England', *Jewish Historical Studies* (2002), vol. 38, 91.
731 Edmund Butcher, The *Beauties of Sidmouth Displayed* (Sidmouth, 1820), 46.
732 Peter Wingfield-Digby, 'The Lousadas of Sidmouth', *The Devon Historian* (2020), vol. 20, 35; TNA, T71/1608.
733 *EPG*, 4 April 1829, 26 July 1834 & 25 Dec. 1834.
734 *EPG*, 17 July 1847.
735 Mogridge, *A Descriptive Sketch*, 42.
736 Article VI, 'Notices of some gardens and country seats in Somersetshire, Devonshire and part of Cornwall', *The Gardener's Magazine* (1843), vol. 19, 238-9.
737 Ancestry, Census, 1851 (Sidmouth); Reginald Lane, *Old Sidmouth* (Exeter, 1990), 19.
738 DHC, 1926B/W/FS/19a. 'Mrs Walrond of Montrath House' exhibited at the Devon & Exeter Botanical & Horticultural Society in 1829: *The Gardener's Magazine* (1829) NS5, 639.
739 *EPG*, 19 Jan. 1828; TNA, PROB 11/37/968; DHC, 74B/MT/201; *Bath Chronicle*, 7 Nov. 1833; *WT*, 30 April 1853; G. T. Bettany, *Eminent Doctors* (1885), II, 148.
740 *Grenada Free Press*, 6 Oct. 1830.
741 NDRO, 3053A/DD35398A; J. E. Taylor (ed.), *Hardwicke's Science Gossip* (1888), vol. 24, 52; Myrtle Ternstrom, 'Lundy History: the course of change', *Lundy Studies* (2007), 44; *Limerick Chronicle*, 13 June 1840.
742 Ancestry, Census, 1871 & 1881 (Lundy); *Bristol Mirror*, 2 Dec. 1837; *Dorset County Chronicle*, 19 April 1838; *EPG*, 13 July 1839; *Perry's Bankrupt Gazette*, 16 Jan. 1841; *Bristol Mercury*, 7 March 1883; *South Wales Echo*, 16 July 1888.

743 https://www.landmarktrust.org.uk>History>Lundy; *Royal Gazette*, 23 Feb. 1822; *Jamaica Journal*, 18 Dec. 1824.

744 *Papers relating to the manumission, government and population of slaves in the West Indies, 1822–1824* (1825), 122-8.

745 Myrtle Sylvia Ternstrom, *'Lundy: an analysis and comparative study of factors affecting the development of the island from 1577 to 1969, with a gazetteer of sites and monuments* (Phd thesis, 1999, Cheltenham & Gloucester College of Higher Education), I, 209-17; *South Wales Echo*, 16 July 1888; *Perry's Bankrupt Gazette*, 16 Jan. 1841.

746 Plymouth Archives, 308/50; Bath Record Office, diary of Thomas Moy.

747 *NDJ*, 9 March 1849.

748 *NDJ*, 28 May 1840.

749 *Evening Mail*, 29 Dec. 1813; TNA, PROB 11/1551/83; Anne M. Powers, *A Parcel of Ribbons* (2012), 334-5; *WT*, 20 Jan. 1838.

750 J. R. Chanter, *Memorials, descriptive and historical of the church of St. Peter, Barnstaple* (Barnstaple, 1882), 176-7; *NDJ*, 16 June 1853; *Bath Chronicle*, 10 May 1890; Hall et al, *Legacies*, 56.

751 DHC, 3053A/35398, 5, 21, 28, 44-6.

752 *NDJ*, 2 July 1840.

753 *NDJ*, 18 Jan. 1872.

754 *List of the Members of the United Company of Merchants of England Trading to the East Indies* (1826), 43.

755 *NDJ*, 25 May 1827, 9 Oct. 1828 & 1 Oct. 1829; *Star*, 19 May 1830; *London Courier*, 18 May 1830; *Taunton Courier*, 1 Oct. 1845; *NDJ*, 6 Aug. 1846; Historic England, Listed Building Survey.

756 Institute of Commonwealth Studies Library, GB 101 ICS 101; https://archiveshub.jisc.ac.uk/data/gb101-ics101, accessed 22 July 2021.

757 Paul Q. Karkeek, *Notes made during a visit to Exmoor and neighbourhood* (Torquay, 1879), 8; John Lloyd Warden Page, *An exploration of Exmoor* (1890), 136.

758 North Devon Athenaeum, 806-01-01-67; Ursula Halliday, *Glenthorne* (Tiverton, 1995); Ancestry, Census, 1841 (Countisbury); Thomas Henry Cooper, *A guide containing a short historical sketch of Lynton* (London, 1853), 11.

759 Kenneth Morgan, 'Bristol West India Merchants in the Eighteenth Century', *Transactions of the Royal Historical Society* (1993), III, 185-6; *DNB*, Madge Dresser, 'Daniel, Thomas (1762–1854), merchant' (2016).

760 Lysons, *Devon*, 465; R. G. Thorne, 'John Nicholas Fazakerley', in R. Thorne (ed.), *The History of Parliament: the House of Commons, 1790–1820* (1986).

761 *Hereford Journal*, 20 Nov. 1844; *EPG*, 11 May 1923.

762 John Nicholas Fazakerley; *Globe*, 6 July 1846; *Barbados Agricultural Reporter*, 27 May 1872. The report had originally appeared in the *Tiverton Gazette* on 30 April.

763 John Bateman, *The Acre-oracy of England* (1876), 52.

764 Hilary Joyce Grainger, The Architecture of Sir Ernest George and His Partners, c1860-1922, PhD thesis (Univ. of Leeds, 1985), 126-30.

765 *EPG*, 16 July 1883; *WMN*, 9 Jan. 1885; 'Stoodleigh Court', *The Gardeners' Chronicle*, NS18 (1882), 103; *The Field*, 24 April 1886 & 28 July 1894; *E&E*, 5 Dec. 1895; *WT*, 20 Dec. 1895.

766 *Sun*, 10 Feb. 1821.

767 John Sugden, *Nelson: A dream of glory* (2004), 309.

768 DHC, DEX/7/b/1/1836/409; *WT*, 16 Aug. 1867; TNA, PROB 37/1395.
769 *RGJ*, 29 May 1813 & 28 Aug. 1813. Abell and Glanville were listed as joint owners in 1816: *RGJ*, 10 Feb. 1816. Abell served as a vestryman in 1819: *RGJ*, 13 March 1819; *Bath Chronicle*, 2 March 1820.
770 *Kentish Weekly Post*, 10 March 1826; *RGJ*, 22 April & 20 May 1826, 2 June 1827; *WT*, 9 Feb. 1833; *EFP*, 26 June 1834; *EPG*, 20 Feb. 1841; *WT*, 20 Feb. 1841.
771 *EFP*, 26 June 1834; *NDJ*, 26 Feb. 1835; Ancestry, Census, 1841 (Alphington).
772 TNA, TNA, PROB 11/1948/120 & T71/69.
773 *Kentish Weekly Post*, 10 March 1826.
774 University of California San Diego, Special Collections and Archives, Mss 220, Hall family papers and sugar plantation records; Ancestry, Hall family tree; TNA, T71/214.
775 *Jamaica Journal*, 24 April 1824.
776 *Morning Chronicle*, 23 June 1812;
777 *Bath Chronicle*, 6 March 1823; *NDJ*, 11 May 1827; *Grenada Free Press*, 19 April 1843; *EPG*, 15 Feb. 1861; Ancestry, Grafton Pollard extended tree.
778 TNA, T71/553 & 529; DHC, QS/118/1; Plymouth Archives, 1676/115/6; *WT*, 23 Dec. 1837; *EFP*, 28 Dec. 1837.
779 *Codrington College in the island of Barbados* (1847), 20; *Westminster Gazette*, 1 Aug. 1899.
780 Agnes Rous Howell, *Hinds Howell, a memoir* (1899); *Norfolk News*, 5 Aug. 1899; *Norwich Mercury*, 5 Aug. 1899.
781 Draper, *The Price*, 309.
782 *The London Gazette* (1843), part 2, 2165.
783 Harrison, *Letter-Books*, 195-8.
784 Harrison, *Letter-Books*, 153.
785 Harrison, *Letter-Books*, 66.
786 Harrison, *Letter-Books*, 234, 236.
787 Harrison, *Letter-Books*, 56.
788 Harrison, *Letter-Books*, 76, 166.
789 Harrison, *Letter-Books*, 263.
790 *WT*, 3 Dec. 1853; *EPG*, 24 May 1861.
791 Harrison, *Letter-Books*, 275-6; *Sherborne Mercury*, 15 Sept. 1834; *EPG*, 7 Oct. 1837.
792 Harrison, *Letter-Books*, 153; *St James Chronicle*, 12 Jan. 1847.
793 *EPG*, 5 Nov. 1880.
794 *Bideford & North Devon Weekly Gazette*, 8 Sept. 1908.
795 Harrison, *Letter-Books*, 264, 268, 291-2; Sarah Harrison, *The Journal of William Rhodes James*, 17; *Morning Journal*, 3 Sept. 1839.
796 http://www.jamaicanfamilysearch.com/Members/JamesWRandHJwills.htm#HJJ.
797 *A list of the officers of the army and Royal Marines on full, retired and half pay* (1827), 561.
798 DHC, 74B/ME/70-2; *RGJ*, 25 May 1816, 1 March & 15 Nov. 1817; *Globe*, 29 Jan. 1818; *Jamaica Almanac* (1824), *RGJ*, 9 Sept. 1826, 16 June 1827, 5 & 26 Jan. 1828; *John Bull*, 25 Feb. 1838; *Shipping & Mercantile Gazette*, 5 Nov. 1840.
799 Somerset Heritage Centre, DD/X/PORT/1.
800 National Records of Scotland, GD/46/17/14, transcript provided by Dr David Alston.
801 George Pinckard, *Notes on the West Indies*, II, 216.
802 *Bath Chronicle*, 11 Aug. 1796.
803 Todd Gray, *The Garden History of Devon* (Exeter, 1995), 192.
804 *EFP*, 12 Oct. 1815.

805 *WT*, 31 Jan. 1852; *Slave Population {Slave Registries}* (1833), 5.
806 *Taunton Courier*, 20 Nov. 1822; *WT*, 31 Jan. 1824; *Salisbury and Winchester Journal*, 9 May 1825; *EPG*, 19 April 1828, 19 March 1831, 30 April & 6 Aug. 1836.
807 National Museum of African American History and Culture, Doug Remley, *The History behind seven early-nineteenth century slave buttons, 2009.32.1-5 and 2014.312.98-99.*
808 *WT*, 23 May 1840 & 31 Jan. 1852; Ancestry, Census, 1841 (Woodbury); *EFP*, 15 June 1843.
809 *LES*, 22 July 1845; *Sherborne Mercury*, 18 Jan. 1845; *Morning Post*, 3 Sept. 1845; *EPG*, 29 May 1847; *WT*, 8 July 1848; *WT*, 31 Jan. 1852; *LES*, 6 May 1857; TNA, PROB 11/1204/196 & 2258.
810 *EFP*, 3 Aug. 1820; *EFP*, 10 May 1821; *Morning Chronicle*, 1 June 1821; *EFP*, 19 Sept. 1822 & 23 March 1826.
811 *Morning Chronicle*, 1 June 1821; James M. Holzman, *The Nabobs in England* (New York, 1926), 138-9.
812 *EFP*, 3 Jan. 1822.
813 *Mockett's Journal* (Canterbury, 1836), 265.
814 *The Gardener's Magazine* (1843), 3rd series, vol. 3, 242.
815 *EPG*, 21 March & 25, 29 April 1829, 10 April & 16 Oct. 1830; *WT*, 26 Feb. 1831; *EPG*, 19 March 1831, 25 Feb., 17 March, 4 Aug. 1832.
816 *EPG*, 4 Jan. 1840.
817 *WT*, 7 Jan. 1843.
818 *EFP*, 11 May 1826.
819 *EPG*, 14 Nov. 1857.
820 *EFP*, 12 Aug. 1858.
821 *WT*, 1 Dec. 1855.
822 *WT*, 1 Dec. 1855.
823 *EPG*, 25 Feb. 1832
824 *WT*, 26 Aug. 1837.
825 *EPG*, 15 Jan. 1842.
826 *EFP*, 21 Oct. 1858.
827 University of Nottingham, Special Collections, Pw L 231/1-2.
828 *WT*, 26 Oct. 1839.
829 *EPG*, 5 Dec. 1840; *EPG*, 5 May 1833; Hunt, *Age of Elegance*, 58; *EFP*, 3 Jan. 1833.
830 J. A. Borome, 'John Candler's visit to British Guiana', *Caribbean Studies* (July, 1964), vol. 4, no. 2, 54-5; Kenneth Joyce Robertson, *The Four Pillars* (2010), 88-9; *EPG*, 11 Jan. 1897.
831 *EPG*, 21 Jan. 1830.
832 DHC, 337B/2/W/P/7; *EPG* & *WT*, 3 Jan, 1829.
833 TNA, T71/178.
834 *NDJ*, 6 April 1843; Ancestry, Census, 1841 (Heavitree), 1851 (Keyingham).
835 Canterbury Museum, New Zealand, T113-114; *WT*, 25 Jan. 1867. For genealogical details of the family see Ancestry, Fenwick/Arlaud family tree.
836 *Pigot*, 189.
837 *Bath Chronicle*, 2 March 1826
838 *EPG*, 28 July 1838.
839 *Timehri being the Journal of The Royal Agricultural & Commercial Society of British Guiana* (1886), vol. 5, 261; *WT*, 25 Jan. 1840; Ancestry, Census, 1841 (Tiverton).

840 White, *Directory*, 235 & 317; *EPG*, 22 March 1867; Ancestry, Census, 1851 & 1861 (Exmouth); *EPG*, 22 March 1867.
841 *E&E*, 24 April 1869.
842 Edwards, *History*, II, 6.
843 Thomas Gisborne, *Essays on agriculture* (1854), 60; *Naval and Military Gazette*, 4 Sept. 1841; *The Atlas*, 7 Jan. 1843; TNA, PROB 11/1978; James Davey and Quinton Colville (eds), *A New Naval History* (Manchester, 2019).
844 TNA, 71/354 & 896; Draper, *The Price*, 215.
845 *Ipswich Journal*, 28 Feb. 1795.
846 Thomas Maxwell Adams, *A cool address to the people of England on the slave trade* (1788); *Kentish Gazette*, 27 July 1792; *EFP*, 15 May 1806 & 3 Jan. 1839.
847 James C. Brandow, *Genealogies of Barbados families* (Baltimore, 1983), 84.
848 Brandow, *Genealogies*, 84; Ancestry, Census, 1851 (Cheltenham), 1861 (Hove), 1871 (Exeter); *Exeter Street Directory* (1865, 1866, 1871), 235; *EPG*, 27 Feb. & 17 Aug. 1877.
849 TNA, T71/520.
850 *Kerry Evening Post*, 31 Aug. 1836; *Salisbury and Winchester Journal*, 21 Nov. 1836; *Hampshire Independent*, 18 May 1839; White, *Directory*, 409; Ancestry, Census, 1851 (Kenton); *EPG*, 15 March 1867.
851 *NDJ*, 27 Dec. 1838; *St James Chronicle*, 23 Aug. 1845; TNA, T17/516; *Western Courier*, 21 May 1851; TNA, PROB 11/2133/499; *WMN*, 21 July 1871.
852 TNA, T71/564.
853 *EPG*, 23 Aug. 1828 & 14 Dec. 1839.
854 H. Tapley-Soper (ed.), *Parish of Topsham*, DCRS (1923), 725 & 741; *EFP*, 8 Aug. 1833.
855 Ancestry, Census, 1841 (Middlesex).
856 TNA, T71/564.
857 *WT*, 28 March 1835 & 28 Jan. 1837; TNA, PROB 11/1824/397.
858 TNA, T71/522, 526, 532 & 564.
859 *Sun*, 16 Nov. 1812; *Bristol Times*, 20 April 1814; *Perthshire Courier*, 5 May 1814; *Globe*, 24 June 1856. Ancestry, Census, 1841 & 1851 (Lympstone).
860 *WT*, 27 June 1857.
861 *NDJ*, 13 May 1847; *Sun*, 11 June 1804; Ancestry, Census, 1841 (Porlock), 1851 (South Molton); *EPG*, 24 April 1852; TNA, PROB 11/2182/109; TNA, T71/1593.
862 Christer Petley, 'Plantations and Homes: the material culture of the early nineteenth-century Jamaican elite', *Slavery and Abolition* (2014), Vol. 35, issue 3, 437-57.
863 Ancestry, Census, 1841 (Bristol) & 1851 (Sidmouth); *Pigot* (1844), 136; *EPG*, 1 Aug. 1846; White, *Directory*, 246; Mogridge, *A Descriptive Sketch*, 43; *EFP*, 16 July 1835; *EPG*, 21 Aug.1852.
864 TNA, T71/242.
865 *EFP*, 20 Dec. 1838; *WT*, 4 Oct. 1845; Ancestry, Census, 1841 (St Sidwell); *EPG*, 9 May 1846.
866 *WT*, 15 Aug. 1846.
867 *Evening Mail*, 15 Sept. 1822.
868 M. K. Bacchus, *Utilization, Misuse and Development of Human Resources in the Early West Indian Colonies* (Waterloo, 1990), 166; *The fourteenth annual report of the Ladies' Society for promoting the early education and improvement of the children of Negroes and of People of Colour in the British West Indies* (1839), 84-5.
869 Bruce M. Taylor, 'Our Man in London', *Caribbean Studies* (Oct. 1976- Jan. 1977), vol.

870 *Western Daily Press*, 30 May 1874; Ancestry, Census, 1851 (St David, Exeter); *E&E*, 9 July 1869.
871 Ancestry, Census, 1851 (Barnstaple); *Tyne Mercury*, 16 Aug. 1803; Chris Lloyd, 'Those Who Left the Dales by the Upper Dales', *The Northern Echo*, 16 March 2011; *Cheltenham Journal*, 29 Jan. 1827; BL, St Vincent Deed Book, EAP688/1/1/76, 264; *The London Gazette*, 1833, 2139; *The Times*, 30 Jan. 1869.
872 BL, St Vincent Deed Book 1826-8, EAP688/1/1/76, 264.
873 *Grenada Free Press*, 22 August 1838.
874 *Bedfordshire Times*, 2 Feb. 1869.
875 *Port of Spain Gazette*, 25 Nov. 1836; TNA, T71/64 & Census, 1841 (Hertfordshire), 1851 (Minehead), 1861 & 1871 (Wiltshire), 1881 & 1891 (Seaton).
876 *NDJ*, 30 Sept. 1875; Tony Moore, 'The first Chief Constable of Shropshire, Captain Dawson Mayne', *Journal of the Police History Society* (2017), vol. 31, 33-5; *Kings County Chronicle*, 2 Oct. 1872; Ancestry, Census, 1841 & 1851 (Shrewsbury), 1871 (Leamington).
877 Ancestry, Census, 1851 (Exeter); *Army & Navy Gazette*, 11 April 1868; *LES*, 10 Sept. 1849; *West of England Pocket Book* (1853), no page number; *Directory of Hampshire and Isle of Wight* (1859), 103; Anita Rupprecht, 'When he gets among his countrymen, then tell him that he is free', *Slavery & Abolition* (2012), vol. 33, issue 3.
878 TNA, CO23/74, Folio 304.
879 *John Bull*, 18 Feb. 1838 & 2 June 1839; *EPG*, 13 June 1840; *E&E*, 9 July 1869; *WMN*, 7 July 1869; TNA, T71/549.
880 *Elgin Courant*, 18 April 1845.
881 TNA, T7/526.
882 *NDJ*, 21 May 1853; TNA, T71/557; White, *Directory*, 235; Ancestry, Census, 1851 (Littleham); *Whitstable Times*, 23 Sept. 1893.
883 TNA, T71/130-1.
884 *The Colonist and Van Dieman's Land Commercial and Agricultural Advertiser*, 23 May 1833.
885 *The Tasmanian*, 30 May 1874.
886 *Colonial Times*, 24 Oct. 1843.
887 Ancestry, Census, 1861 & 1871 (Torquay); *Torquay Times*, 5 Feb. 1870.
888 *WT*, 11 Aug. 1838; Ancestry, Census, 1851 (East Teignmouth), 1861 (West Teignmouth), Farr Heney Port Robbtom family tree; *EFP*, 4 May 1864; *Western Daily Mercury*, 4 May 1864; TNA, T71/125, 130 & 48.
889 Ancestry, Census, 1841 (Liverpool), Marr family tree; *The Atlas*, 13 June 1846; *Grenada Free Press*, 7 April 1830; TNA, CO 318/74; *WT*, 15 Oct. 1842.
890 https://www.spanglefish.com>slavesandhighlanders.
891 *WT*, 15 Oct. 1842.
892 Michael Rhodes, *Devon's Torre Abbey* (Cheltenham, 2015), 95-100; Ancestry, Census, 1841 (Southampton); 1851 (Tormohun); *Western Courier*, 10 March 1852.
893 Ancestry, Fiona Russell family tree; *Northampton Mercury*, 11 Oct. 1856.
894 *Westmorland Advertiser*, 6 Aug. 1814; *EFP*, 29 Oct. 1857; Ancestry, Census, 1851 (Littleham); *Liverpool Mercury*, 14 Sept. 1838; *Limerick Chronicle*, 6 Feb. 1839; *Pigot* (1844), 150; TNA, T71/510.
895 TNA, T71/520 & 542; *Bristol Mercury*, 27 July 1839; *St James Chron*icle, 14 Nov. 1844;

Ancestry, Census, 1851 (West Teignmouth); *Bristol Mercury*, 14 Oct. 1854.

896   *EFP*, 10 Sept. 1818; *Morning Post*, 18 June 1867; Ancestry, Census, 1851, 1861, 1881 (Topsham), Janes + Thickett family trees; *LES*, 6 Oct. 1885.

897   *EFP*, 12 Nov. 1835; *Sun,* 3 Nov. 1835; *EFP*, 27 July 1837; *RGJ*, 15 June & 28 Sept. 1816; Ancestry, West family tree; TNA, T71/147 & 145.

898   Ancestry, Census, Exmouth, Totnes & Clyst St Mary (1851).

899   *Sun*, 22 May 1838; *Morning Post*, 23 May 1838.

900   James Fox, *Five Sisters: The Langhornes of Virginia* (New York, 2000), 21-44.

901   Gray, *Not One of Us*, 258.

902   *Tiverton Gazette and East Devon Herald*, 28 May & 4 June 1867.

903   W. Jeffrey Bolster, *Black Jacks* (Harvard, 1997), 120-1; Nathaniel Hawthorn, *Yarn of a Yankee Privateer* (New York, 1926), 239; Nathaniel Hawthorne, 'Papers of an old Dartmoor prisoner', *The United States Magazine and Democratic Review*, vol. 18, 461.

904   Ancestry notes three sixteenth-century examples of Devon as a first name in London, Oxford and Lancashire and another dozen seventeenth-century instances across the country but these are errors in transcription or of the technology. There are also misunderstood naming of individuals in the census of 1841. These have normally been caused by misreading the written source in substituting Devon for Dixon or Dickson.

905   *WMN*, 23 June 1884.

906   Jackson, 'Elizabethan Seamen', 16.

907   Fox, *Five Sisters*, 21-4, 43-6.

908   *The Sessional Papers printed by order of the House of Lords* (1845), vol. 10, nos 191 & 1944, 253, 255-6.

909   *Barbados Mercury*, 11 June 1814; *St James Chronicle*, 5 April 1827; *Morning Post*, 31 May 1830; *Sussex Advertiser*, 11 Oct. 1830 & 30 Dec. 1839; *Accounts & papers* (1820), vol. 10, no. 194; *Sussex Advertiser*, 10 Oct. 1848; *Dorset County Chronicle*, 5 Feb. 1829; *GM* (1832), 102, pt 1, vol. 151; *EPG*, 17 June 1837; *EFP*, 24 April 1856 & 3 Dec. 1862.

910   https://www.antislavery.org.

Index

Illustrations are noted in **bold**

Abell, Catherine 207; Eliza 121, 140, 207; Margaretta 207; William 207, 279 n.769
abolition xii, 5, 8, 36, **48**, 51-2, 60-62, 100, 148, 153, 171, 196-7, 204, 232; medals **61**, **241**; motto 60
Acland, Thomas Dyke 196-7
Adams, Ann St John 225; Margaret 179; Thomas Maxwell 225, 280 n.846
Adderley, Mrs 72
Addison, Catherine 104; Eliza Jane 159; Joseph 159
Africa xi, xii, xiii, 2, 5, 8, 12, 14, 17, 19, 21, 24, 26, 27, 28, 29, 30, 35, 36, 43, 44-9, 52, 56, 58, 59, 60, 62, 64-6, 70, 72, 73, 76, 79, 80-2, 84, 85, 87, 88, 91, 92, 94, 95, 125, 127, 129, 133, 136, 137, 144, 171, 175, 178, 180-1, 184, 187, 196, 197, 208, 222, 238, 243; Algeria 24; Angola 65; Benguela 136; Benin 65; Congo 65, 223; East 94; Gabon 65; Ghana 65; Guinea 14, 65; Libya 24; Madagascar 94; Morocco 24; Mozambique 94, 133; Nigeria 65; North xii, 2, 5, 8, 24; Senegal 12, 65; South 6, 45, 94, 96, 135, 205; Tunisia 24; West 6, 9, 24, 27, 65, 91
Alleyne, Elizabeth Mary 226; family 159; James Holder 226
Allwood, Elizabeth 162
Alphington 30, 121, 139, 160, 207, 268 n.510; ponies 30
Anderson, Clementia Grant 214; John 112, 162, 226
Anguilla 96, 132, 136, 268 n.507
Angwin, Robert Hilton 51, 115
animals and insects, bears 148; birds 6, 43, 148, 218; caterpillars 26; cats 148; dogs 137, 148; horses 50, 94, 122, 148, 178, 184; rabbits 30; rats 30; shark 122; snakes 148
Anson, Thomas 196
Antigua 52-3, 64, 66, 68, **69**, 70, 71, 75, 88; 132, 139, 168, 174, 179, 200, 222; Body Ponds 70, 186; Five Islands 166; Lady Cooke 166; Lower Walrond 200; Old Road 193; Otto 165; Upper Walrond 200
Arlington 132; Court 191, 196
Ashburton 129, 244
Ashbury 130
Ashprington 26, 173
Asia 6, 17, 26, 62; Ceylon 94, 189; China xi, 62, 65, 76, 85, 91, 92, 185; Hong Kong xi, 6; India 26, 62, 76, 81, 85, 88, 91, 92, 94, 95, 98-9, 125, 131, 140, 189, 190-1, 203, 217; South xii, 65, 73, 80, 85, 88, 91; South East 62; Sri Lanka 62, 94
Astor, Nancy 197, 240, 244

283

Attlay, Stephen Oakeley 53, 114, 140; Stephen Oakeley Junior 59
attorneys 9-10, 32, 51, 81, 137, 149, 154, 161, 162, 174, 179, 187, 189, 238, 246, 272 n.629
Austen, Jane 53
Australia 6, 35, 94, 135, 163, 174, 182, 189, 211, 212
Axminster 170; carpets 98

Backey, John 227
Bahamas xiv, 47, 56, 64, 66, 68, 71-3, 92, 100, 132, 139, 144-56, 232, 242; Cat Island 72, 150, 154; Great Exuma 72, 144, **145**, 146, 149-56, 246, 270 n.556; Nassau 149-50, 152, 246; Pompey 150, **151**, 152-4
Baijer, Baijer Otto 70, 165; family 165-6; John Otto 165
Bailey, John 227; Mr 56
Baker, Florence 137; John Pool 51; John Pool Wilkinson 51; Mrs 56; Samuel White 137
Balfour, Blayney 246-7
Bancroft, Edward 76
Barbados 11, 19, 42, 56, 64, 65, 66, 67, 68, 73, **74**, 75, 81, 132, 135, 139, 140, 141, 159, 160, 161, 163, 166, 179, 186, 192, 193, 198, 204, 208, 209, 214, 225, 226, 227, 229, 232-3, 238; Adams Castle 225; Arthur Seat 238; Chamber of Commerce 225; Chance Hall 226; Chimborazo 159; Codrington College 209; Crab Hill 227; Durants 232; Edgcumbe 67; Greggs 226; Harrow 227; Haynesfield 229; Oxford 226; Pickerings 227; Saltram 67; The Hope 226; Thorpe Cottage 159; Thurban 159; Villa Nova 229; Vineyard 163
Barham, John Foster 39
Barnes, Ann 120; Hannah 35, 103, 140, 163, 186-7; Joseph 186-7
Barnstaple 24, 26, 30, 55-6, 62, 65, 66-7, 98, 115-117, 119, 122, 137, 142, 146, 158, 171, 174, 189-90, 203, 212, 229, 231, 239, 254, n.50, 258 n.181; Holy Trinity Church, 203; Newport Terrace 171, 189
Barrett, Edward Barrett Moulton 100
Barrow, John 227
Barthurst, Thomas 133
Barton, Henry Charles Benyon 42; Mary Ann 42; Robert 92, 136
Bass, Frankey 85
Baston, Henry 100
Bath 9, 168, 186, 187, 219, 224, 225, 233
Beaufort House 9
Batt, Elizabeth Caroline 70
Beacher, John 187
Bealey, family 51
Beare, George 70, 174-5; James 174-5
Beckford, Mr 56
Bedford 66, 231
Bennett, Margaret Taylor 35-6
Bent, Anne 167; John 127, 161, 244; Mary 167
Berbice 75, 127
Berkshire 173, 175, 178, 185, 222, 233; Hungerford 173; Reading 22; Windsor 66
Berry Pomeroy 127, 167, 244; Weston House 127, 167, 244
Berry, John 2
Bickell, Richard 68
Bickford, James 63
Bickleigh 193-4
Bicton 139, 142, 146, 153, 174, 197, 242
Bideford xiii, 12, 26, 34, 35, 40, 65, 67, 84, 97, 115, 116, 117, **118**, 119, 122, 135, 137, 143, 148, 165, 189, 212, 262 n.303; 266 n.442; Bridge Street 35; Glenburie 212; Grammar School 35; Hallsannery 212; North Down Hall 212; Springfield Terrace 165
Bideford, Mary 67
Binney, Anna 125, 173; John 173
biscuits 12
Bishop, Sarah 81

Bishop's Tawton 162, 165, 171; Newport Row 162
Bishopsteignton xiv, 27
Bittadon 130
Black, James 26-7
Blake, Caroline 193-6; Catherine 234; Patrick 30
Bocas, Abraham 29
Bond, John Nelson 115, 161, 187
books 189, 210; *And Then There Were None* 26; *Froudacity* 8; *Life in the Trenches before Sebastopol* 220; *Mansfield Park* 53; *My Devonshire Book* 6; *Seaton Beach* 182; *Slave Life in Georgia* 62; *The Book of Beauty* 218; *The English in the West Indies* 8; *The Grand Gazetteer* 117, 120; *The King's Beard* 14; *The narrative of a five years expedition against the revolted Negroes of Surinam* 30; *The Power of Woman* 143; *The Universal Gazetteer* 109; *The vision and other poems in blank verse* 73; *Westward Ho*! xiii, 12
Bovell, William 75, 92, 157, 226
Boy, Tom 233
Boyd, John 73
Bradninch 137, 139, 174, 238, 268 n.510; Byrleigh House 208
Brampford Speke 174, 181-2; Lower Cleeve 181
Braunton 56; Buckland 56
Brave, Judith 234
Brazil 73, 136, 184
Bremner, William 53-5
Bretton, Thomas 133
Brice, Andrew 120
Bridestowe 209-10
Brisco, Wastel 197
Bristol xii, 1, 32, 53, 59, 66, 85, 117, 119, 122, 124, 140, 142, 162, 166, 170, 171, 173, 178, 186, 187, 193, 200, 202, 204, 210, 228, 238, 242; Berkeley Square 204
British Guiana **41**, 64, 66, 67, 75-9, 127, 132, 139, 161, 179, 185, 218, 220, 222, 223, 232, 244; Amersfoort 223; Exmouth 67; Mary's Hope 127; Nieuw Oosterbeck 223
Broadclyst 239
Broadhembury 70, 173, 200
Broadwoodkelly 66
Brodbelt, Anna Maria 34; Anne Gardner 34; Charlotte Jersey 32; Francis Rigby 34; Eliza Lee 34; James 32; James Lee 32-4, 140, 161, 163, 212; Thomas 32, 34
Brook, Charles 193
Broomfield, Alexander Scott 92, 115, 186
Brown(e), Henry 132; John 62; Joseph 212
Browning, Elizabeth Barrett 97, 99-100, 111
Brunton, James 98-99; Mary 264 n.366
Bryan, Elizabeth 107, 171
Buckerell 50
Buckfastleigh 98
Buckinghamshire 91
Buckland Filleigh 159-60
Buckland Tout Saints 130
Buckley, Louisa 177
Budleigh Salterton 75, 98, 100, 133, 135, 139, 163, 171, 181, 188, 209, 225, 227, 268; Fore Street 188; Kersbrook 135; Umbrella Cottage 188
Bunbury, Benjamin 175; Edward 175; Hugh Mill 161, 173, 174, 175-7
Burdon, John Dennis 158
Burke, Dorothy 141, 168
Burlescombe 81
Burn, William Gardner 140, 208
Burton, Elizabeth 42; William Godfrey Pollard 42
Bush, John 127
Butterleigh 40
Byam, George 70; Henrietta 70

Cadbury 75
Cadeleigh 59

Cadogan, Sarah Oxley 75, 226-7, 232; Ward 98, 226-7
Cambridge 35, 36, 40, 159, 175, 196
Cambridge, John 227
Camden, William 124
Campbell, Duncan 96, 188; John 140, 163, 188, 227; M. 10; Mary 188
Canada 92, 140, 211, 238; Newfoundland 6, 44-5, 112, 114, 117, 119; Nova Scotia 184
Carmichael, Alison 23, 89
Cary, George Stanley 87, 127, 140, 197, 239; Robert Shedden Sulyarde 236
Cash, Johnny 36
Caymans 96, 132, 268 n.507 & n.508
Chambers, Ann 179
Champneys, Thomas 56
Channel Islands, Guernsey 119; Jersey 32, 119, 189
Chaser, Thomas 133
Cheldon 130
Cheshire, Warrington 117
Christie, Agatha 26
Christopher, Richard 187
Chudleigh 34, 260 n.237; Lawell House 70; Ugbrooke 196
Chulmleigh 79
Churston Ferrers 66, 260 n.234
Circassians 24
Clannaborough 130
Clark, Mary Bucknor 112, 165
Clarke, Alexander Campbell 227; Caroline Haughton 193; Charles 227; Clarissa 227; David 231; Edward James 227; Eliza Claudia 227; Frances 227; Hannah 127; John 202, 227; John Tharp 100, 140, 227-8; Louisa 227; Mr & Mrs 247; Philippa 227-8; Thursa 227; Myra 227
Clarkson, Thomas 60
Clements, James 135
Cleveland, John 119
Clinton, Elizabeth Ann 159

cloth 97; dyes 44, 70, 89; industry 1, 51, 70, 97-8, 120-1, 122, 124-5, 127, 216
Clyst St George 160; Knowle 160
Clyst St Mary 139, 217-223, 268 n.510; Winslade 217-223
Cobham, Susannah Cobham 11
Cock, Scipio 66
Cocks, Philippa 227
Codrington, Edward 171, **172**, 173, 200
Coke, Edward Francis 40
Colbiornsen, Maria Roselle 190
Colcroft, Mary Gerald 229-31
Cole, George 103, 112, 161, 174, 177
Colleton family xiv, 45-51, 98, 238; John 45, 73, 75; Louisa Carolina 47-51, 170; Peter 73
Collins, Richard 121, 140, 163, 272 n.636
Columbus, Christopher 26, 44, 82, 87, 88
Colyton 24, 42, 85, 170, 182 184, 262 n.315; Fore Street 42
Commissioning, Cinderella 112
Common Sense xi
Compton Castle 196
Connett, Edward 32, 112, 174
Copper, Scipio 66
Cornish, Emily 31
Cornwall 66, 160, 171, 173, 242, 250; Falmouth 66, 173, 268; language 21; Mount Edgcumbe 55, 120, 196; Penzance 66, 171; Redruth 62
Cosens, Grace 51
Countisbury 109, 202-4, 268 n.510; Glenthorne 109, 203-4
Courtenay family 6, 45, 211
Cowan, Thomas 100
Cox, George John 89, 228; Harry Alexander 228
Craftus, Richard 129
Cranstoun, Anne 232
Creacombe 130
Crediton 27, 133
Crosby, Mercury 236

Crosse, Eliza 56
Cuba 150
Cullompton 66, 98, 123, 200
Cunningham, James 112, 141, 159, 163, 228-9
Cure, Mary 38
Cuthbertson, Mr 219
Cutting, Joseph 133

D'Urban, Mary xix, 80, 104, 126, 140, 160, 174, 179; William James 179
dahlia xiii
Dallas, Charlotte 236
Dalrymple, Tom 236
Dalzell, Mary 170, 186, 274 n.681
Daniel, John 204; Thomas I 204; Thomas II 161, 163, 173, 204; Thomas III 204; Thomas Carew 205
Dartmoor Prison 129, 243; Thespian Company 243
Dartmouth 26, 32, 65, 127
Davis, Mary Ann 239
Davy, Caroline 66; Edward 66, 179; Elizabeth 66; Hannah 66; Helen 66; Isabella 66; James 66, 126, 179; James Lewis 66, 207; John 179; Joseph 66; Louisa 66; Rebecca 179; Richard 66; Rosa 66; Ruth 66; Thomas 84, 123, 140, 174, 179-81; William 66
Dawlish 10, 35-6, 59-60, 98, 101, **102**, 103, 112, 131, 139, 159-60, 163, 174, 177, 186-7, 192, 210-212, 236, 264 n.366 & n.368; Barton Cottage 187, 238; Laurel Cottage 177; Marine Parade 236; Park House 211; Plantation Terrace xiv; Public Rooms and Library **16**; Weech Street 177
Day, John 227
de Benguela, Antonio 136-7; Fernando 137
Delve, John 239
Demerara 11, 31-2, 39, 40, 51, 65, 75-6, 77, 79, 98, 135, 140, 150, 161, 173, 175, 177, 179, 190, 214, 216, 217, 222, 223-4, 234, 236; Adventure 216; Devonshire 161, 175; Devonshire Castle 161, 175; Endraught 166; Enmore 216, 222; Friendship 77; Good Faith 216; Good Hope 135; Hope 216; John 77; Mon Repos 166; Ondereeming 190; Paradise 77, 216; Pomeroon 77; St Christopher 135
Dennis(s), Philip 187; Sarah 187
Dent, Digby 158; Frances 85, 158
Devon, Charles 188
Devon, Black population 24-7, 129-37; coastal resorts 99-115; history 1-9, 97-128; immigration 130-4; names for estates 67; urban areas 115-28
Devonport 55, 66, 98, 120-1, 123, **134**, 166, 185; hustings 60, 171; Ker Street 185; Navy Row 158; Officer's Row 158; Upper Somerset Place 166; Victualling Yard 185
Devonshire, Maryann 127
disease 8, 71, 73, 109; cholera 32
Divine, George 146
Dixon, Manley 104, 120, 140, 184
Doddiscombsleigh 158
Dolmage, Adam 9; Sarah 9
Dominica 53, 64, 68, 79-80, 132, 139, 196; Aberdeen 53; New Hampshire 196
Dorset 160, 170, 231, 242; Dorchester 66; Weymouth 66
Douglass, Charles 231
Downer, William 202
Doyle, John Hyde 70, 140, 186
Drake, Elizabeth Charity 170; Francis xix, 2, 44; William 170
Drane, Augusta 188-9; Thomas 95, 115, 141, 188-9
Ducarel, Jane 26; Mary 26
Dunbar, Charles 136
Duncan, Queen 236
Dunning, Edward Harris 205
Duntze, John 52, 216
Durnford, Andrew 30; Barbara 30; sisters 30
Dyer, Mr 246

Ealsworthy, Miss 79
Easdon, William 136
East Allington 24
East Budleigh 100, 170, 181, 227; South Promenade 100; Tidwell House 181; Woodbeer Villa 100
East Down 11, 42, 174
East India Company 9, 62, 97, 98, 190, 264 n.365
Eaton, Richard 10
Edward, John 233
Egg Buckland 160
Elliot(t), Mr 214; Nathaniel 59
Ellis, Jane 185; John 55
emancipation 62, **90**, **138**, 242, 246-7; Act 9, 40, 59, 62-3; Day **xv**, 63, 70-1, 75, 92, 100, 103, 104, 107, 109, 11, 114, 116, 119, 120, 121, 122, 123, 124, 125, 126, 127, 139, 192-3, 210, 229; mockery 127-8
English Heritage 197
enslaved people 65; branding 35, 158; language 50; metal-making skills 57-9; names 30, 65-7, 178, 193, 196, 227, 232, 238; North African xiii, xiii, 5, 8; punishment **37**, **48**, 87, 89, 146, 150, 152, **183**, 192; shops 88; terminology 19-30, 49, 52; unions 27-35
enslavement 64; colonies 64-96; history 1-2, **3**, **4**, 5-6, 8-9, 12, 14, 21, 25-6, 43-60; modern 244; morality 60, 62, 153; perspective 12-14, 234, 236; supporters 62
Erskine, James St Clair 200
Escott, John 227
Essequibo 75, 77, 175, 179
Essex 197, 232; Woodford 184, 250
ethnicity **245**; Black 24-7; blackface 135, 243; Caucasian 23-4; Chinese 29, 65, 76, 81, 82, 85, 91, 92; Creole **18**, 19, **20**, 21, 23, 29, 35, 65, 68, 82, 84, 94, 125, 127, 146, 152, 163, 175, 178-9, 180, 187, 238, 239; Indians 65, 76, 80, 81, 82, 85, 88, 91-2, 95, 98-9, 125, 131, 244; Indigenous Americans 44, 64-5, 70, 71, 73, 76, 77, 79, 80, 82, 85, 87, 88, 91, 143, 196; Jews 28, 63, 82; mixed 19, **20**, 21, **22**, 23-32, **33**, 34-5, 64, 65, **74**, 79, 82, 84, 85, 88, 95, 100, 196, 202, 212, 242, 244; terminology 19-30; whiteface 243
Europe, Belgium 111; Denmark 44, 64, 190; France 42, 44, 50, 57, 75, 76, 79, 80, 82, 84, 85, 87, 88, 89, 91, 92, 94-5, 107, 115, 120, 142, 189, 214, 223, 238; Germany x, 39, 76, 82, 84, 85, 91, 143; Holland 44, 64, 75, 76, 165, 194, 214, 223-4, 232; Italy 50, 79, 104, 111; Portugal 44, 64, 76, 80, 81, 82, 88, 91, 92, 136; Spain 14, 24, 26, 29, 44, 50, 64, 68, 71, 79, 82, 91, 116, 144, 194, 236; Sweden 44, 64; Switzerland 76, 88, 159, 202
Exeter xii, xiv, 1, 10, 11, 14, 21-3, 24, 27, 29, 38, 39, 42, 43, 45, 50, 51-2, 59, 60, 62, 63, 67, 73, 75, 79, 81, 85, 89, 91, 97-8, 100, 103, 112, 115, 117, 120-1, 125-6, 127, 129, 135-7, 139, 149, 153, 158, 159, 160, 161, 163, 165-6, 168, 173, 174, 175-7, 178, 179, 186, 187, 189, 191, 197-8, 207, 208, 216, 217-22, 224, 225, 226-7, 229, 231, 232-3, 238, 240, 243; ball **xx**; Baring Crescent 232; Bedford Chapel 218; Bellair 197; Blackamoor's Head 135; Bradninch House 165; Bystock Terrace 121, 232; Cathedral 38, 208; Colleton Crescent 50, 121, 208; Colyford Villa 229, 232; Devon & Exeter Female Penitentiary 218; Devon & Exeter Hospital 218; Dix's Field 79, 136; Duryard Lodge 225; Eaton Place 100; Franklyn House 165; Guildhall 29, 197; Higher Summerlands 121, 229; Hill's Court 11; Hoopern House 52; Jeffery's Row 39; Longbrook Street 229; Lunatic Asylum 170, 216; Mont Le Grand 11; Mount Radford 238; Northbrook

Lodge 121, 126, 227; Radnor Place 238; Rougemont Castle 137, 165; Royal Albert Memorial Museum 224; St David 136; St Edmund 226; St Mary Arches 11; St Mary Major 24, 136; St Sidwell 31, 39, 59, 100, 136, 166; St Thomas 96, 165-6, 187, 218; Seldon Cottage 238; Southernhay 42, 121, 136, 163, 226; statue of St Peter 23; Victoria Terrace 178; West of England Infirmary 216; West Quarter 29; Whipton 137; workhouse 12
Exminster 52
Exmouth 26, 38, 45, **96**, 133, 179, 184, 186, 205, 207, 208, 217, 223-4, 227-8, 233, 236, 239; Beacon Hill 104, 159, 179, 205, 217, 224; Claremont Terrace, 167, 224, 233; Louisa Place 205; Manor House 26, 227; Moorlands 179; Prospect Place 236

Faith, Amy 236
faiths, African 49; Anglican 1, 2, 5, 10-11, 40-42, 59, 70, 72, 101, 104, 109, 119, 136, 158, 159, 160, 161, 163, 166, 179, 202-204, 209, 242-3; Baptists 171; Islam 5, 24, 29, 44; Judaism 19, 28, 63, 73, 84, 198; Methodism 60, 63, 100; Moravians 229; Palatines 143; Roman Catholicism 28, 63, 160, 204; Society of Friends 60; Unitarianism 28, 60; Voodou 14, 36
Farington, Joseph 190
Farquharson, Elizabeth 11; William Tatham 12
Farwell, Christopher 244; George 167
Fazakerley, John Nicholas 204
Ferguson, Charlotte 178
Filleigh, Castle Hill 196
Fisher, John 140, 158, 181; John Campbell 42, 141, 158, 181
Flannigan, Frances Langham 70
Fleming, Gilbert Fane 197
Floyd, Elizabeth Powys 109, 111; George xi; Henry 111; Mary 111

Follet(t), Frances 9; Joan 21
Foot, Jesse 107
Ford, Elizabeth 238
Fortescue, John Dicker Inglett 84, 103, 159-60; Rebecca 159
Fox, Harold ix
Frances, Molly 208
Fraser, C. H. 185; Jane Agnes Wilhelmina 185; John Nugent 166
Fremington 55; Bickington 55
French, Leonard 26
Froude, J. A. 6, **7**, 8
Fulford, family 47; John 47
Furse, Ann 32

Gale, Thomas 26
Gander, Sarah 135
gardens 39, 45, 55, 146-7, 153, 165, 168, 189, 196, 202, 208, 224, 238
Garner, Nicholas Russell 100, 140, 163
Gates, Thomas 2
Ghosh, Nanda Lal 125
Gibbes (Gibbs), George 60; Samuel 81
Gilbert, Adrian 26; Humphrey xix, 44
Gillis, Suckay 85
Glanville, Francis 160; Samuel 207
Gloucestershire 141, 200, 204; Cheltenham 226; Gloucester 66; Henbury 204
Goldsworthy, Sam 202
Goodridge, Mary Ann 209-10
Gorges, Ferdinando 26
Goss, Dr 211; Mr 211
Graham, Barbary 178; Catherine 178; Dahlia 12; Harriet 178; Joseph 158
Grant, Alexander Cray 36-8, 174, 177-8; Governor 150; John Thomas 40
Graves, Louisa Carolina Graves 45-51, 170; Richard 47, 50; Samuel 50; Sophia Louisa 45, 51
Gray, Mr 191
Great American Slave Troupe 243
Great Fulford 47

Great Torrington 34-5, 119, 121-3, 137, 148, 163, 256 n.115; Beam 34, 122, 142
Greenwich 66
Greig, Samuel Alexander 10
Grenada 9, 32, 42, 64, 66, 68, 80-2, 88, 91, 105, 112, 132, 139, 160, 167, 171, 174, 175, 179, 191, 196, 216, 222, 238; Belmont Estate 9; Chemin 179; Hope Vale 179; New Hampshire 196; Samaritan 191
Grenville, Richard 14
Griffith, Catherine Campbell 117, 119-20, 189-90; Frances 189; John William Spencer 189; Mary 189
Guscott, Francis 165
Gutteres, Moses 111

Hackett, James 190
Haley, John Daniel 79; Josephine 79
Halfyard, Ann 136-7; Richard 136-7
Hall, Jasper Taylor Hall 160; Thomas 104, 159, 207-8
Halliday, Walter Stevenson 42, 109, 140, 203-4
Hamilton, Alexander Hamilton 80, 126, 140, 190-2, 216; Franky 178; Sarah 178
Hampshire 38, 140, 177, 184, 185, 232; Southampton 160, 226, 255 n.75
Harberton 98, 239
Harding, William 202
Hare, Isabella 178; Jennet 178
Harpford 158
Harris, Andrew Hector 45; Mr 133
Hartland 26, 196
Hatherleigh 24
Haverfield, Mary 34-5, 119, 122; Robert Tunstall 34, 256 n.115
Hawkins, Henry Adolphus 84, 119, 141, 159, 174, 178; John 2, **3**, 6, 21, 44, 244; William 26
Hay, Harriet 42

Haynes, Edmund 75, 229, 232; Lucretia 11, 229, 232
Heanton Satchville 197
Heaven, Alick 202; William Hudson 141, 200-2, 238
Heavitree 31, 67, 121, 133, 139, 222-3; 234, 238, 268 n.510; South Wonford House 223; Stafford Terrace 222
Hembury Fort 50
Hemmington, Ulric Theodore 91
Hereford 34
Heron, Samuel 196
Herring, Mr; Mrs 99
Hertfordshire 67, 231
Hewitt, Eliza 208; Elizabeth Mary 231-2; Mary Kelitt 208; Raby Williams 208; William Kellett 208
Hicks, William Surmanid 133
Hiern, Charles 122-3
Highatt, Henry Stogdon 174, 181-2
Highweek 127
Hiles, Samuel 125
Hill, Rowland 231
Hinds, Ellen Lytcott 208
Hodder, Ceasar 67
Holder, John Hooper 115
Holman, James 95
Holmes, William Henry 79, 120
Honduras 66, 96, 132, 268 n.507
Honeychurch 130
Honeychurch, Edwin 202
Horn, Ben 233; James 173
Hoskins, W. G. ix
Houstoun, Robert 9, 10, 80, 115, 157
Howell, Hinds 42, 75, 141, 161, 209-10
Huggins, Edward Rodon 140, 185; Emily 185
Hughes, Edward 202
Hunt, Jane 239
Huxtable; Anthony 117; Thomas 117
Hyndman, Catherine 76

Index

Ideford 163, 165, 212
Ilfracombe xiv, 31, 60, 62,105, **106**, 107, 131, 139, 170, 171, 186, 212, 224, 268 n.510; Coronation Terrace 31
Inglett, Richard 159
Instow 26, 40; Tapley 119
Ipplepen 207
Ireland, 6, 45, 51, 70, 73, 88, 107, 115, 117, 119, 121, 129, 130-1, 166, 167, 175, 228, 231, 268 n.517; Dublin 66, 188, 194; Munster 45
Isle of Wight 226
Ives, Maria 171

Jackson, Elizabeth 135; Sarah 29; William 165
Jamaica 28, 32, 34-6, 40, 42, 51-3, 55-8, 64-8, 70, 82, **83**, 84-5, 99, 100, 105, 115, 117, 119, 123, 125, 129, 132, 139-41, 150, 162, **165**, 167-8, 170-3, 177-9, 181-2, 184-9, 192, 193, 198, 200, 203, 205, 207-12, 214, 223, 226-31, 234, 236, 238; Agent General 51-2; Albion 177; Archibald 181; Assembly 28, 56, 162, 258 n.188; Barnstaple 67; Bean 200; Bellfield 228; Berkshire Hall 163, 165; Berwick 177; Biddeford 171, 228; Bideford 67; Castle Wemyss 203; Cedar Valley 100; Chatsworth 166; Cold Spring 43; Content Hall 208; Devon 67; Essex Valley 205; Exeter 51, 67; Exmouth 67; Flower Hill 226; foundry 55-9; Galloway 231; Golden Grove 200; Green River 167; Hall's Delight 171; Hall's Prospect 184; Haughton Hall 192; Heavitree 67; Hopewell 228; Kingston 10, 11, 35, 163, 173, 186, 192; Knowsley Park 180; Lower Warminster 205; Lowlayton 193; Luana 181; Montego Bay 14; Morant Bay 55; Morgan's Valley 160; Mount Edgcumbe 67; Mount Moses 163, 173; Newry 55; Old England 11; Orange Grove 181; Palmyra 192; Pear Tree Grove 178; Ramble Pen 200, 202, 228; Retrieve 228; Rio Magno 177; Rose Hall **13**, 14, 192; Rothiemurchas 214; St Andrews 10; St Catherine 185; Saltram 67; Saltspring 188; Silver Grove 200; Silver Hill; Sportsman's Hall 171; Spring Vale 177; Stewart Castle **235**, 236; Stoney Gut 170; Topsham 67; Torrington Castle 67; Trelawny 171; Union 181; Upper Warminster 205; Wear 67; Williamsfield **206**, 207-8; Windsor **237**, 238; Worthy Park 40
James, Herbert Jarrret 10, 192, 210-212; Hugh 11; Jane Caroline 35, 103; John 227; Mary Partridge 193; Philip Haughton 192-3; Richard Boucher 212; Sam 202
Jameson, Richard 158
Jeremiah, John 58-9
Johnson, Edgar 267 n.487; Elizabeth Williams 11; Eliza Gardener 34; John 227; Mary Theresa 163; Thomas Lewis 12
Johnstone, William 62
Jones, Elizabeth Sophia 179; William 231
Jopp, Eliza 123; John 123
Jordan, Robert 53
Julian, G. H. 198

Kean, John 97
Kearton, Mary Gerald 229-31
Kekewich, Samuel Trehawke 160
Kent 66, 173; Folkestone 187; Hastings 187; Tunbridge 173
Kentisbeare 27
Kentisbury 11
Kenton 51-2, 158, 186, 228; Staplake Mount 52
Keppel, Frederick 40
King, Sarah 9; William Brooks 9, 114, 157, 159

291

Kingsbridge 36; Boweringsleigh 177
Kingsley, Charles xiii
Kingsnympton 32
Kingsteignton 67
Kragelius, Agnes Theresa 79; Arabella Caroline Constantia 79; Caroline 79; Dick Horatio 79
Kuhn, Jan Hendrick 224

Lamb, Alexander 91
Landmark Trust 197, 202
Lane, William 129
Latter, Exeter 66
Lawrence, Thomas George 132
Lee, James 32, 34
Lees, A. J. 154, 247-8
Lewis, John 191-2; Matthew 36
Lincoln, Abraham 157
Lindsey, Leonora Hankinson 168
Liverpool xii, 1, 51, 117, 127, 166-7, 226, 234, 236
London x, 1, 10, 19, 26, 31, 32, 34, 38, 39, 40, 44, 51, 55, 57, 59, 73, 97, 99, 101, 199, 124, 125, 127, 140-1, 143-4, 161, 163, 165, 168-71, 174, 175, 177-8, 185-9, 192-3, 197, 198, 200, 202, 204, 205, 207, 212, 214, 217, 223, 225, 227, 229, 231, 232, 236, 242, 247; Adelphi 55, 188; Bloomsbury 194; Cavendish Square 34; Cheapside 101; Kensington 165; Paddington 159; Portman Square 207; Regent's Park 175; Wandsworth 175; Whitechapel 101; Whitehall Gardens 177
Lopes, Manesseh Masseh 59
Lord, Benjamin 146
Loscombe, Clifton Wintringham 104, 166; Maria Frances 166
Loudon, John Claudius 198, 217
Lousada, Emanuel 198; Emanuel Baruh 109, 198
Lowman, Martha 171
Lundy 182, 197, **199**, 200-202, 238; Millcombe House 197, 200-202
Luxton, Scipio 66
Lympstone 92, 133, 158, 216, 217, 227
Lynmouth 107, **108**, 109, 139
Lynton 107-9, 160, 167, **201**, 202-3, 204; Clooneavin 204; Combe Park 109, 202-3; Watersmeet 202-4
Lyon, Edmund Pusey 51-2; family 51-2

McCaul, James 31; William 31, 107
McClean, George 105; Lauchlan 126; Thomas Scott 133
McClery, Ann Clarke 112, 231; Judith 231
McIntosh, Sarah Oxley 226-7
Mackenzie (McKenzie), Eliza 194; Francis 214, Henry 202
McMillan, Donald 32, 80
Madden, Richard Robert 64, 68
Mais, Amelia 170-1
Malta 80, 81
Mamhead 55; Newhouse 59
Mansong, Jack 55
Marchant, Elizabeth 45
Mariansleigh 66
Marshall, Anna 125, 126; Edward 163; Elizabeth 100, 125
Marsham, Charles 88
Martell, John 120, 141, 185
Martin, John 85; Richard Montgomery 73, 77, 82, 84; Thomas 85
Mauritius 64, 68, 94-6, 129, 131, 132, 139, 141, 189, 242
Mayne, Dawson 231; Elizabeth Mary 112, 231
medicine 32, 34, 49, 209, 210-211, 233; apothecary 53
Mellis, George 62
Membland 168
Merton 158
Middle East 70; Lebanon 85, 92; Syria 91
Middlesex 67, 167, 178, 188, 194
Mill, Mary 175

Miller, J. 116
Mills, John 184
Mitchell, Mary Elizabeth Stewart 179; Samuel 179
Modbury 63
Modyford, Thomas 75
Monck, George 73
Montserrat 30, 96; Plymouth 67
Moody, Martha 232; Thomas 232
Moore, Thomas 5
Morchard Bishop 11, 133, 174
Mowatt, Mary Bucknor 165
Munro, George 125
Murphy, Patrick 208

Napier, Ann 166
National Trust xi
Nelson, Frances 205; Horatio 205
Nembhard, Elizabeth 42; Henry 40-2, 119
Nevis 64, 66, 68, 85, 86, 132, 139, 205, 262 n.314
New Zealand 189
Newton Abbot 190; Courtenay Terrace 190; Sandford Orleigh 137
Neyle, Margaretta Parsons 207
Nibbs family 52-3; James Langford 52-3
Nicholas, Elizabeth 55
Nicoll, Hannah 186-7
Nitre, John 227
Norfolk 38, 202, 209
North Huish 21, 31
Northumberland 226; Brinkburn Abbey 226

O'Halloran, Ellen 205; William Adlam 115, 205
Oakford 40, 205
Ogilvie, Clementina Perry 53, **54**; family 53; George 53, **54**
Okehampton 62, 122
Orgill, Mingo 34
Ottery St Mary 27, 31, 84, 123, 139, 174, 179-81, 207, 268 n.310; Mill Street 180; Raleigh House 180
Ourry, Paul Henry 171
Oxenham, John 2
Oxfordshire 42; Oxford 178, 200, 209, 222, 223, 282 n.904

Paignton 161
Palmer, Annie 14, 36; John 192; Rebecca Ann 14, 36, 192
Parkin, James 40
parliament 35, 36-8, 47, 51-2, 59, 60, 62-3, 95, 149, 152, 153, 159, 177; members 62, 119, 127, 146, 148-9, 160, 171, 177, 185, 204, 231, 244; Reform Act 63, 120
Parr, Samuel 160
Passley, John Panton 114, 140, 214
Patch, Edmund 239
Paul, Robert 262 n.314
Payne, Frederick 39; John 39-40
Paynter, Rose 218
Pearce, Mr 187; Mrs 187
Pearse, George 161, 174, 208
Peat, John 231
Peel, Ann 133
Pellew, Edward 2-5
Penoyre, Thomas Stallard 34
Perry, Richard Vining 53
Petgrave, Wilhemina 170
Philips, John Randall 115, 232; Philip Lovell 232
Phillpotts, Henry 40, 159
Phoenix, Charles 133, 267 n.488
Pince, Mr 218
Pinder, Humphrey Senhouse 42
Pitt, William 56, 148
Plummer, Barham & Plummer 39
Plymouth 60, 62, 67, 79, 85, 95, 98, 123-4, 127, 129, 131, 135, 143, 158, 173, 184-6, 226, 243; Bedford Terrace 53-5; City Council 197, 244; Clowance Street 79; Elliot Terrace 197; Hamoaze 55; Hoe 123;

Plymouth (cont.):
  Laira Green Cottages 185; Mannamead 12; museum 6; Mutley 12; Napier Terrace 12; North Hill Place 226; Saltram 67, 171, 196; Saltram Place 226; South Devon Place 12; South View 12
Plympton St Mary 170, 208; asylum 170, 208
Poland, Misses 97; Mrs 97
Pole 197; William 184; William Templer 87, 140, 174, 182-4
Policy Exchange xi
Porcher, Josias Du Pre 98, 217, 264 n.365
Porter 77; Henry 38, 76, 140, 173, 217-222, 239-40; Ludovico 222; Thomas I 214-216; Thomas II 19, 76, 79, 140, 173, 190, **213**, 216-7, 240; Thomas III 222
Potter, James 223; Rebecca 121, 140, 222-3
Powderham Castle 6, 196
Powell, Rhys Davis 9
Poyer, James 226
Prentice, Eliza Jane 159
Preston, Alice Ann 167
Prettejohn, John 104, 233, 239
Price, John 40
Prideaux, John 60
Prince, John 2
prostitution 143-4
Pusey, Venus 236

Rackenford 188; Cruwyshayes 188
Radcliffe, Tristram 51
Ralegh, Walter 2, 24, 26, 44
Redlegs 65
Reece, Emma 166; John 166
Reed, James 11; James Groscourt 11; Lucretia 11; Mary 11
Reeder, John 55-9, 81, 258 n.181
Repton, George Stanley 197
Rice, Thomas Dartmouth 135, 243
Rich, George Frederick 120, 185; Thomas 185

Richard, John 227
Richards, Elizabeth 60; James 59-60
Ridout, Miss 111
Robertson, Robert 168
Robley, Adelaide 193; Caroline 125, 173, 193-6; Fanny Ann 193; John 193-4; John Horatio 193
Roborough 5; Maristow House 59
Rockbeare 38, 39-40, 77, 139, 190, 214, 216-217, 222, 240; Ford House 39; Rockbeare House 19, 216, 217
Rodd, Federata 158; James 158
Rodon, Elizabeth 107, 171
Rogers, Anne 165
Rolle xiv, 30, 47, 142-56, 197, 243; Alexander **155**; Cuffin 30; Denys 56, 72, 122, 142, 143, 148, 149, 150; Elizabeth 56; John 30, 34, 38, 56, 71, 72, 92, 104, 122, 140, 142-6, **147**, 148-56, 173, 174, 179, 181, 232, 239, 240, 242, 246-7; Kitty 30; Malachi 30; Peggy 30; Pompey 30; Sukey 30
Romney, Lord see Marsham
Rose, Peter 98-9
Ross, Elizabeth 34; James 34; Lindsay 196; Mary 34-5, 119; Robert 34; William 119
Rossiter, Thomas 84, 125, 140, 174, 178-9, 212
Rowe, Elizabeth 11; Frances 250; James John 9-11, 42, 174, 179; Joshua 250; Judith 123; Juliana 123; Miss 40, 42
Rowlandson, Thomas 53
Russell, Henry 217; Whitworth 218

St Croix 197
St Helena 62
St Kitts 30, 59, 64, 66, 68, 85, 87, **88**, 107, 132, 136, 139, 158, 166, 184, 197; Golden Rock 184; Grange 197; Grove 158; Mills 184; Shadwell Park 197; Westhope 197

St Lucia 96, 132
St Vincent 31, 64, 66, 68, 88-9, 100, 132, 139, 160, 175, 193-4, 228, 229; Calliaqua 31, 193; Hope 160; Kearton 229, **230**, 231; Pembroke 193; The Villa 193
Sambo, John 227
Sanders, Frances 158; Thomas Finnimore 165
Sandford 239
Sandiford, William 226
Satterleigh 130
Saville, Albany 62
Sayers, John 51
Scarborough, John 85; Mary 85
Schaw, Charles 115, 233-4
Scotland 73, 119, 130, 140, 168, 177, 185; Aberdeen 196; Edinburgh 32, 34, 232; Glasgow 177, 186, 234; Perthshire 168
Scott, Henry Cussens 160; John 92
Seaman, Catherine 114, 234; Christian Anne 234; William Boog 234
Seaton 231; Beer Road 231; Violet Terrace 231
Semple, Robert 115, 163, 234-6
Serpell, H. O. 12
Sewell, William 84
Seymour, Henry 227
Shakespear, Catherine 189-90; Fatima Campbell 190
Shaldon 114
Shedden, Robert 236
Shepperd, Barbara 32; Maria 32; Rebecca 32; Sarah 32
Shillingford St George 130
ships 57, 105, 117, 124, 153, 173, 188, 189, 190, 191, 197; HMS *Africa* 133; *Altmark* x; HMS *Andromache* 185; *Brookes* 160; *Daniel & Henry* 6; *Devonshire* 144; *Elizabeth & Jane* 212; *Grenada* 216; *London* 107; *Peace & Plenty* 146; *Spitfire* 166; *Two Friends* 142
Shobrooke 209

Shute 87, 139, 174, 182-4, 196, 197, 242
Sidmouth 14, 36, 66, 75, 79, 80, 91, 97, 99, 104, 109, **110**, 111-112, 114, 125, 131, 139, 163, 165, 166, 177, 192-3, 196, 198, 212, 228-9, 231-2; Bedford Hotel 166; Belle Vue 111; Belmont 111; Clifton Terrace 231-2; Cotmaton 111, 196, 276 n.723; Denby Place 165; Fortfield Terrace 177; Helens 100, 111, 192-3; May Cottage 177; Peak House 111, 198; Powys 111; Witheby 111, 228-9; Woolbrook Cottage 109
Sidmouth, Robert 67
Simcoe, John Graves 50
slander 21, 26-7
slave-holders 139-239; attraction of 47; character 9-11, 36-9, 42, 52, 148, 162, 163, 182, 188, 190-1, 193, 194, 209, 216, 220-2, 229, 233-4, 240; compensation payments 157-239; Devon-born 173-84; mixed-race 32-6
Sleep, Catherine 114
Sleigh, Joseph 165, 271 n.605
Sloane, Ann 79; family 77; William 91
Smart, Sally 234
Smith, Caroline 234; Eleanor 190; Fanny 137; Lewis 62; Mary 234; Mr 187; Mrs 187; Moses 137; Sarah 234
Smyth, Elizabeth 158; Federata 158; Francis George 158; Richard 133; William Gould 228
Sober, Harrison Walke 160
societies, Central African Mission 62; Church Missionary Society 229; Colonial Society 73; Devon & Exeter Anti-Slavery Committee 62; Devon & Exeter Horticultural Society 218; Devonshire Association 6; Exeter Humane Society 216; Ladies' Society for promoting the early education and improvement of the children of Negroes and of People of Colour in the British West Indies 229;

societies (cont):
 Royal Society for the Encouragement of Arts, Manufactures and Commerce 146, 184; Society for Promoting the Education of the Poor 216; Society for the Prevention of Cruelty to Animals 30; Society for the Promotion of Christian Knowledge 218; Statistical Society of London 73
Somerset, 11, 34, 42, 66, 85, 100, 109, 141, 158, 166, 170, 171, 174, 177, 181, 187, 203, 214, 217, 222, 228, 231, 242; Bath 9, 38, 49, 53, 168, 186-7, 219, 224-5, 233; Bridgwater 66; Chard 66; Enmore 222; Ilminster 231; Minehead 66, 100; Porlock 228; Stogumber 42; Taunton 66, 109, 171; Wellington 177
Sorzano, Maria 236
South Molton 89, 228; Fort House 228
Sparke, John 21
Sparkes, Joseph 62
Stafford 234
Staple, Mary 231
Starcross 32, 80, 112, 174, 220, 226; Warren House 226
Stedman, John 30, 194, **195**, 196
Stevenstone 56, 72, 122, 142, 148, 197, 268 n.510
Stewart, Houston Shaw 120, 185; Thomas 117
Stirling, Ann 166
Stoke Damerel 65, 120, 133, 158, 185; James Terrace 158; Wyndham Place 158
Stoke Gabriel 26
Stonehouse 120, 124, 133, 158, 160, 186; Durnford Street 160, 186; East Emma Place 158
Stoodleigh 204-5
Strickland, Maria 92, 103, 104, 236; Martin 236
Styles, Clarissa 32; Jane 32; Mary 32
Surinam 30, **79**, 92, 194, **215**, 244

Surrey 167, 207; Egham 207
Sussex 66, 244; Bohemia Mansion 197; Brighton 109, 166, 187
Sutton, Lydia 38
Swarbeck, Elizabeth Upton 34
Swete, John 42, 70
Symons, Mr 116

Tarleton, Henry 167
Tasmania 233-4; Schawfield 233
Tavistock 98; School 85
Tawstock 196
Taylor, Edward Butler 114, 238; Margaret 35-6, 103, 140, 212; Mr 221
Teignmouth 9, 30, 53, 59, 60, 85, 98, 101, 112, **113**, 114, 139, 159, 161, 166, 175, 212, 214, 220, 234, 238, 268 n.510; Bitton Street 234; Carlton Place 234; East Cliff House 53; Hennons 10; Landscore Villa 234; Mare Platt House 53; Reed Vale 159; Tucker's Garden 238
Teschemaker, John 76, 104, 107, 139-40, 223-4; Thomas 76, 104, 125, 139-40, 157, 223-4
Tharp, Mary 238; Thomas Reid 238; William 238
Thomas, John 107, 227
Thorne, John 227
Tilly, Richard 23
Tiverton 30, 36, 42, 52, 62, 66, 70, 81, 84, 97-8, 115, 124-5, 133, 139, 166-7, 171, 173, 174, 178-9, 194-6, 204, 209, 212, 223-4, 268 n.510; Blundell's School 167, 224; Brunswick House 167; Franca Villa 167; Gotham House 224; St Peter Street 224; Westexe 178
Tobago 32, 64, 66, 67, 68, 89-91, 132, 139, 161, 166, 185, 186, 193, 194, 214, 216; Betsey's Hope 194; Cove 194; Friendship 194; Golden Grove 194; Goldsborough 194; Nutmeg Grove 32; Perry Wood 216; Richmond 194; Sherwood Park 186;

Town of Plymouth 67
Tobin, George 85, 114
Toby, Anne 91, 186; Isaac 91, 186
Top, John 227
Topsham 9, 31, 60, 66, 67, 80, 98, 112, 121, 125-7, 135, 139, 160, 173, 174-5, 179, 190, 222, 226-7, 238, 268 n.510; Barton Cottage 238; Headon Cottage 98; Newport 121, 126, 179; Seabrook 126, 238; the Retreat 126, 190-1; the Strand 31, 126
Torquay 9, 11, 30, 51, 76, 80, 114-5, 168, 186, 187, 189, 205, 207, 232-6; Adlamville 205; Babbacombe 189; Bishopstowe 189; Brotherton House 236; Castle 115; Cheltenham Villa 234; Hampton House 51; Lower Union Street 115; Melville Lodge 189; Middle Westhill 189; Modena Terrace 234; Oldway 197; Park Hill Road 168; Parkwood 168; Thornton 9; Tor Hill Road 187; Torre Abbey 197, 236; Torville 232
Tortola 174
Totnes 26, 27, 31, 51, 53, 66, 91, 125, 127, **128**, 129, 139, 167, 173, 242, 244; Follaton 239
Toynes, Elijah 29
Trefusis, Ann St John 225; Captain 247; family 225; Mark 156
Trent, Constantine Estwick 160
Trevelyan, George 42
Trim, James 133
Tringham, Eleanor 166-7; William 125, 166-7
Trinidad **90**, 91-2, **93**, 94, **138**; Mount Stuart 177; Torrecilla 236
Trutch, William 187
Tucker, Elizabeth 239; James 21; Margaret 21
Tuckett, George Lowman 107, 171
Turner, Dr 211; Francis 136; George 137; John 136; John Fisher 136; Sophia 136

United States xi, 32, 65, 66, 85, 88, 92, 94, 98, 167, 211, 223; Boston 223; Detroit 62; Florida xiv, 47, 56, 142-8, 242; Georgia 45, 62, 73, 137, 144, 217; New England 26, 73, 223; New York 10, 243; North Carolina 45, 73; Ohio 32; Philadelphia 117; South Carolina 45, **46**, 47, 49, 50, 73, 217; Virginia 12, 26, 45, 72, 117, 119, 236
University of Exeter 225
Upham, Anne 163-5; John 163-5
Urquhart, Walter 31; William 105

Vassall, William Junior 167; William Senior 167
Victoria, Queen 109, 148
Vidal, Elizabeth 117, 162-3, 212; Francis 163; John James 162-3
Virgin Islands 66, 96, 132
von Ketelhodt, Maximilian August 51

Waite, George 202
Walcott, James Percy 98, 133, 135
Wales ix, 9, 12, 105, 107, 116, 119; 184, 236; Cardiff 171; Craig Y Nos 9
Walker, Peter 81
Wallen, Edward Pinnock 238; Elizabeth 43, 238
Walrond, Bethell 173, 200; Janet 200; Lyons 70, 200
War, 1812 5, 117, 129; American Civil xi, 12; American Revolutionary 19, 47; Great 137; Peninsular 11; Second World x, 129, 229
Ward, John Abel 85; John William 159
Warner, Richard 101
Washfield 52-3, 70, 75, 209, 268 n.510; Beauchamp House 52
Waters, John 187
Waymouth, Charles 42, 59; Mary 103
Webber, John Incledon 56; Mary 133; Philip 56

Weekes, John 52; Nathaniel 163; Rebecca Ann 97, 112, 163, 192-3
Welch, Alice Anne 104, 109, 167; Arthur 167; Richard 167
Went, James King 42, 114, 159, 166, 248; James King Junior 159
Werrington 66, 260 n.234
West Alvington 59, 174
West Ogwell 42
West Putford 40
West, Charles Southcott 133
Westcote, Thomas 2
White, James 60
Whitlock, Edward 31; Emily 31; George 31; Hubert 31-2; William 31
Wichalse, Mary 24; Nicholas 24
Wilkinson, Elizabeth 51
Willesford, Elizabeth 85
Williams, Ann 11; Ceclia 178; Charles 133; Elizabeth 11; Grace 133; James 231; John 135; Mary 135, 187, 267 n.487; Patty 178
Williamson, John 133
Willis, Mary 38-9, 104; Sophia 174

Wilson, Martha Euphemia 114, 161
Wiltshire 231; Salisbury 85, 189
Wiltshire, Thomas 187
Windsor, Henry George 75, 100, 140, 159, 224, 249
Winkleigh 66
Withycombe Raleigh, see Exmouth
Wolseley, Charlotte 222; William Bertie 222
Wonda, John 227
Wonnacott, William 135
Woodbury, Lodge 91; Upper Nutwell 217
Worger, Mr 177
Worsely, John 133
Wylly, William 100

Yearwood, Seale 75; Susan R. 75
Yorkshire 140, 182, 223; York 178
Youings, Joyce ix
Young, William 91, 193

Zeno, Charles 133
Zoolah, Nancy 96

59. Sketches of Jamaica by William Berryman, c1808–1815. ▶

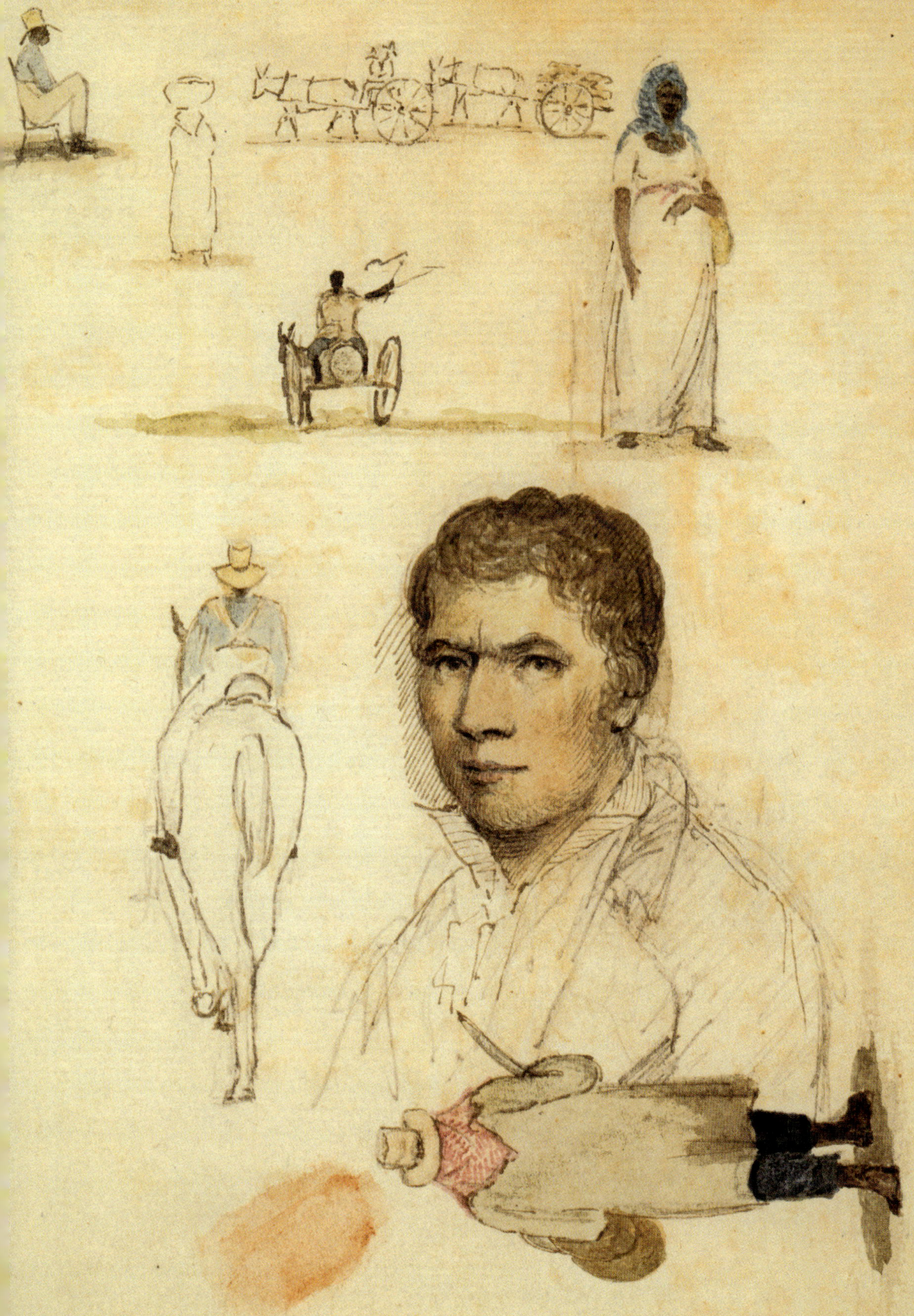

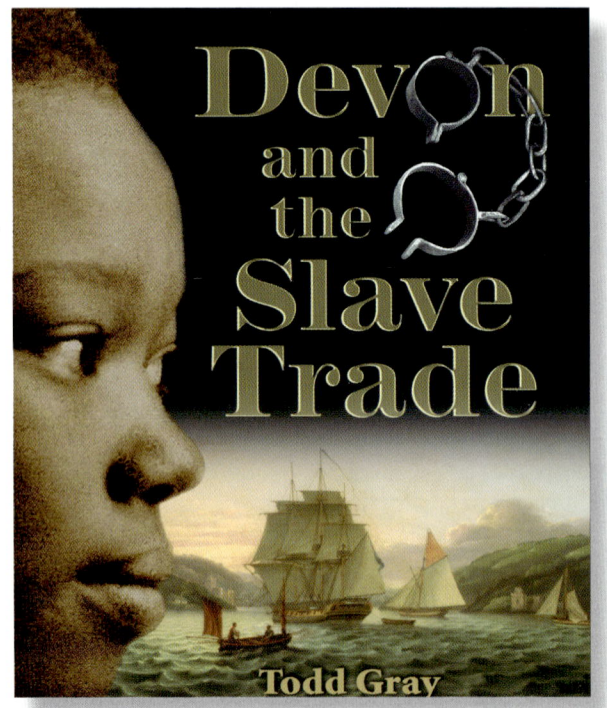

HISTORY THAT HURTS

Also from The Mint Press

Direct through Stevens Books or from all booksellers

Taddyforde House South, Taddyforde Estate, New North Road, Exeter EX4 4AT

web: www.stevensbooks.co.uk
telephone: 01392 459760
email: sales@themintpress.co.uk